The Which? Guide to

Pub Walks

ABOUT THE AUTHORS

Tim Locke is a travel researcher and writer of long standing, with particular expertise in Britain, Europe, New England and the Far East. He has also written guides to the Lake District, the West Country, and Yorkshire and the Peak District for Which? Books.

Sue Gordon, his co-author, is a travel writer specialising in Great Britain, Boston and New England. She has devised and written up walks for various publications.

The Which? Guide to
Pub Walks

TIM LOCKE and SUE GORDON

CONSUMERS' ASSOCIATION

Which? Books are commissioned and researched by
Consumers' Association and published by
Which? Ltd, 2 Marylebone Road, London NW1 4DF
Email address: books@which.net

Distributed by The Penguin Group:
Penguin Books Ltd, 27 Wrights Lane, London W8 5TZ

First edition May 2000

British Library Cataloguing in Publication Data
A catalogue record for this book is available from the British Library

ISBN 0 85202 807 5

Authors and publishers wish to thank
Jack Pleasant, Kim Lewis and Sophie Gumpel
for their contribution to the pub information.

Cover design by Sarah Watson
Cover photograph by Britain on View
Text design by Julie Martin

Typeset by Saxon Graphics Ltd, Derby
Printed and bound in England by Clays Ltd, St Ives plc

Contents

Symbols used in maps and walks 7

Key map 8

Introduction 11

Hertfordshire

1 Ardeley and Benington 21
2 Tring Reservoirs and the Grand Union Canal 25
3 Brocket Park and Ayot St Lawrence 29
4 Ivinghoe Beacon and the Ashridge Estate 34

Essex

5 Terling and Fairstead 38
6 Tollesbury Wick Marshes and Shinglehead Point 42
7 Dedham Vale and Flatford Mill 46
8 Clavering and Arkesden 51
9 Great Bardfield and Finchingfield 55

Kent

10 Appledore and the Royal Military Canal 60
11 Ide Hill and Emmetts Garden 64
12 Trottiscliffe and the Coldrum Long Barrow 68
13 Wye Downs and Crundale 72
14 Stodmarsh and Grove Ferry 76
15 St Margaret's Bay and South Foreland 80
16 Shoreham and Lullingstone 85
17 Penshurst and Chiddingstone 89
18 One Tree Hill and Ightham Mote 94

East Sussex

19 Berwick and Alciston 99
20 Ticehurst and Bewl Water 104
21 Winchelsea and the Brede Level 108
22 The Long Man and Lullingstone Heath 113
23 Streat and Ditchling Beacon 117
24 Friston and the Seven Sisters 121
25 Ashdown Forest and Pooh Sticks Bridge 126

West Sussex

26 Arundel Park and the Arun Valley 131
27 Kingley Vale and the Devil's Humps 135
28 Devil's Dyke 139
29 The Chidham Peninsula 143
30 Hooksway and Harting Downs 147

London

31 Dulwich and Sydenham Hill Wood 150
32 Richmond and Ham 155
33 Hampstead and Kenwood House 160
34 Barnes Common and Chiswick Mall 166

Surrey

35 Elstead, Ockley Common and Thursley Nature Reserve 172
36 Abinger Roughs and Friday Street 177
37 Hascombe and Hydon's Ball 182
38 St Martha's Hill and the Gunpowder Mills 186

Hampshire

39 Bramdean and Hinton Ampner 190
40 Selborne and Noar Hill 194
41 Greywell and the Basingstoke Canal 198
42 East Meon and the Downs 203

Oxfordshire

43 Dorchester-on-Thames and Wittenham Clumps 207

Berkshire

44 Henley, Hambledon Lock and the Regatta Course 211
45 Cookham, Winter Hill and the Thames 215
46 Windsor Great Park 219

Buckinghamshire

47 The Chess Valley 223
48 Turville and Stonor Park 227
49 Marlow and the Thames towpath 232
50 Burnham Beeches and Littleworth Common 236
51 West Wycombe and the Chiltern Hills 240
52 Little Hampden and Coombe Hill 244

Symbols used in maps and walks

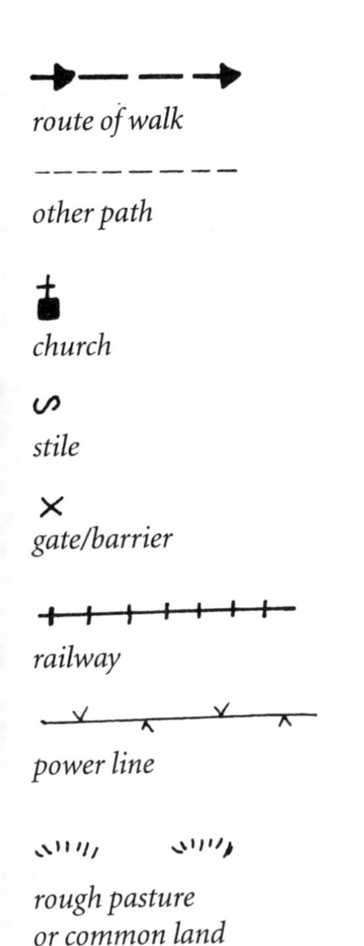

route of walk

other path

church

stile

gate/barrier

railway

power line

rough pasture or common land

woodland

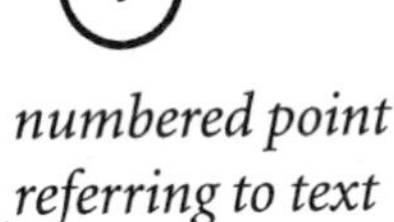

numbered point referring to text

pub

Editor's Choice pub

other refreshments

WC
public conveniences

PT
public transport

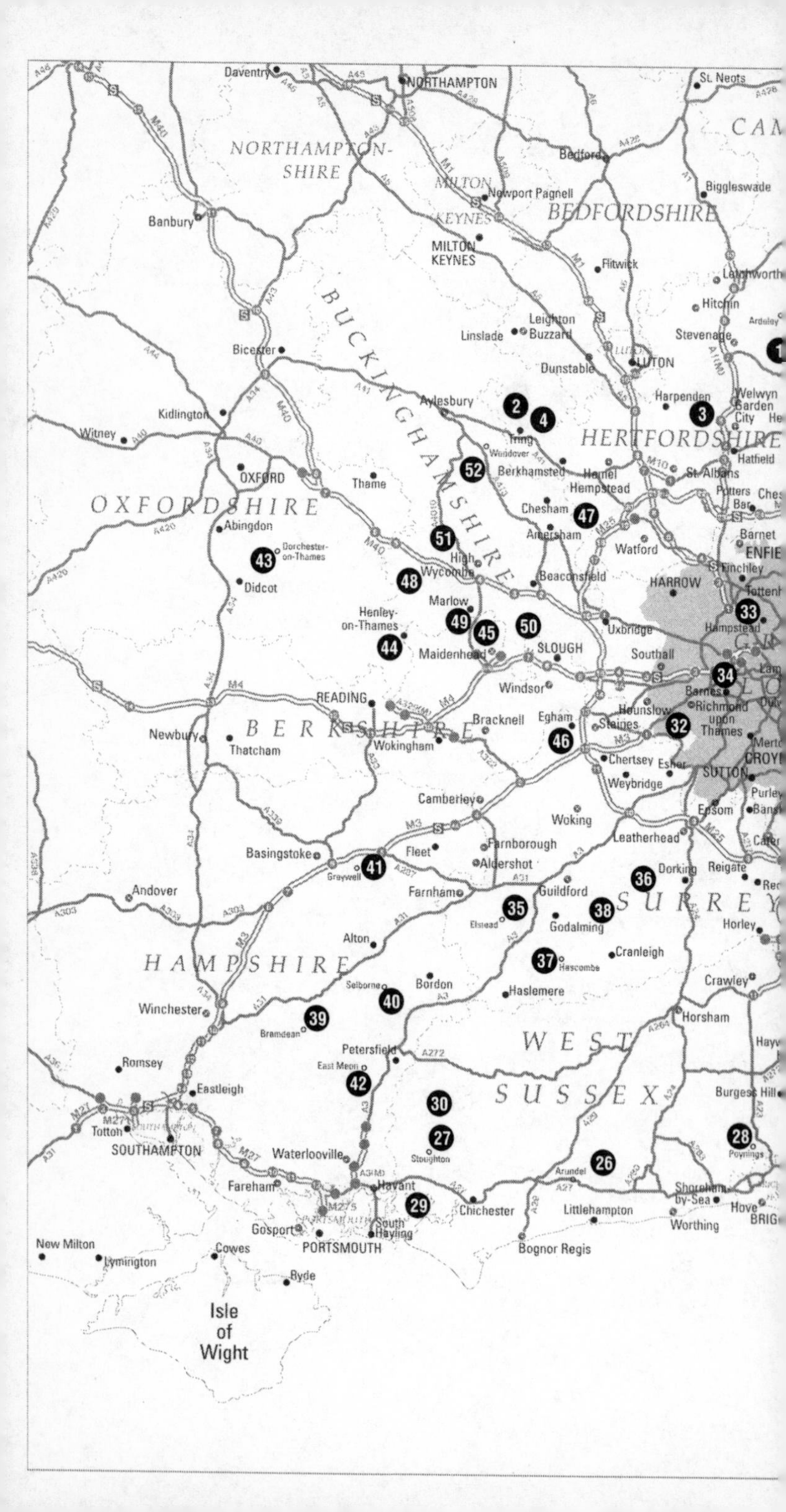

Daventry
NORTHAMPTON
St. Neots
NORTHAMPTON-
SHIRE
Bedford
MILTON
KEYNES
Newport Pagnell
BEDFORDSHIRE
Biggleswade
Banbury
MILTON
KEYNES
Flitwick
Letchworth
Hitchin
Stevenage
BUCKINGHAMSHIRE
Leighton
Buzzard
Linslade
Bicester
Dunstable
LUTON
Aylesbury
Harpenden
Welwyn
Garden
City
Kidlington
Tring
HERTFORDSHIRE
Witney
Wendover
Hatfield
OXFORD
Thame
Berkhamsted
Hemel
Hempstead
St. Albans
Potters
Bar
OXFORDSHIRE
Chesham
Abingdon
Amersham
Watford
Barnet
Dorchester-
on-Thames
High
Wycombe
Finchley
Didcot
Beaconsfield
HARROW
Marlow
Henley-
on-Thames
Uxbridge
Hampstead
Maidenhead
SLOUGH
Southall
Windsor
READING
Barnes
Hounslow
Richmond
upon
Thames
Newbury
BERKSHIRE
Bracknell
Egham
Staines
Thatcham
Wokingham
Chertsey
Esher
SUTTON
Weybridge
Camberley
Epsom
Woking
Leatherhead
Basingstoke
Fleet
Farnborough
Aldershot
Greywell
Dorking
Reigate
Andover
Farnham
Guildford
SURREY
Elstead
Godalming
Horley
Alton
Cranleigh
HAMPSHIRE
Hascombe
Selborne
Bordon
Crawley
Haslemere
Winchester
Horsham
Bramdean
WEST
SUSSEX
Petersfield
Romsey
East Meon
Eastleigh
Burgess Hill
Totton
SOUTHAMPTON
Waterlooville
Stoughton
Poynings
Arundel
Fareham
Havant
Shoreham-
by-Sea
Hove
Chichester
Littlehampton
Worthing
Gosport
South
Hayling
PORTSMOUTH
Bognor Regis
New Milton
Lymington
Cowes
Ryde
Isle
of
Wight

CAMBRIDGE
SUFFOLK
ESSEX
KENT
EAST SUSSEX
Stowmarket
Haverhill
IPSWICH
Saffron Walden
Sudbury
Clavering
Finchingfield
Great Bardfield
Dedham
Felixstowe
Harwich
Braintree
COLCHESTER
Bishop's Stortford
Terling
Witham
Clacton-on-Sea
Harlow
Tollesbury
Chelmsford
Maldon
Epping
Chipping Ongar
Chigwell
Billericay
Brentwood
Wickford
Rayleigh
Rochford
Romford
BASILDON
Ilford
Hadleigh
South Benfleet
SOUTHEND-ON-SEA
Dagenham
Rainham
Canvey Island
Erith
Grays
Tilbury
Dartford
Gravesend
Sheerness
Sidcup
BROMLEY
Rochester
Gillingham
Chatham
Whitstable
Hern Bay
Margate
Broadstairs
Ramsgate
Orpington
Sittingbourne
Faversham
Stodmarsh
Shoreham
Canterbury
Sevenoaks
MAIDSTONE
Ide Hill
Deal
Tonbridge
Wye
Ashford
St. Margaret's at Cliffe
Penshurst
Dover
Royal Tunbridge Wells
Folkestone
Hythe
Ticehurst
Appledore
Uckfield
Winchelsea
Hailsham
Hastings
Bexhill
Newhaven
Seaford
Eastbourne
Location of pub walk
0
10 miles
0
10 kms

Introduction

Even to those who have lived in the region for years, the countryside of the apparently crowded South-East is full of surprises. Within only 50 miles of Trafalgar Square it is possible to find terrain of great rural beauty belying its proximity to the capital – beech forests, marshy coasts, chalk downlands, water meadows and rolling pastures. Essentially it is a civilised landscape too, of farms, country estates, village greens, church towers and (often) welcoming pubs.

None of the land rises to any great height – the regional Everest is Leith Hill in Surrey, which reaches 965 feet, with only its summit tower taking it above the 1,000-foot mark. But much of the South-East is ideal for walking – folded and complicated enough to change in character over the course of a few miles, and sufficiently elevated in places to give some remarkably sweeping views.

And largely because it is so much revered by walkers, the network of public rights of way is on the whole extremely well maintained, with sturdy stiles, gates that open properly, clear waymarking and good signposting.

Pubs for walkers

Many of the region's country pubs are ideally located for walkers. For this book we have, with the aid of the team from our sister publication *The Which? Guide to Country Pubs*, routed walks past some of the finest pubs in the South-East. The best are flagged up as 'Editor's Choice', represented in the text by the symbol ✪. For all the other pubs on each walk we give the address, phone number, opening times, food times as well as short descriptions of beers and food on offer. We also indicate whether children and dogs are welcome; details change, and it may be worth phoning ahead to be absolutely sure. Please note that we are not necessarily recommending pubs that we include other than those which are Editor's Choices.

For a few walks we were unable to find a pub on the route that merits the Editor's Choice accolade, but in some instances we have also given a nearby Editor's Choice a short drive away.

Many walks in this book can be joined at a number of points, so you can plan ahead to arrive at the pub at the beginning, in the middle or at the end of the walk.

Before you go

We give **timings** based on an average walker (without stops) – generally at about two miles per hour. If that sounds slow, bear in mind that stiles, gates and even reading the directions all hinder progress.

We also indicate **difficulty** – easy, moderate or energetic, based on terrain, any steep ascents or descents, and length – so it is inevitably a somewhat subjective scale. To this we add any particular warnings about mud or steep climbs.

Mud of course is pretty much a fact of life at certain times of year. The varied geology of the South-East makes mud similarly diverse. In the sandy soils of the Surrey hills and the Ashdown Forest, the mud does not really cling even when the ground is waterlogged. Conversely on the South Downs you can find yourself striding over well-drained chalk one moment and in glue-like clay the next.

Not much in the way of specialist equipment is needed. **Walking boots** are strongly recommended, as they cushion the roughness of an uneven path and give ankle support. They are virtually essential if there is likely to be a lot of mud around. In bone-dry conditions, stout shoes or trainers would do. Indeed, trainers with a really springy sole can be comfortable when it is really hard underfoot. Wellingtons can be useful for short strolls when it is really muddy or waterlogged but are not ideal for longer walks.

A **small backpack** is the best way of carrying your gear, which should include some food and drink even if you intend to eat at a pub. In view of the fickleness of the English climate, it is worth taking spare **clothing**. Include waterproofs and perhaps socks and headgear too.

Many walkers wear a pair of both thin and thick (wool loop-stitch) socks. Avoid jeans or any long trousers that restrict your knees when they get wet; stretchy trousers are much better. Shorts or skirts are obviously pleasant to wear in summer, but stinging nettles can be a problem. When vegetation is likely to be dense, a stick or pair of secateurs might be handy.

A **map case** is invaluable for protecting this book and any map you carry, as you can keep the book or map open, with the carrying cord around your neck so that your hands stay free.

Finding your way

We have tried our best to make the directions as clear and concise as possible. The circled numbers cross-refer to the sketch map for easy reference. Where relevant, we have also indicated whether the walk is likely to be easy or difficult to follow.

Directions can easily go out of date: for example, fences get removed or erected, signposts get re-worded, stiles get replaced by gates or disappear altogether, new stiles appear where there was none before, and path junctions come and go. Accordingly, we have tried to give enough information for each walk to confirm that you are on the right route.

Paths are usually signposted where they leave a public road.

- **Signposts** vary in style and prominence, some being obvious and clearly placed on poles, others being easily missed concrete tablets only a few inches off the ground.
- **Waymarks** may appear on paths or bridleways. These take the form of coloured arrow motifs placed on posts, stiles, gates and the like.
- **Yellow arrows** Public footpath (open to walkers only).
- **Blue arrows** Public bridleway (open to horse riders and cyclists as well as walkers).
- **Red arrows** Byway (open to all traffic).
- Sometimes you may see **white arrows** (permissive or licensed path, not a right of way, but the landowner allows public access for the time being), and other coloured waymarkers for self-guided trails through land owned by the National Trust, Forestry Commission and certain other bodies.
- **Acorn motifs** National Trail (a long-distance path set up by the Countryside Commission), such as the North Downs Way, the Ridgeway, the South Downs Way and the Thames Path). Many other long-distance routes such as the Greensand Way and Essex Way have their own logos.

Public transport

Some of the walks can be reached by train, and many more by bus. If there is no rail station, we have indicated bus services (usually from the nearest place that has a rail station), and whether buses run daily or at weekdays only. We have not included details where there is only one daily or weekly bus.

For more information on public transport services, contact the following helplines (note that some are open only during normal office hours):

Buckinghamshire (0345) 382000
East Sussex (01273) 474747 or (01797) 223053
Essex (08457) 000333
Hampshire (01962) 846924
Hertfordshire (0845) 7244344
Kent (08457) 696996
Surrey (01737) 223000
West Sussex (0345) 959099
National train enquiry line (08457) 484950

Note that there is no general helpline covering **Berkshire**.

For details of any **tourist information centre** or **public transport operator** in Britain, Tel: (0800) 192192 (freephone).

By car

All the walks in this book have a feasible **parking** space, either roadside parking, or in a designated parking area; we usually state whether a charge is made. Additionally it may be possible to use pub car parks, but please check with the pub itself first.

Landscape in the South-East

Finding really good walks in the region can be a bit hit and miss, and we have taken great pains to steer you well clear of the more humdrum agricultural tracts and areas dominated by main roads and creeping suburbanisation. All the walks in this book were chosen as being special, and taken as a whole they form a balanced and varied cross-section of the best of the South-East. The most rewarding areas for walking tend to be to the south and west of London, and accordingly there is a geographical bias in those directions. But we have also ventured into Hertfordshire and Essex, as well as London itself.

Thatched roofs, pargeted (ornately plastered) and timber walls, village greens and quiet farmland punctuated by strips of woodland are among the East Anglian elements of **northern Essex** and **eastern Hertfordshire**. Some of the most interesting walking is from village to village, around Saffron Walden, Benington, Clavering and the 'Constable country' of the Stour Valley near Dedham. East of Chelmsford the partly wooded commons around Danbury are laced with paths, while further south there is virtually unlimited access through Epping Forest (where finding the way can be a challenge). The **Essex coast** has hundreds of miles of sea wall, from Manningtree on the Stour to Purfleet on the Thames, and most of it is followed by rights of way. This can be wonderfully exhilarating, with vast skies and plenty of bird life apparent on the surrounding marshes and mudflats, such as around the Crouch and Blackwater estuaries; Tollesbury and Mersea Island are good areas to head for.

The **Chiltern Hills**, or 'Chilterns', describes the chalk hills of Buckinghamshire and its neighbours, including such summits as Ivinghoe Beacon in Hertfordshire, the Dunstable Downs in Bedfordshire (from where you can explore the unique Tree Cathedral, a First World War memorial plantation laid out in the plan of a cathedral) and Coombe Hill, the highest point in Buckinghamshire. You will find a lot of unspoilt countryside here, with glorious beechwoods around the National Trust-owned village of West Wycombe, for example, and most famously the forest known as Burnham Beeches, where trees are at their most spectacular in autumn.

Part of the **Thames Valley** runs along the southern edge of the Chilterns, which offers a heady mix of gracious trees and elegant riverside architecture, particularly in the section from Maidenhead, past Cookham, to Marlow and then on to Henley. This is the archetypally English landscape of the Regatta, Stanley Spencer, Windsor (where walkers have access to Windsor Great Park), *The Wind in the Willows* and *Three Men in a Boat*. The level towpath provides almost effortless walking and now forms part of the 180-mile **Thames Path**, which runs from the river's source near Kemble in Gloucestershire to the Thames Barrier in east London.

Another National Trail is the **North Downs Way**, along the chalk hills of the North Downs from Farnham in Surrey to Dover on the Kent coast. Parts of this path make a useful basis for circular walks, including around Ranmore Common and St Martha's Hill in Surrey, the cliffs between Folkestone and Dover, and the delectably rural hills around Wye Down in Kent.

Between the two chalk ridges of the North and South Downs stretches an area known as the **Weald**, which rises to the intricate wooded greensand heights of Leith Hill, Pitch Hill and Holmbury Hill in Surrey, and Black Down on the West Sussex/Surrey borders. It becomes predominantly heathy further west into Surrey and north-east Hampshire, around the Devil's Punch Bowl near Hindhead, and around Thursley Common and Frensham Ponds. Further east, in East Sussex, is the Ashdown Forest, where the sandy tracks, heaths and clumps of Scots pines are familiar from the illustrations of the Winnie-the-Pooh books. Many Wealden villages are remarkably unspoilt, and local buildings typically timber-framed, brick, weatherboarded or tile-hung. In Kent you will see great numbers of oast-houses – circular or square towers that were built as kilns for drying hops but have now been converted for other uses. Orchards and hop gardens are less common than they once were, but still form a component of the Kentish scene.

The 101-mile **South Downs Way** follows the crest of the lofty South Downs from Winchester, in Hampshire, to Beachy Head near Eastbourne in East Sussex. For much of the way, the path follows ancient tracks past prehistoric burial mounds, with vast panoramas north across the Weald and sometimes south over the Channel. Some sections of the route are surprisingly remote, leading for miles without encountering a village, and taking in such mysterious places as the chalk carving known as the Long Man of Wilmington (which the South Downs Way encounters from the top, upside down, although our featured walk approaches 'him' in the logical direction). The exciting coastal finale beyond Cuckmere Haven takes in a series of sheer, rapidly crumbling cliffs known as the **Seven Sisters** before rising to the massive Beachy Head itself.

Many downlands in the South-East are now intensively farmed, but there are still pockets that form important wildlife habitats, such as the primeval yew forest of **Kingley Vale** in West Sussex, and the wooded slopes (or 'hangers') of **Selborne Hill** and **Noar Hill** in Hampshire. **Mount Caburn** near Lewes in East Sussex is one of several National Nature Reserves, valued for its chalkland flora (including orchids). **Denbies Hillside**, near Dorking in the Surrey North Downs, harbours virtually every species of British grassland butterfly.

The rugged sandstone cliffs above Hastings old town – itself an intriguing warren of former fishermen's houses, stepped alleys and snoozing cats – offer an inviting coastal walk for a couple of miles to **Fairlight Glen**. Other undeveloped parts of the Sussex coast worth a stroll are **Chichester Harbour**, particularly around Chidham, Bosham and East Head, **Pagham Harbour** and at **Atherington**, west of Littlehampton.

London has some charming semi-rural walks through patches of woodland and common and through former villages such as around Wimbledon Common, Sydenham Hill Woods and Hampstead Heath. The Thames provides another focus, and in addition to our featured walks at Barnes and Richmond, you will find plenty of scope for strolls by the river skirting Hampton Court Park and Kew Gardens. Canal towpaths provide another angle for enjoying the capital: one absorbing stretch is the 3 miles or so from Little Venice to Camden Lock, fascinating for its glimpses of back gardens, London Zoo and moored narrowboats.

Walking in the countryside: law and practice

To the best of our knowledge, none of the walks in this book involves trespassing or following obstructed footpaths. But if you are walking in the countryside it is useful to have an understanding of the rights and duties of visitors to it. The countryside is not an open playground through which we can wander at will, but the law in England and Wales gives you specific rights of access to parts of it. And even where there are no such rights, many landowners are happy to allow you on part of their property.

Paths for the walker

Public rights of way On these, you have a legal right of passage, and no one can stop you using it. Most rights of way are marked on Ordnance Survey (OS) maps. You can walk along a public right of way, whether it's a public footpath, a public bridleway (where you can also ride or cycle) or a byway (or 'road used as a public path', which you can often drive along). Such paths should, by law, be signposted where they leave a road, but in practice signs may be missing. On the way, a landowner, local authority, local footpath group or private individual may have waymarked the route, but waymarkings are far from universal (see page 13).

There is no obligation to waymark paths after they leave the road, but a farmer must make the line of the path apparent after ploughing, within 14 days if it is the first disturbance for that crop or within 24 hours of any subsequent disturbance (unless a longer period has been agreed with the highway authority).

Forestry Commission tracks and paths i.e. those that are not public rights of way. You have permissive access – which means that you are generally welcome, but that you cannot insist on any legal rights of access. This is so that the farmer has the right to close off the tracks, notably during tree-felling.

Canal towpaths Unless there is a sign to the contrary, you can usually use them.

Other tracks and paths If you find a well-trodden path or track but an OS map does not show it as a right of way, it is not safe to assume you can use it. However, some landowners, including some private ones as well as, for example, local councils and water authorities, give permissive access to parts of their land (signposts or waymarks will confirm if this is so), and occasionally a new public right of way may have been created.

Land you are allowed on

Some commons A common is simply an area of land over which local people have various rights, such as to graze cattle. There is not necessarily any legal right for the public to walk or picnic. But some privately owned common land is open to the public, and any local authority-owned common will have been set aside for public use.

Areas where 'access agreements' have been made Occasionally, a local authority will have made a formal agreement with a landowner to allow public access (except in some cases in the lambing or shooting seasons). These have occurred in some National Parks, but otherwise are rather uncommon. Notices are usually displayed where public access is permitted.

Country parks and picnic sites The public has access if they are owned by a local authority.

Beaches Access is allowed if they are owned by a local authority, and usually if privately owned, too.

National Trust land including open land, beaches and woodland, often marked by signs and shown on OS maps. The public is allowed access unless there are notices to the contrary.

Minimum widths

The Rights of Way Act 1990 stipulates minimum widths for paths on cultivated land:

- ☐ if the width of a path is recorded, then that is the minimum width
- ☐ if the width is not recorded then the minimum width is:
  - for a footpath, 1 metre across the field, 1.5 metres on the field edge
  - for a bridleway, 2 metres across the field, 3 metres on the field edge
  - for other rights of way, 3 metres across the field, 5 metres on the field edge.

Ardeley and Benington

HERTFORDSHIRE — WALK 1

This route offers landscape strongly reminiscent of East Anglia, a rolling terrain dotted with secretive estates and crossed by quiet tracks. Benington is a rather wonderful place to walk into from the fields, and Ardeley provides the other focal point. Route-finding is fairly straightforward.

Jolly Waggoner, Ardeley SG2 7AH. ☎ (01438) 861350. Open Tues to Sat 12 to 2.30, 6.30 to 11, Sun 12 to 3, 7 to 10.30; food Tues to Sun 12 to 2, Tues to Sat 6.30 to 9. Greene King IPA and Abbot Ale. Inside are beams and open timbers, with dried flowers and paintings of the pub. The food might be omelette stuffed with smoked haddock and served with a béchamel sauce, or home-made beef burgers, sirloin of Scotch beef provençale, or open toastie sandwiches with salad. Children over 7 welcome in bar eating area. No dogs.

Bell Inn, Town Lane, Benington CM7 4SA. ☎ (01371) 811097. Open Mon to Sat 11.30 to 3, 6.30 to 11, Sun 12 to 3, 7 to 10.30; food 12 to 2, 7 to 9.30 (exc. Tues). Greene King IPA and Abbot Ale. A la carte menu including butterfly Pacific prawns in garlic butter or home-made soup to start, and steak and kidney pie, peppered pork or chicken breast and prawn as a main course. Blackboard menu, sandwiches, bar snacks, including sandwiches, ploughman's and jacket potatoes. Children welcome in dining area only. Dogs welcome in public bar only.

Start: Wood End, on minor road signposted south-east from Ardeley and east of Walkern; limited roadside parking near small grass triangle with road signpost at the junction in the centre of the hamlet. Grid reference 326255.
Length: 8½ miles (13.5 kilometres), 4 hours.
Difficulty: Moderate. Most of the going is along gentle farm tracks, although it can get very muddy after rain.
OS maps: 1:25,000 Explorer sheet 194; 1:50,000 Landranger sheet 166.
Shop in Benington.
PT Buses to Benington (Mon to Sat only) from Hertford, Ware and Stevenage.

❶ From the signpost on the grass triangle, with the direction for Great Munden on your left, turn right along a cul-de-sac, passing a post-box on your right. Keep to the principal road, which becomes an unsurfaced track at the end of the village. Fork right at a major fork of tracks (just before a lone brick bungalow); 100 yards after the bungalow keep on the track as it bends left.

After ⅓ mile ❷, fork left; 250 yards later ignore a sharp right turn. 500 yards later, bear right at a track junction by a waymark post with a blue arrow, following a track along the right edge of the field towards **Ardeley**. Emerge at a housing estate, go forward to a

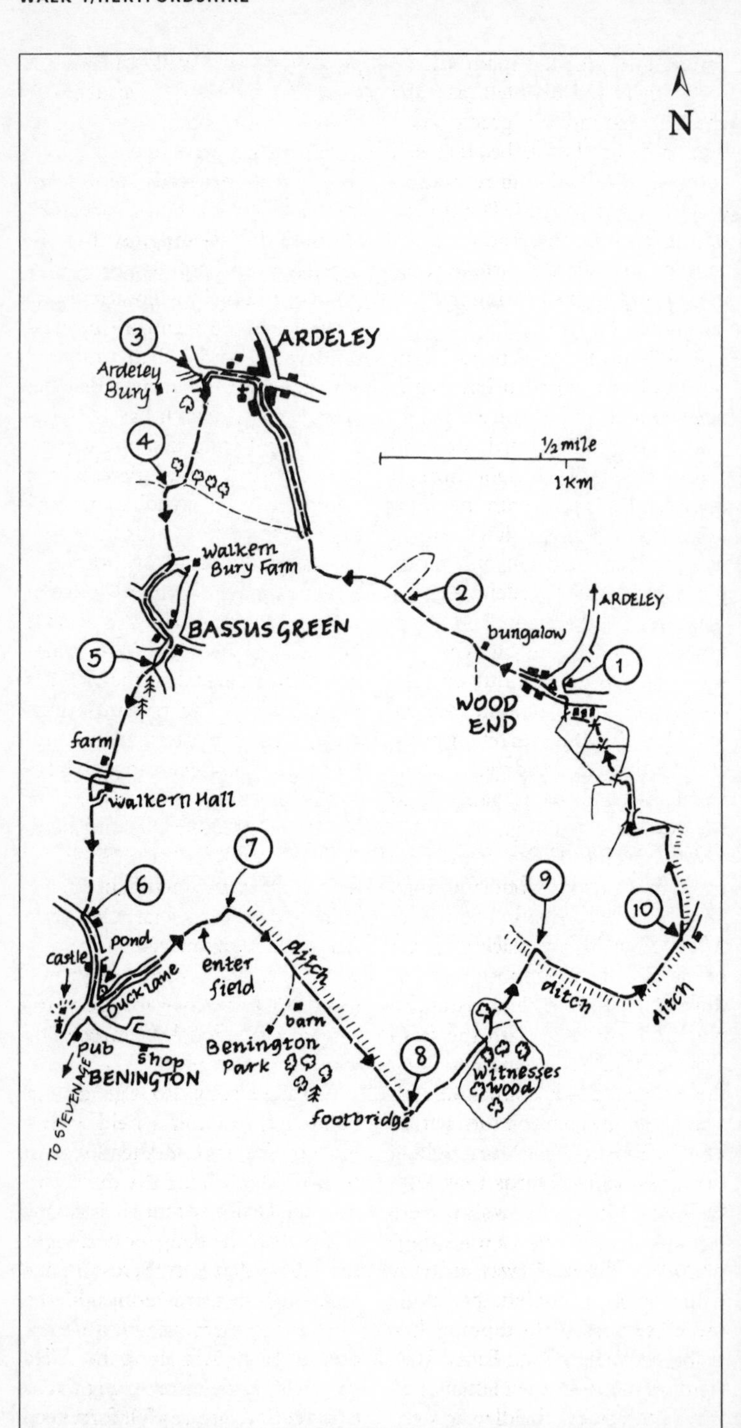
N
ARDELEY
Ardeley Bury
½ mile
1 KM
Walkern Bury Farm
ARDELEY
bungalow
BASSUS GREEN
WOOD END
farm
Walkern Hall
pond
castle
Duck Lane
enter field
ditch
barn
Benington Park
pub
shop
BENINGTON
TO STEVENAGE
footbridge
Witnesses Wood
ditch
ditch
1
2
3
4
5
6
7
8
9
10

T-junction with the main village road, where you turn left, past the church. Around the green lies a semi-circle of whitewashed thatched cottages, a painstaking recreation of a rural idyll in 1917. The church opposite has interesting 15th-century roof tracery, ornate roof-bosses, and angels bearing musical instruments.

❸ Where the road bends right (after 400 yards) turn left (signposted Public Byway) on a concrete track, keeping forward after 30 yards where it bends right through a gate, now on a path between hedgerow trees, and later with a hedgerow on the right only along the edge of a field. **Ardeley Bury** is seen away to the right. The house has a late-Tudor core, but what you see is an engaging indulgence of 1820, built for a Mr John Murray, with fanciful flint turrets, pinnacles, Gothicised windows, a baronial hall, a musicians' gallery and wedding-cake vaulting.

At the end of the field, pass through a strip of woodland, then ❹ turn right at a path T-junction. After 80 yards, you reach a corner of the track by a signpost; turn left downhill, dipping then rising, to reach a farm road with the farm away to your left. Bear right along the farm road to a T-junction with a lane, along which you turn left. At houses (Bassus Green) turn right at the crossroads, towards Clay End. ❺ After 150 yards, where trees begin, fork right on to a track signposted Public Bridleway, initially with woods on your left, then along the left edge of a field, dipping then rising to Walkern Hall Farm. Turn right on the road, then left after 50 yards by a public bridleway signpost, on a track. **Walkern Hall** (on your left) is early 19th century with a Greek Doric porch.

The track merges into a concrete track and proceeds along an avenue. ❻ On reaching a road, turn left on it, into **Benington**. The village has an enchanting green with a pond overhung by willows and surrounded by 16th-century plaster-rendered and half-timbered cottages, with the ancient Bell Inn close by. The church has 14th-century chapel windows, one depicting Edward II being pierced by a sword, medieval arcading and wall paintings. The Lordship is a Georgian house incorporating a strange mock-Norman folly of 1832 made out of ruins of a castle demolished in 1212. With gatehouse and portcullis, the effect is eye-opening. The romantic gardens, rich in rockery plants and herbaceous borders, and with lakes to stroll around, are open 1 April to 31 August, Wednesday and bank holiday Monday 12 to 5, Sunday 2 to 5. At the road junction in the village centre, turn sharp left into Duck Lane (signposted Clay End). Where the lane becomes an unsurfaced track, go forward; 50 yards later, at a junction, keep forward by a blue waymark post.

The track soon drops gently and bends left to enter a field with a ditch on the right. ❼ After 80 yards, turn right, crossing the ditch and now on a track with a ditch alongside on the left, along the bottom of the valley. After ⅓ mile cross a track and keep forward alongside the ditch, soon merging into a better-defined track, still along the valley floor. 200 yards before going under a power line, ignore a left fork; keep the ditch on your left, go under the power line and ❽ immediately cross a footbridge on the left and go uphill with a fence on your right and soon a wood on the right.

Enter the wood at a recessed corner, keep forward inside the woods (immediately ignoring a minor right fork) to reach a field after 100 yards. Turn right for 20 yards and then left along a grassy strip (an old field boundary) which soon becomes a hedgerow (walk along the right-hand side of it), leading towards power lines. ❾ At the end of the hedgerow, you reach a waymark post and ditch, and turn right at a T-junction with a track.

Follow this down to the bottom of the valley where you turn left at a junction, on a track with a ditch on the right. ❿ Where a bridge and road appear on the right, ignore them and keep forward (or to avoid the field route, if it is overgrown, you can turn left along the road, then left at the next junction to return to Wood End), still with the ditch on your right. Soon you pass another bridge on your right, ignore a major left fork, and turn left at the end of the field, with the hedgerow and ditch on your right.

At the next field corner, turn right over a low brick bridge to enter a second field, where you go forward up the right edge, turning left at the top right-hand corner, then after 50 yards take a gate on the right into a third field. Go diagonally left across to a gate in line with the nearest house (with dormer gables) in this and the fourth field.

Enter the fifth field, proceed on the right edge (past the house on your right) and soon take a gate on the right by an open-sided barn (not through the farmyard just before this) to follow a concrete track to the road. Turn left to the centre of Wood End.

Tring Reservoirs and the Grand Union Canal

HERTFORDSHIRE/BUCKINGHAMSHIRE WALK 2

Locks, canalside pubs and narrowboats supply the keynotes for this unusual circuit. It is almost entirely on towpaths of the Grand Union Canal, its branches (including a derelict one) and the banks of its feeder reservoirs. Known collectively as the Tring Reservoirs, they provide some of the best bird-watching opportunities in the region and even attracted the great zoologist Sir Julian Huxley in the early years of the 20th century to study the courtship display of grebes. There are short, easily followed link sections. You can start the walk from Tring station, following the canal all the way to join the main route.

Birds you might see by or near the canal include reed and sedge warblers, flycatchers, coots, water rail, metallic blue kingfishers, tawny and barn owls and herons.

Half Moon, 60 Tring Road, Wilstone HP23 4PD. ☎ (01442) 826410. Open Mon to Sat 12 to 2.30, 6 to 11, Sun 12 to 3, 7 to 10.30; food 12 to 2, 7 to 9 (exc. Mon eve). 4 real ales. Bar snacks, sandwiches, traditional pub dishes with chips, blackboard specials. Children welcome. Dogs welcome.

Grand Junction Arms, Bulbourne Road, Bulbourne HP23 5QE (just off the main walk). ☎ (01442) 890677. Open Mon to Fri 12 to 3, 6 to 11, Sat and Sun 12 to 11 (10.30 summer); food Oct to Easter Tues to Sat 12 to 2.30, 7 to 9.30, Easter to Sept 12 to 2.30, 6.30 to 9.30. Tetley, Adnams beers. Lunch-time curry buffet, blackboard specials, traditional pub dishes. Children welcome. Dogs welcome.

White Lion Inn, Startops End, Marsworth HP23 4LJ. ☎ (01442) 822325. Open Jan Mon to Sat 12 to 3, 6 to 11, rest of year Mon to Sat 11 to 11, Sun 12 to 10.30; food Mon to Fri 12 to 2.30, 7 to 9.30, Sat 12 to 9, Sun 12 to 5. Courage, Fuller's London Pride. Blackboard specials, Sunday roasts, à la carte menu, buffet, bar menu. Children welcome in restaurant until 7pm. Dogs welcome in bar (but not during food times).

Red Lion, 90 Vicarage Road, Marsworth HP23 4LU (just off the route near bridge 130). ☎ (01296) 668366. Open Mon to Fri 11 to 3, 6 to 11, Sat 11 to 11, Sun 12 to 10.30; food all week 12 to 2, Tues to Sat 6 to 8.30. Fuller's London Pride, Tetley, guest beers and house bitter. Traditional pub food, including scampi or cod and chips, chilli con carne, vegetable curry. Sandwiches available at lunch-times Mon to Sat. Children welcome in games room. Dogs welcome.

Angler's Retreat, Startops End, Marsworth HP23 4LJ. ☎ (01442) 822250. Open Mon to Sat 11 to 3, 6 to 11, Sun 12 to 3, 7 to 10.30; food 12 to 2, 7 to 9.30 (exc. Sun eve). Fuller's London Pride, Courage, Ruddles beers. Blackboard specials, bar snacks and sandwiches. Children welcome in garden room. Dogs welcome on a lead.

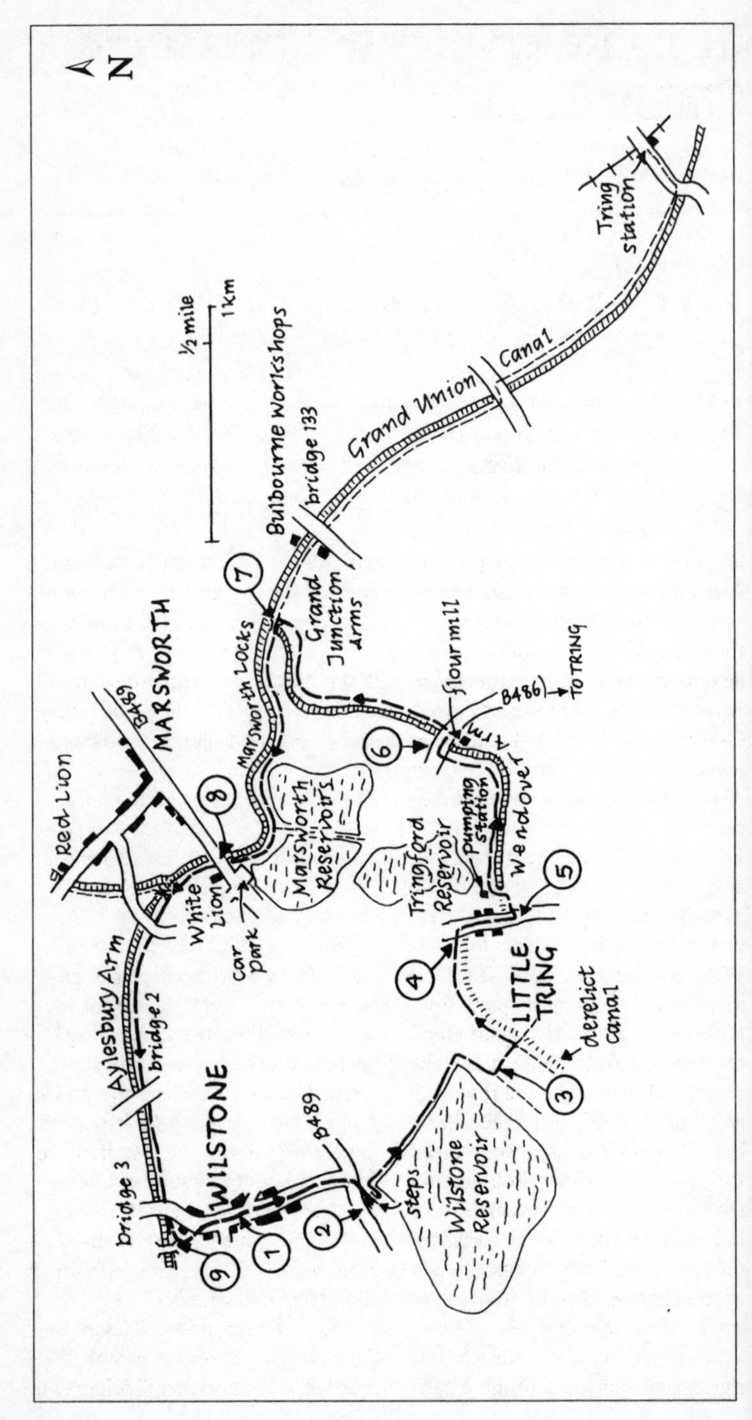
N
½ mile
1km
Tring station
Grand Union Canal
Bulbourne Workshops
bridge 133
Grand Junction Arms
Marsworth Locks
MARSWORTH
B489
Red Lion
White Lion
car park
Marsworth Reservoirs
Tringford Reservoir
Pumping station
Wendover Arm
flour mill
B486
TO TRING
LITTLE TRING
derelict canal
Wilstone Reservoir
steps
B489
WILSTONE
Aylesbury Arm
bridge 2
Bridge 3
1
2
3
4
5
6
7
8
9

Start: Village centre, Wilstone (¼ mile off B489 and 8 miles east of Aylesbury). Grid reference 905140.

Alternative start: Marsworth Reservoir car park, on B489 just south-west of Marsworth and opposite the White Lion (marked by a British Waterways sign 'Welcome to Tring Reservoirs'). Start walk at ❸. Grid reference 919142.

Length: 5 miles (8 kilometres), 2½ hours; 8 miles (14.5 kilometres), 3½ hours if starting from Tring station.

Difficulty: Easy; virtually all on the level.

OS maps: 1:25,000 Explorer sheet 181; 1:50,000 Landranger sheet 165.

Shop (open seven days a week) in Wilstone. Tea room/kiosk by the towpath opposite the White Lion, Marsworth.

PT Tring station (frequent services from London Euston, Watford Junction and Milton Keynes). Turn left out of the station and follow the road past the Royal Hotel, and after 200 yards turn right on the towpath along the right side of the canal. At the first bridge (¾ mile) cross to the other side of the canal. Continue under the second bridge ½ mile later. After 400 yards cross a footbridge to take the right branch of the canals (signposted Braunston). Join the walk at ❼.

---

❶ With the Half Moon pub on your left follow the street out of Wilstone. In 1751 the pub hosted the coroner's inquest following the last witch hunt in Hertfordshire, when locals murdered Ruth Osborn, whom they had accused of witchcraft.

Beyond the end of the village, reach the T-junction with the busy B489. Cross over and turn right along the pavement. After 100 yards this continues as a path beneath the large grassy bank of **Wilstone Reservoir** ❷. Turn left just before a small car park up a flight of steps and left again along the embankment for ½ mile. The reservoir is a local nature reserve, a wetland habitat of reed beds, marsh, open water and woodlands. It supports a heronry; hobbies and reed and sedge warblers can be seen in summer. After the far corner of the reservoir, the track passes a belt of trees and reaches a T-junction of tracks: turn right here.

❸ After 300 yards, turn left as signposted (ahead, through a gate, is private), on a path between hedges, leading up to a path junction by a deep ditch, the drained and spectacularly derelict portion of the **Wendover Arm** of the Grand Union Canal. Turn left along this former towpath. This branch originally extended to Wendover, a distance of 6 miles, but suffered from leaks and fell into disuse in 1904. Today only the last 1¼ miles are navigable; there is a long-term campaign for its restoration.

❹ After ¼ mile turn right on the road, follow it for 300 yards past houses (Little Tring), then at the top of the rise ❺ turn left, on a signposted footpath, to rejoin the drained canal. Just where the canal proper starts, cross to the left-hand towpath. Just on the left here is **Tringford pumping station**, built by the Grand Junction Canal Company in 1818 to pump water from the Marsworth, Wilstone, Startop's End and Tringford reservoirs.

The towpath passes **Heygates' flour mill** on the opposite bank; the modernised Victorian mill originally had a windmill in the centre of the complex. ❻ After ½ mile, cross via the road bridge to the right-hand towpath. Follow this for ½ mile to the junction with the main portion of the Grand Union Canal ❼.

For Tring station or for a ¼ mile detour to the Grand Junction Arms, turn right. Opposite the Grand Junction Arms are the canalside **Bulbourne workshops**, where traditional wooden lock-gates are made. The 3 miles eastward from here past Tring station to Cow Roast is a stretch known as Tring Summit, the highest point on the Grand Union Canal (a climb through 57 locks and up nearly 400 feet from its beginnings at Brentford). Each time a boat passes through a lock at either end of the summit, 56,000 gallons of water are used, and new supplies have to be pumped from the Tring Reservoirs.

To continue to Wilstone, cross the bridge to the towpath in the direction signposted Braunston. Follow the towpath for ¾ mile, past a flight of seven locks and, on your left, **Marsworth Reservoir** and **Startop's End Reservoir**. A path just above the towpath gives an excellent view of this important nature reserve. The two reservoirs are divided by a dyke which you can walk along. There are great numbers of black terns and great crested grebes.

You reach bridge number 132 (the number is on a plaque above the arch of the bridge) by a car park on the left ❽. Cross the road and continue on the towpath opposite, passing the White Lion Inn. Take the left fork of canals after 300 yards. (For the Red Lion cross the footbridge by the lock, go past the British Waterways buildings, cross the road and follow the towpath opposite on the left bank until the next bridge, which you cross into the village; the Red Lion is almost immediately on the left.)

Follow the towpath of the **Aylesbury Arm** for 1 mile. This branch was opened in 1815, and the Tringford and Startop's End Reservoirs were built to cope with the additional demand for water. At the junction is a staircase lock, effectively two locks in one, with the bottom gates of one acting as the upper gates for the other.

❾ 200 yards after passing under bridge 3, and just by a footbridge, turn left to leave the canal for a footpath leading to houses at the edge of Wilstone village. Turn right on reaching the road; this leads to the village centre.

Grand Union Canal

The Grand Union network, linking London with Birmingham, Leicester and Nottingham, and totalling over 300 miles, used to be the backbone of the inland waterways system. It resulted from the amalgamation in 1929 of several independent canals, the most significant and successful of which was the Grand Junction, a late-18th-century waterway running between the Thames in London and Braunston in the Midlands. Commercial transport survived on the Grand Union until the 1970s (by the late 1930s the company had the largest fleet of narrow boats in the UK) and today it is one of the UK's most popular cruising waterways.

Brocket Park and Ayot St Lawrence

HERTFORDSHIRE WALK 3

This route begins on a path into the woods of the Brocket Estate, leading on to landscaped parkland and the miniature valley of the River Lea (here not much more than a brook), which winds its way between marshes to Waterend and is followed by the waymarked Lea Valley walk. A parkland avenue leads from Lamer House towards Ayot St Lawrence, where you have the chance to visit Bernard Shaw's house and village. The final sections take in farmland tracks and the Ayot Green Way, a dismantled railway line. The short version of this walk follows the River Lea before returning along the Ayot Green Way. The views are more extensive on the full version of the walk.

Waggoners' Inn, Brickwall Close, Ayot Green AL6 9AA. ☎ (01707) 324241. Open Mon to Sat 11.30 to 3, 5 to 11, summer Mon to Sat 11 to 11, all year Sun 12 to 10.30; food 12 to 2.30, 6 to 9. 4 real ales. A la carte menu, blackboard specials, sandwiches and bar snacks. Children welcome in family area. No dogs.

Brocket Arms, Ayot St Lawrence AL6 9BJ. ☎ (01438) 820250. Open 11 to 11; food 12 to 9. Adnams and guest beers. The Brocket Arms dates from the 14th century, and little has changed; the bar is beamed, with an inglenook at one end, and is said to be haunted by a priest hanged here during the Reformation. Bar snacks, including sandwiches and jacket potatoes during the day and early evening. On the evening menu (from 7pm) might be salmon, rib-eye steaks and specials. Children welcome. Dogs welcome.

Start: Ayot Green Way car park (open 10 to 8, winter 10 to 4), near Ayot Green, west of A1(M) and Welwyn Garden City. Take B197 (which runs closely parallel to A1(M) from Welwyn southwards), and turn off at signpost to Ayot St Lawrence and Ayot St Peter. After crossing the bridge over the motorway, follow the road markings, forking right in the village green; the car park is signposted on the right after ¼ mile. There is also roadside parking by the Waggoners' Inn: fork immediately left into Brickwall Close on crossing the A1(M). Grid reference 222144.

Alternative start: Ayot St Lawrence (roadside parking; also car park by the 'new' church (the classical church, as opposed to the ruined one near the pub). Begin with the pub on your left, follow the village street to Shaw's Corner and join the walk at ❻. Grid reference 194167.

Length: Full walk 8 miles (13 kilometres), 4 hours; short walk from Ayot Green omitting Ayot St Lawrence 5½ miles (9.5 kilometres), 2¾ hours; short walk from Ayot St Lawrence omitting Ayot Green 5½ miles (9.5 kilometres), 2¾ hours.

Difficulty: Moderate. Muddy after rain; some uneven ground but only gently undulating.

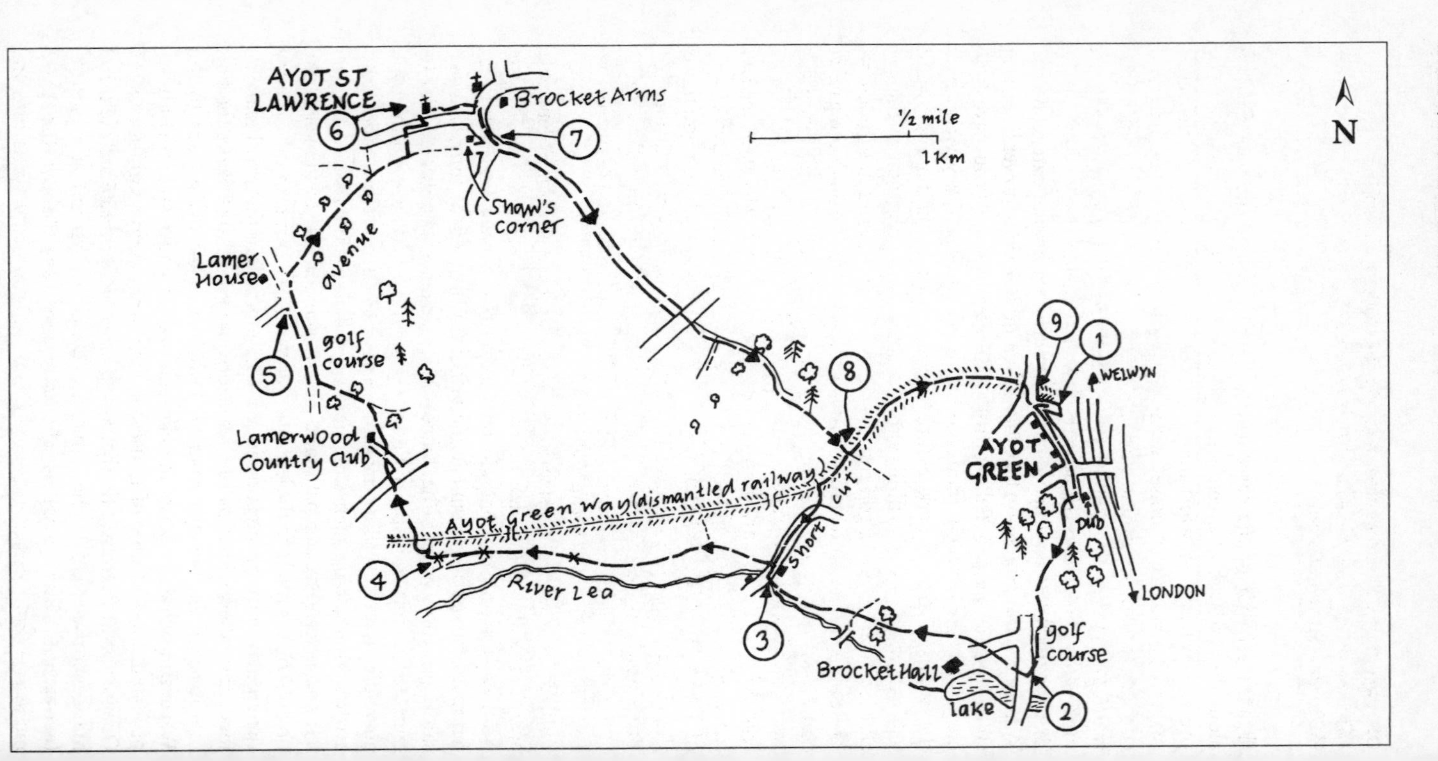
AYOT ST LAWRENCE
6
Brocket Arms
7
Shaw's corner
½ mile
1km
N
Lamer House
avenue
golf course
5
Lamerwood Country Club
8
9
1
WELWYN
AYOT GREEN
pub
Ayot Green Way (dismantled railway)
Short cut
4
River Lea
3
LONDON
golf course
Brocket Hall
lake
2

OS maps: 1:25,000 Explorer sheet 182; 1:50,000 Landranger sheet 166.
PT None on the route; the centre of Welwyn Garden City (served by buses and trains) is 1½ miles east of Ayot Green.

❶ Turn left out of the car park, along the road to Ayot Green, a very pretty setting (unfortunately marred by motorway noise) with cottages and houses around a large triangular green. Just before the motorway bridge fork right into Brickwall Close, leading to the Waggoners' Inn, where you take the stile opposite the pub. Follow this clearly waymarked path, soon into the woods of Brocket Park. Follow yellow waymarks downhill and across the fairways of a golf course. ❷ Reach a surfaced estate road; the route continues opposite, on the waymarked Lea Valley Walk (a path leading to the right, between fences), but first turn left for a view of 18th-century **Brocket Hall** from the elegant stone bridge over the Broadwater, an artificial lake.

Return to take the waymarked Lea Valley Walk, which you follow until ❹. On reaching the estate road again, cross it and turn left into a field. Proceed initially alongside the fence on your left, then maintain the same direction where the fence ends, to enter woodland; continue ahead, following yellow marker arrows, soon joining a fence on the left and descending to a path junction, where the tracks to the left and right are signed as private. Continue forward on the enclosed path.

After ⅓ mile, reach a road at **Waterend**, which consists merely of a ford and a couple of houses. One is West End House, a fine brick manor-house (1610); the other (across the River Lea) is the medieval White Cottage.

Turn right on the road ❸, then left after 50 yards on the Lea Valley Walk. After ¼ mile, fork left, parallel with the River Lea (here not much more than a brook). The track soon follows the left edge of two long fields.

Beyond a kissing-gate, continue forward following power lines, and ❹ leave the field (you have now also left the Lea Valley Walk) by a kissing-gate in the far right-hand corner, just to the right of the last power post. Beyond it, turn left on a track and go through the gate at the end of the field and turn right at a T-junction of tracks.

For the short walk back to Ayot Green Carry on 130 yards to a junction of tracks and turn right: this is the Ayot Green Way, a dismantled railway, which you follow for 2 miles until dropping to the road at ❾.

To continue to Ayot St Lawrence Turn left up steps and through a gate after 70 yards, head diagonally to cut the corner of a field, through a gate and across an old railway track (the Ayot Green Way). Go up the bank opposite and follow the path beyond. Cross the road to the gate opposite and just to the left of the driveway to Lamerwood Country Club, and follow the grass beside the driveway until (just before the fork where the left drive leads to the clubhouse and restaurant) a waymark arrow points right across the driveway and immediately left. 100 yards later turn left at a path T-junction, and follow the path, ignoring any side turns into the golf course, to a tall metal gate. Turn right on the hard track.

❺ After ⅓ mile the track merges into a tarmac estate road: proceed along it for 100 yards, then fork right. The left turn is private, into **Lamer House**. Only a pretty stable-block is visible from the route. Apsley Cherry Garrard, co-traveller with Scott on the doomed Antarctic journey and author of *The Worst Journey in the World* (a title reputedly inspired by Shaw) lived here.

The track runs along an avenue of trees. Where the avenue ends, turn right at a path junction, to proceed along a woodland fence on your right. At the end of the second field on the left, and 50 yards before the woods end, take a stile on the left, and follow the right edge of the field to a road. Turn right on the road, then after 50 yards take the next track on the left, to ❻ **St Lawrence Church**. Go through the gate on the right, just before the church, and pass in front of the imposing Grecian façade. Beyond the church go through an ornate iron gate and immediately turn right through a kissing-gate, and follow the left edge of two fields to the road at **Ayot St Lawrence** (see box opposite). The village centre, old church and pub lie to the left, but the route continues to the right.

❼ At **Shaw's Corner** ignore the right turn but keep forward, signposted Wheathampstead. This road soon bends left, then, where it bends right 20 yards later, keep forward on the signposted bridleway. ¾ mile later cross the road and take a bridleway opposite alongside woods. After the first field, where the fence on your right ends, avoid the path to the right but continue along the left edge of the next field. At the end of this large field (which is subdivided by a line of trees marking an old field boundary), the track bends right (still alongside woods), then 70 yards later bears left to leave the field and enter the woods: keep forward, soon emerging into a field. The track follows the left edge of this field for 50 yards, then bears left into the next field, turning right and following the right edge in the same direction.

❽ At a former railway bridge, go up on to the old railway track (the **Ayot Green Way**). Opened in 1860, the railway once linked Hatfield and Dunstable via Welwyn and Wheathampstead. It was closed to passenger traffic in 1965. When the gravel workings nearby were shut in 1971, it ceased operation completely.

For the short walk back to Ayot St Lawrence Turn right along the Ayot Green Way for ¼ mile, then turn left on a path signposted Waterend, up into a field, then turn right along the field edge and right again on a quiet road downhill. After ¼ mile turn right opposite a large brick manor house (West End House) on the Lea Valley Walk and rejoin the walk at ❸.

To continue to Ayot Green Turn left along the Ayot Green Way.

❾ When you reach the road junction, take the signposted road half right for Ayot Green.

Ayot St Lawrence and Shaw's Corner

The idyllic backwater village of Ayot St Lawrence has two churches: the first encountered on this walk is the 'new' one, designed by Revett in 1778–9, its giant portico modelled on the Temple of Apollo at Delos; its position completes a vista from Lamer House. The second church is a Gothic, ivy-clad ruin, partly demolished by the Lord of the Manor in the 1770s and saved only by the intervention of the Bishop of Lincoln: the roof was lost, but the tower was saved. Close by are early-18th-century Ayot House and a group of half-timbered cottages adjoining the Brocket Arms.

George Bernard Shaw lived at the house he named **Shaw's Corner** from 1906 until his death in 1950. Since then it has been kept as it was during his life, with his books, desk and walking sticks seemingly awaiting his return. He allegedly settled here because of an epitaph in the churchyard to a woman who died at the age of 70, which said simply 'Her life was short'; he thought that a village considering 70 a short life must be a good one to live in. The house is maintained by the National Trust and is open to the public (1 April to 1 November, Wednesday to Sunday plus bank holiday Monday).

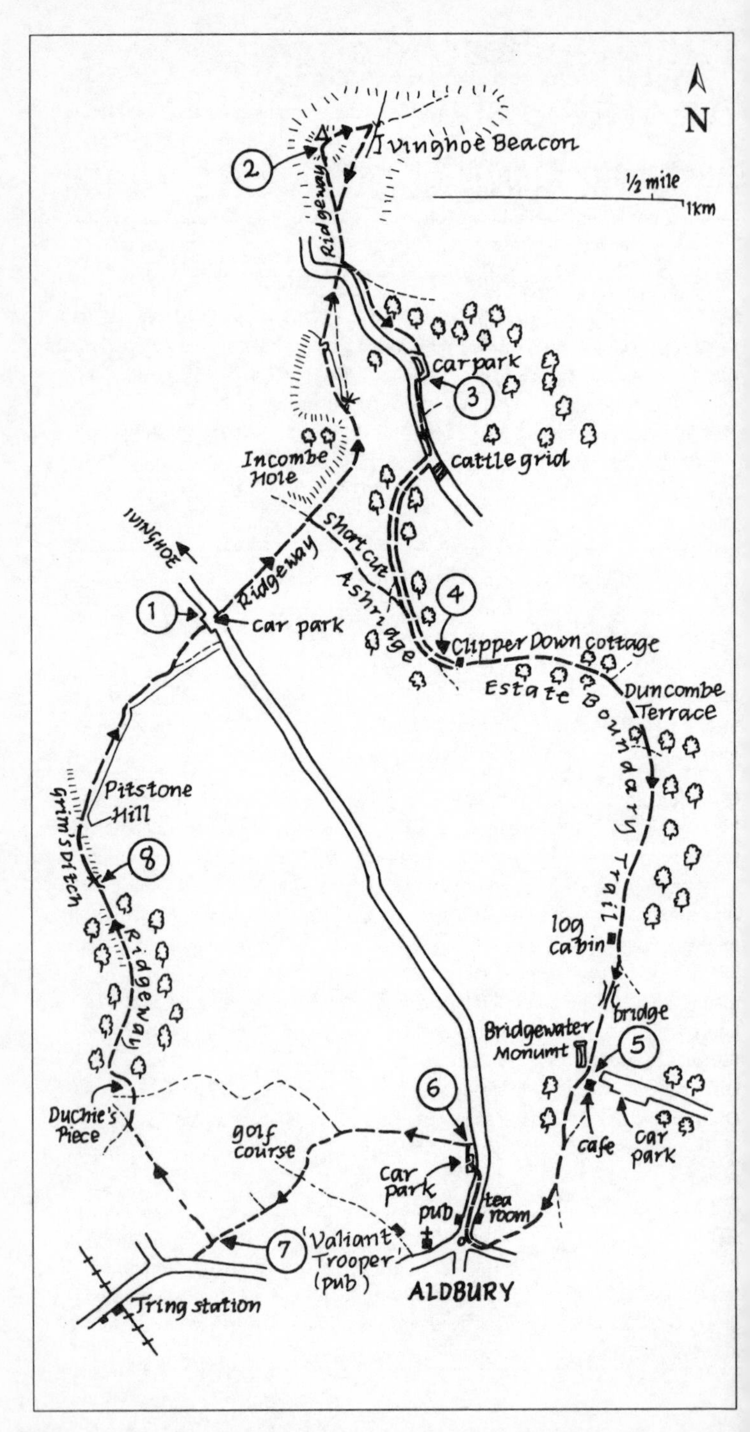

N
Ivinghoe Beacon
½ mile
1km
Ridgeway
car park
cattle grid
Incombe Hole
IVINGHOE
Short cut
Ridgeway
Ashridge
Car park
Clipper Down cottage
Estate Boundary Trail
Duncombe Terrace
Pitstone Hill
Grim's Ditch
Ridgeway
log cabin
bridge
Bridgewater Monumt
Duchie's Piece
golf course
Car park
pub
tea room
cafe
car park
'Valiant Trooper' (pub)
ALDBURY
Tring station
1
2
3
4
5
6
7
8

Ivinghoe Beacon and the Ashridge Estate

HERTFORDSHIRE/BUCKINGHAMSHIRE WALK 4

This route in cherished countryside takes in some of the very best of the Chiltern escarpment, passing through the stately beech woods of the National Trust's huge Ashridge Estate and emerging on to spectacular open chalk downs.

Valiant Trooper, Aldbury HP23 5RW. ☎ (01442) 851203. Open Mon to Sat 11.30 to 11, Sun 12 to 10.30, closed 25 Dec exc. 1 hour at lunch-time; food 12 to 2, (2.30 Sun and bank hol Mon), Tues to Sat 6.30 to 9.15; restaurant closed Mon L. Bass, John Smith's, Fuller's London Pride and 2 guest ales. The pub dates from about 1752. Jacket potatoes, ploughman's, sandwiches are all on offer as well as steak and kidney pie. Fillet steak or salmon and prawn en croûte are to be found on the blackboard menu. Children welcome in family room. No dogs in restaurant.

Greyhound, 19 Stocks Road, Aldbury HP23 5RT. ☎ (01442) 851228. Open Mon to Sat 9am (for coffee), 11am (bar) to 11pm, Sun 9 (for coffee), 12 (bar) to 10.30; food Mon to Sat 12 to 2 (3 for cold food), 7 to 9.15, Sun 12 to 4. Badger beers. Steaks, scampi, soup and sandwiches available during the day. A la carte and specials menus in the evenings. Children welcome in garden room. No dogs in restaurant.

Start: Free National Trust car park 1½ miles north of Aldbury and 1 mile south-east of Ivinghoe. From Aldbury take the road signposted Ivinghoe and Stocks Hotel; the car park is at the top of a rise, on the left, marked by a vehicle height restriction barrier and a National Trust sign for Ashridge. Grid reference 955149.

Alternative start: National Trust car parks just south of Ivinghoe Beacon (grid reference 964160; start walk at ❸) and by the Bridgewater Monument (grid reference 971130; start walk at ❺). Free car park 200 yards from Aldbury village centre on the road to Ivinghoe, and on the left (grid reference 965127; start the walk at ❻).

Length: Full walk 8½ miles (14 kilometres), 4 hours; short walk omitting Ivinghoe Beacon 6 miles (10 kilometres), 3 hours.

Difficulty: Moderate, with steady but not steep climbs; muddy after rain.

OS maps: 1:25,000 Explorer sheet 181; 1:50,000 Landranger sheet 165.

Refreshment kiosk by Bridgewater Monument, Town Farm tea room and shop in Aldbury.

WC At the visitor centre by the Bridgewater Monument.

PT Tring station (frequent services from London Euston, Watford Junction and Milton Keynes). Turn right out of the station and follow the road, ignoring a left turn to Ivinghoe after 150 yards; 100 yards later turn left on a concrete track (signposted Ridgeway Path). Where the track bends left, after 50 yards, keep straight on; turn left at the junction immediately beyond a gate. Join the walk at ❼.

❶ Cross the road from the car park and take the Ridgeway Path opposite. You cross a large field, at the end of which is a path junction beyond a kissing-gate.

For the short walk Turn right (waymarked the Ashridge Estate Boundary Trail, which you follow to the Bridgewater Monument). Cross two stiles as you rise up through the woods. Turn right at a T-junction with a track and rejoin the walk at ❹.

For the full walk Carry straight on and continue to follow Ridgeway Path signs and acorn waymarks to Ivinghoe Beacon. The track bends round to the left above a spectacularly steep-sided valley. Keep to the left of a gate, as signposted, along the fence on your right, into trees and down a grassy slope, over a stile and down to the road. Cross over to take the left-hand of two tracks, ascending gently to the summit of **Ivinghoe Beacon** ❷, the northern end of the 85-mile Ridgeway Path, which leads south-west to Overton Hill near Avebury in Wiltshire. Bronze Age settlers left numerous barrows, while at the summit is the site of a hillfort.

At the triangulation pillar at the summit, turn right and follow the path to a stile: do not cross this stile but turn right, initially along the fence on your left, and retrace your steps to the road. Just before the road, take a path on the left which runs parallel to the road as far as a National Trust car park at the top of the hill ❸. Turn left out of the car park along the road. After 250 yards, just before the road crosses a cattle-grid, turn right on a track signed to Clipper Down Cottage. Keep to the main track, which later joins the waymarked Ashridge Estate Boundary Trail; glimpses through the trees reveal **Pitstone Windmill (NT)**, between Ivinghoe church and the huge chimney of the nearby cement works. Dating from 1627, it is one of the oldest surviving post mills in the UK (it is open to the public on Sunday and bank holiday afternoons from June to August).

❹ Where the track ceases to rise, fork left, and pass through a gate just to the right of Clipper Down Cottage. Follow this broad path for 1 mile, avoiding side turnings, then 150 yards after a large log cabin on your right (with a National Trust sign for Ashridge beside it) keep to the main path, which bends half right and crosses a footbridge. This emerges by the 100-foot-high **Bridgewater Monument**, erected in 1832 in memory of the third Duke of Bridgewater (who then owned the Ashridge Estate), the 'Father of Inland Navigation'. The first of his numerous waterway projects was the Bridgewater Canal (in Lancashire and Cheshire), engineered by James Brindley in 1761. From April until the end of October you can climb up the 172 steps within the monument for a small fee (NT).

❺ Take the track between the Bridgewater Monument (right) and Monument Cottage (left; by the tea garden) and follow it downhill through woodland, ignoring all left turns, to **Aldbury**. Turn right on the road into the village centre. Around the village you will see 16th-and 17th-century cottages, some half-timbered. Within the church is the impressive 15th-century Pendley Chapel, enclosed by a handsome Perpendicular stone screen and containing the effigies of Sir Robert Whittingham and his wife. Outside is the tomb of Mrs Humphry Ward (1851–1920), novelist and opponent of female emancipation; she lived at Stocks House (now a hotel).

Turn right at the centre of Aldbury (signposted Ivinghoe), by the pond, triangular green, stocks and whipping-post. Go past the Greyhound Inn on your left. ❻ After 200 yards, go into the car park on the left. Immediately turn right, continuing parallel with the road, on a track along the edge of the sports field, to pass to the right of a brick pavilion, then turn left on a bridleway track. Ignore all side turns and keep to this enclosed bridleway (avoid a signposted footpath on the right, and then a footpath crossing). The bridleway later skirts a golf course (where you ignore another bridleway to the right). Reach a junction with the Ridgeway Path (which you follow all the way to ❶ (and on to ❷ if you began from one of the alternative starting points); it is signposted and waymarked with acorn motifs throughout) and turn right ❼.

The path runs first between hedges and then turns half right at a junction as signposted. You pass **Duchie's Piece** on your left, an area of downland given to the Queen Mother, and home to the Duke of Burgundy butterfly – now extinct in the rest of Hertfordshire.

The path then turns left up a flight of steps and continues through woodland (avoid side turnings). ❽ After ½ mile emerge on open downland and continue forward uphill; on the right is a sunken grassy track known as **Grim's Ditch**, a long earthwork that runs for 25 miles through the Chilterns. It is thought to have been an Iron Age boundary marker. This section runs around **Pitstone Hill**. The views of the Chiltern escarpment and the southern Midlands are superb. At the top of the slope, the path continues forward at a fence corner, alongside the fence on the right. As you near the road, fork left into the car park.

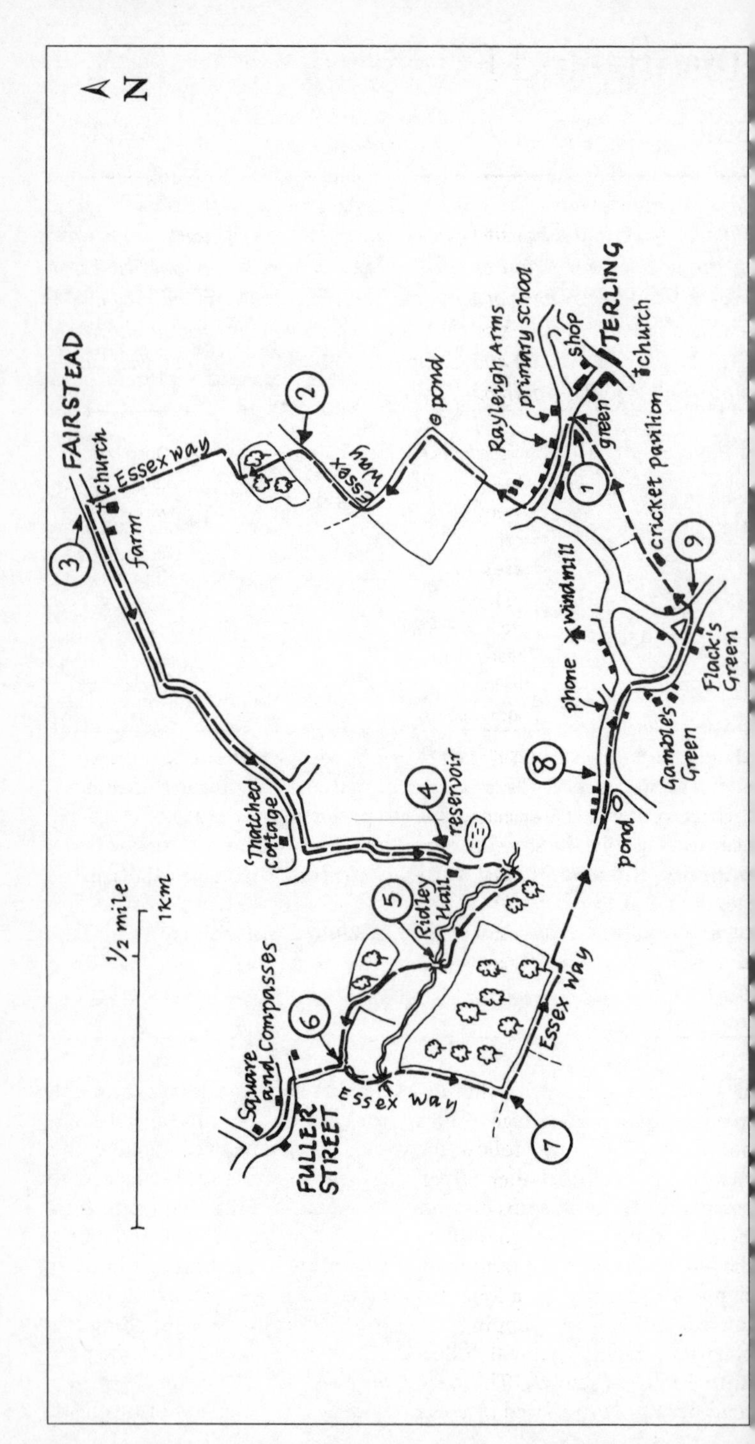
N
FAIRSTEAD
church
Essex way
farm
3
2
pond
Essex Way
TERLING
primary school
shop
church
Rayleigh Arms
green
1
cricket pavilion
9
windmill
phone
Flack's Green
Gamble's Green
8
pond
Thatched cottage
4
reservoir
5
Ridley Hall
Essex Way
6
Square and Compasses
FULLER STREET
Essex Way
7
1/2 mile
1KM

Terling and Fairstead

ESSEX WALK 5

Village greens and expansive East Anglian skies are keynotes to this walk in the peaceful farmland of central Essex. The well-waymarked Essex Way is followed for most of the route, with pleasant lane-walking and a few field paths for the link sections. Beyond the ancient-feeling church at Fairstead lies the Square and Compasses pub at Fuller Street, well worth aiming for before the path back to Terling.

Rayleigh Arms, Owls Hill, Terling CM3 2PW. ☎ (01245) 382223. Open Mon to Sat 12 to 3, 6 to 11, Sun 12 to 4, 7 to 10.30; food Mon to Sat 12 to 2, 6.30 to 10, Sun 12 to 3, 7 to 9.30. Courage beers. Traditional pub food, steaks and sandwiches. Children welcome. Dogs welcome.

Square and Compasses, Fuller Street, ☎ (01245) 361477. Open Mon to Sat 11.30 to 3, 6.30 (7 winter) to 11, Sun 12 to 3, 6.30 to 10.30; food Mon to Fri 12 to 2, 7 to 9 (9.30 Fri), Sat 12 to 3, 7 to 9.30 Sun 12 to 2.30, 7 to 8.30. Ridleys IPA and guest beers. The pub serves hearty country cooking, has hanging baskets and a rear garden and is popular with the locals. Children welcome in eating areas, small children welcome during day only. Dogs welcome in bar only.

Start: Terling (pronounced 'Tarling'). Park on road near green and road junction by primary school and close to Rayleigh Arms (by signpost to Hatfield Peveril; Boreham, Chelmsford; Great Leighs, Braintree, Fuller Street). Grid reference 772151.
Length: 6 miles (10 kilometres), 3 hours.
Difficulty: Easy, over arable land, mostly well waymarked but occasionally rough underfoot.
OS maps: 1:25,000 Explorer sheet 183; 1:50,000 Landranger sheet 167.
Shop at Terling (just off the route, near the church).
PT Generally no useful bus service, although on Saturdays 2–3 buses from Braintree serve Terling.

❶ From the green, with the primary school and village notice board on your right, follow the road signposted to Fuller Street, passing the Rayleigh Arms on your right. Just after a road goes off to the left, turn right on a farm road, signposted **Essex Way**, a long-distance path from Epping to Harwich, which you will follow until Fairstead church. The farm road becomes unsurfaced by some derelict farm buildings, and the route carries on into the left-hand field as waymarked. Follow the right edge of the field to its corner by a pond on the right, then turn left, still inside the field. At the next corner the route continues into the right-hand field (following its left edge), then turns right along the edge of a third field (avoid the path ahead).

❷ Towards the end of this field,

the route turns left across the field and through a small coppiced wood. Turn right along the edge of the next field, then left after 150 yards just after passing beneath the power lines and proceed through the churchyard of **Fairstead Church**. The spire dates from about 1600 and is a landmark seen from far around. Medieval wall paintings enliven the whitewashed interior, most strikingly the Passion painted over the Norman chancel arch. The building is lit by slender 13th-century lancet windows and spanned by great beams. A grotesque carved head at the west end of the church sports curious horn-like headgear.

❸ Turn left along the road (you leave the Essex Way which leads to the right along the road), and fork right after ½ mile, signposted Great Leighs/Braintree. After Thatched Cottage (despite its name it is not thatched) on the right, turn left on an unsignposted lane.

At the end of the road pass a house (Ridley Hall) on your right, and keep left (avoiding the driveway ahead), now along an unmade track. Cross a bridge and turn right. The track leads through a small plantation, across a field towards a pylon (ignore a stile at the end of the field; the track leaves by a corner to the right of this) and through another plantation.

❺ Where the track bends markedly left, take the footbridge (in summer this may be rather hidden by nettles) on the right. In the field, bear half left to the top then walk alongside woodland into the next field, where you follow the right edge and take the first field entrance on the right (where power lines cross at a field corner); turn left, along the edge of the next field to its corner ❻.

To continue the walk, omitting the Square and Compasses at Fuller Street turn left on the Essex Way.

To detour to the Square and Compasses at Fuller Street Turn right towards houses, then left on the road; just before the pub on the left-hand side of the road is the **former village shop** with an unusual old advertising sign for Lifebuoy Soap where the message changes as you move (to 'No Wear, No Tear, No Care').

Retrace your steps to ❻ from the pub (if starting from here this point is found by following the road in the Terling direction until an open field appears on your left), where you turn right on the Essex Way, along the right edge of a field. At the end of this field, turn right on the Essex Way.

Both routes Continue on the Essex Way (which you follow until ❽): it immediately turns left along the edge of the next field for 50 yards, then goes left downhill where the hedge ends. Cross a footbridge and head to the right of a pylon, up the left edge of a field alongside a wood.

❼ At the top, turn left along a track (still along the outside edge of the wood), and at the end of the field, where the track bends right, keep forward, continuing alongside the wood. Where the wood ends, turn left alongside the wood, then at the next projecting corner of woodland bear half right along a grassy strip towards the houses. Cross waymarked stiles then follow a track which becomes surfaced beyond the first house. ❽ At a road junction (just after a pond on the right), turn left, soon past a phone box (where Oakfield Lane joins from the left) and then turn right (where the left turn is Hull Lane). You pass a group of cottages ranged around Gamble's Green and get a distant view of a sailless smock windmill away to the left. At the next green (Flack's Green) follow the principal road ahead (ignoring a left turn) in the Chelmsford direction. ➒ 30 yards after the end of Flack's Green, turn left through a gate and follow the left edge of this field. Maintain this direction for ½ mile (ignoring paths leading to the left), passing to the left of a cricket pavilion, then past a playground and a tennis court where the route now follows a track to the road junction at Terling.

The centre of **Terling** lies to the right (signposted Chelmsford) and is worth a short stroll for its red-tiled and cream-washed houses, and green presided over by the church with its brick tower of 1732. Nearby Terling Place was the former home of Edward Strutt, a 19th-century agricultural improver.

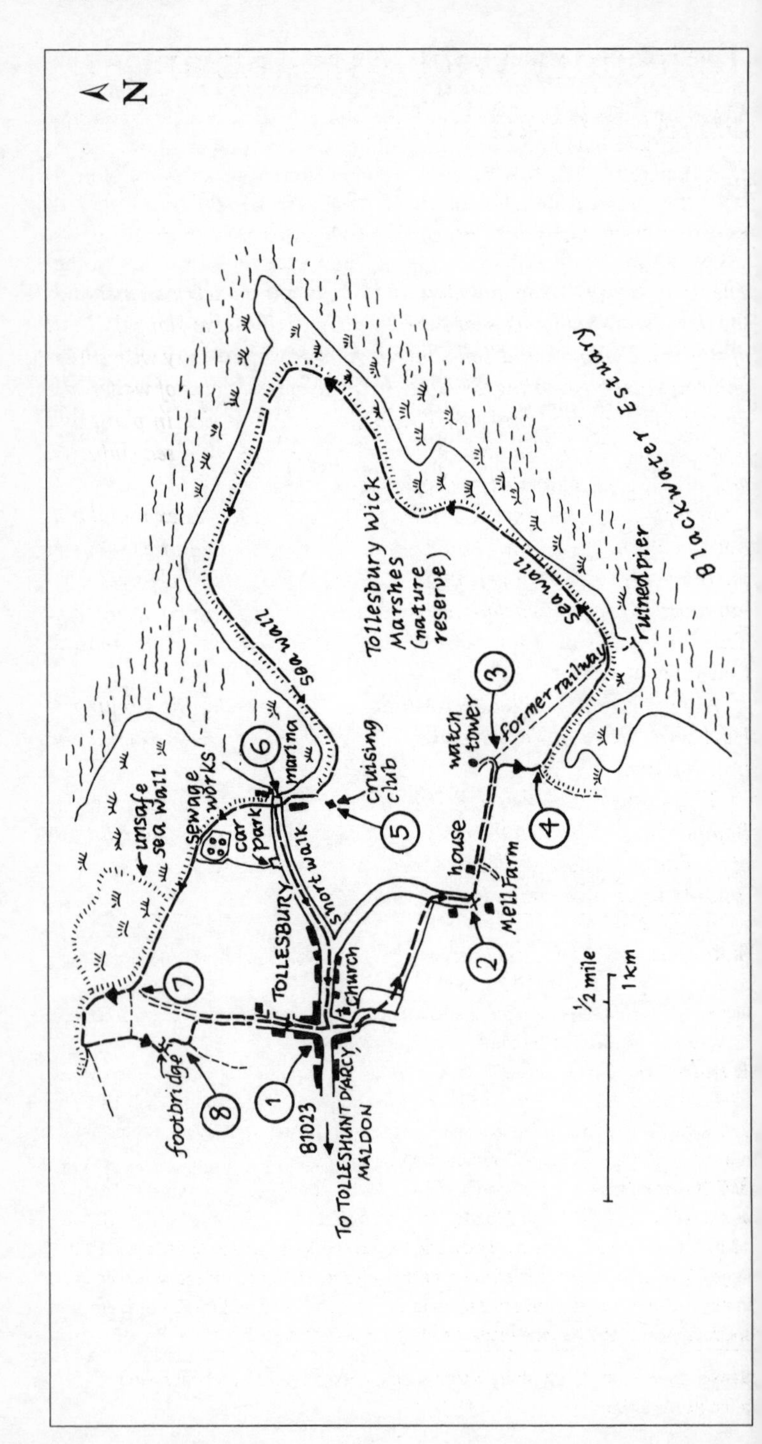
N
Blackwater Estuary
Tollesbury Wick
Marshes
(nature
reserve)
sea wall
sea wall
ruined pier
former railway
watch
tower
house
Mell Farm
cruising
club
marina
car
park
sewage
works
unsafe
sea wall
TOLLESBURY
short walk
church
footbridge
B1023
TO TOLLESHUNT D'ARCY,
MALDON
1
2
3
4
5
6
7
8
½ mile
1km

Tollesbury Wick Marshes and Shinglehead Point

ESSEX

WALK 6

There's a strongly elemental character about these lonely marshes, and the elevated sea wall makes for superb walking as it snakes along the limit of cultivated land around Tollesbury, a village formerly busy with smuggling and oyster gathering. Skylarks, brent geese and flocks of waders are among the abundant bird life. The marshes are also rich in plant and insect life, with brackish areas of common reed, sedge and sea clubrush, and small pools frequented by dragonflies.

In total there are some 400 miles of sea wall on the Essex mainland, from Manningtree on the Stour to Purfleet on the Thames; this is one of the finest stretches, with variations of mood as the scenery changes from salt marsh to open sea before reaching civilisation by a forest of masts at Tollesbury's marina. Our nearest recommended pub is on the road to Colchester at Peldon.

At the head of the Blackwater Estuary is more waterside strolling at Heybridge Basin, at the sea end of the Chelmer and Blackwater Canal near Maldon.

To the north, Colchester is Britain's oldest-recorded town, razed by Boudicca in AD60 when the Iceni attacked the Romans. The foundations of the Roman temple of Claudius were incorporated into the castle, which is now a museum, and the Roman vaults can be visited.

Kings Head, 1 High Street, Tollesbury CM9 8RG. ☎ (01621) 869303. Open Mon to Sat 11 to 11, Sun 12 to 10.30; food 12 to 2.30, 6.30 to 8.30. Champion Mild, Ridleys IPA. Sandwiches, and bar snacks including jacket potatoes, ham, egg and chips. Children welcome. Dogs welcome.

Hope Inn, 16 High Street, Tollesbury CM9 8RG. ☎ (01621) 869238. Open Mon to Sat 11.30 to 11, Sun 12 to 10.30; food Wed to Sat 12 to 2, 6.30 to 9, Sun 12.30 to 2. Greene King IPA. Set menu, bar snacks, specials including fresh fish and chips, for example. Children welcome. Dogs welcome in public bar.

Peldon Rose, Mersea Road, Peldon CO55 7QJ (off the route, between Tollesbury and Colchester). ☎ (01206) 735248. Open Mon to Sat 11 to 11, Sun 12 to 10.30; food 12 to 2, 6.30 to 9.30. Adnams, Wadworth 6X, Flowers IPA as well as guest beers. This large 600-year-old half-timbered inn is ideally suited for visitors to the many wildlife sites in the area. It has an extensive menu, using seasonal and local produce. Desserts are a speciality. Most food is home-made. Children welcome. No dogs.

Start: Church Street, Tollesbury village centre, near the church and pubs. Grid reference 956105.

Length: Full walk 7 miles (11 kilometres), 3½ hours; short walk omitting part of sea wall 5 miles (8 kilometres), 2½ hours.
Difficulty: Easy. All on the level, but the wind can make it hard going. Dog-friendly stiles and gates all the way.
OS maps: 1:25,000 Explorer sheet 176; 1:50,000 Landranger sheet 168.
Shops in Tollesbury.
WC On the short walk, by the road just inland from the marina.
PT Buses to Tollesbury from Maldon, Colchester and Witham (not Sun).

❶ From the central crossroads by the Kings Head, take Church Street, past the church on your left, then fork left (where the right turn is Elysian Gardens). Just after an old red-brick garden wall ends on the left, take the signposted path on the left, diagonally across a field, then go through a gate and carry on to reach a road. Turn right on the road, then ❷ just before the double gates to Mell Farm, take a kissing-gate on the left, and follow the track beyond, along a field and then keep forward by a modern red-brick house and barns on the left (avoiding tracks to the right and left). ❸ Where the hedge ends, turn right on an enclosed, signposted path (with a fence on your left and a hedge on your right) towards the coast. ❹ Turn left at the sea wall (a raised grassy dyke), which snakes above the extensive saltmarshes. You soon enter **Tollesbury Wick Marshes**, a nature reserve maintained by the Essex Wildlife Trust and part of the Blackwater Estuary Site of Special Scientific Interest, a wetland of international importance. This point is Mill Creek, named after a now vanished tide mill.

Just after the first bend to the left, look for a gate away to the left: this is across a grassy strip, which is all that remains of the **Tollesbury Light Railway**, opened in 1904 in an attempt to develop a continental packet station and yachting resort here. But the seaside resort failed to materialise, and the line closed in 1951. At low tide you can still see the remains of the pier on the seaward side; it was dismantled in 1940 to foil any attempted enemy landing.

Also in view are a series of rectangular enclosures marked out with wooden stakes on the seaward side of the sea wall; these brushwood **polders** were an attempt to build a coastal defence in the 1980s, but the structures failed to slow the tidal waters. These have been succeeded by another experimental **sea defence** technique, in the form of huge mounds of sand and shingle that run in a line from Blockhouse Bay to Shinglehead Point. These are the dredgings from Harwich harbour used by the Environment Agency for what is termed in the trade as 'beach recharge'. They are helping to protect the remaining saltmarsh strip at the toe of the sea wall.

Carry on along the sea wall for 2½ miles; **Bradwell nuclear power station** is seen across the Blackwater estuary, then eventually Tollesbury marina comes into view. The sea wall makes a major turn at **Shinglehead Point**, where a Second World War pillbox is adorned with anti-nuclear graffiti. This is a good spot for sighting overwintering duck, waders and geese, and more unusually great northern divers and common seals; little terns are breeding summer visitors. At very low tide it may be possible to see, about ¼ mile out to sea, a low line of stumps. These are the remains of **Saxon fish weirs**, many of which survive in the area. They have been radio carbon-dated to between the 7th and 10th centuries, and some retain bark and tool marks. It is thought that the weirs were monastic property.

❺ At the marina, pass the mast-topped Tollesbury Cruising Club on your left, following a gravel track, then fork left on to a stony path in front of a row of modern brick and weatherboarded houses on the left.

❻ Reach the road by a magnificent group of wooden **sail lofts** built in 1902, when Tollesbury had a fleet of over 100 fishing smacks; they were restored in 1983.

For the short walk turn left along the road and return to Tollesbury.

For the long walk take the path opposite, by the concrete steps, and continue along the sea wall, with a huge area of saltmarsh on the seaward side. You pass a sewage works away to the left, and 300 yards later fork left at a junction of sea walls (where a notice announces that the right-hand sea wall is unsafe). In the interests of nature conservation, the **marshes** to the north are being expanded by abandoning parts of the sea wall.

❼ ¼ mile later the sea wall makes a major right turn (avoid a path going off to the left), and soon after the unsafe sea wall rejoins on the right (by another danger notice). The sea wall now bends left and where it is about to bend right 200 yards later, go forward across a ditch and turn left (avoiding a prominent track ahead towards a road) inland, soon with a hedgerow on the left. In the corner of the field, avoid entering the field on your left but turn right, with hedgerow trees and ditch on your left, crossing the ditch by a footbridge after 200 yards, and proceeding with the hedge on your left.

❽ 130 yards later, the path turns left through the hedgerow; beyond, keep forward (avoiding another path to the right) and follow the hedged path to reach a stony track. Turn right to the edge of Tollesbury, where a residential road leads back to the village centre.

Tollesbury Wick Marshes

The word Wick denotes a sheep walk. Great flocks of sheep grazed here during the 16th and 17th centuries. This 600-acre nature reserve is outstanding for birdlife, especially overwintering species. In summer you can see redshank, lapwing, pochard, skylarks and meadow pipit. Winter brings great numbers of brent geese, lapwing and golden plover, as well as wigeon, teal, hen harriers and short-eared owls.

The sea wall, which is thought to date from between 1400 and 1500, divides the salt marsh from the coastal grazing marsh. It was substantially raised following the 1953 floods. The reserve is owned by the Essex Wildlife Trust, a registered charity (for more information tel (01206) 729678).

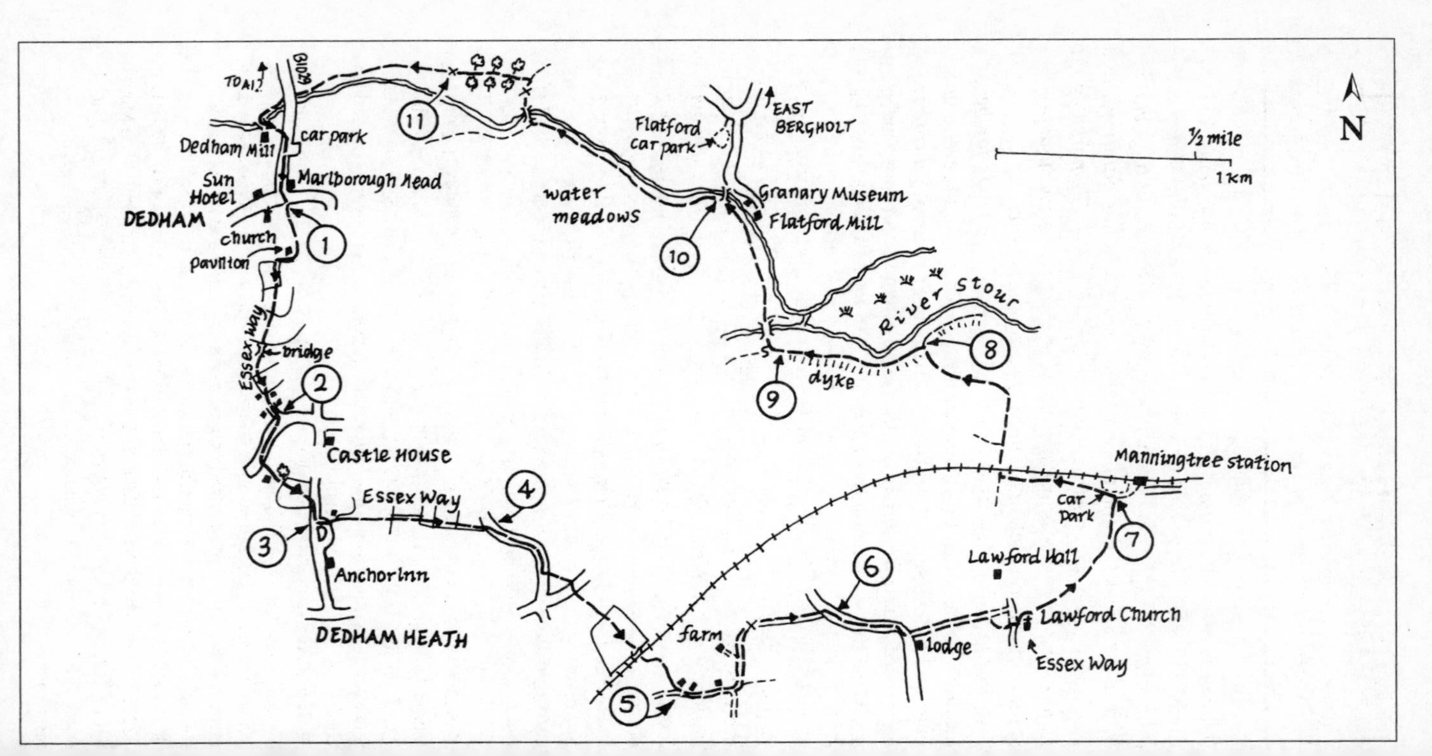
N
½ mile
1 km
TO A12
B1029
car park
Dedham Mill
Marlborough Head
Sun Hotel
DEDHAM
church
pavilion
Essex Way
bridge
Castle House
Essex Way
Anchor Inn
DEDHAM HEATH
water meadows
Flatford car park
EAST BERGHOLT
Granary Museum
Flatford Mill
River Stour
dyke
Manningtree station
Car Park
Lawford Hall
Lawford Church
Essex Way
lodge
farm

Dedham Vale and Flatford Mill

ESSEX/SUFFOLK WALK 7

'I love every stile and stump, and every lane in the village' remarked John Constable of his native East Bergholt. The area of Dedham Vale occupies a hallowed place in the history of English landscape painting: Flatford Mill is the subject of one of Constable's most familiar paintings, and Dedham church appeared in many of his landscapes. Remarkably the watermeadows of the Stour Valley have survived the agricultural progress of the centuries and retain a haunting pastoral character.

Constable Country, as it has become known, extends far beyond Dedham Vale. Stoke-by-Nayland church tower features in several paintings, and the classic East Anglian qualities of the plaster and timber villages spread to such gems as Lavenham, Long Melford, Clare, Cavendish and Thaxted. Sudbury has a museum to its most famous son, Thomas Gainsborough.

The route starts from the strikingly well-preserved old village of Dedham, where Constable attended school, passing the former house of the artist Alfred Munnings (see box). The opening stages follow the intermittently waymarked Essex Way across elevated land with views over the Stour Valley. You have a glimpse of Lawford Hall, then after a gentle descent to the Stour the rest of the walk is quite different in character, following the river closely for most of the way and briefly straying into Suffolk.

Boat hire for exploring the Stour further is available at Flatford (from the Granary Museum) and from the Riverside Café at Dedham.

Marlborough Head, Mill Lane, Dedham CO7 6DH. ☎ (01206) 323124. Open Mon to Fri 11 to 3, 6 to 11, Sat 11 to 11, Sun 12 to 10.30; food Mon to Fri 12 to 2.30, 7 to 9, Sat 12 to 3, 7 to 10, Sun 12 to 9.30. Greene King IPA and Abbot Ale, Adnams, Tetley beers. A la carte menu, daily blackboard specials, sandwiches and bar snacks. Children welcome in family room. No dogs.

Sun Hotel, High Street, Dedham CO7 6DF. ☎ (01206) 323351. Open Mon to Fri 11 to 3, 6 to 11, Sat 11 to 11, Sun 12 to 10.30; and food Mon to Fri 12 to 2.30, 6 to 10, Sat and Sun 12 to 10 (9.30 Sun). Courage Best and Directors, Adnams. A la carte menu and specials board, sandwiches, baked potatoes, pasta and fish. Children welcome in family room and restaurant. No dogs in restaurant.

Anchor Inn, Heath Road, Dedham DO7 6BU (200 yards south of ❸). ☎ (01206) 323131. Open Mon to Sat 11.30 to 3, 6 to 11, Sun 12 to 3, 7 to 10.30; food Mon to Sat 12 to 2, 7 to 9, Sun 12 to 2. Adnams, Greene King IPA. Restaurant menu, bar snacks, blackboard specials, sandwiches. No children in bar area, No dogs in restaurant.

Kings Head, Burnt Oak, East Bergholt CO7 6TL (off the route). ☎ (01206) 298190. Open Mon to Sat 12 to 3, 6.30 to 11, Sun 12 to 3, 7 to 10.30; food all week 12 to 2, 7 to 9. Greene King IPA, Flowers Original, Wadworth 6X. Lovely garden. Bar food, sandwiches, baguettes, ploughman's, specials menu and à la carte menu. Children welcome in restaurant. Dogs welcome in public bar.

Start: Dedham. Parking in the village centre or in the large free car park 250 yards north on the B1029 (Mill Lane; turn off high street by Marlborough Head; turn left out of the car park for the start of the walk). Grid reference 057333.
Alternative start: Flatford National Trust car park (fee); exit by the information board about Flatford at the bottom of the car park, follow the road down to a thatched cottage, where fork right and cross the river; turn right on the riverside path and join the walk at ⓾. Grid reference 075335.
Length: 7 miles (11 kilometres), 4 hours.
Difficulty: Moderate, mostly over pasture, but with occasional arable.
OS maps: 1:25,000 Explorer sheet 196; 1:50,000 Landranger sheet 168.
Tea rooms, shop and restaurants in Dedham. Ice cream kiosk at Flatford.
WC Just after the start of the walk in Dedham, and at Flatford.
PT Trains to Manningtree. Turn half right out of the main exit (platform 1), then just before the car park take the path half left signposted Flatford, turning right again at a T-junction with a track (soon ignore a left turn signposted Lawford church). Join the walk at ❼.

---

❶ From the village centre by the church, take the small lane by the war memorial opposite the Marlborough Head and signposted to the tourist information office and to toilets. This leads into playing fields: turn right immediately after a modern cricket pavilion (where the route ahead continues as a road), along the edge of the cricket field, then just before a dog litter bin take the signposted stile on the left.

The first part of this walk as far as Lawford church follows the Essex Way, which is sporadically waymarked as such.

Follow the left edge of the first field to take a kissing-gate (ignore another path to the left), then forward across the second field to another kissing-gate. In the third field the path passes an old oak tree to reach a stile and footbridge. In the fourth field bear half left to an unprominent footbridge just to the right of the right-hand power post. Follow the right edge of the fifth field, past sheds (one with a memorial to two horses 'Fred the character and Shem the gentleman, now forever in Trapalanda'). The route leads round the right side of a pink house, along its drive and then along a small residential lane to a T-junction ❷.

Turn right to continue. Alternatively you can detour left and right at the main road to see **Castle House**, the former house of Alfred Munnings (see box).

The route continues past more houses. Just after a house on the left called Hunters Moon, turn left on a gravel driveway between hedges. This bends left by a house: go over the paved area in front of the house (it looks rather private, but is a public right of way) to find a woodland path leading to the right. Go up a bank, then forward across a field to a signposted stile beside a gate (not initially visible but it soon comes into view).

Turn right on the road. ❸ 100 yards later turn left into Anchor Lane (the Anchor Inn is 200 yards further down the road). In a few yards, where the lane bends right, keep straight on, along the driveway to Winterflood House, and keep forward again as the driveway bends left to the house. Initially the path has the hedge on the left, then maintains the same direction, along edges of a series of fields via waymarked stiles.

❹ Turn right on the road, and 30 yards before 30mph signs take a stile on the left and bear half right across the field to a stile near a power post. Turn right on the road and immediately left on a signposted enclosed path. This reaches an open field: go forward down to a stile, cross the railway with care and go up the slope into a wood, bending left after 70 yards by a waymark post.

❺ Just past a woodshed, turn left on a track by a wooden barn, and go past a house on your left. 300 yards later, just after another barn on the left, ignore a track to the right, and 40 yards later keep left on the main track (avoiding a stile ahead) which soon bends right (ignore a left fork to some barns). You pass a farm on the left and enter a field, continuing slightly round to the right along a grassy track.

❻ Turn right on the road, and 40 yards after it bends markedly to the right, go through a gate by a Victorian lodge on the left, and follow a semi-surfaced estate road. **Lawford Hall** comes into view away to the left, its square, red-brick Georgian façade of 1756 concealing a timber Elizabethan core.

50 yards before the right-hand field ends, bear half right over a waymarked stile to another stile and reach a road by **Lawford church**. Inside is a rich array of chancel monuments, and the choir is lit by eight windows beneath arches carved with flowers, beasts and birds. In the nave is an oil painting of the church with a pitchfork-wielding peasant depicted in the churchyard.

Take the signposted path into the churchyard and round the left side of the church, leaving by an ornate gate near the far end. An enclosed path leads gently downhill. After ½ mile turn left below the railway embankment near Manningtree station at a T-junction with a track, signposted Flatford ❼.

500 yards later, turn right under the railway bridge; ignore gateways and side turns (mostly marked 'private'), as this track bends left and then right.

❽ Turn left at a T-junction of paths by the river bank. The walk from here to Dedham Mill passes through the lovely scenery of **Dedham Vale**, where kingfishers may be seen on the river, and snipe and redshank frequent the marshes. In the far distance Dedham church tower is soon seen ahead beyond a foreground of reeds, and the path loses sight of the river.

❾ After ½ mile, ignore a stile ahead but turn right over a concrete dam-like structure (marked '56 gates'), over a small tributary (ignoring a path on the right) and then rejoin the main river. You later pass **Willy Lott's Cottage** and **Flatford Mill** on the other bank. The cottage and mill pool were immortalised in Constable's famous painting *The Haywain*. You can cross the bridge and turn right to see the mill, which has belonged to the National Trust since 1943 and is now a field studies centre, but there is no access to its interior. Close by is the **Granary Museum** of bygones, from where boats may be hired.

⑩ The riverside path skirts water meadows that have changed little since Constable's time. After ½ mile cross a prominent footbridge, signposted Dedham and East Bergholt. Follow the enclosed path, through a gate and then where the left-hand field ends turn left on a semi-hidden path bounded on either side by hedgerow trees and between fields. ⑪ Go through a kissing-gate and continue forward, soon rejoining the river. Turn left on the road and immediately right on the riverside path (signposted Stratford St Mary), and cross the river by the next bridge, over locks and past the left side of Dedham Mill to rejoin the road. Turn right into Dedham village centre.

Dedham

As a boy Constable crossed the Stour and walked through the meadows from East Bergholt to the Grammar School in the Square. He had not enjoyed his school in Lavenham and attended Dedham as a day boy. One of his earliest paintings was of the headmaster, who soon appreciated the boy's artistic potential.

Presiding over this most handsome of village streets, the 131-foot tower of St Mary's Church is itself familiar from many of Constable's paintings. On the north wall inside the church, a plaque records the death in 1747 of Judith Eyre, who swallowed a pin in a Christmas pudding.

In 1919 Alfred Munnings purchased Castle House (Open Sunday to Wednesday, May to October, spring bank holiday, plus Thursday and Saturday in August; 2 to 5pm), 'the house of my dreams'. It is now a museum dedicated to his life and work. Dedham also has an Arts Centre, housed within a former Victorian chapel, with crafts displays and demonstrations.

Clavering and Arkesden

ESSEX WALK 8

At either end of this walk are two wonderful villages. Clavering's old street dips down to a ford, and its magical, rather sombre, churchyard abuts a mysterious-looking castle site. Arkesden village is all cream walls and sloping greens. In between you follow some ancient-feeling paths bounded by hedgerow trees; elsewhere there are good paths and tracks along field edges. On one appreciable stretch of quiet road you pass two sailless windmills before continuing on a private farm road.

For some rewarding East Anglian townscape nearby, Saffron Walden has some splendid examples of pargeting (decorative exterior plaster-work), as well as an enigmatic 'turf maze' cut into the grass on the common. On the west edge of the town, Audley End House (English Heritage; 1 April to 30 September, daily 11 to 6; October, Wednesday to Sunday 10 to 3) is a palatial Jacobean house, with pictures and furniture largely accumulated in the 19th century by the then owner the third Lord Braybrooke.

Fox and Hounds, High Street, Clavering CB11 4QR. ☎ (01799) 550321. Open Mon to Thurs 12 to 3, 5 to 11, Fri to Sun 12 to 11 (10.30 Sun); food 12 to 2.30, 6 to 9.30 all week. Bass, Courage Directors, Theakston beers. A wide range of food is available, including jacket potatoes, lasagne and steak as well as vegetarian options. Roasts are served on Sundays. There is also a specials board. Children welcome. No dogs.

Axe and Compasses, Arkesden CB11 4EX. ☎ (01799) 550272. Open Mon to Sat 11.30 to 2.30, 6 to 11, Sun 12 to 3, 7 to 10 (closed 25 Dec); food all week 12 to 2, 6.45 to 9.30 (no food Sun eve). Greene King, Morland Old Speckled Hen, Marstons beers. This low-slung brick and thatch pub, with its bare boards and traditional pub games in one bar and knick-knacks and horse brasses in the other, serves a decent choice of fresh food with Mediterranean hints. Main courses might be monkfish in saffron, duck, venison, or a roast on Sundays. Children welcome in dining-room. No dogs.

Cricketers, Clavering CB11 4QT (off the route, ¾ mile north-east of Clavering village centre on the B1038). ☎ (01799) 550442. Open all week 10.30 to 3, 6 to 11 (closed 25, 26 Dec); bar food all week 12 to 2, 7 to 10, restaurant Sun 12 to 2, Mon to Sat 7 to 10. Adnams Broadside. The Cricketers is bright and modern with an open-plan layout, a log fire, brass knick-knacks, and a very low ceiling in the main bar. Food is traditional Sunday roast style with a slight continental influence: examples include roast pheasant, half a lobster and prawn salad, or suprême of chicken wrapped in puff pastry. The specials board is popular with regular diners, fish is plentiful, and puddings are home-made. Children welcome in bar eating area. No dogs.

Start: Clavering's decorative pheasant-topped village sign and shelter, by B1038 at junction with Middle Street. Roadside parking easiest in side roads; there is a small

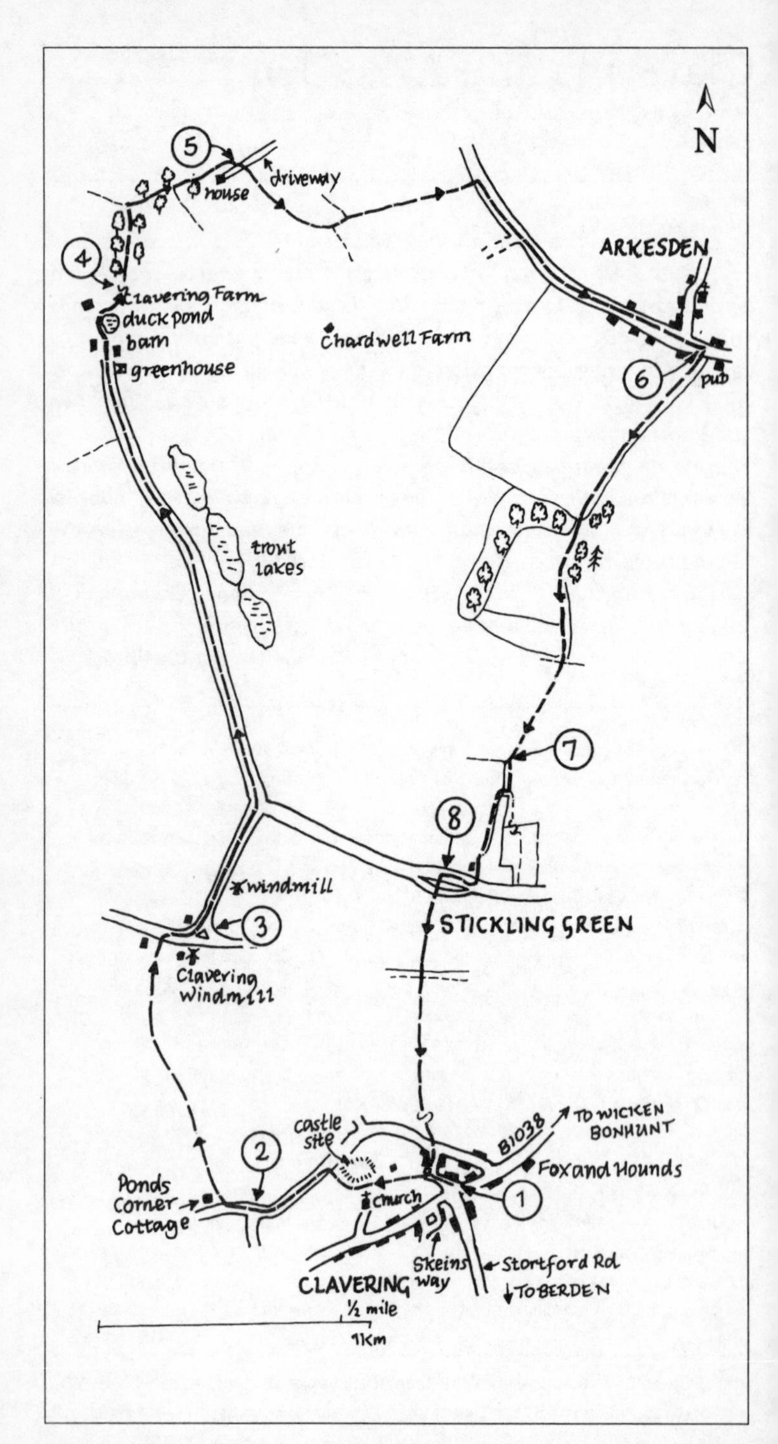
N
5
driveway
house
4
Clavering Farm
duck pond
barn
greenhouse
Chardwell Farm
ARKESDEN
6
pub
trout lakes
7
8
windmill
3
STICKLING GREEN
Clavering Windmill
castle site
2
B1038
TO WICKEN BONHUNT
Fox and Hounds
Ponds Corner Cottage
Church
1
Skeins Way
Stortford Rd
TO BERDEN
CLAVERING
½ mile
1Km

layby in nearby Stortford Road, by the United Reformed Church; also in Skeins Way (near phone box); both these turnings are on the left as you approach via Wicken Bonhunt from the east (past the Fox and Hounds). Grid reference 474318.
Length: 6½ miles (10 kilometres), 3½ hours.
Difficulty: Easy, though the paths running between field hedgerows have a tendency to get muddy.
OS maps: 1:25,000 Explorer sheets 194 and 195; 1:50,000 Landranger sheet 167.
PT Limited bus service from Haverhill to Saffron Walden via Audley End station to Clavering

---

❶ Take Middle Street, by the village sign and the road sign warning of the ford. Where this street bends right in the charming old centre, with its rendered and half-timbered cottages, keep forward on a gravel drive past The Bury (the former manor, which dates from the 13th century). Just before the garden holly hedge ends on your right, keep forward at a track junction (the right turn is private). Enter the yew-shaded churchyard and keep forward along the right-hand fence; it is, however, worth looking inside the **church**, and along the tiny street of cottages just above it. The church is 15th-century Perpendicular, with a fine screen depicting saints on one side, and elaborate memorials to the Barlee (or Barley) family, and a 1591 memorial brass to one Lady Welbore. An effigy of a medieval knight in the north aisle predates the rest of the church by two centuries.

Resuming the walk, carry on along the path along the bottom edge of the churchyard, then just past a point level with the church tower, turn right through a kissing-gate and proceed with a fence away to the left and the outer defences of the site of **Clavering Castle** – founded in 1052 by a French adventurer called Robert Fitz-wimarc, and now an area of bushes and banks – down to your right. A clear path soon leads over a foot-bridge and on to a road on which you turn left.

❷ Keep forward at a junction with a road joining from the left, and 50 yards later (just before Ponds Corner Cottage) turn right on a track signposted 'bridleway', which leads ½ mile to a road. Turn right on the road, then ❸ turn left at the next road junction (signposted Stickling Green), by the sailless **Clavering windmill** (a tower mill) on your right. You pass another sail-less brick **tower mill** dated 1811, then where the road bends right keep left on a private road (footpath only) for 1 mile to Clavering Farm. This road passes a chain of trout lakes on the right and becomes a concrete track at the farm. Here you pass a greenhouse and two barns then turn half left by a noisy duck pond, through a pair of brick pillars, along a house driveway and then half right (waymark on telegraph post) across the grass just before another pair of pillars near the modern farmhouse. Cross two stiles, then ❹ go forward on a path along a woodland strip, avoiding any side paths into fields; the path later bends right and passes a house. ❺ Emerge on a driveway and take the signposted track opposite.

This takes a meandering course between hedges (again, avoid any paths into fields) for over ½ mile. Turn right on a road, into **Arkesden**, with its assemblage of cream-walled thatched cottages set back behind greens enclosed by white railings. The church has an imposing Elizabethan canopied tomb to Richard Cutte and wife.

❻ At Arkesden village centre, by the grassy triangle, village pump and road junction, take the road in the Clavering and Newport direction for 30 yards, then shortly before the Axe and Compasses pub turn right on a signposted path along the left edge of a field. At the end of the field, keep forward (now on a wider track), ignoring a track to the right and another track through woodland to the left. Your track continues alongside trees on the left through two fields, then bends slightly right, now alongside a lower hedgerow.

❼ At the end of this field, where the track bends right, enter the left-hand of two fields ahead and continue forward alongside the hedgerow. 100 yards later cross a plank bridge in the hedgerow on the right and in the next field follow the left-hand hedgerow, immediately bending left, and later continuing along an enclosed path to emerge on a track by a house. Turn left to the road at the hamlet of Stickling Green. Turn right along the road for 100 yards, then ❽ turn left in the middle of the green by a footpath signpost beside a water hydrant sign and take a narrow path between garden hedges. This enters a field via a footbridge and continues as a grassy strip along power lines, over the brow of the hill (by the crossing of power lines), then down to Clavering via a stile. Emerge on the road near a ford; just to the right is tiny thatched, weatherboarded **Chestnut Cottage**, erected in the 17th century and measuring just 8 feet by 10 feet; probably built as the ford-keeper's cottage, it is one of the smallest houses in the UK. Continue opposite over a footbridge to return to the village sign.

Great Bardfield and Finchingfield

ESSEX WALK 9

This route encompasses two outstandingly attractive villages, each with a village green, medieval church and a windmill. In between, the walk follows brooks and tracks across gently rolling farmland, with wide skies and empty horizons lending an unmistakably East Anglian flavour.

The walk can tie in with a visit to any number of the area's unspoilt villages such as Thaxted, Clare and Cavendish. A short distance east lies Hedingham Castle, with its remarkably well-preserved Norman keep and its walls still standing at their original height. Close by is the Colne Valley Railway, with diesel and steam trains operating most Sundays (tel (01787) 461174).

Fox Inn, The Green, Finchingfield CM7 4JX. ☎ (01371) 810151. Open Mon to Fri 11 to 11, Sat 12 to 11, Sun 12 to 6; food Mon to Sat 12 to 2.30, 6 to 9.30, Sun 12 to 3. Greene King IPA and Abbot Ale. The beautifully pargeted (see box) pub has poll position on the village green overlooking the pond. A la carte menu, home-made pies, fish, jacket potatoes and baguettes. No children in restaurant in evenings. No dogs during food times.

Red Lion, 6 Church Hill, Finchingfield CM7 4NN. ☎ (01371) 810400. Open Mon to Sat 11.30 to 11, Sun 12 to 10.30; food 12 to 3, 6.30 to 9.30 (8.30 Sun). Ridleys beers. A la carte menu might include duck paté with cranberry compote or garlic mushrooms to start, and smoked chicken with cream and tomato or fillet of pork in a mustard and cream sauce as a main course. Specials might be seafood stir-fry or Arabic lamb rice and salad. Bar meals could include pies, home-made soup, all day breakfast or cottage pie and chips. Sandwiches are also available. Children welcome in restaurant. No dogs in restaurant.

Three Tuns, Weathersfield Road, Finchingfield CM7 4NR. ☎ (01371) 810165. Open Mon to Fri 5 to 11, Sat and Sun 12 to 3.30, 7 to 11, food see opening times. 4 real ales. Bar snacks and teas available. Children welcome. Dogs welcome.

Vine, Vine Street. Great Bardfield CM7 4SR. ☎ (01371) 810355. Open Mon to Sat 11 to 3, 6 to 11. Sun 12 to 3, 7 to 10.30; food 12 to 2, 7 to 10. Ridleys, Greene King beers. Blackboard specials and sandwiches. No children in bar. Dogs welcome in public bar only.

Bell, Great Bardfield CM7 4SA. ☎ (01371) 811097. Open 12 to 3, 7 to 11 (10.30 Sun). Greene King beers. No food (except when delicatessen opposite is open, as food is bought in). Children welcome. Dogs welcome.

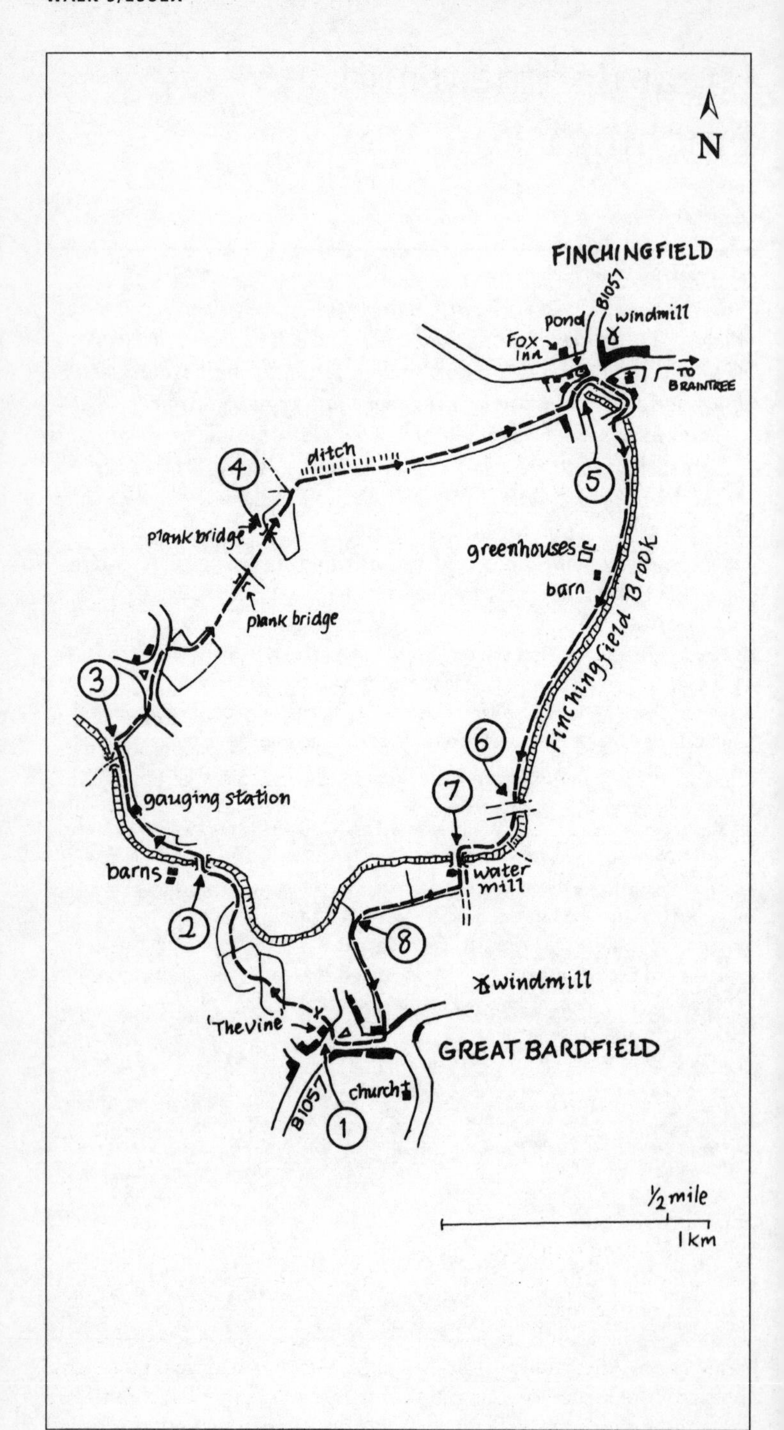
N
FINCHINGFIELD
B1057
pond
windmill
FOX INN
TO BRAINTREE
ditch
4
5
plank bridge
plank bridge
greenhouses
barn
Finchingfield Brook
3
6
gauging station
7
barns
water mill
2
8
windmill
'The Vine'
GREAT BARDFIELD
church
B1057
1
½ mile
1 km

Start: War memorial cross in Great Bardfield village centre near the Vine public house; on B1057, east of Thaxted. Grid reference 675305.
Alternative start: Village green at Finchingfield (junction of B1053 and B1057). Join walk at ❺. Grid reference 685328.
Length: 4½ miles (7 kilometres), 2½ hours.
Difficulty: Easy, with no appreciable slopes; short stretches may cross arable fields. Stinging-nettles in summer make shorts or skirt unsuitable.
OS maps: 1:25,000 Explorer sheet 195; 1:50,000 Landranger sheet 167.
Tea rooms in Finchingfield. Both Finchingfield and Great Bardfield have a village shop.
WC Finchingfield (signposted from the green, and near the village hall).
PT Infrequent bus service from Braintree to Finchingfield and Great Bardfield (not Sun).

---

❶ Take the signposted track to the right of the Vine pub, passing a walled garden on your left with a curious flint folly in it. Soon you enter the first field. Go half left to a stile in the hedgerow, emerging into a second field where you ignore another stile immediately to the left but drop down the slope slightly to the right to find a footbridge and stile in the opposite hedgerow.

Proceed diagonally in the third field to a gate, and go forward in the fourth field down to a stile. Keep right, along the right edge of the fifth field (with a brook just to your right).

❷ Cross the footbridge over the brook shortly before a group of barns, and turn left on the other side, now alongside the brook on your left.

By a weir and brick hut (a water-gauging station), the path is now fenced on the right-hand side. Soon ignore a footbridge on your left, but just after it ❸ cross a stile into the field and turn right, up the field edge to a stile on to a road. Turn left on the road, and go forward at a junction, signposted Pitley Farm. After 100 yards, take the signposted gate on your right and follow the farm track in the first field. After 100 yards, in the middle of the field (immediately after the hedgerow away to your left reaches a projecting corner), turn left and enter the second field, proceeding along the left edge alongside a hedgerow with a deep ditch on its far side.

After 250 yards, at the end of the field, enter the right-hand of two fields ahead via a plank footbridge, to follow the left edge of the third field for 150 yards until taking a plank footbridge (rather hidden in the hedgerow) on the left in the field corner ❹. Bear diagonally left across the middle of the fourth field (roughly in line with the direction given by the footbridge itself) to the far end of the left-hand hedgerow (if the field-path is obscured by crops, you are entitled to cross the field and will be doing a service to others by treading the correct route).

Emerge at a junction of well-defined farm tracks (leading left, ahead and right), and turn right. The track immediately bends left, then right alongside a ditch on the left and heads for Finchingfield village, later with a fence on the right. Emerge into the village and turn left on the road to reach the village green. The village centre of **Finchingfield** makes a beautiful composition, with its green, duck-pond and colour-washed cottages (the pargeted walls (see box overleaf), adorned with decorative plasterwork, are very much the local style) leading the eye to the weather-boarded postmill of 1775. Opposite a group of almshouses, enter the churchyard under an overhanging building that was the hall of a Guild of the Holy Trinity up until the Reformation. The church has a wealth of features, including an outstanding 15th-century carved screen, a Norman doorway and a monument to one William Kempe who in the early 17th century 'did by a voluntary constancy, hold his peace for seven years' – a penance of silence he undertook after falsely accusing his wife of infidelity.

❺ Standing on the green with the Fox Inn to your left, take the right-hand of the two bridges over the pond, and just past the decorative village sign on the green and a red-brick Georgian house on the right turn right on a small lane. This lane runs between walls for a short distance; 50 yards after the left-hand wall ends, take the signposted path on the right. As soon as you cross a footbridge, fork left and follow the enclosed path, soon through woods and into a field. Continue always alongside Finchingfield Brook on your left. After ¼ mile, in a field containing greenhouses, the path passes to the left of a small barn, still beside the brook and soon across the end of a private garden.

❻ 500 yards later, emerge on to a farm track by power lines and continue opposite and slightly to the right, to enter a field where you keep along the left edge (still alongside the brook which has, however, disappeared from view); at the corner of the field avoid the wooden footbridge and stile to the left, but keep right, still along the field edge.

❼ Cross by the next footbridge on the left (a larger, metal one) and go forward over a field past a watermill and house, then 30 yards later turn right. Enter a field, with the brook about 50 yards to your right: keep to the left edge of two fields until ❽ you reach a ditch ahead, where the route continues over a stile to the left, now along the right edge of a field with back gardens on the right (ignore a plank bridge on the right) and a windmill away to the left. Keep forward at the end of the field and follow an enclosed path to join the road at Great Bardfield. Turn right and keep right at the next junction (or left to detour to the church) to reach the war memorial.

Great Bardfield, with its greens punctuating the street line, repays exploration. The main street is wide and gently sloping, with a variety of medieval timber-framed and Georgian brick houses. Between the two world wars the village was something of an artists' colony. The church has a magnificent 14th-century stone screen. Tie-beams above the chancel are dated 1618, and there is (under a cover) a fine Tudor memorial brass.

Pargeting

The art of raised decorative plasterwork is local to Suffolk, Essex and Hertfordshire. The technique dates from the 16th and 17th centuries, when plaster was applied over the timber-framed gables and façades. While the plaster was wet, various moulds were pressed into it, making up elaborate patterns. Originally these depicted animals, plants and people; later designs were geometric. 'Pargeting' derives from the French *pour jeter*, which means to throw.

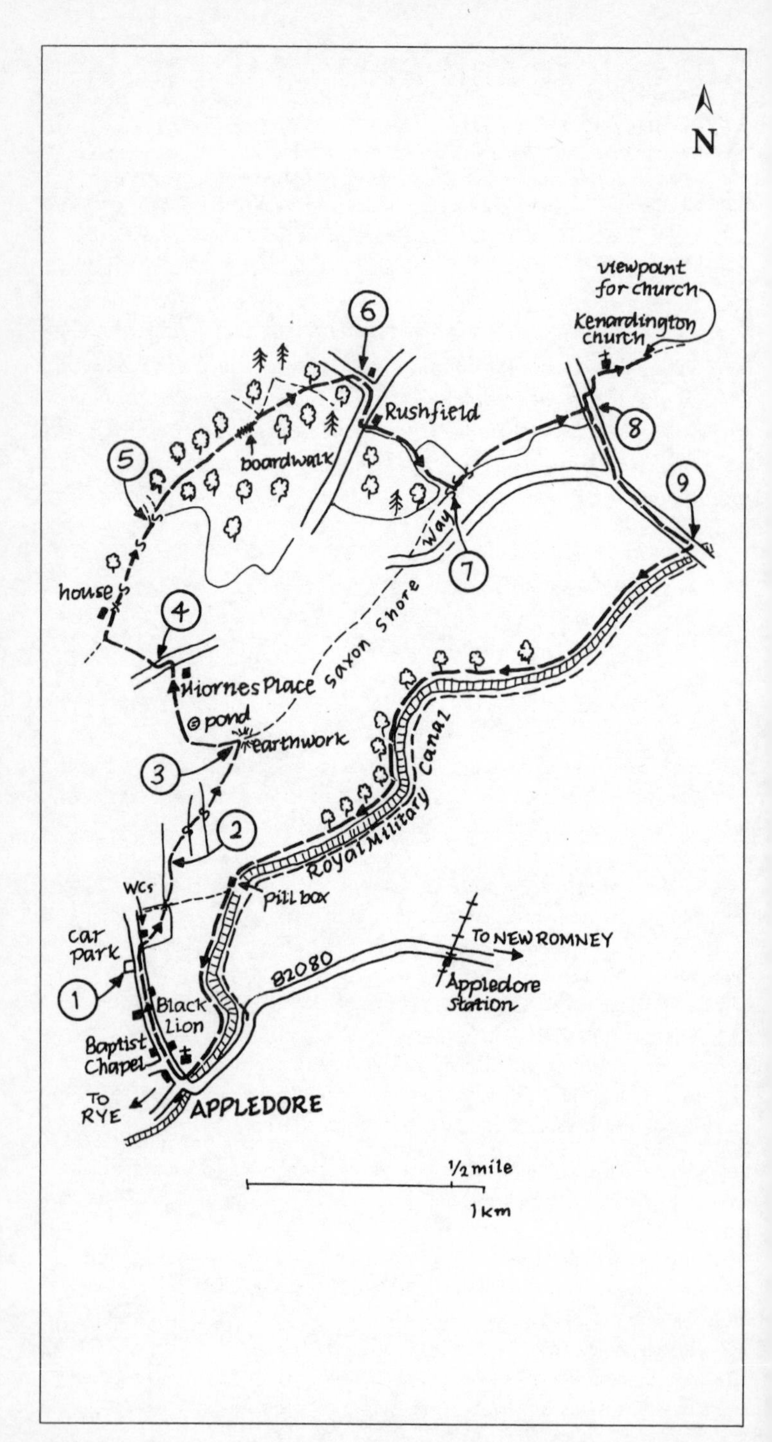
N
viewpoint for church
Kenardington church
6
Rushfield
boardwalk
5
8
9
7
Way
house
Saxon Shore
4
Hiornes Place
pond
earthwork
3
Royal Military Canal
2
WCs
pill box
Car Park
TO NEW ROMNEY
B2080
1
Appledore Station
Black Lion
Baptist Chapel
TO RYE
APPLEDORE
1/2 mile
1 km

Appledore and the Royal Military Canal

KENT WALK 10

The peripheries of Romney Marsh may not be obvious walking terrain but the land rises enough to get views towards the coast. Fascinating historic survivals include Appledore village, Hiornes Place, Kenardington Church and the Royal Military Canal. On the way you pass through a sizable broad-leaved woodland, bright with bluebells in spring. There are arable fields to cross, and some mud, but negligible ascent; part of the route follows the waymarked Saxon Shore Way. Nettles can be a problem in summer.

Black Lion, 15 The Street, Appledore TN26 2BU. ☎ (01233) 758206. Open Mon to Sat 11.30 to 11, Sun 12 to 10.30; food 11.30 (12 Sun) to 10. Hancock's and Bass beers. A la carte menu, blackboard specials and fish, bar snacks and sandwiches on weekdays. Children welcome. Dogs welcome.

Ypres Castle, Gun Garden, Rye TN31 7HH (off the route). ☎ (01797) 223248. Open 12 to 11 (10.30 Sun); closed eve 25 Dec; food 12 to 2.30, 7 to 10.30 (all day at certain times in summer). Half a dozen fine cask-conditioned ales, including Charles Wells Bombardier, Adnams Broadside and Harveys beers. Much of the food served at this 17th-century freehouse is reliant on local produce: perhaps soup or a fishy starter; and for a main course lamb in red wine and rosemary gravy or duckling in morello cherry and brandy. Those wanting something lighter at lunch-time could choose from baguettes, jacket potatoes and ploughman's. A carvery is available at Sunday lunch-time. Children welcome in family room. Dogs welcome on a lead.

William Caxton, West Cross, Tenterden T30 6JR, on A28, 10 miles south-west of Ashford (off the route). ☎ (01580) 763142. Open 11 to 3, 5 to 11, Sat 11 to 11; food Mon to Sat 12 to 2.30, 7 to 9.30, Sun 12 to 2.30. Shepherd Neame beers. The menu at this large, white-painted and tile-hung pub includes a large range of pub food: sandwiches and baguettes, fish and chips, lasagne, steak and Guinness pie. Children welcome in restaurant if eating. Dogs welcome in bar area.

Start: Appledore, on B2080 south of Ashford. Free car park signposted by the parish hall at the north end of the village.

Length: 6.5 miles (10.5 kilometres), 3 hours.

Difficulty: Easy to moderate.

OS maps: 1:25,000 Explorer sheet 125; 1:50,000 Landranger sheet 189.

Shop in Appledore.

WC In the playing field near the start of the walk.

PT A few buses from Tenterden and Appledore (not Sun). Appledore station (Ashford–Hastings line) is 1 mile east (turn left out of the station along the B2080).

❶ Turn left out of the car park, then after 80 yards, take the path on the right opposite the drive to Magpie Farm. Cross a playing field (a toilet block is here) and go diagonally left to the gate in the corner. Keep left along the edge of the next field, following the yellow waymarks of the Saxon Shore Way, ❷ turning half right midway through the field to a stile, taking the right-hand of two stiles into a small copse and across more fields.

The **Saxon Shore Way** is well marked in this section. This 135-mile long-distance path explores the line of the Kent coast as the Romans knew it (the sea has since receded in many places, and hereabouts the fertile farm land of Romney Marsh has since been reclaimed). On its journey from Gravesend to Rye it passes a chain of coastal defences erected against Saxon raiders.

❸ The path leads up to a prominent ancient mound. From here you have a wide view over Romney Marsh, with pylons radiating out from the massive distant bulk of Dungeness Power Station. About 50 yards after this mound, turn very sharp left to leave the Saxon Shore Way (which is about to go along a line of trees). Follow this pleasant old green track, which now heads past a pond and **Hiornes Place**. Adjacent to this most attractive old tile-hung house (not open) is a private 14th-century chapel, glimpsed from the path. Wat Tyler attacked the house in the Peasants' Revolt of 1381.

❹ Turn left along the road for 30 yards, then right by a telegraph post on a wide path. This can be a little overgrown, but should be manageable in high summer, and the route is obvious. Beyond a stile you emerge on to a driveway, along which you turn right past a red-brick house. Yellow waymarks lead you through an area partly planted with orchards, and then into much denser woodland by a stile ❺.

As soon as you enter the woods, cross another stile and keep right at a T-junction of paths just after. Avoid any turnings to the left and follow the main path, which continues to be clearly marked with yellow arrows. After a section along a boardwalk, take the middle of three paths as waymarked. The trees are delightfully mixed, both mature and coppice, and mostly hazel, oak, chestnut and silver birch. In spring the carpets of bluebells are spectacular.

❻ At the road, turn right and right again at the T-junction. Just past a weatherboarded cottage called Rushfield on the left, turn left on a track with coppiced woodland on your right. The path can get a little overgrown in summer, but should be passable.

❼ After ⅓ mile the waymarked Saxon Shore Way crosses the path, indicated by steps up to stiles on either side; turn left. Beyond a small paddock you enter a large field (with its far boundaries virtually out of sight); the route is not visible here, but you should have no problems finding the route if you walk close to the right-hand hedgerow. ❽ Reach a road: right is the continuation, but first detour a few yards to **Kenardington church** by taking the path roughly opposite.

The lonely, unmodernised country church overlooking

Romney Marsh has no electricity, and a tall, primitive interior of whitewashed walls beneath a beamed roof. Follow the Saxon Shore Way into the field below the church for a fascinating exterior view, where you can see how the 12th-century tower has been bricked up on the side of the original nave, which has long since vanished. The present building evidently occupies what was a side aisle. From there you can also discern the line of the bank of a Saxon camp (stormed by the Danes in 893) around the churchyard. Return to the road, walk along it and keep left at the next junction.

❾ At the swan-populated Royal Military Canal, turn right along either bank: the north bank delves more into the woods, and from it you get only occasional glimpses of the canal (although it opens out later), but there are opportunities for observing woodland birdlife. The south bank path eventually joins a road, which is followed for ¼ mile to Appledore Bridge.

At Appledore Bridge turn right through **Appledore** to return to the start. The village has one of Kent's most charming streets, with many timber-framed, tile-hung and brick cottages dating from its days as a prosperous medieval weaving centre. In 1380 the French destroyed the church and village.

The Royal Military Canal

It is hard to credit, but this peaceful stretch of water, populated only by swans and moorhens busying themselves amongst the waterlilies and duckweed, was originally conceived as a barrier against marauding Napoleonic armies. It was thought that the French might try to invade England on the flat beaches between the cliffs of Hastings and Folkestone. At a cost of £230,000, a vast sum in Georgian times, the canal and a parallel military road, screened by a bank, were constructed to ward off the enemy. Dog-legs every 500 yards allowed for a clear line of fire along any section, while troops could be transported quickly in barges or along the road. The invasion never materialised, and the whole project became something of a military folly. The canal operated commercially until the mid-19th century, since when it has become a wildlife haven owned by the National Trust. During the Second World War, when invasion threatened again, pillboxes were built along the canal, some of which survive today. A canalside path now runs along the entire length.

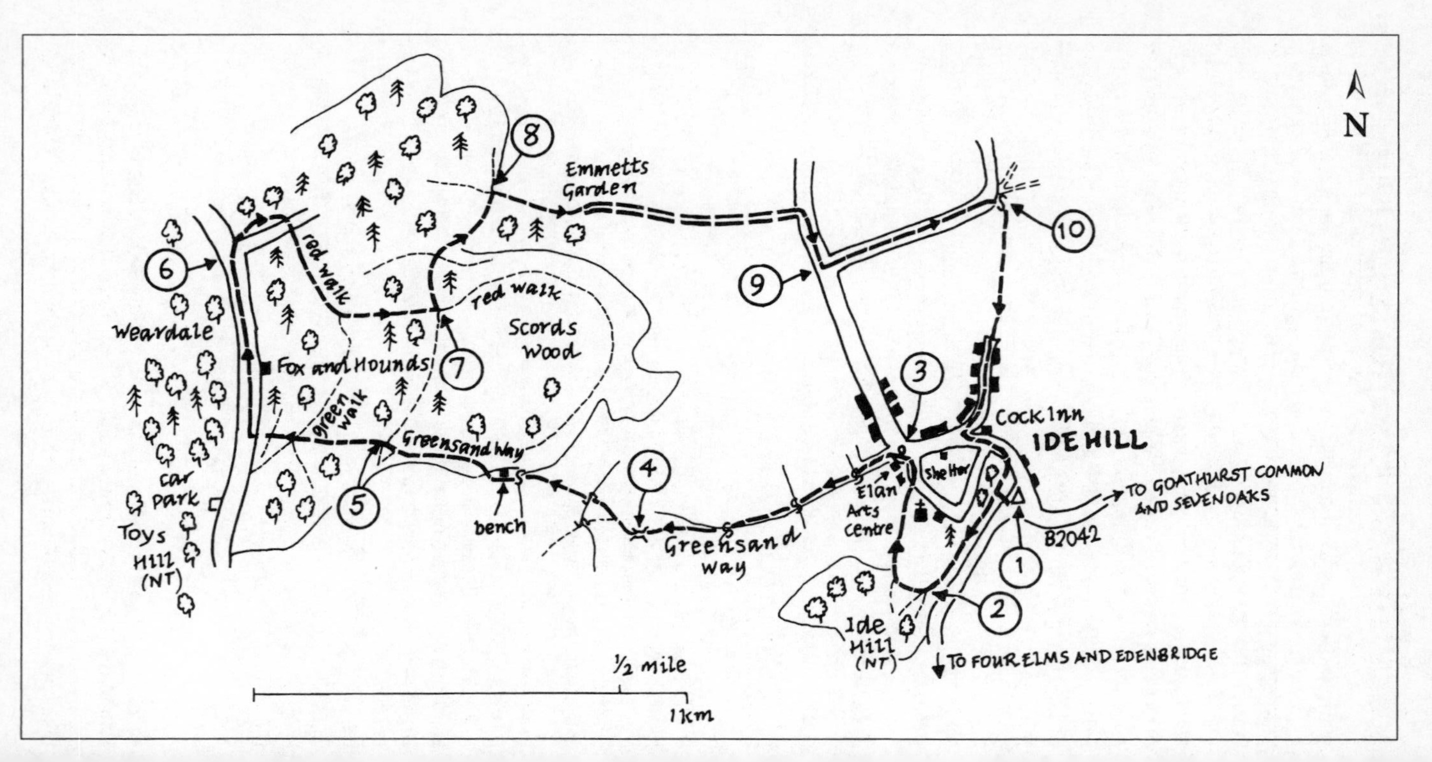
N
Emmetts Garden
red walk
red walk
Scords Wood
Weardale
Fox and Hounds
green walk
Greensand Way
car park
Toys Hill (NT)
bench
Greensand Way
Cock Inn
IDE HILL
Shelter
Elan Arts Centre
TO GOATHURST COMMON AND SEVENOAKS
B2042
Ide Hill (NT)
TO FOUR ELMS AND EDENBRIDGE
1/2 mile
1km
1
2
3
4
5
6
7
8
9
10

Ide Hill and Emmetts Garden

KENT WALK 11

Ide Hill is both a wooded hill and a very attractive village set around a wide green – both are high up on the greensand escarpment amid some of the lushest and most varied of Kent's countryside. This short exploration packs in a surprising amount – hillside, open pasture fields for the opening stages, then some of the best of the area's woodlands, now owned by the National Trust. You also have the chance to visit the Trust's glorious Emmetts Garden; if this is closed you still get a fair view of the site from this walk, which follows the driveway between two parts of the garden. A short drive north-west are two National Trust houses: Winston Churchill's Chartwell and General Wolfe's Quebec House at Westerham.

Fox and Hounds, Toys Hill TN16 1QG. ☎ (01732) 750328. Open Mon 12 to 2.30, Tues to Fri 11.30 to 2.30, 6 to 11, Sat 11.30 to 3, 6 to 11, Sun 7 to 10.30; food Sundays and bank holidays only. Greene King beers. The Fox and Hounds is a remote cottage tucked away in the forest by itself. Rolls and snacks on Sundays and bank holidays only. Children welcome in restricted area at lunch-times. Dogs by arrangement only.

Cock, Ide Hill TN14 6JN. ☎ (01732) 750132. Open Mon to Sat 11.30 to 2.30, 6 to 11, Sun 12 to 3, 7 to 10.30; food 12 to 2, Tues to Thur 6 to 8.30, Fri, Sat 6 to 9, no food Mon or Sun eves. Greene King IPA and Abbot Ale. A la carte menu, Sun sandwiches only. No children. Dogs welcome.

Castle Inn, Chiddingstone (off the route; for details, see Walk 17)

Start: Car park on B2042 ¼ mile south-east of Ide Hill (between Edenbridge and Sevenoaks), by the signpost to Ide Hill and by the toilet block. Alternative parking around the green at Ide Hill village.

Length: 3½ miles (5 kilometres), 2 hours.

Difficulty: Easy to moderate, over undulating terrain, with the steepest sections near the start.

OS maps: 1:25,000 Explorer sheet 147; 1:50,000 Landranger sheet 188.

Elan Arts Centre in Ide Hill serves teas Wed to Sun 10 to 5/5.30; there is also a shop in the village. Visitors to Emmetts Garden can use the toilets and tea room there.

WC In the car park at the start.

PT Some buses to Ide Hill from Sevenoaks, Mon to Sat, plus (summer only) about six a day on Sun.

❶ With toilets on the right and the B2042 on the left, cross the road signposted Ide Hill ¼ mile and take the rising woodland path by the National Trust sign for Ide Hill and signposted **Greensand Way**, which you will follow for the next mile of the walk. This long-distance route running 55 miles from Haslemere to Limpsfield takes in some of the most pleasantly varied terrain in the south-east of England, crossing the Devil's Punchbowl, Hascombe Hill, Leigh Hill and Reigate Heath.

Continue to follow Greensand Way signs, keeping left after 20 yards, and ignore the next right turn uphill just before a stone bench in memory of Octavia Hill, overlooking a fine view of the Weald. Octavia Hill (1838–1912), a campaigner for housing reform and public open spaces, was one of the co-founders of the National Trust in 1894. A woodland owned by the National Trust and reached later in this walk is also named after her.

Just after the bench take the rightmost of three paths. ❷ Keep forward at the next junction on Greensand Way where another path joins from the left; views now open out to the left. Past the Victorian church, go down the road down the left-hand edge of the village green of Ide Hill, past a roundabout with a Greensand Way sign at the bottom of the green.

❸ 25 yards later, just before the primary school, turn left on a drive-way. This enters a field: follow Greensand Way signs down field edges to a small bridge in the trees ❹, then go steeply up the centre of the next field (the route was not very clearly marked when this walk was inspected): avoid a stile in the top left corner but take another stile to the right of this, rise to cross a stile by the woodland fence, then follow the top of the field.

Just after a memorial bench take a stile on the right into the woods. Keep forward along the Greensand Way as another path almost immediately joins from the right, and fork right where the left fork goes along a fence. ❺ 70 yards later keep forward on the Greensand Way and Red Walk.

These **woodlands** are part of the National Trust's Toys Hill estate, which include some of the finest ancient woodlands in Kent. The estate was badly damaged by the 1987 storm; some fallen trees were cleared, but others were left to allow natural regeneration. The area supports a diversity of fungi and woodland birds.

At a five-way junction leave the Greensand Way and take the rising path waymarked as Weardale Walk ahead uphill; at the top, go straight on at a junction, on the Weardale Walk. Turn right on the road, past the Fox and Hounds pub, then ¼ mile later ❻ turn right, signposted Emmetts Garden, but immediately fork left on to the Red Walk and Green Walk.

In 100 yards the Red Walk crosses the road; continue on the Red Walk, which forks left from the Green Walk after ¼ mile, and drops to a junction with a blue waymarked bridleway ❼, where you turn left to leave the Red Walk.

Carry on past the first cross-junction, then turn right at the next cross-junction ❽ (Weardale Walk), waymarked with a yellow arrow. This path drops down past Emmetts Garden and continues along the main driveway.

Emmetts Garden (National Trust, open late March to late May, Wednesday to Sunday and bank holiday Mondays; 11–5.30, last admission 4.30) looks far over the Weald and includes exotic shrubs and trees, a rose garden and rock garden and fine spring displays of daffodils and bluebells.

Turn right at the T-junction with the road, then ❾ take the first road on the left (Norman Street). Ignore a stile on the right just after passing under power lines. ❿ After ¼ mile, where the road bends left, take the right-hand driveway, then immediately right over a stile. Cross a field (aiming to the left of a house on the far side), then follow a residential road into Ide Hill village centre.

Turn left, past the Cock Inn on your left. Opposite a house called Deansfield, and before the next right road turn, fork right on a path by a National Trust sign for Ide Hill. Immediately turn left (where the path ahead climbs steps) through a small field with a strategically sited picnic bench and view of Bough Beech Reservoir, then follow a path through woods. The next turn leads down to the car park.

Weather tiling

A feature of many Wealden houses is the tile-hung wall, a practice dating from the late 17th century in the region. This weatherproofing measure spread to other parts of England but is essentially a speciality of Kent, Surrey and Sussex. In many cases, the same type of tile is used for the roof. Frequently, the tiles are hung on to wooden battens or affixed by pegs. Older tile-hung houses are commonly wooden framed and covered with pantiles. These are large tiles, known as Flanders tiles before 1700, when they were imported from Holland. An Act of Parliament at the time of George I stipulated that their measurements should be at least 13½ x 9½ x ½ inches. Their design required only a single overlap, making them lighter; this in turn economised on the amount of roof timber required.

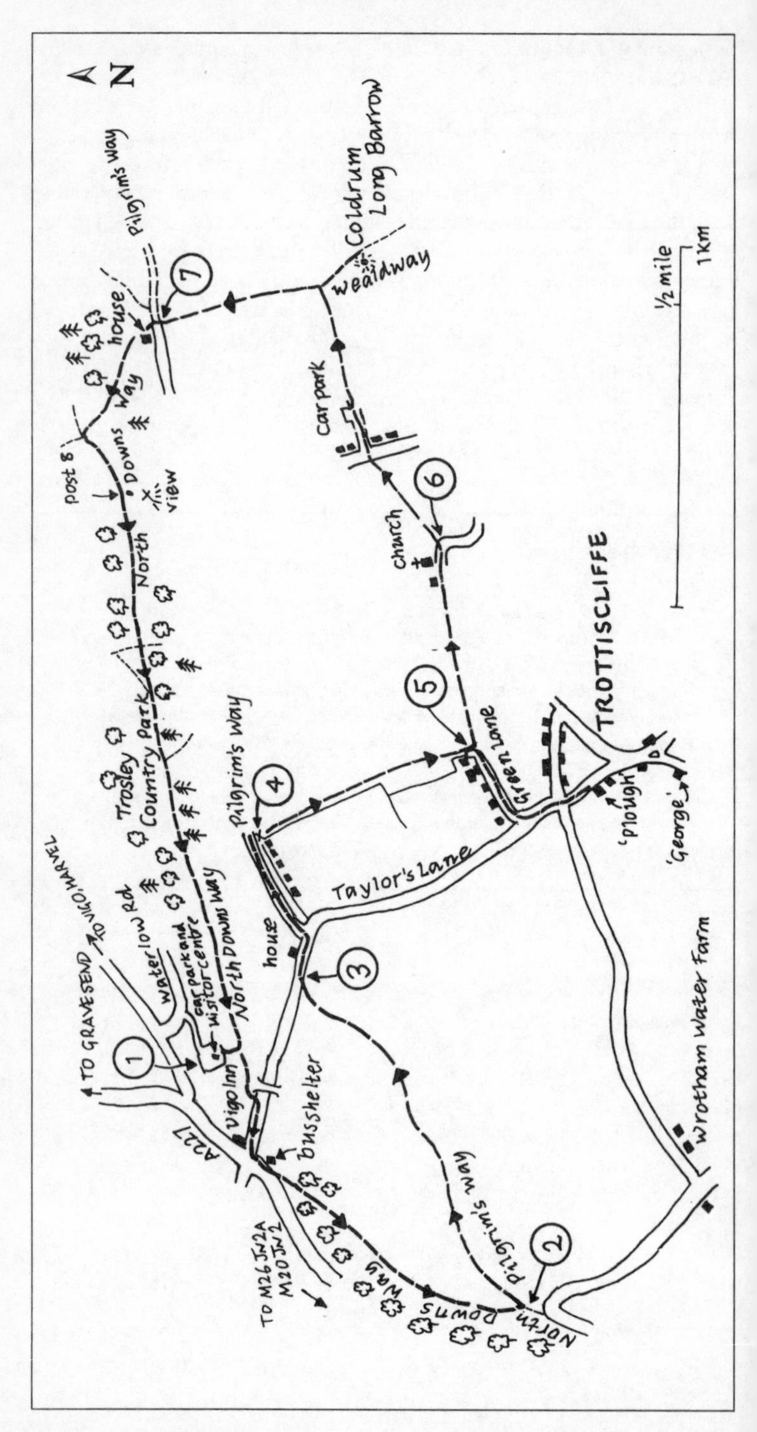
N
Pilgrim's Way
Coldrum Long Barrow
Wealdway
7
house
North Downs Way
post 8
view
Trosley Country Park
Pilgrim's Way
4
5
6
church
car park
Green Lane
TROTTISCLIFFE
'Plough'
'George'
Taylor's Lane
house
3
Waterlow Rd
car park and visitor centre
North Downs Way
1
TO GRAVESEND
A227
Vigo Inn
bus shelter
TO M26 JN2A
M20 JN2
North Downs Way
Pilgrim's Way
2
Wrotham Water Farm
½ mile
1 km

Trottiscliffe and the Coldrum Long Barrow

KENT WALK 12

The best of the views are reserved for the later stages, as you look up to the North Downs from the foot of the escarpment and glimpse the paper mill chimneys of the Medway Valley in the far distance. The North Downs Way along the top of the slope leads under a dense woodland canopy, but with occasional views southwards. The Plough Inn in the pleasantly rural village of Trottiscliffe (pronounced Trozly) merits a deviation from the route before you head on along rolling farmland to the Coldrum Long Barrow, one of the archaeological wonders of Kent.

Plough, Taylors Lane, Trottiscliffe ME19 5DR. ☎ (01732) 822233. Open 11.30 to 11; food 11.30 to 2, Mon to Sat 6 to 9.30. Adnams, Wadworth 6X, Flowers and Fuller's beers. The starters at this 500-year-old, weatherboarded inn can be refreshingly different, perhaps goats' cheese served with home-made chutney. The pub's dishes are listed on a specials board – for example, ribeye steaks, home-made meat curries. Other choices include ploughman's and jumbo rolls. Children welcome in bar eating area. Dogs welcome in one bar.

George Inn, Taylors Lane, Trottiscliffe ME19 5DR. ☎ (01732) 822462. Open Mon to Fri 11 to 3, 6 to 11, Sat 11 to 11, Sun 12 to 10.30; food Mon to Sat 12 to 2.30, 7 to 9.30 (9 Sun). Shepherd Neame beers. Sandwiches, bar snacks and blackboard specials available. Children welcome in children's room and restaurant. No dogs in restaurant.

Start: Trosley Country Park, well signposted off the A227 (turning is also signposted Vigo and Harvel). Take the first right turning – Waterlow Road – and the entrance is almost immediately on your right; small fee for parking). Park by the visitor centre and refreshment kiosk. Grid reference 635611.

Length: 5 miles (8 kilometres), 2½ hours.

Difficulty: Moderate, with a rutted and uneven descent, and one climb on to the North Downs.

OS maps: 1:25,000 Explorer sheet 148; 1:50,000 Landranger sheet 177 or 188.

Uncle Bob's Cabin in Trosley Country Park car park sells hot and cold snacks.

WC In the car park at the start of the walk.

PT Buses from Wrotham, Sevenoaks and Tunbridge Wells (Mon–Sat) and Gravesend (daily) pass the Vigo Inn near the start of the walk; start with the pub on your left, go past the bus shelter and fork left on the North Downs Way, which drops steadily, with occasional views on the left; join the directions at ❷.

❶ With the Visitor Centre and refreshment kiosk on your left, take the broad path immediately to the right of the map information board (with roofed top). 20 yards later, turn right at a T-junction with the North Downs Way (by a map of the North Downs Way), which you follow for the first stages of the walk. This leads through barriers, keeps to the right of a stone bridge over the road and reaches the road, where you turn right up to the A227 by the Vigo Inn. Turn left (along the pavement) for 20 yards, then just after the bus shelter fork left on the North Downs Way, which soon drops steadily, with occasional views on the left.

❷ Emerge into the semi-open at an oblique T-junction of paths at the foot of the North Downs. Turn sharp left (signposted Byway), leaving the North Downs Way – you are now following the age-old Pilgrim's Way *(it is possible to shorten the walk slightly by following roads: turn right here, then left on the road, and left again into Trottiscliffe, where you will find the Plough Inn on your right).*

❸ After ¾ mile turn right on the road, then left at the next junction (on a road called Pilgrim's Way) where the main road continues as Taylor's Lane. ❹ After ¼ mile, just after the end of the houses down on your right, turn right on a signposted path through a kissing-gate into a field, where you follow the right edge and maintain this direction (along field edges and eventually past garden fences) to a T-junction with a path ❺ (leading to Trottiscliffe church to the left). Left is your continuation.

For the pubs at Trottiscliffe, detour right here – soon joining the end of a residential road (Green Lane), and then turn left at the road junction into the unspoilt village centre. (To return to the route from the Plough, turn left out of the pub, then right into Green Lane. At the end of the road continue forward into a field, with Trottiscliffe church ahead.)

To continue carry on along the field edge towards **Trottiscliffe church**. Standing beside Trosley Court and dedicated to St Peter and St Paul, this early Norman structure is a simple oblong, with box pews, and a grandiose pulpit of 1781 brought from Westminster Abbey. The artist Graham Sutherland and his wife, who lived in Trottiscliffe, are buried here.

Past the church, continue on the road for 25 yards, and as it is about to bend right (just after some attractive stone-built cottages on the left) take the path on the left ❻ (rather obscurely waymarked) over a field. Cross the road and take the lane opposite signposted to Coldrum Long Barrow car park: this becomes a path, leading along a field edge and reaching a path T-junction with the Wealdway in a group of trees: left is the continuation, but first detour right a short distance to see the **Coldrum Long Barrow**. This is one of the most impressive Neolithic burial places in the south-east of England, consisting of sarsen stones within a stone circle. It dates from the latter half of the 3rd millennium BC. In 1910, remains of 22 skeletons were excavated, their short stature, delicate bone structure and long heads being characteristics of a Mediterranean people.

Return to the path junction and follow the Wealdway uphill (there are distant views of Medway Valley paper mills to your right). ❼ At the end of a small road by a house, turn right and immediately left, steeply uphill. At the top, the North Downs Way (which you now follow all the way back to the start) leads to the left, back into **Trosley Country Park** through woodland, with some fine canopies of yews; in a couple of places the woodland has been cleared to open out the view. You can get a good view by taking a path on the left (by a post numbered 8 – facing the other way) to a gate on to open downland. Eventually the North Downs Way reaches the map sign on the left, where the car park and picnic area are visible a few yards to your right.

Trosley Country Park

The 160 acres of woodland and downland that form the country park were prevously part of the estate of Trosley Towers, a huge Victorian pile demolished in the 1930s. It was owned by the Waterlows (a printing family). Sydney Hedley Waterlow made his fortune in railway stationery and printing. A philanthropist by nature, he became a local MP, and as Lord Mayor of London opened the Guildhall Library to the public.

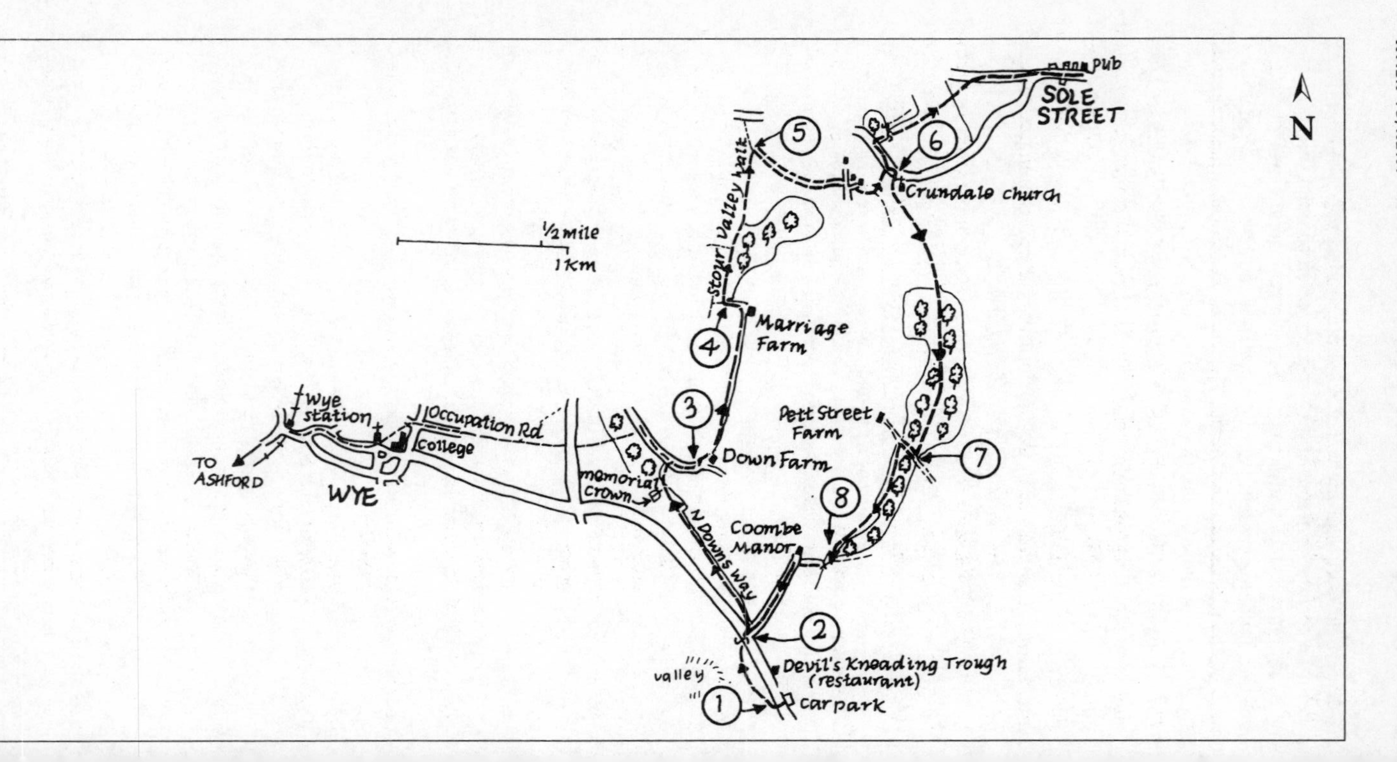
N
pub
SOLE STREET
Crundale church
Stour Valley Walk
½ mile
1 Km
Marriage Farm
Pett Street Farm
Down Farm
Wye station
Occupation Rd
College
TO ASHFORD
WYE
memorial Crown
N Downs Way
Coombe Manor
Devil's Kneading Trough (restaurant)
valley
car park
1
2
3
4
5
6
7
8

Wye Downs and Crundale

KENT WALK 13

This is one of the very deepest parts of the North Downs, with a superb view in the opening sections before the landscape becomes more folded and secretive. Paths are well maintained and waymarked. You can shorten the walk by omitting the Compasses Inn and instead driving to it afterwards; if the field path used for visiting the pub is ploughed, it may be better to go round via the extremely quiet lane.

A worthwhile detour by car is into Wye, which has scarcely a jarring note in the village centre. You can also start the walk from the church (see public transport information); this adds an extra 2 miles (3 kilometres).

Compasses Inn, Sole Street, Crundale CT4 7ES. ☎ (01227) 700300. Open 12 to 3, 6.30 to 11 (10.30 Sun); food Mon to Sat 12 to 2.30, 6.30 to 10, Sun 12 to 3, 6.30 to 9. Fuller's London Pride. Pub snacks, steak and chips, sandwiches and blackboard specials are available. No children in front bar. No dogs.

Tickled Trout, 2 Bridge Street, Wye TN25 5EB (off the route). ☎ (01233) 812227. Open Mon to Sat 10.30 to 2.30, 6 to 11, Sun 12 to 3, 6.30 to 10.30; food Mon to Sat 12 to 2.30, 6 to 9.30, Sun 12 to 2.30, 7 to 8.30. 5 real ales. A la carte menu and daily specials as well as sandwiches are served.

Start: Car park on Wye Down; from the centre of Wye, with the church on your left follow the road, keeping straight on at the crossroads (Scotton Street) by Wye College on your left, and carry on towards Hastingleigh (ignoring a right fork) up on to the North Downs. Park on the left in a free car park with English Nature sign ¼ mile after the Devil's Kneading Trough Restaurant on the left. Grid reference 079454.

Alternative start: Free car park (with donations box) by Crundale church at ❻. Grid reference 085487.

Length: Full walk 8 miles (13 kilometres), 4 hours; short walk omitting pub 6 miles (10 kilometres), 3½ hours.

Difficulty: Moderate, all on undulating downland but no really steep sections.

OS maps: 1:25,000 Explorer sheet 137; 1:50,000 Landranger sheet 179 or 189.

Devil's Kneading Trough Restaurant serves morning coffee, teas, lunch and other meals. Full range in Wye (not on the route unless you start from Wye station).

PT Train to Wye. You join the walk by following the North Downs Way for 1 mile (return same way). Turn left out of the station, and fork left into Churchfield Way. Take the path (North Downs Way) into the churchyard, to the right of the church, then on to emerge by the Department of Biological Sciences of Wye College, where the route bends right to reach a road junction. Take Occupation Road opposite; this becomes a track. Cross the next road and take the North Downs Way opposite, up the side of a field and through woodland. Turn right along a small road, ignore the North Downs Way as it branches off right and join the route at ❸.

❶ From the middle of the car park, cross the road and take the gate by the sign about **Wye Downs National Nature Reserve**, an area of downland with many characteristic species of birds, insects and flora (including orchids). Turn half right to reach the top edge of the escarpment, above the Devil's Kneading Trough – a spectacularly steep valley with a magnificent view over Ashford, towards the cliffs near Hastings, and the nuclear power station at Dungeness. Do not descend but keep right, soon along a fence on your left; ignore a gate in the fence but take the metal kissing-gate ahead, marked North Downs Way, and follow the path near to the woodland on the left. ❷ Cross the road to the small road opposite, and immediately turn left, continuing on the North Downs Way. Beyond a gate, this proceeds along a fence on your right until you enter a hummocky area where you head on to a fence corner by a bench and a gate (which you do not go through). You are now just above the memorial crown, cut into the hillside in 1902 by Wye College students to commemorate the coronation of Edward VII; it has recently been restored at great expense, with wire holding together the thousands of pieces of flint.

Carry straight on, with the fence on your right until you cross a stile on the right (marked North Downs Way), and proceed along the left-hand fence, then beyond the next stile along the right-hand fence (ignore a path leading to the left). Turn right along a small road. ❸ Where the road ends at a fork by Down Farm, fork left on a level track. ½ mile later, where the track ends at the next farm (Marriage Farm) take the gate ahead, and turn left at a T-junction by a power post. ❹ After 150 yards, at the next junction (where the field on the right ends), turn right on the Stour Valley Walk, through woodland, and down to a field. Turn left along the top edge of the field, enjoying glorious downland views. ❺ At the end of the field, the path enters trees: turn right at a junction (leaving the Stour Valley Walk which goes left), soon re-entering the field, and then carrying straight on, soon between hedges. At a junction of farm roads by a house, keep forward on a concrete road, then keep to the right of the next house (with silo) on a rising grassy path. Turn half left at the next junction, on a broad path rising to reach a road.

For the Compasses Inn at Sole Street (detour 1 mile each way) The simplest route (road walking all the way, but along a very quiet road) is to follow the road up to the right, then right at the junction to Sole Street. A more interesting route via field paths (which may be ploughed out at some times of the year) is to turn left down the road (if you started from Crundale church, turn left out of the car park and along this road), then take a path on the right into woodland and marked by a stone 'public footpath' sign. In the woods, enter the right-hand field by a stile (avoid a stile leading into another field to the left) and turn left along the hedgerow to its corner, then continue in the same direction into the next field, then slightly left up to an entrance in the opposite hedgerow; turn right along the road into Sole Street.

To continue turn right at the point you joined the road to reach **Crundale church ❻**. This much-restored building stands separately from Crundale village. Inside, to the left of the door, is a fine incised slab to a 15th-century vicar.

Take the signposted byway just below (to the right of) Crundale church (benches here make useful picnic places), and follow this track along the top of Crundale Downs for just over a mile; it begins in the open, then goes through woodland (which may be waterlogged in places, but there are always ways round the muddiest parts); finally it drops. ❼ Turn right at a track junction, downhill. After 250 yards, take a waymarked bridleway on the left into the bottom edge of the woodland. This later continues along a field edge with Coombe Manor farm visible ahead, then enters a small patch of woodland and emerges into a field ❽: keep along the fence on your right for 50 yards, then turn right through a gate, along the right edge of a field to a farm road serving Coombe Manor, along which you turn left. At the road junction, return on the North Downs Way ahead, through woodland into Wye Downs Nature Reserve (if you have started from Crundale church, it is still worth making this detour, although the walk route continues along the North Downs Way to the right at the road junction).

Wye

Seen from the Downs from the memorial crown, this is the smallest university town in Britain. In 1447 Archbishop Kempe founded a college of priests there, and part of the 15th-century building is incorporated into the Oxbridge-like 19th-century college that originated as the South Eastern Agricultural College in 1894. In 1948 it became formally incorporated into the University of London. Close by are greenhouses where research is carried out, and Coldharbour Farm, the college's countryside management centre. In the village itself, it takes only a few minutes to walk round the delightfully unspoilt streets, past the fine medieval church partly rebuilt in 1703.

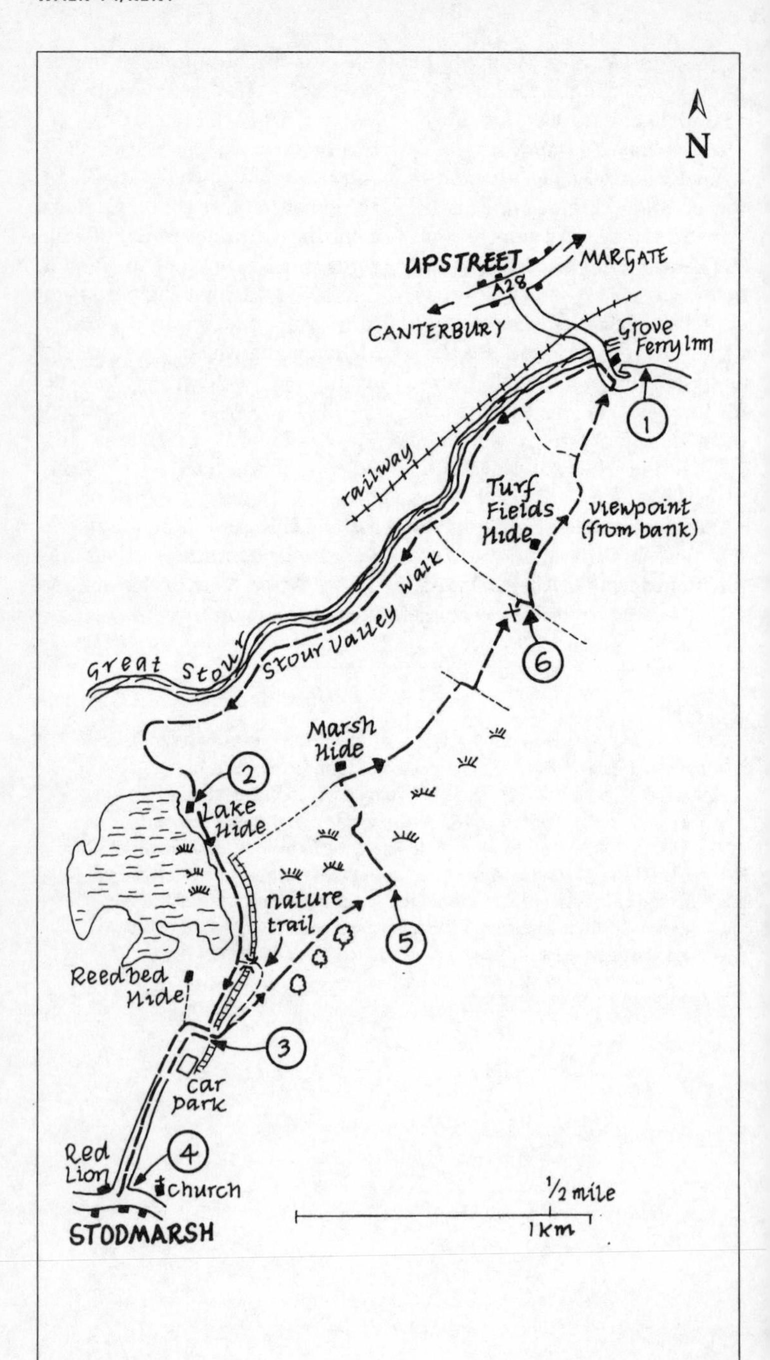
N
UPSTREET
MARGATE
A28
CANTERBURY
Grove
Ferry Inn
1
railway
Turf
Fields
Hide
viewpoint
(from bank)
Stour Valley walk
6
Great Stour
Marsh
Hide
2
Lake
Hide
nature
trail
5
Reedbed
Hide
3
Car
Park
Red
Lion
4
church
STODMARSH
1/2 mile
1km

Stodmarsh and Grove Ferry

KENT WALK 14

Bring a pair of binoculars for this tour of one of the major wetland bird sanctuaries of southern England, in the Stour Valley east of Canterbury. The peaceful little village of Stodmarsh with its pub and church makes a worthwhile detour from the reserve. Paths are clearly marked but can be very wet over the meadows; when the walk was inspected the reeds beside the paths had been cut down to allow walkers to bypass the deeper puddles. The section along the river is well drained. It is advisable to have waterproof boots, however. You can end the walk with a boat trip or boat hire from Grove Ferry.

Close by is Fordwich, the smallest town in Britain, with a very pretty centre around its jettied town hall of 1544. Wickhambreux is perhaps the pick of the nearby villages. Farther east is Sandwich, with its impressively intact medieval centre and three medieval churches, and Richborough Roman Fort and township site, dating from the Roman landing of AD43.

Grove Ferry Inn, Upstreet CT3 4BP. ☎ (01227) 860302. Open summer Mon to Sat 11 to 11, Sun 12 to 10.30, winter Mon to Fri 11 to 3, 6 to 11, Sat and Sun 11 to 10.30; food 12 to 2, 6 to 9. 2 real ales. A la carte menu, blackboard specials and bar snacks are available. Boat trips are available from here. Children welcome. Dogs welcome in bar area.

Red Lion, Stodmarsh CT3 4BA. ☎ (01227) 721339. Open Mon to Sat 11 to 11, Sun 12 to 10.30, bar food 12 to 2.30, 6.30 to 9.30, Greene King beers. The Red Lion has an open fire in a low-ceilinged room and is hung with hops and decorated with sheet music. It also has a pretty hedged garden. A la carte menu, blackboard specials, bar snacks, soup and sandwiches. Children welcome. Dogs welcome.

Fordwich Arms, King Street, Fordwich CT2 0DB (off the route). ☎ (01227) 710444. Open Mon to Sat 11 to 11, Sun 12 to 3, 7 to 10.30; food all week 12 to 2, Mon to Sat 6.30 to 10. Flowers, Wadworth 6X, Shepherd Neame Master Brew. The Fordwich Arms is a brick mock-Tudor pub with gardens leading down to the Stour. The food is cooked fresh and prepared to order. Choices include numerous sandwiches, 'double-filled' cottage rolls, salads, jacket potatoes and ploughman's. All dishes on the blackboard menu are served with four fresh vegetables and potatoes. Children welcome in dining-room. No dogs in dining room.

King William IV, 4 High Street, Littlebourne CT3 1ST (off the route). ☎ (01227) 721244. Open Mon to Sat 11 to 11, Sun 12 to 10.30; food all week 12 to 2.15, 7 to 9.15. Bass, Shepherd Neame Master Brew. Inside this sturdy white-painted brick freehouse are a log fire, hoppy decoration, and golfing and cricketing paraphernalia. You can choose from a set two-course meal at lunch-time, bar snacks or an à la carte menu. Food could include Stilton and celery soup with herby croutons, rabbit braised in red wine with parsley dumplings, or simple egg and chips or fried cod. No children. No dogs.

Start: Grove Ferry Inn. Approaching from the west, cross the level crossing and river, and turn off just after the pub at a brown sign for the picnic site. There is a small fee for parking in the picnic site.
Alternative start: Stodmarsh. Free car park for the nature reserve (turn off in the centre of the village, by the pub; the car park is on the right after ¼ mile); turn right to start the walk, along the track leading away from the village; join walk after ❹. Roadside parking opposite the Red Lion pub in Stodmarsh is limited.
Length: 5 miles (8 kilometres), 2½ hours.
Difficulty: Easy.
OS maps: 1:25,000 Explorer sheet 150; 1:50,000 Landranger sheet 179.
WC In car parks at Grove Ferry and Stodmarsh.
PT Frequent daily buses from Canterbury, Sturry, Margate and Ramsgate to Upstreet (¼ mile off the route), from where you take the road towards Preston to Grove Ferry.

---

❶ With the Grove Ferry Inn on your left, follow the road away from the river for 20 yards, then go through a gate on the right, signposted Stour Valley Walk. This walk is a long-distance route from Ashford to Sandwich via Wye and Canterbury. Follow this along the bank of the River Stour for 1½ miles.

The path then leaves the river, bending left and passes the Lake Hide ❷, a tower built for observing bird life on the lake. This **lake** was caused by mining subsidence, and by the 1930s began to form lagoons. Avoid a bridge on the left (nature trail). ❸ At a junction with a track leading left (signposted Marsh Hide) and by an information board about bitterns, detour right for Stodmarsh (the first turn on the right at a nature reserve sign numbered 6 can be taken for the Reedbed Hide). ❹ In **Stodmarsh village centre**, look into the church, with its 15th-century Perpendicular screen; on the outside arch of the door, carvings of crosses were carved by crusaders on their way to the coast and are still visible; the 13th-century tenor bell is thought to be the oldest in Kent.

Retrace steps from Stodmarsh (if you are starting the walk here, take the small side turning to the right of the Red Lion as you face the pub), past the car park, which has a dispenser for maps and information leaflets about the reserve. Keep right at the junction where straight on leads to the Reedbed Hide, and turn right at the next junction (which you have already reached if you started from Grove Ferry), signposted Marsh Hide. Avoid side turnings over bridges, and follow the path to Marsh Hide: this soon bends left, with water channels on both sides, and after ½ mile emerges into a field ❺. Turn left, cross bridges, keep left and continue past the Marsh Hide.

Pass the Nature Reserve sign numbered 4, and go through a gate. Go right and immediately left. Soon ignore a footbridge to the right, but take the bridge ahead. Emerge into a field, continue to a wooden gate inscribed 'English Nature' (with a metal kissing-gate alongside), beyond which ❻ you turn right at a T-junction with a track, then just 15 yards later turn left. This leads past the Turf Fields Hide. Just after this, the track bends left: the bank up to the right is worth climbing for a fine view of the reserve. Continue along the stony track to the road at Grove Ferry.

The long-serving ferry service over the Stour that gives **Grove Ferry** its name ended with the building of the road bridge in 1959. In medieval times this point was in the tidal Wantsum Channel, which cut off the Isle of Thanet and made it a true island. There are boat trips at weekends and certain other times (for details ask at the pub) and opposite the pub, rowing boats, pedalos and motor boats may be hired.

Stodmarsh National Nature Reserve

The name Stodmarsh signifies an alluvial marsh where a 'stud', or herd, of stallions was kept. The marshes were reclaimed by refugee Protestants from Flanders; in the early 18th century they erected the Lampen Wall as part of the great drainage scheme. Today the watermeadows and reedy lagoons are designated as Stodmarsh National Nature Reserve. During winter the water levels are raised by the operation of sluices to flood the meadows as flocks of wildfowl arrive to shelter and feed. In spring the water levels are dropped to allow birds to feed on the mud.

The huge bird population includes kingfishers, harriers, reed buntings and wild ducks, while the spring and autumn migrations bring purple herons, little egrets, avocets and sandpipers. A variety of insect life includes moths, dragonflies and damselflies, while among the fauna you may see stoats, weasels, water voles and exceptionally water shrews and otters. The walk passes all the reserve's specially constructed hides, as well as the starting point of the short nature trail. A free descriptive leaflet is available in the car park at the Stodmarsh end of the walk.

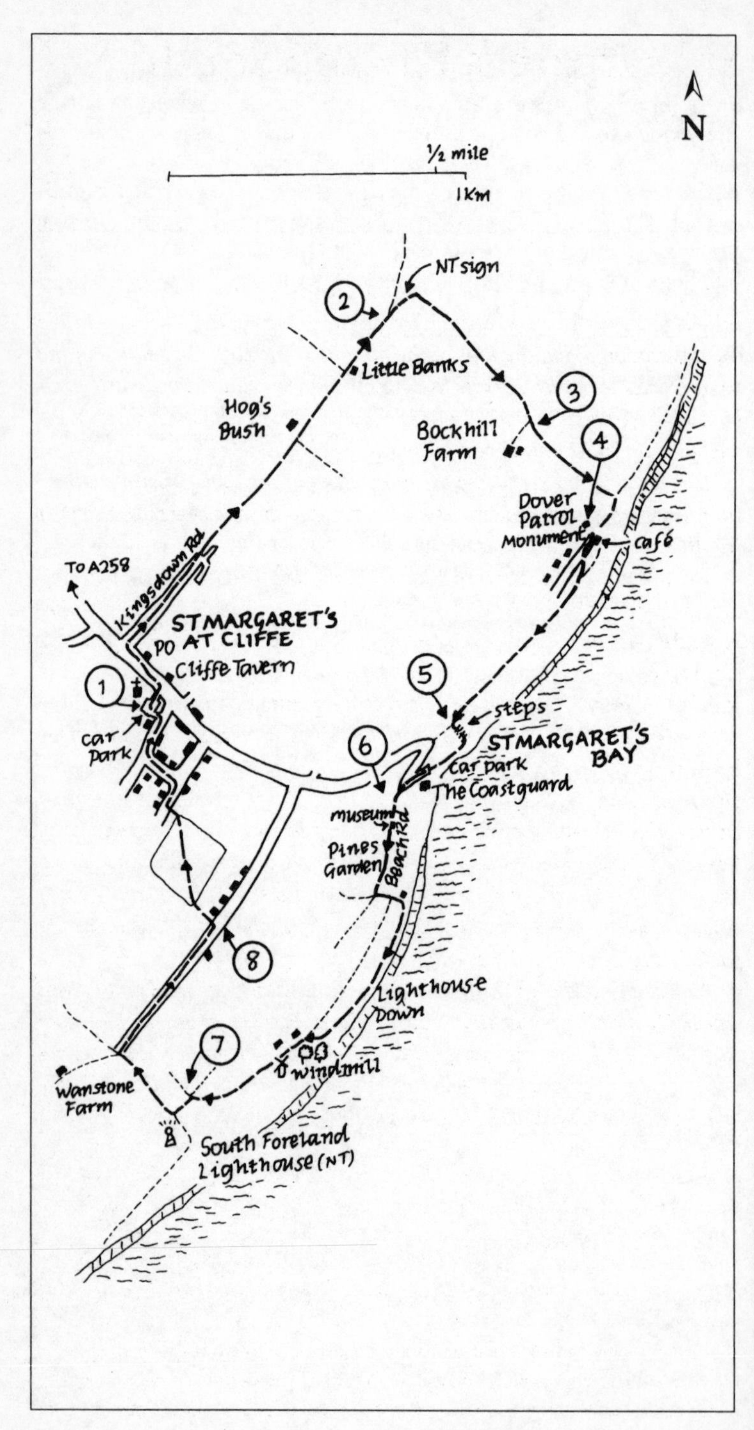
N
½ mile
1Km
NT sign
2
Little Banks
Hog's Bush
3
Bockhill Farm
4
Dover Patrol Monument
café
To A258
Kingsdown Rd
ST MARGARET'S AT CLIFFE
PO
Cliffe Tavern
1
Car Park
5
steps
ST MARGARET'S BAY
6
Car park
The Coastguard
museum
Pines Garden
Beach Rd
8
Lighthouse Down
7
windmill
Wanstone Farm
South Foreland Lighthouse (NT)

St Margaret's Bay and South Foreland

KENT WALK 15

The pubs and fine Norman church at St Margaret's at Cliffe give an inland focus to the walk, but the scenic glory undoubtedly belongs to the coastal section along the tops of the famous white cliffs. For much of the year, France is in view, across the busiest shipping lane in the world, and by way of contrast the walk drops to shore level at St Margaret's Bay. Keep well in from the crumbly and dizzyingly sheer cliff edge.

It is feasible to extend the coastal section of the walk in either direction, towards Dover or Deal. It is also possible to walk the entire stretch from Dover to Deal and return by rail.

Recommended add-ons include Henry VIII's Tudor rose-shaped castles at Deal and Walmer (English Heritage; open daily 10 to 6, November to March 10 to 4; Deal closed winter Monday and Tuesday; Walmer closed January and February Monday to Friday), and at Dover the Roman Painted House (open April to September 10, closed Monday except bank holidays in July and August), which retains its under-floor heating system and remains of painted walls. Dover Castle (English Heritage; daily 10 to 6, November to March 10 to 4) is one of the great castle visits, deserving at least half a day. In addition to the Norman keep, Saxon church and Roman lighthouse, the Dover Castle site includes a labyrinth of tunnels, from which the evacuation of British and French troops at Dunkirk was conducted in May 1940, and which subsequently sheltered the Combined Headquarters.

Curiosity-seekers may like to pay a visit to Samphire Hoe on the west side of Dover. This is the newest part of Great Britain, created out of spoil dug from the Channel Tunnel excavation, and being naturalised with wild flowers. It gives a great view of the foot of the cliffs – something hitherto visible only by boat.

Hope Inn, High Street, St Margaret's at Cliffe CT15 6AT. ☎ (01304) 852444. Open Mon to Sat 11 to 11, Sun 12 to 10.30; food Mon to Sat 12 to 2.30, 7 to 9, Sun 12 to 2, 7 to 9. Shepherd Neame. Sunday roast, blackboard menu, bar snacks, sandwiches. Children welcome. Dogs welcome.

Cliffe Tavern, High Street, St Margaret's at Cliffe CT15 6AT. ☎ (01304) 852400. Open 11 to 11, Sun 12 to 10.30; bar food 12 to 2.30, 7 to 9.30; restaurant Thur to Sat D only 7 to 10. 3 or 4 regularly changing ales. The white weatherboarded building has been considerably extended from original 16th-century house. Morning coffee and cream teas are served, as well as traditional pub fare – soup, hot baguettes or curry of the day. There is also a specials board, with pork or beef with stir-fried noodles or a dozen fish options. Children welcome in eating areas. No dogs in restaurant.

Red Lion, 1 Kingsdown Road, St Margaret's at Cliffe CT15 6AZ. ☎ (01304) 852467. Open Mon to Sat 11 to 11, Sun 12 to 10.30; food 12 to 2.30, 6.30 to 9. 1 real ale. Bar snacks, basket meals, sandwiches and summer blackboard specials. Children welcome in restaurant area. Dogs welcome in bar area.

Smugglers, The High Street, St Margaret's at Cliffe CT15 6AU. ☎ (01304) 853404. Open Mon to Fri 12 to 3, 5 to 11, Sat 12 to 11, Sun 12 to 4, 7 to 10.30; food Mon to Sat 12 to 2, 6.30 to 9.45, Sun 12 to 2.45, 7 to 9.30, tapas served all day. John Smith's, 2 other real ales. Full menu, including home-made soup or coarse Ardennes paté to start, and mushroom stroganoff or fillet of chicken prosciutto or a choice of fish as a main course plus specials. Tapas, bar snacks, ploughman's, baguettes and salads at lunch-time, Mexican and pizza menus. Children welcome in restaurant. Dogs welcome in bar area.

The Coastguard, St Margaret's Bay CT15 6DY. ☎ (01304) 853176. Open Tues to Sat 11 to 4, 7 to 11, Sun 12 to 4, 7 to 10.30 (12 to 11 April and May), closed Mon; bar food 12 to 3, 7 to 9.30 (9 Sun). 1 real ale. Traditional pub food, baguettes, sandwiches, bar snacks, Sunday roasts. Children welcome. Dogs welcome.

Start: Free car park signposted in the centre of St Margaret's at Cliffe (near the Cliffe Tavern and Hope Inn), 1 mile off A258 between Dover and Deal. Grid reference 358447.
Length: 5 miles (8 kilometres), 2½ hours.
Difficulty: Easy. On good paths and tracks, with no particularly steep climbs.
OS maps: 1:25,000 Explorer sheet 138; 1:50,000 Landranger sheet 179.
Blue Birds tea rooms by the Dover Patrol Monument. Pubs, shops and tea room at St Margaret's at Cliffe.
WC In the car park at St Margaret's at Cliffe and on the shore at St Margaret's Bay.
PT Buses (Mon to Sat) to St Margaret's at Cliffe from Dover, Folkestone and Canterbury.

---

❶ Turn left out of the car park (exiting the way you entered). Walk along the main street, past the Cliffe Tavern on your right, and the complete and impressive **Norman church** on your left (well worth a look; get the key from the nearby village stores).

Turn right in front of the Red Lion pub into Kingsdown Road. Past the last house, continue forward on an unmade track (ignoring a right turn called The Freedown, and another right turn shortly after). Views open up over a valley on the left. After ¼ mile you pass a house called Hog's Bush: continue straight ahead (ignore tracks to the right), and later ignore a waymarked path descending to the left opposite a house called Little Banks. ❷ Just as the main track bends slightly left and is about to descend, take a level grassy path between bushes straight ahead. This soon passes a National Trust sign for Bockhill Farm and bends right, down into a slight valley and along a grassy strip between fields. After the path rises it bends right. ❸ Just where the path bends further right (with the huge Dover Patrol

Monument in view ahead) and is about to enter Bockhill Farm, keep left, into the left-hand of two fields, alongside the hedgerow to the sea (it should be possible to walk along the path beside the hedgerow*). Turn right at the T-junction with the coastal path.

❹ Join the end of the road between the old coastguard station (now Blue Birds tea rooms) and the **Dover Patrol Monument**. This commemorates the patrol that maintained a fleet of destroyers that controlled cross-Channel shipping during the First World War. It proved essential for getting supplies through, and an annual memorial service is held here. In clear weather the cliffs on the French side of the Channel look extremely near; the most prominent feature is **Cap Gris-Nez**, between Calais and Boulogne.

Take the gate on the left, opposite the monument, and take the lower of two paths (starting in line with another gate in the left-hand fence) leading to the right, along the cliff top. Eventually this becomes more enclosed. ❺ Take steps down on the left (immediately before railings, giving a sea view, above a derelict concrete structure, and beneath tall gabled buildings on the right; there were low branches over the top of the steps at the time of inspection. Alternatively continue along the main path to the corner of the road and turn left down to the bay), down to the shore, then turn right to **St Margaret's Bay**, the nearest point of the mainland to France, which is just 21 miles away; the bay is the traditional starting point for cross-Channel swimmers.

From the Coastguard pub take the road up. (Ignore a path on the left just before a wooden fence begins: it is permanently closed, but still signposted). At the first very sharp bend in the road, take the unmade turn ahead signposted to the Pines Garden and Museum. ❻ 30 yards later fork left on Beach Road, past **St Margaret's Museum** (open summer Wednesday to Sunday, 2 to 5) of local history, and the **Pines Garden** (open all year daily 10 to 5, later in summer, closed 25 December) a three-acre site created in 1970 out of a rubbish dump and now with a lake, rockery, waterfall, Romany wedding caravan and bronze statue of Winston Churchill.

At the end of the Pines Garden, turn left at a four-way track junction. As the track bends right by a bungalow and a National Trust sign for Lighthouse Down you can go forward to pick up the cliff-top path, leading to the right and rejoining the track just before some woodland. Continue to the left along the track, past a sailless **windmill** on the left, erected as an electricity generator in 1928.

Just before **South Foreland Lighthouse**, the track bends right inland. ❼ Take the next left turn, at a track junction, to the lighthouse (NT, open Easter to end October, weekends and bank holidays, 12.30 to 5 or dusk if earlier), which Marconi used for his pioneering radio experiments.

Just before you reach the lighthouse, turn right inland for ¼ mile then go right at a T-junction (where left is a private farm track and ahead is a path across a field), along a broad road. ❽ After 600 yards and immediately before the first house on the left (called Kestrels) take a woodland path on the left, alongside the garden fence and then diagonally right across a field to the edge of St Margaret's at Cliffe. Turn right on the residential road, then first left (in the middle of a housing estate), and right on the main road to the village centre (the car park is signposted to the left).

*The National Trust has asked us to point out that although it is nearly always possible to walk along a path along the field edge to the sea here, they may once in six or seven years plough out the path completely for a day or so. The path is a permissive path, not a public right of way.

Shoreham and Lullingstone

KENT WALK 16

A favourite Sunday escape for Londoners, this Green-Belt terrain lies close to the capital but is quite rural in character and gives scope for a walk taking in the River Darent, Shoreham and the North Downs. The golf course in Lullingstone Park is largely screened by woodland, through which the paths pass. Lullingstone Roman Villa and Lullingstone Castle can be seen in the final stages. A charming riverside path concludes the walk. Paths are waymarked throughout.

Lullingstone Park and golf course is managed by Sevenoaks District Council and is designated as a Site of Special Scientific Interest for its ancient pollard trees and other woodland supporting lichens, breeding birds and over 500 species of fungi (including some rarities). Trail leaflets are available from the Countryside Centre, where this walk starts.

The alternative starting point gives you rather more walking before you arrive at the pubs at Shoreham; it is also nearer London than the main starting point.

Ye Olde George, Church Street, Shoreham TN14 7RY. ☎ (01959) 522017. Open Mon to Sat 10 to 11, Sun 12 to 10.30; food Mon to Sat 12 to 3, 6 to 10, Sun 12 to 4. Greene King IPA and Abbot Ale, Morland Old Speckled Hen, Courage Best. Roasts, steaks, salads, sandwiches. Children welcome. Dogs welcome.

Kings Arms, Church Street, Shoreham TN14 7SJ. ☎ (01959) 523100. Open Mon to Sat 11 to 3, 6 to 11, Sun 12 to 4, 7 to 10.30; food Mon to Sat 12 to 2.30, 6.30 to 9.30. Courage Best, Morland Old Speckled Hen, Ruddles Best Bitter and County and 1 guest ale. This pub claims to have the last surviving Ostler Box, a kind of cubby hole giving access to the bar from the street for the convenience of horsemen. Steaks, fish, lasagne, chilli, pies. Children welcome. No dogs.

Two Brewers, 30 High Street, Shoreham TN14 7TD. ☎ (01959) 522800. Open Mon to Sat 11.30 to 3, 6.30 to 11, Sun 12 to 10.30; food Mon to Sat 12 to 2, 7 to 9.30, Sun 12 to 2.45, 7 to 9. Courage Best, Shepherd Neame, Spitfire. A la carte and blackboard menus, Sunday roasts and sandwiches. Children welcome. Dogs welcome in public bar.

Start: Lullingstone Park Visitor Centre, ½ mile (1 kilometre) south of Eynsford station, off A225. Free car park. Grid reference 526638.

Alternative start: Sevenoaks District Council car park near golf club house at ❽. From Polhill roundabout on A21, follow brown signs marked 'Lullingstone Park and Golf Club'. To join the walk, pass through the gate at the far right-hand corner of the car park. Grid reference 506646.

Length: Full walk 8 miles (13 kilometres), 4 hours; short walk omitting Lullingstone Villa and Lullingstone Castle 5½ miles (9 kilometres), 3 hours.

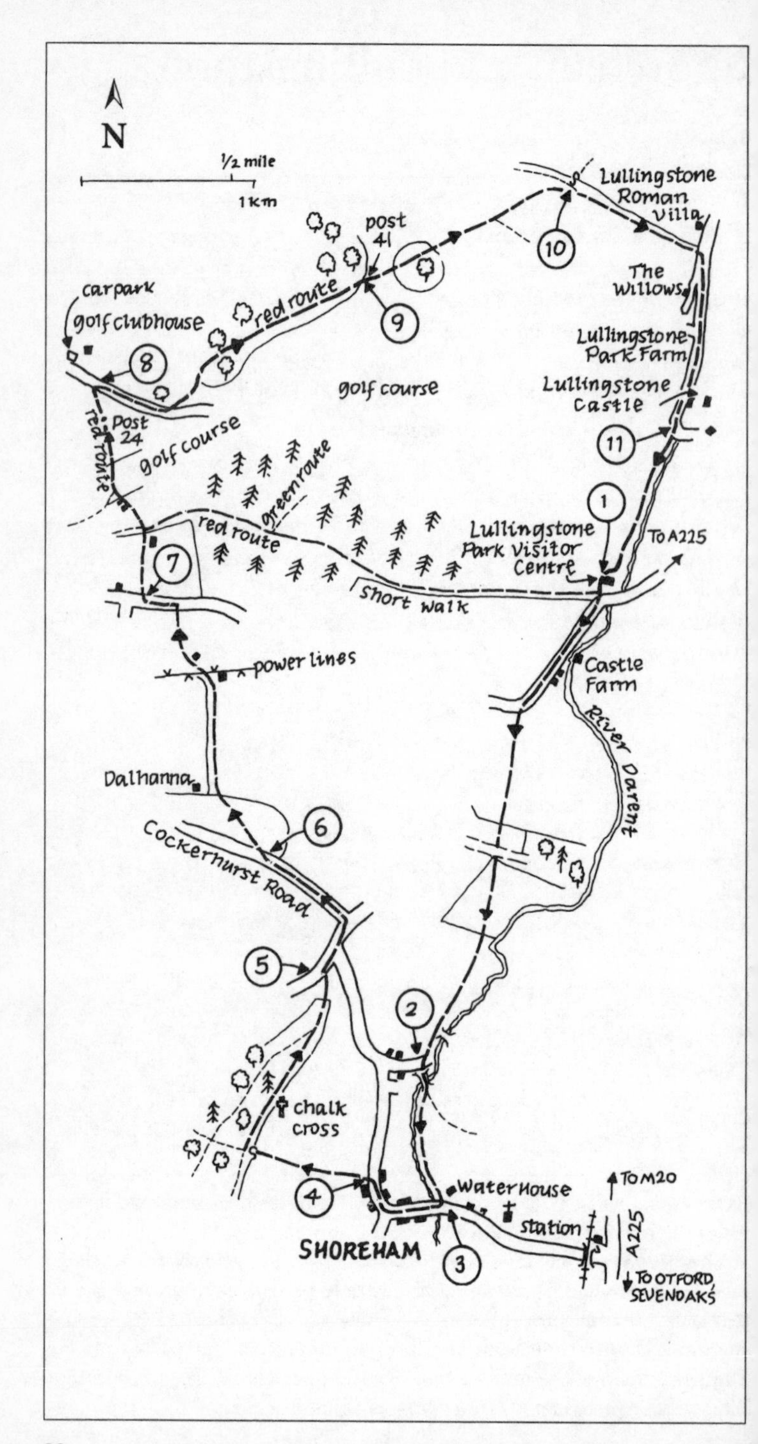
N
1/2 mile
1km
carpark
golf clubhouse
8
post
41
9
red route
10
Lullingstone
Roman
Villa
The
Willows
Lullingstone
Park Farm
Lullingstone
Castle
11
golf course
post
24
red route
golf course
green route
red route
7
1
Lullingstone
Park Visitor
Centre
To A225
Short Walk
power lines
Castle
Farm
River Darent
Dalhanna
6
Cockerhurst Road
5
2
chalk
cross
4
Water House
To M20
station
A225
SHOREHAM
3
To OTFORD,
SEVENOAKS

Difficulty: Moderate. Muddy after rain.
OS maps: 1:25,000 Explorer sheet 147; 1:50,000 Landranger sheets 177 and 188.
☕ Cafeteria at Lullingstone Park Visitor Centre (open daily 10 to 4 winter, 10 to 5 summer).
WC Lullingstone Park Visitor Centre.
PT Train to Shoreham. Turn right out of the station, and right again down the road to Shoreham village and join the walk at ❸.

❶ Go out to the road and turn right along it. **Hop gardens** are seen on both sides of the road. On the left the Hop Shop sells hop products, dried flowers and more.

Past a group of houses as the road is about to bend right, take a track on the left with yellow arrow markers (Darent Valley Path), through a field and follow all the way to Shoreham. ❷ Emerge on a road by some houses, turn left and immediately right on to a path by the river. Cross over a footbridge and keep right on the other side; along the river emerge at the centre of the village by the road bridge, where you turn right ❸.

Shoreham is an unspoilt village nestled among the North Downs and with a river along part of its street. The visionary artist Samuel Palmer lived at Water House (where the walk enters the village) from 1827 to 1834, the most productive years of his life (many of his paintings have a local setting). Palmer attracted a group of young disciples, who called themselves The Ancients; sceptical and suspicious villagers called them the Extolagers. William Blake paid a visit to Palmer here in 1827.

The late-Perpendicular **church** is restored but has some outstanding features, notably the rood screen spanning the width of the building. Stained glass by the eminent Pre-Raphaelite artist Burne-Jones was installed in 1903, after the artist's death.

Carry on along the village street of Shoreham, then turn right at a T-junction. ❹ After 60 yards, bear left by house no. 13 (near **Shoreham Aircraft Museum**, a small museum about Second World War aircraft; open May to October), on a signposted path uphill, between hedges. Further up, emerge by a stile on to downland. This fine **view** extends over Shoreham and the Darent Valley. The **chalk cross** seen to the right was cut into the hillside as a memorial for those who died in the First World War. The woodland crowning the slope was partially destroyed in the great storm of 1987.

Go up alongside the fence on your right to the next stile into Meenfield Wood, then right at a cross-junction of paths. The path now goes along the level, with fine views of the valley, then drops slightly (beyond a barrier, ignore a sharp left turn), finally bending left to a road ❺.

Turn right on the road, follow Well Hill signs (ignore a right turn for Shoreham at the first junction), then turn left at the second junction to go up Cockerhurst Road. ❻ Take the signposted path on the right opposite a bungalow gate; the path goes uphill through rough land and bearing left; it then gets fainter (maintain direction uphill, finding a stile 100 yards to the right of a red-roofed house which comes into view). Follow a field path along the left-hand edge of a field to a bungalow under some power lines, where the path continues to the left and is now enclosed; past the last bungalow it becomes a concrete track until the road.

Turn left on the road, then ❼ right after 100 yards over a stile (where overhead wires cross); the path goes along the left edge of a field, and is then enclosed; emerge by a stile (said to be the tallest in Kent) in the woods and reach a signpost at a four-way crossing.

For the short walk turn right and follow the red marker posts back to the start.

For the full walk go forward and follow the woodland path downhill until you emerge on the golf course. Carry on ahead and follow the red marker posts carefully; the route crosses over a fairway, goes into the woods (past a red marker post) and emerges, soon ❽ joining a park road (the club house is in view to the left). You go right along it and then bear left into the woods, where you follow red or blue markers (which follow almost the same route, soon merging again).

❾ Finally, the red route emerges from the woodland. Go forward along the left-hand side of a field to find a marked barrier into a strip of woods, then proceed out into the open (down and up). Keep ahead on the red route (avoiding side turns), reaching a fence where ❿ you turn right and follow the path downhill.

At the bottom, you reach the estate road; **Lullingstone Roman Villa** is immediately to the left (English Heritage; open 1 April to 1 November, daily 10 to 6, until dusk in October; rest of year 10 to 4). Discovered in 1939, and now protected from the elements by a large modern shed, this country villa was begun in about AD100 and was occupied and adapted for much of the Roman period. It retains superb mosaics. A particular feature of the villa is that it has four very distinct periods of occupation by different owners; one had a room with a natural spring, intended as a shrine for pagan worship and has frescoes of water nymphs; another owner converted some rooms into a Christian chapel. The audio tour gives the full story.

Go right on the road, past the 15th-century gatehouse (one of the earliest all-brick buildings in the UK) to **Lullingstone Castle** (open April to September, 2 to 6 weekends and bank holidays). This is a family mansion with a great hall, library and state rooms, containing collections of porcelain, furniture and portraits. The castle estate formerly included Lullingstone Park.

⓫ As the road bends left go forward to find a riverside path leading to Lullingstone Park Visitor Centre.

Penshurst and Chiddingstone

KENT WALK 17

This is an attractive cross-country route linking two charming Wealden villages, with quintessential Kentish views. The terrain is low-lying but by no means flat, with enough changes in elevation to sustain interest. Paths are mostly defined or waymarked, but, because of the intricate nature of this landscape, the route is not always obvious.

Penshurst and Chiddingstone villages both give their names to local vineyards, one of which is passed on the early stages of this walk.

Leicester Arms, High Street, Penshurst TN11 8BT. ☎ (01892) 870551. Open Mon to Sat 11 to 11, Sun 12 to 10.30; food 12 to 2.30, 7 to 10. Larkins Traditional Ale and Porter. A la carte restaurant, bar food including gammon, lasagne and chicken. Children welcome. Dogs welcome in some parts of pub.

Rock Inn, Chiddingstone, Hoath TN8 7BS. ☎ (01892) 870296. Open Mon to Sat 11.30 to 3, 6 to 11, Sun 12 to 3, 7 to 10.30; food 12 to 2.30, 7 to 10. Larkins beers. Cooked food including lamb casserole or ham, egg and fries, ploughman's and sandwiches. No children. Dogs welcome.

Castle Inn, Chiddingstone TN8 7AH. ☎ (01892) 870247. Open Mon to Sat 11 to 11, Sun 12 to 10.30; bar food 11 to 10.45, Sun 12 to 10.15; restaurant 12 to 2, 7.30 to 9.30. Larkins Traditional Ale and Young's beers. An artists' paradise, the Castle Inn is now the National Trust's responsibility. The heavily beamed building has been an inn for 250 years and was a private residence for 300 years before that. The pub serves simple appetising dishes such as egg mayonnaise, a plate of smoked salmon, or the pasta dish of the day. Children welcome. Dogs welcome.

Start: Penshurst village centre, on B2176 south-west of Tonbridge; park on village street near the Leicester Arms. Grid reference 526438.

Alternative start: Chiddingstone village centre at ⑩. Roadside parking (crowded at peak times). Grid reference 501452.

Length: 6½ miles (10.5 kilometres), 3 hours.

Difficulty: Moderate, with uneven ground but no particularly steep sections; stinging nettles may be a slight problem on some sections in summer.

OS maps: 1:25,000 Explorer sheet 147; 1:50,000 Landranger sheet 188.

Shops and two tea-rooms in Penshurst (Fir Tree House tea room has a charming garden). Tea room/restaurant in Chiddingstone.

WC Penshurst.

PT Buses (Mon to Sat, plus Sun in summer) from Tunbridge Wells and Edenbridge to Penshurst. (Note that Penshurst railway station is more than 2 miles north of the village.)

❶With the Leicester Arms on your left, walk along Penshurst village street, avoiding a right turn and passing the village hall on your right and the Penshurst Stores on your left. You also pass on your left

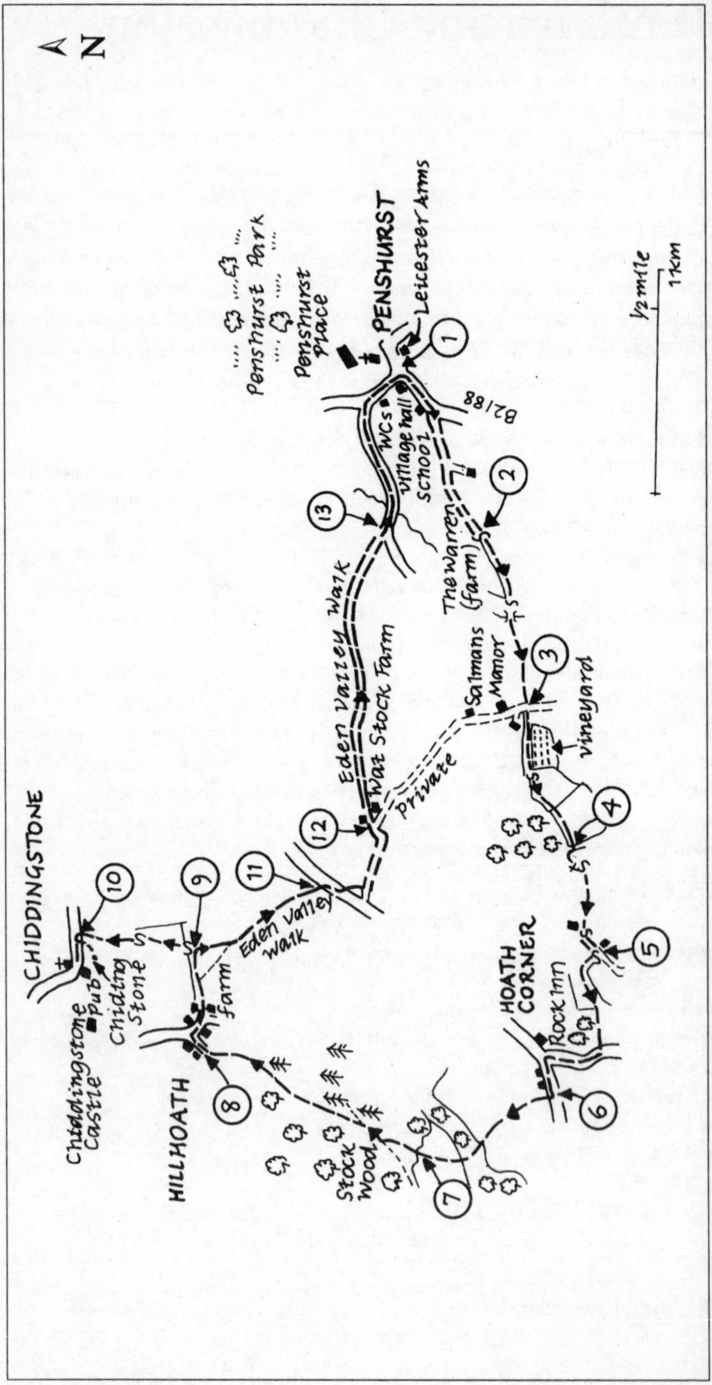
N
PENSHURST
Leicester Arms
Penshurst Park
Penshurst Place
B2188
WCs
Village hall
School
The Warren (farm)
Salmans Manor
Vineyard
Private
Eden Valley Walk
Wat Stock Farm
CHIDDINGSTONE
Chiddingstone Castle
Pub
Chiding Stone
Farm
Eden Valley Walk
HILLHOATH
HOATH CORNER
Rock Inn
Stock Wood
½ mile
1 km
1
2
3
4
5
6
7
8
9
10
11
12
13

the quaint garage/filling station/ shop, with its horseshoe-shaped doorway, a legacy from its former days as the smithy.

Just after the primary school on your right, turn right into a lane called The Warren; ignore side turns and continue past a row of cottages. ❷ At Warren Farm the lane ends: keep forward, entering a field by a stile and proceeding along the right-hand edge. On the other side of the hedge on the right is a brick **pillbox**, one of a great number built to guard against invasion during the Second World War.

In the second field cross to a footbridge ahead. From this an enclosed path leads to a third field, which you cross diagonally right to a stile by a gate in the corner (in line with an oast-house in the distance), and go forward along the right edge of the next field.

❸ Emerge on a driveway and take the rising path opposite, immediately to the left of the brick pillar of the gate of Salmans Manor, passing along a tall hedge on the right and with a field on the left. This path later passes a **vineyard** on your left. At the top of the main ascent and after the vineyard ends, take a stile on your left and continue forward along the right edge of two fields. At the end of the second field, a stile leads to a narrow path emerging over a plank bridge spanning a ditch on to a track ❹; turn right along this track, which immediately bends left. At the end of the woodland, enter the left-hand of two fields ahead by a stile and keep right to follow the right-hand edge of the field. Just past a tile-hung house on your right, take the stile on the right and follow the path to the end of a driveway (emerging by a garage).

Follow the driveway for 100 yards, then opposite a house ❺ take steps leading up to a stile on your right. Follow the left edge of the field; where the hedge on the left reaches a corner, turn left on a path between the hedge and a fence. At the end of the field on your right, keep forward by a rock outcrop, on a rising track. This track passes along a ridge of the upper greensand, giving views northwards to the North Downs.

Reach a road and turn right along it; the **rock outcrops** along the road are of the distinctive greensand rock. A huge outcrop is seen on the left side, just before the hamlet of Hoath Corner.

In the centre of Hoath Corner, take the next road turning on the left (towards Markbeech; The Rock pub, which illustrates the outcrop on its sign, is a few yards to the right) for 100 yards, to pass Cares Cross (house) and Pear Tree Cottage (both on the right), then immediately ❻ take a signposted stile on the right. This enclosed path descends, then goes along the edge of a field (with a hedge on your right), then into woodland to the bottom of a slope. On emerging into a field, keep right, up a rise, alongside the woodland on the right until you reach a corner, where you go forward across the field to take a path into more woodland ❼.

This leads to a T-junction with a broader track: turn right along this and in 80 yards ignore a right fork. A series of horse jumps appears alongside the track.

❽ After ½ mile emerge by a gate at the end of an unmade road by houses at Hill Hoath. Go forward, then turn right at a T-junction. 70 yards later, opposite a house on the right, take a track on the left, passing a pair of modern cottages (Hill Hoath Cottages) on your left and a farm and barns on your right. Past the barns, pick up a path alongside a fence on your left. 30 yards beyond the next stile ignore a path to the right but keep forward close to the fence.

❾ This reaches a path junction at a stile; the continuation of the route is to the right (i.e. not crossing the stile itself) but first detour to Chiddingstone by crossing the stile and turning left on the field path, which later continues as an enclosed path, finally emerging on the road at **Chiddingstone** ❿. This is a one-street village of rare perfection, with a group of 16th- and 17th-century half-timbered houses, built at the height of the Wealden iron industry, and the ancient Castle Inn under the ownership of the National Trust. Opposite them the church dates from the 13th century and has a Perpendicular tower and a Jacobean font and pulpit. Continue along the street (i.e. with the church on your right) for a glimpse across the ornamental lake of **Chiddingstone Castle**, a Gothic revival manor house rebuilt in the early 19th century. It has Egyptian and Oriental pieces in its collection of art and antiquities (open Good Friday and Easter Monday, then end of May to end of September, Wednesday, Thursday, Friday, Sunday and bank holiday Monday, and the first two Sundays in October).

The **Chiding Stone** (signposted) is worth a look as it is only a short walk away. This sandstone outcrop, adorned with a century's worth of graffiti, has given its name to the village. In less civilised times this was the place to which men brought their nagging wives so that the assembled villagers could nag them back by way of retribution.

Return the same way to the path junction mentioned above (at ❾). If you are starting the walk from Chiddingstone, this point is reached by beginning with the Castle Inn on your right and the church to your left. Follow the street, past the primary school, then 50 yards after the path on the right, signposted to the Chiding Stone, turn right on another signposted path. Soon cross a stile (ignore a gate into a recreation ground on your left), then follow the path, which soon goes down a field to cross a stile where you rejoin the main walk. On rejoining the main walk, bear left.

Soon a broader path (part of the 15-mile **Eden Valley Walk** from Haxted in Surrey to Tonbridge), lined with trees, joins from the right; keep to the left here, through a gate and keep left as waymarked at the next fork.

⓫ At the road, turn right, and after 30 yards take the Eden Valley Walk on the left and continue across a field. As you cross the field, note a rather striking **pink house** prominent through the trees to the left (you may have spotted it earlier). All is not what it seems (as you will soon see). Carry on to a stile beside a gate on to a track. Turn left.

⓬ At a farm (where you have reached the strange pink house that turns out not to be a house at all but an ingenious *trompe-l'oeil*), fork left, and 100 yards later keep straight on, ignoring a track that enters a field to the left. ⓭ After 1 mile join a road; keep left, over a bridge. Turn right at the main road to enter Penshurst village.

Penshurst

The village has a charming corner around the churchyard, entered by an archway beneath a picturesque half-timbered house. Next to the village is Penshurst Place, one of the great manor houses of the Weald (open weekends in March, and daily from April to the end of October) and birthplace of Philip Sidney, the Elizabethan poet. The house dates from about 1350 and has a magnificent Great Hall; the gardens are noted for double herbaceous borders and clipped yew hedges. A public footpath just to the left (west) of the church, and heading northwards, enters the Penshurst Place estate and gives some glorious views of the house.

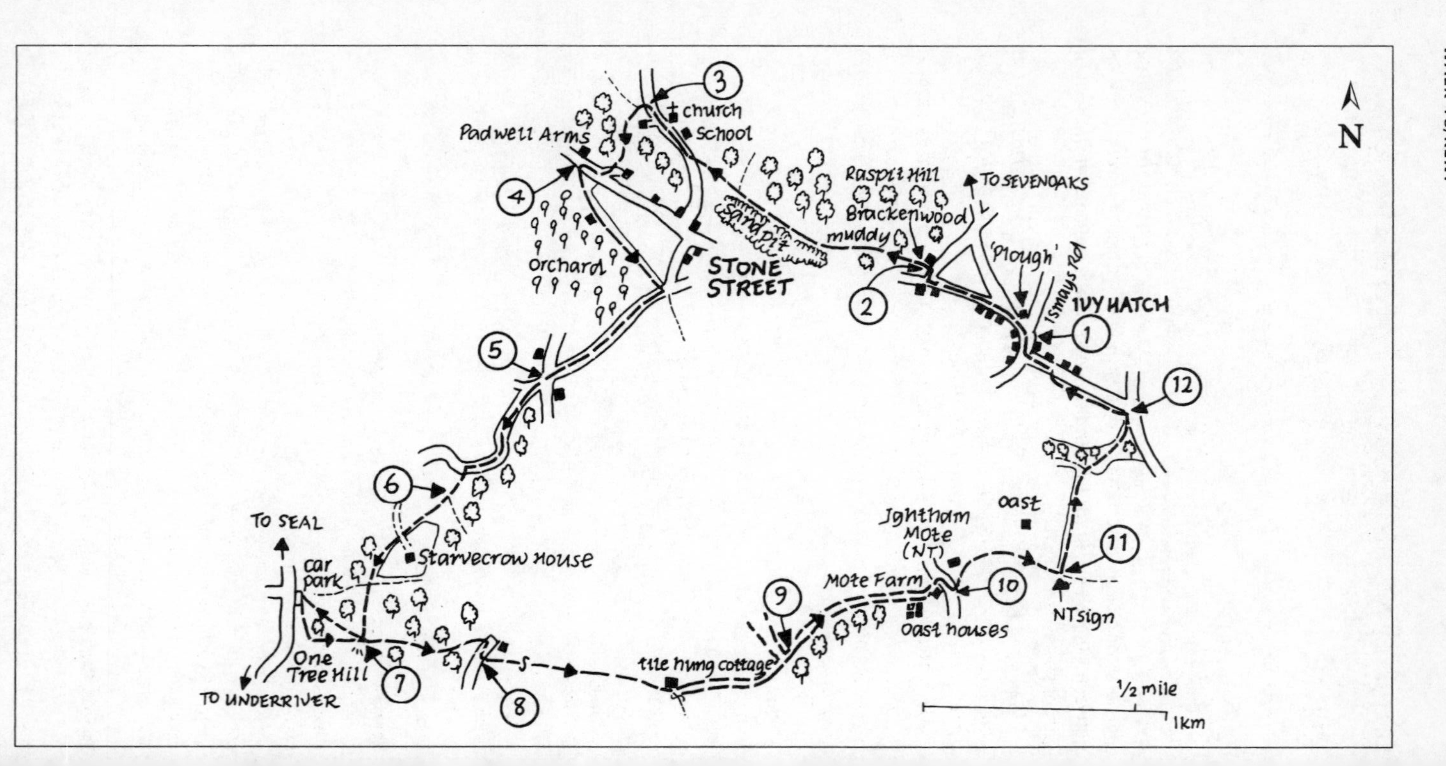
N
church
School
Padwell Arms
Raspit Hill
TO SEVENOAKS
Brackenwood
sandpit
muddy
'Plough'
Ismays Rd
orchard
STONE STREET
IVY HATCH
oast
Ightham Mote (NT)
TO SEAL
Starvecrow House
car park
Mote Farm
NT sign
oast houses
One Tree Hill
tile hung cottage
TO UNDERRIVER
1/2 mile
1km
1
2
3
4
5
6
7
8
9
10
11
12

One Tree Hill and Ightham Mote

KENT WALK 18

Some of Kent's most rewarding walking is found in the greensand country, where the sandy soils give rise to a distinctive vegetation and the landscape is predominantly woodland and pasture. One of the crowning glories is the escarpment, notably on the well waymarked Greensand Way between One Tree Hill and Ightham Mote, which appears in the second part of this varied route.

If you want more walking before arriving at the Padwell Arms, start at One Tree Hill: from there it is 2 to 2½ hours to the pub, which is nearly three-quarters of the way round the walk.

The ascent from Ivy Hatch goes through woodland; mud is often a problem in these first stages. You need to look for the route with some care before dropping down to the Padwell Arms. Orchards and oast-houses follow.

Plough, High Cross Road, Ivy Hatch, Kent TN15 0NL. ☎ (01732) 810268. Open Mon to Sat 11.30 to 3.30, 6 to 11, Sun (April to October) all day, (winter) 12 to 3; food Mon to Sat 12 to 2, 6.30 to 10, Sun 12 to 3. Larkins beers. This is more a restaurant than a conventional pub, though it has a small bar. On offer are perhaps soup, steamed fresh asparagus or grilled goats' cheese crostini to start, or fresh dressed lobster salad, roast Aylesbury duck or roast local pheasant as main courses. Children welcome. No dogs.

Padwell Arms, Stone Street TN15 0LQ. ☎ (01732) 761532. Open Mon to Sat 12 to 3, 6 to 11, Sun 12 to 3, 7 to 10.30; food 12 to 1.45. 7 real ales. Often packed with walkers and horseriders, this rural local has a nicely positioned terrace in the front overlooking orchards. Set menu, including steak and kidney pie and chips, or steak. Also blackboard specials and Sunday roasts. Children welcome in some eating areas. Dogs welcome.

Start: Ivy Hatch (east of Sevenoaks and south of Ightham), roadside parking in village centre by the Plough public house. Grid reference 587546.

Alternative start: One Tree Hill National Trust car park, on the east side of the road between Seal and Underriver.

From Underriver (from the south) go northwards, up a long hill, and then the car park is on the right (just before a turn on the left to River Hill 1½, Sevenoaks 3).

From Seal (from the north), travel along Seal's main street from the Sevenoaks direction, past the Crown pub, then turn right for 2¼ miles, through Godden Green (past the Buck's Head on the right), over a crossroads; the car park is on the left just before the road dips down a long hill with a 14% gradient sign.

To join the walk: Start with the road to your right, and go past the barrier to the left of the National Trust sign for One Tree Hill and the locked gate. Ignore the path to the left going alongside the wooden railing but continue forward through the woodland.

This brings you 130 yards to a T-junction at the top of the main slope; turn left (waymarked Greensand Way) to the stone bench and viewpoint, where the route continues ahead (avoid the path to the left, just after the bench); join the walk at ❼. Grid reference 559533.

Length: 6 miles (9.5 kilometres), 3½ hours.

Difficulty: Moderate; up and down, on sandy soils and mostly through woods and along tracks; muddy in places.

OS maps: 1:25,000 Explorer sheet 147; 1:50,000 Landranger sheet 188.

Tea-room at Ightham Mote for visitors to the house.

PT About five buses a day from Sevenoaks to Ivy Hatch and Stone Street (Mon to Sat).

---

❶ Take the main village street in the Sevenoaks direction, passing the Plough on your right and the bus stop on your left, forking left at the first junction, signposted Stone Street. Take the next right turn (Pine Tree Lane), then ❷ turn left after 30 yards on a path between houses (just to the left of a house called Brackenwood), climbing through the woods. The (often muddy) path climbs on to a greensand ridge: the sandy nature of the soil is apparent on the path. At the top, an **abandoned sandpit** down on the left has created a precipitous cliff-like drop.

Ignore the bridleway signposted through a gate on your right after ¾ mile. Turn right at the road, past the school and church (ignore the driveway to Cone Hill on the left) then, just as the road is about to bend right, fork left on a signposted bridleway into the woods.

❸ After 20 yards take the footpath on the left at a signpost. This path is not defined at the start. Go at right angles to the bridleway for 30 yards, then as the slope steepens bear slightly left to pick up a narrow but defined path which hugs the slope and descends. Keep forward at the next waymarked junction (avoiding the path to the right), near a building, and follow an enclosed section between fences, past brick and stone houses to a driveway (with St Lawrence Vicarage up to the left) and carry on down to a road. Turn right along the road to the Padwell Arms.

❹ Take the bridleway through the orchard opposite the Padwell Arms. This passes to the left of a house in the orchard. Turn right along the road (ignoring the bridleway ahead). ❺ At a crossroads keep forward (signposted Fawke Common and Underriver). The road drops; after ¼ mile, as the road is about to bend right uphill, take a signposted footpath on the left into woods.

❻ After 150 yards, fork right, uphill. You are soon joined by a field fence on the left. Cross over a track that goes to Starvecrow House to your left, and continue with the fence on your left. Where this fence ends at a corner, go forward at a path junction, past a National Trust sign for One Tree Hill, taking a path with wooden railings on the left. Where both the path and the railings bend right, go forward, under the railings and across turf (the site of a long-vanished house) to a viewpoint with a stone bench at the top of the slope (if you have started from One Tree Hill car park, the shortest way back is along the path to the right immediately before you reach the stone bench). Turn left just beyond the bench ❼.

One Tree Hill is owned by the National Trust and comprises an area of mixed woodland, with remnants of ancient woodland cover on the escarpment and a good view over Tonbridge and the Weald. A copper beech near the summit stands on the site of a great beech tree that gave the hill its name, and nearby is the reputed site of a Roman cemetery.

You follow the level path parallel to the top of slope on your right (this is the **Greensand Way**, from Haslemere in Surrey to Hamstreet in Kent, well signposted in this section; the walk follows it to Ightham Mote). Turn right at a T-junction 100 yards later, and fork right after further 50 yards. The Greensand Way leads over a stile and through trees. Reach the end of a lane, turn right downhill along it for 70 yards, then ❽ turn left over a stile on a signposted path. This soon leads to the bottom of a small cliff, with greensand boulders at its foot. In the distance at the 2 o'clock position, and to the right of Shipbourne church, is **Hadlow Tower**, a slender Gothic-revival folly erected in 1838 but sadly damaged by the 1987 storm.

On the left, after ½ mile, is a **covered well**. Just beyond the well is a cottage (a good example of Wealden domestic architecture); here take the track ahead (ignore a stile on your right, leading into a field).

❾ ½ mile later, ignore a track rising to the left at a waymark post. The track bends left at a fine group of **oast-houses** (originally kilns for drying hops) by Mote Farm, to reach the road. Turn right along the road and ❿ almost immediately left between the brick gateposts of Ightham Mote. Follow this estate road (which bends right in front of the iron gates to Ightham Mote, then rises). **Ightham Mote** (National Trust; open March to end October, daily except Tuesday and Saturday) is an outstanding example of a medieval moated manor house. It has a brick and timber exterior, though the half-timbering was covered over with plaster until the early years of the 20th century. The Great Hall, the Old Chapel, 14th-century crypt and painted ceiling of the Tudor Chapel are among its glories.

As the track bends left keep forward on a track between fields. ⓫ After passing below a converted oast-house away to your left, you reach a National Trust sign for Ightham Mote (facing the other way); here turn left and follow the path (waymarked with a red arrow denoting the National Trust's 'Red Walk') up the left side of the field. Just after you enter woodland, fork right (ignoring the left fork, which is again waymarked with a red arrow) and follow it to a road ⓬. Turn left to reach Ivy Hatch, using the parallel path between hedgerows along the left side of the road as far as possible before you are forced back on to the road. At the road junction in the village, carry on, signposted Ightham and Seal, to the Plough.

Local strolls

The best short amble based on the walk described here is from One Tree Hill car park eastwards in the direction of Ightham Mote.

Knole Park, north west of One Tree Hill, is a fine expanse of parkland dominated by the largest stately home in the UK (365 rooms and 52 staircases). The park has a population of deer (not to be approached) and is crossed by public rights of way. Godden Green is a useful starting point.

Further west are walks from Westerham into Squerries Park, where the signposted Tower Walk takes you to a ruined tower in the middle of the estate. More paths are open to the public than are shown on OS maps.

Berwick and Alciston

EAST SUSSEX WALK 19

Berwick and Alciston are two charmingly unspoiled villages tucked beneath the South Downs, each with pleasant old pubs. Alfriston is larger and busier, definitely Sunday afternoon teashop territory, but with some most attractive corners: in particular, it is worth making time to visit the Old Clergy House. The walk begins along shady paths and tracks (which can be muddy), before the scenery opens up near Berwick church. After exploring the length of Alciston's single street, the route climbs quite steeply up the escarpment of the Downs, before the high-level finale, with wide views over the sea and far across the Weald. Paths are very clearly marked, with good waymarking.

This route can be combined with Walk 22, Long Man and Lullingstone Heath, to make a 13-mile 'figure of eight' ramble taking in the Long Man of Wilmington.

Close by is Charleston Farmhouse, the bohemian country retreat of the Bloomsbury group of post-Victorian artists, writers and intellectuals: Vanessa Bell (Virginia Woolf's sister), Duncan Grant and David Garnett set up home here in 1916. The house, restored after Grant's death in 1978 and preserved by the Charleston Trust, is full of colourfully painted and improvised decoration which had much influence on 20th-century design: the house, garden and visitor centre are open to the public (2 to 6 Wednesday to Sunday and bank holidays from April to October and 2 to 5 at weekends in November and December); see also Berwick church below.

For superb coastal views, drive into nearby Seaford, park at the eastern end of the esplanade and walk up Seaford Head: from the top you look along the length of the Seven Sisters cliffs.

George, High Street, Alfriston BN26 5SY. ☎ (01323) 870319. Open Mon to Sat 11 to 11, Sun 12 to 10.30; food Mon to Sat 12 to 2.30, 7 to 9 (9.30 Sat), Sun 12 to 3, 7 to 9.30. 4 real ales. Large back garden. A la carte menu, with specials board in the restaurant during the day. Blackboard menu including soup, salads, ploughman's and pasta. Sandwiches are available in the bar at lunch-time. Children welcome. Dogs in bar only.

Star, High Street, Alfriston BN26 5TA. ☎ (01323) 870495. Open 7am to 11pm (10.30 Sun); food 12 to 2, restaurant 7 to 9, Sun 12.30 to 2.30, 7 to 9. Bass beers. This hotel-like dining pub has a red figurehead lion from a 17th-century ship adorning its handsomely carved exterior. It has a set and à la carte menu in addition to sandwiches and daily specials. Starters might include seafood terrine on mixed leaves with a cucumber dressing, while main courses might be seared scallops, savoy cabbage with a mustard dressing or pan-fried chicken breast wrapped in bacon with

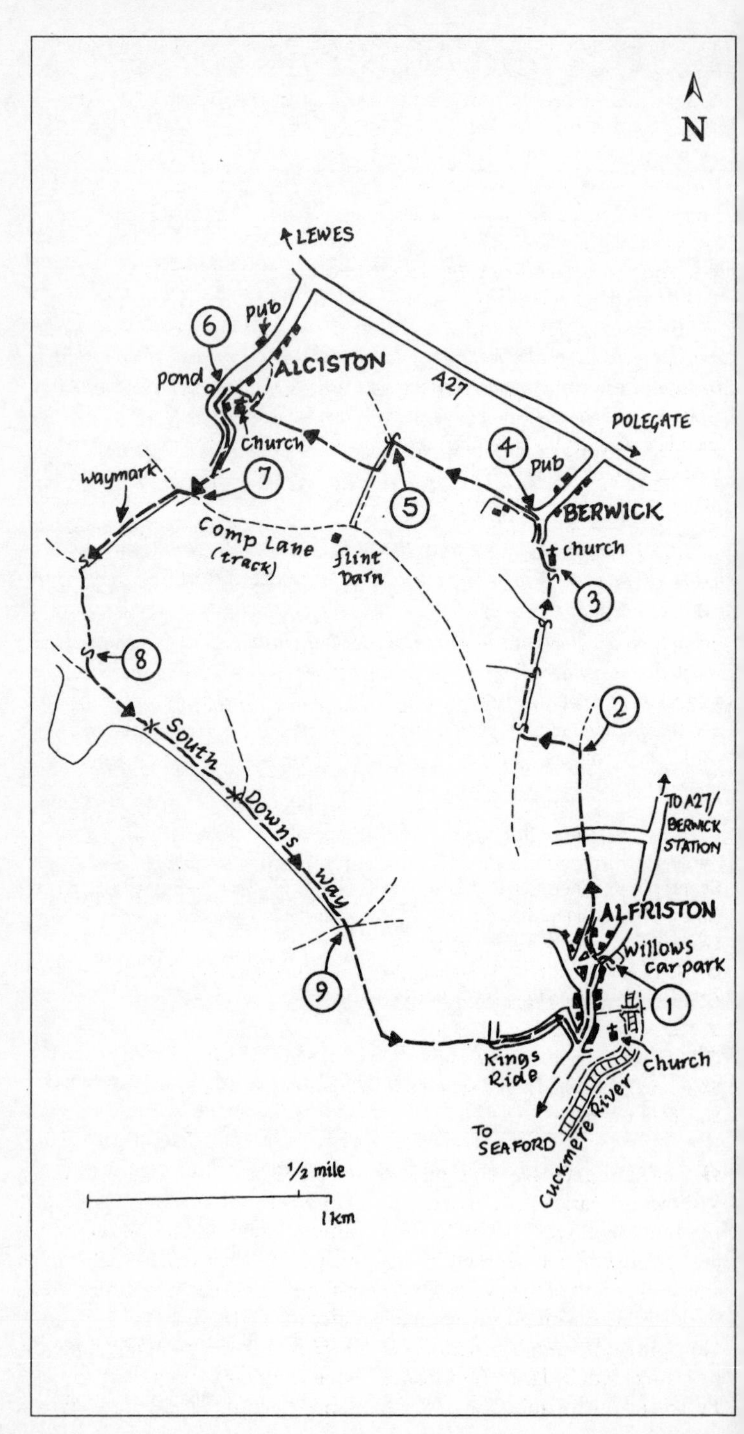
N
LEWES
pub
ALCISTON
A27
pond
church
POLEGATE
pub
BERWICK
waymark
Comp Lane
(track)
flint barn
church
South Downs Way
TO A27/
BERWICK
STATION
ALFRISTON
Willows
car park
Kings
Ride
church
TO
SEAFORD
Cuckmere River
½ mile
1km

an asparagus sauce. Bar snacks are available from 6 to 9 every evening. No children in bar area. No dogs in restaurant.

Smuggler's Inn (also known as the Market Cross), 6 Market Cross, Waterloo Square, Alfriston BN26 5UE. ☎ (01323) 870241. Open Mon to Sat 11 to 3, 6.30 to 11, Sun 12 to 3, 7 to 10.30; food 12 to 2, 7 to 9. John Smith's, Harveys beers. A former smugglers' haunt, this pub serves steaks, gammon, fish, sausages. Ploughman's and sandwiches also available at lunch-time. Children welcome in restricted area. Dogs welcome.

The Cricketers' Arms, Berwick BN26 6SP. ☎ (01323) 870469. Open Mon to Sat 11 to 3, 6 to 11 (all day Sat in summer), Sun 12 to 10.30 (12 to 3, 6 to 10.30 winter); closed 25 Dec; food 12 to 2.15, 6.30 to 9 (all day Sat in summer), Sun 12 to 9. Harveys beers. A very pretty village pub formed from the conversion of two flint-faced cottages, the Cricketers' Arms has attractive gardens at front and rear, with picnic tables for summer eating. Inside are creaky floors, old wooden tables and chairs, cricketing prints on the walls, and log fires in winter. Light dishes might include deep-fried Camembert or garlic mushrooms. Jacket potatoes, ploughman's, sausages or home-cooked ham are also on offer as well as daily specials. Fresh fish, game in winter, and shellfish in summer. Children welcome in eating area. Well-behaved dogs welcome.

Rose Cottage Inn, Alciston BN26 6UW. ☎ (01323) 870377. Open Mon to Sat 11.30 to 3, 6.30 to 11; Sun 12 to 3, 7 to 10.30; food 12 to 2, 7 to 9.30 (9 Sun); restaurant Mon to Sat 7 to 9. Harveys beers and a guest ale. Small and cottagey village pub serving dishes made from seasonal produce. Fresh fish is caught locally, and most vegetables are organically grown. Starters might be home-made soup or coarse farmhouse paté with toast, while main courses could include venison braised in port and Guinness or traditional Sunday roast. Specials include rabbit and bacon pie, chicken in tomato and basil topped with mozzarella or Thai-style curries. Salads. On the evening bar menu are dishes such as half pound of Lincolnshire pork sausages with chips or fried scampi with chips. Full bar menu including ploughman's is available at lunch-times. No sandwiches. No children in bar. Dogs welcome on a lead in the bar.

Start: Alfriston (north-west of Eastbourne and south of A27); park in Willows Car Park (small fee), well signposted on north edge of village. Grid reference 522034.
Length: 5½ miles (9 kilometres), 3 hours.
Difficulty: Moderate, with one steep climb; farmland and downland.
OS maps: 1:25,000 Explorer sheet 123; 1:50,000 Landranger sheet 199.
Shops and tea rooms in Alfriston.
WC In Alfriston (in short stay car park a few yards from the start).
PT Buses to Alfriston from Lewes and from Berwick railway station (hourly Sat and Sun, May to Sept).

---

❶ Leave the village end of the Willows car park, by a tourist information board, cross the main road and go up the narrow road opposite, to the right of the short stay car park (marked with no entry signs). Go right at the next T-junction, on a rising small lane signposted Berwick Court 1 mile. You pass the entrance to White Lodge Country House Hotel on your right and after the houses end the route continues as a earthy path between hedges. Eventually drop to a road. Take the path opposite.

❷ At a path junction, where the view suddenly opens out towards Berwick church spire, turn left on a track between fields (towards a flint barn, although you won't go that far). At the end of the first field on the right, cross the stile on the right (with yellow waymark). You are now on the long-distance **Vanguard Way**, a 63-mile route from East Croydon station to Seaford via the Ashdown Forest.

The path crosses three fields to Berwick church; turn right at the end of the third field, then left into the churchyard. Go round the left-hand side of the church to the porch ❸. The stained-glass windows at **Berwick church** were destroyed by a Second World War bomb blast; their plain glass replacements create a much lighter interior. The Charleston artists (see introduction above), Vanessa Bell and Duncan Grant, and Vanessa's son Quentin, were commissioned in 1941 to decorate the plain walls. Local people, friends of the artists and servicemen stationed in the area acted as models, and Sussex landscapes provided the background for their striking religious and seasonal scenes.

On the far side of the church, go under the metal arch and lantern and down steps, turn right on a gravel path between walls, leading on to a driveway. You reach a road junction at a small grassy triangle; the Cricketers'Arms is to your right, but turn left to continue the route.

❹ Where the road ends (with a concrete farm road to the left), go forward on a concrete track (signposted Alciston) initially. Keep going in the same direction as the track bends left at some barns, now on a chalky track, first alongside a hedge and then (after hedge corner) along a grassy strip between fields.

❺ At the end of this field, avoid the stile ahead but turn left towards the South Downs. After about 200 yards go right at a waymark post through a deliberate gap in the hedge, towards Alciston church.

At the end of the field, turn right and immediately cross a stile on the left, through a small field and beside the churchyard wall to the road ❻. The Rose Cottage pub is to your right. Turn left to continue.

Court House Farm, on the left, has a ruined medieval dovecote. As the road bends left you pass the farm's huge **tithe barn**, of church-like dimensions and 170 feet long; it is not open to the public, but you may be able to glimpse its roof timbers and tie-beams from the road when its doors are left open. Medieval tithe barns like this were built for storing the 'tithe' – one-tenth of agricultural produce, which was paid to the church as a tax.

The road becomes an unmade track and rises to a track junction ❼: turn right (this is Comp Lane, the old **carriage road**) and then left 50 yards later as soon as you enter a field. The path rises up the left edge of the field and then after 100 yards, at a waymark post, continues through a tunnel-like hedge.

After a stile, turn left and immediately right uphill steeply to the next stile ❽. Bear half left as waymarked to join the South Downs Way along the crest of the ridge; this soon has a fence on the right and is waymarked with acorn motifs. Views extend towards Hastings, with the prominently circular Arlington Reservoir to the left.

❾ At a path junction, go forward on the South Downs Way, which drops to Alfriston via a residential road called Kings Ride. Emerge on the main street by the Star Inn, with its red lion known as Old Bill (thought originally to have been a Dutch ship's figurehead) on its exterior; the car park is to the left, but it is worth detouring to the church and Clergy House: turn right, past the George Inn, and left by the United Reform Church. You can also continue to a pretty bridge over the Cuckmere River, where the riverside Kissing Gates Walk leads to Litlington Bridge.

Alfriston

Looking on to a tiny chestnut-shaded square with the only surviving market cross in East Sussex stands the Smugglers' Inn. During the early years of the 19th century this pub was the headquarters of the notorious Alfriston gang of smugglers who led an excise man to his death on the nearby cliffs. The spacious church, built of small, knapped flints, dates mainly from the 14th century, and its grand proportions have made it known as the Cathedral of the Downs. Across the green from the church stands the Clergy House, a 14th-century timber-framed and thatched 'hall house' that in 1896 became the first property to be acquired by the recently formed National Trust (who paid just £10 for it). The interior and its cottage garden are open to the public.

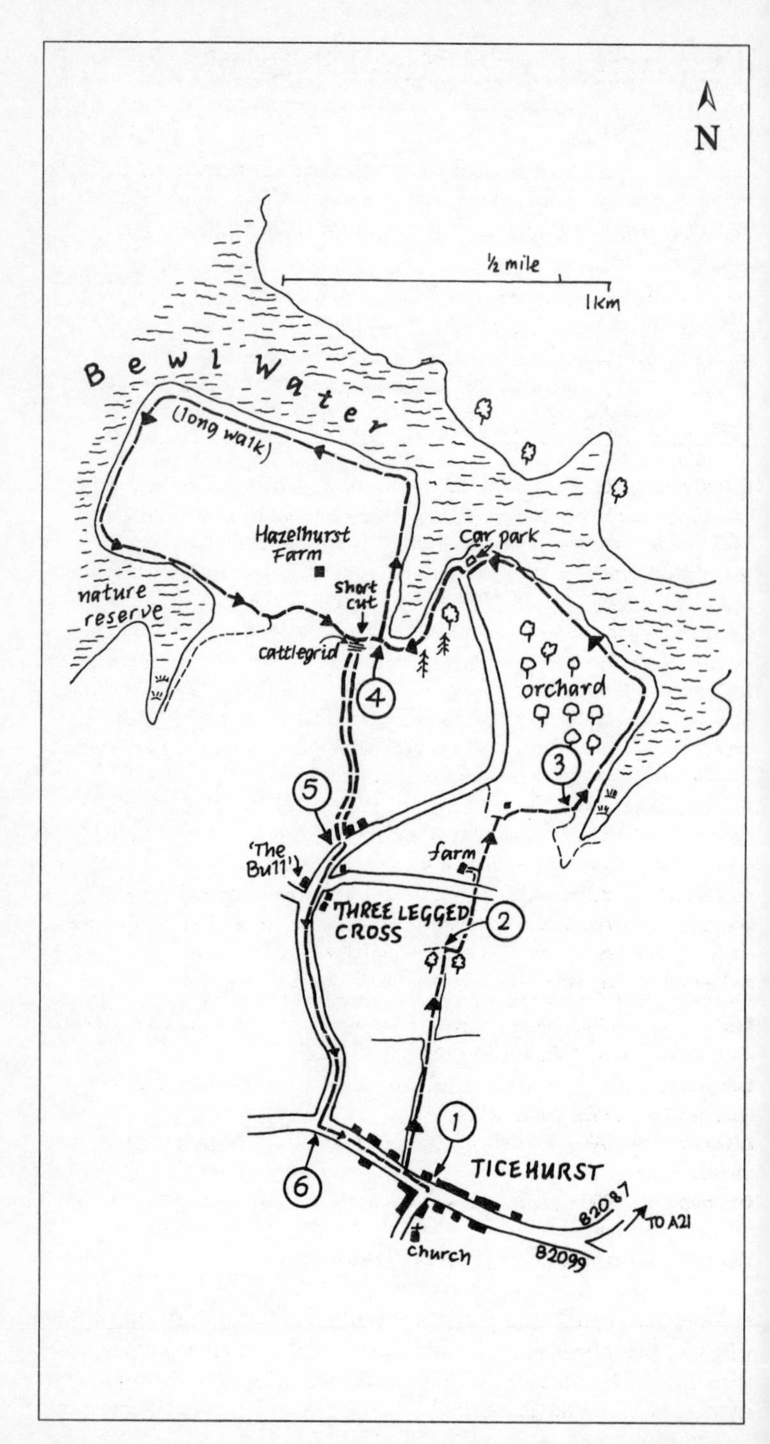
N
½ mile
1km
Bewl Water
(long walk)
Hazelhurst Farm
Car park
nature reserve
short cut
cattlegrid
orchard
4
3
5
'The Bull'
farm
THREE LEGGED CROSS
2
1
6
TICEHURST
B2087
TO A21
Church
B2099

Ticehurst and Bewl Water

EAST SUSSEX WALK 20

The largest lake in south-east England forms the focus of a shortish ramble in the oast-house and orchard country of the Sussex Weald, with the Bull Inn a welcoming stop towards the end. Most of the interest is from the waterside vistas, but the approach to Bewl Water is also attractive in its own right.

For a longer route you can tackle the full 13 miles of the lake's perimeter path, taking about six hours.

Bell Hotel, Ticehurst TN5 7A5. ☎ (01580) 200234. Open 11 to 3.30, 6 to 11; food 12 to 2, 7.30 to 9. Harveys beers. 14th-century coaching inn. Sandwiches, bar snacks and grills available. Children welcome. Dogs welcome on a lead.

Duke of York, High Street, Ticehurst TN5 7BD. ☎ (01580) 200229. Open Mon to Sat 11 to 11, Sun 12 to 10.30; food 1 to 9. Harveys, John Smith's, Boddingtons's beers. Seasonal specials, sandwiches, bar snacks available. Children welcome. Dogs welcome.

Chequers Inn, High Street, Ticehurst TN5 7BQ. ☎ (01580) 200287. Open Wed 6 to 11, Thurs 12 to 2.30, 6 to 11, Fri and Sat 12 to 11, Sun 12 to 3, 7 to 10.30, closed Mon and Tues; food 12 to 2, 7 to 9. 1 real ale. Snacks, steaks and sandwiches are all on offer. Children welcome. No dogs in restaurant.

Bull, Dunster Mill Lane, Three Legged Cross TN5 7HH. ☎ (01580) 200586. Open Mon to Sat 11 to 11, Sun 12 to 10.30; closed 25 Dec; food all week 12 to 3, 6.30 to 9.30. Harveys, Bass, Rother Valley beers. The low-ceilinged tile-hung hostelry is set in a pretty garden with two *pétanque* pitches and a weekend bouncy castle. The interior has sturdy black beams, exposed stonework and flagstone floors. On the menu are filled baguettes, ploughman's and soup as well as pheasant, venison, fish, steak and kidney pudding and steak. Children welcome. Dogs welcome on a lead.

Start: Ticehurst village centre; roadside parking near the church or in a small square by the Duke of York. Grid reference 689303

Length: Full walk 5 miles (8 kilometres), 2½ hours; short walk omitting part of lakeside path 3½ miles (6 kilometres), 2 hours.

Difficulty: Easy. All on the level, through pasture and woodland and along the lakeside path.

OS maps: 1:25,000 Explorer sheet 136; 1:50,000 Landranger sheet 188.

Shops in Ticehurst.

PT Hourly buses from Tunbridge Wells to Ticehurst (not Sun).

❶ From the central road junction with the Bell Hotel opposite and with the Duke of York to your right, turn left on the B2099 in the Wadhurst/Tunbridge Wells direction. After 70 yards, just after house no. 32 (Wisteria House) and Gunning & Co. Estate Agent, turn right on a path between houses. Keep in this direction (after the wall on the left ends ignore a stile on your right into a playing field) for the first ½ mile, during which the path emerges into a field and goes forward along field edges towards a distant oast-house, then drop into a small wood.

❷ 100 yards into the wood, turn right at a T-junction of tracks; the route immediately bends left to enter the right-hand of two fields, up a grassy strip along the field edge to a small road.

Cross to the driveway opposite, and after 25 yards, where the driveway bends left into a pantile-hung house, keep forward on an enclosed path between hedges. Where the right-hand field ends (on the other side of the hedgerow), turn right at a path junction (if you reach a corner of a vehicle-width track you have overshot by 20 yards), past a weatherboarded summerhouse with a cockerel weather vane (over the hedge to the left).

Emerge into the open and ❸ turn left at the path T-junction. The edge of **Bewl Water** soon becomes visible: you are now following part of the 13-mile Round Bewl Water Walk; there is an orchard to the left for the first section. Past a gate (and a car park on your right) turn right at a T-junction with a lane, through the barrier; the Round Bewl Water Walk continues immediately left to regain sight of the lake. It goes into woods – past a fine timber-frame Wealden house to the left.

❹ At the junction with the Round Bewl Water Walk, signposted to the left through a gate, and a footpath signposted ahead over a stile:

For the short walk turn left on the Round Bewl Water Walk to reach a concrete track with Hazelhurst Farm (private) to the right. Turn left over a cattle grid and follow the track (leaving the Round Bewl Water Walk) to reach a road T-junction by houses at the edge of Three Legged Cross.

For the full walk go forward over the stile on a path skirting the peninsula, on the edge of the lake (keep to the path). It is slightly confusing where a Sussex Trust for Nature Conservation sign says 'keep to the path' and there is a temptation to follow a concrete track left through a gate (which says 'private, no right of way') – but just keep ahead.

Eventually at the recess of the inlet, turn left at the junction with the Round Bewl Water Walk, through a gate. At the concrete track with Hazelhurst Farm (private) to your left, turn right over the cattle grid, and follow the track to reach houses at the edge of Three Legged Cross.

Both routes ❺ Turn right past weatherboarded cottages, and pass the Bull on your right; follow Cross Lane ahead.

❻ At end of Cross Lane, turn left on the B2099 to Ticehurst. **Ticehurst** itself is a handsome Wealden village, with many cottages tile-hung or weatherboarded. St Mary's Church is a spacious structure with a richly ornate 16th-century font cover and a medieval brass of a knight. The stained glass features a 'doom window' of grinning devils transporting erring souls to an unpleasant fate in hell. There is also a large second-hand bookshop close by.

Bewl Water

Created in the 1970s, this huge reservoir on the Kent/Sussex border has become a valued landscape asset for the south-east. Over 120 acres of the reservoir and its surrounding land are managed by the Sussex Trust for Nature Conservation, and nesting rafts and special islands have been made to enable nesting birds to avoid potential predators. Geese, ducks, divers and waders winter here, and migrants include warblers, wheatears, redshank, greenshank, common and green sandpiper and terns. Herons can often be spotted feeding on shallow water, and moorhen, mallard, coot and great crested grebe nest year-round. Butterflies such as the common blue and gatekeeper are seen on the sheep-grazed grasslands around the reservoir, where flora includes vetch and early purple and spotted orchids.

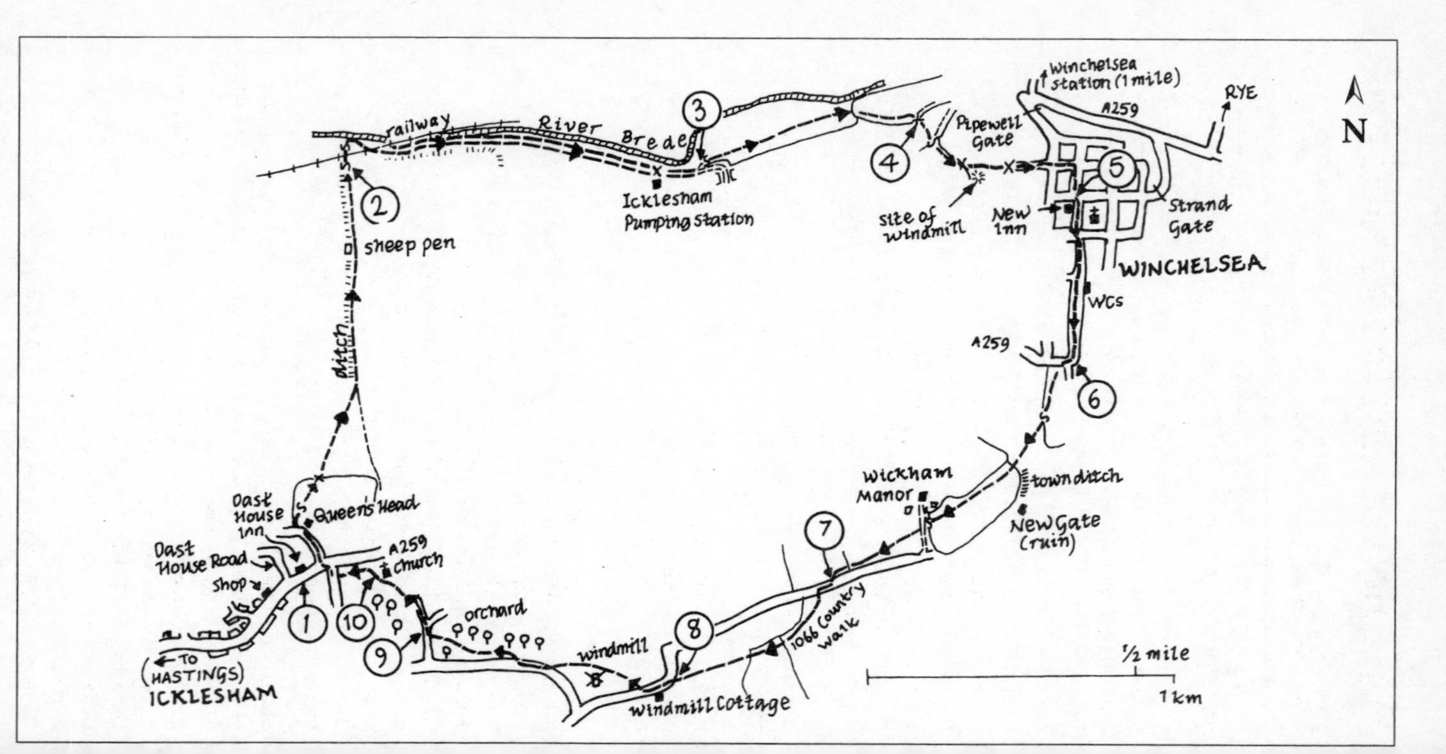
N
Winchelsea station (1 mile)
RYE
A259
railway
River Brede
Pipewell Gate
Icklesham Pumping Station
site of windmill
New Inn
Strand Gate
sheep pen
WINCHELSEA
WCs
A259
ditch
Wickham Manor
town ditch
Oast House Inn
Queens Head
New Gate (ruin)
Oast House Road
A259
church
Shop
orchard
1066 Country Walk
windmill
TO (HASTINGS)
ICKLESHAM
Windmill Cottage
1/2 mile
1 km

Winchelsea and the Brede Level

EAST SUSSEX WALK 21

The first view from this walk is over one of the most unspoilt tracts of Romney Marsh, edged by slopes that constituted what was the coastline in Roman times. Here the canalised River Brede winds through a sweep of drained marshland known as the Brede Level, and now grazed by sheep. Its open, fenny character contrasts with the undulating terrain of the second part of the walk. We recommend you start and finish at Icklesham, itself of limited interest (apart from the church), as Winchelsea is a highly rewarding place to arrive at on foot and the second part of the walk has the edge scenically, with some particularly attractive parkland around Wickham Manor.

After you have done the walk, the old Cinque Port town of Rye is well worth a visit, and there is a long sandy beach nearby at Camber Sands.

Oast House Inn, Main Road, Icklesham TN36 4AJ. ☎ (01424) 814217. Open Mon to Fri 10.30am to 11pm, Sun 12 to 10.30; food 12 to 11 (10.30 Sun). Bass. Bar snacks, roasts and steaks are all available as well as specials on a blackboard. Children's menu. Children welcome. Dogs welcome.

Queen's Head, Parsonage Lane, Icklesham TN36 4BL. ☎ (01424) 814552. Open summer 11 to 3, 6 to 11, winter 12 to 5, 7 to 10.30; food Mon to Sat 12 to 3, 6.15 to 9.45, Sun 12 to 3, 7 to 9.45. Old Forge, Swale, Rother Valley and Woodforde's beers. Built in 1632, the 'Queen's Head' is picked out in slates on the roof and has a fine view over Romney Marsh towards Rye. On the menu might be steaks, pies, sandwiches, ploughman's and Sunday roasts. No children in bar, no under-12s after 8.30pm. Dogs welcome.

New Inn, German Street, Winchelsea CN36 4EN. ☎ (01797) 226252. Open 11 (12 Sun) to 3, 6 to 11 (10.30 Sun); food 12 to 2, 6.30 to 9. Harveys beers. Home-cooked food on an à la carte menu could include crispy deep-fried Camembert or crispy mushrooms and garlic mayonnaise to start, and sirloin steak, local fish, including skate and cod, or grilled leg of English lamb steak to follow. Daily blackboard specials, bar snacks and sandwiches are also available. No children in public bar. No dogs.

Start: Oast House Inn, Icklesham, on A259 2 miles west of Winchelsea. Roadside parking in side roads (such as Oast House Road between the shop and the Oast House Inn; or Manor Close just west of this). Grid reference 878165.

Alternative start: New Inn, Winchelsea (by the churchyard). Roadside parking. Join the walk at ❺. Grid reference 905174.

Length: 5 miles (8 kilometres), 3 hours.

Difficulty: Moderate. On the level or over gently rolling farmland. Sections over arable land may be very uneven underfoot.

OS maps: 1:25,000 Explorer sheet 125; 1:50,000 Landranger sheet 189.

Shop and tea room in Winchelsea. Shop in Icklesham.

WC In Winchelsea, just after the start of the walk.

PT Hourly buses Mon to Sat (two-hourly on Sundays) to Icklesham and Winchelsea from Brighton, Eastbourne, Bexhill, Hastings, Rye and Folkestone. Winchelsea station is a mile north of the village, and a rather dull walk along the road (turn right out of the station).

---

❶ With the Oast House Inn on your left, walk along the A259 pavement, then take the first left turn (Parsonage Lane; signposted to the Queens Head). Where the road bends left, turn right and pass to the left of the Queen's Head to take the stile in the rear right corner of the pub car park (this was obscured by a caravan on semi-permanent-looking hard standing at the time of writing). The hilltop town of **Rye** is visible in the distance.

Bear half right down to a gate (the path is not visible on the ground), then in the next field head in the same direction. At the bottom of the slope keep forward (slightly left) on a track along the right-hand side of a drainage ditch, heading towards the two white tops of a distant oast-house.

❷ After ½ mile cross a stile and go carefully over the railway. On the other side, cross a small bridge and immediately turn right to take another stile and re-cross the railway. Turn left along a stony path beside the railway for 20 yards, then take the stile and steps down on the right to emerge on to a high dyke between two ditches (the left one containing the River Brede). After ¼ mile the right-hand ditch bends away; keep forward for another ¼ mile to pass a flat-topped brick pumping station.

❸ 100 yards beyond the pumping station, where the Brede bends markedly left and the track leaves it and heads to a bridge, take the stile between the Brede and the track, and follow the right-hand fence. Where the fence ends, keep forward (if the field is ploughed up a strip of vegetation should show the route) towards distant buildings. After an uneventful plod (not the highlight of the walk) you reach the end of this large field. Go through the gate beside a stile and turn right to skirt the edge of this hummocky field and to pass through a signposted gate ❹. Turn right uphill (ignoring a path to the left) and beyond the next stile join a rising sunken grassy track. At the top, take the gate on the left and go round the left-hand side of a mound, on which stand the millstone and a few sad remains of **St Leonard's Windmill**, destroyed in the 1987 storm. Carry on to join the end of a road and go forward across the A259 into **Winchelsea** (see box). Take the next right and reach the New Inn, by the church ❺.

After you have explored the village, resume the walk with the New Inn on your right and the churchyard on your left, and walk along the pavement on the right side of the road, past **Wesley's Tree** (the descendant of an ash from where the founder of Methodism preached his last open-air sermon in 1790). You later pass the toilets on your left.

❻ ¼ mile after the end of the

village, the road bends right (signposted Hastings; avoid Wickham Rock Lane ahead); just after this bend take the 1066 Country Walk signposted on the left. This well signposted long-distance route leads back to Icklesham.

Carry on half right to a stile and into the next field, where you continue half left. At the end of this field you can see, on your left, part of the medieval town ditch and the ruined **New Gate**, built by Edward I as the southern entrance to the town, which never expanded as far as this. Go up the next field, heading to the left of stone-built Wickham Manor, to take the stile just to the left of a fine old tile-hung barn. Views open out over Romney Marsh and the coast.

Cross over the driveway to the manor and cottages; the path bears half left, and in the next field follows the left edge of the next field and then emerges onto a small road ❼. Turn right along the road then immediately left into a field: the path joins a hedgerow corner, by a Second World War pillbox, and follows the right edge of this and the next field – with views of Dungeness power station in the distance (on an exceptionally clear day you might see the French coast), then crosses the third field to a gate.

❽ Turn left on a road, then 100

Winchelsea

From 1191 Winchelsea was admitted as one of the Cinque Ports, a confederation of Channel ports formed for the defence of the coast, supplying ships and men for the royal fleet in return for certain privileges.

Originally Winchelsea was below its present hilltop site, but in 1287 a great storm washed the town away and altered the course of the River Brede. The new town was begun on top of the hill the following year, laid out in its strikingly regular grid plan. Cellars were dug at the king's expense, and wharves were developed. However, the build-up of shingle from the 15th century gradually cut the town off, and now it stands more than a mile inland.

The town's commercial decline was compounded by the Black Death during the 14th century and by repeated attacks from the French in the 14th and 15th centuries. What you see today is predominantly later – tile-hung, weatherboarded or Georgian – although many vaulted medieval cellars survive, and there are three town gates.

St Thomas's Church fills one square of the grid plan and is partly ruined and partly incomplete, its tower demolished and its transepts and nave gone. Nevertheless, what remains is impressive, especially its rich array of canopied tombs.

Writing in about 1725, Daniel Defoe found Winchelsea 'rather the skeleton of an ancient city, than a real town.' Its population has shrunk, from about 6,000 in its heyday to only a few hundred today.

A model of medieval Winchelsea is on display with seals of the Cinque Ports in the stone-built Winchelsea Court Hall Museum (open May to September, Tuesday to Saturday and bank holidays 10.30 to 12.30, 2 to 5, Sun 2 to 5) near the churchyard. The former gaol is on the museum's ground floor.

yards later turn right on a path rising to the right of the hilltop **windmill**, then down to a stile in the bottom left-hand corner of the field to turn right on a small lane. 40 yards later take a path on the right (the entrance is rather hidden in the hedgerow), and turn left as waymarked in the apple orchard, then right after 100 yards, then immediately left again across the middle of the orchard. ❾ Join a road, and turn right on it, forking left in front of Manor Farm Oast, then at the end of the orchard on the left, turn left on a grassy track (past Stable Cottage on the right). ❿ At the entrance to Icklesham churchyard, either continue round to the left on the path, or go into the churchyard to see **All Saints Church**, a restored Norman building with a variety of carved capitals and a central tower rising in three stages. Turn left after 20 yards by the hexagonal church porch on a gravel path past a lamp-post and car park. Either way, turn right on the road to reach the A259 opposite Parsonage Lane.

The Long Man and Lullingstone Heath

EAST SUSSEX WALK 22

This walk starts and finishes with views of one of the most mysterious hill figures in England, the celebrated Long Man of Wilmington. On the top of the Downs it is a different world, with huge vistas over the sea, and larks for company. A chalky track leads gently down to Alfriston, where the walk can be combined with Walk 19 to make a 13-mile walk taking in Berwick Church. The final stages head alongside the swan-populated Cuckmere River, then across fields past the Sussex Ox pub and on to Wilmington church.

Plough and Harrow, Litlington BN26 5RE. ☎ (01323) 870632. Open 11 (12 Sun) to 4, 6.30 to 11 (10.30 Sun); food 12 to 2.30, 7 to 9 (10 Sat and Sun). 6 real ales. Pies, soup, bar snacks, steak, sandwiches, fish and specials. No children. No dogs in restaurant.

George, Star and The Smuggler's Inn, Alfriston (see Walk 19 for details).

Sussex Ox, Milton Street BN26 5RL. ☎ (01323) 870840. Open Mon to Sat 11 to 3, 5.30 to 11 (6 to 10.30 winter), Sun 12 to 3, 5.30 to 10.30, closed 25 Dec; food Mon to Sat 12 to 2, 6 to 9, Sun 12 to 9. Greene King Abbot Ale and Harveys beers. The Sussex Ox is a large white weatherboarded pub with great views of the South Downs. On offer are ploughman's, jacket potatoes and open sandwiches as well as dishes such as grilled whole plaice or duck cassoulet. There are also blackboard specials. Children welcome in dining room. Dogs welcome on a lead.

Start: Free car park at Wilmington (signposted as Litlington and Long Man from A27) between Lewes and Polegate; the car park is at the far end of the village, on the right. Grid reference 544041.

Alternative start: Alfriston (Willows car park; small fee). Walk to the river bridge. *Either* turn left out of the car park, along the main street, then turn left just after the George Inn and the United Reformed Church, on a paved path leading downhill, then go half left down to the river (where the right turn goes to the Old Clergy House); *or* exit the rear of the car park, on a paved track near a modern house called the Willows – this becomes a stony track and leads past a stile and locked gate, and bends right to the river bridge. *Both routes* Cross the bridge and turn left along the riverside path (signposted Milton Street) and join the walk at ❼. Grid reference 544041.

Length: 7½ miles (12 kilometres), 3½ hours.

Difficulty: Moderate, with one climb on to the Downs.

OS maps: 1:25,000 Explorer sheet 123; 1:50,000 Landranger sheet 199.

Litlington Tea Gardens, Litlington (a Sussex institution, going strong since the early 19th century, when it was set up as a pleasure garden). Tea rooms and shops in Alfriston.

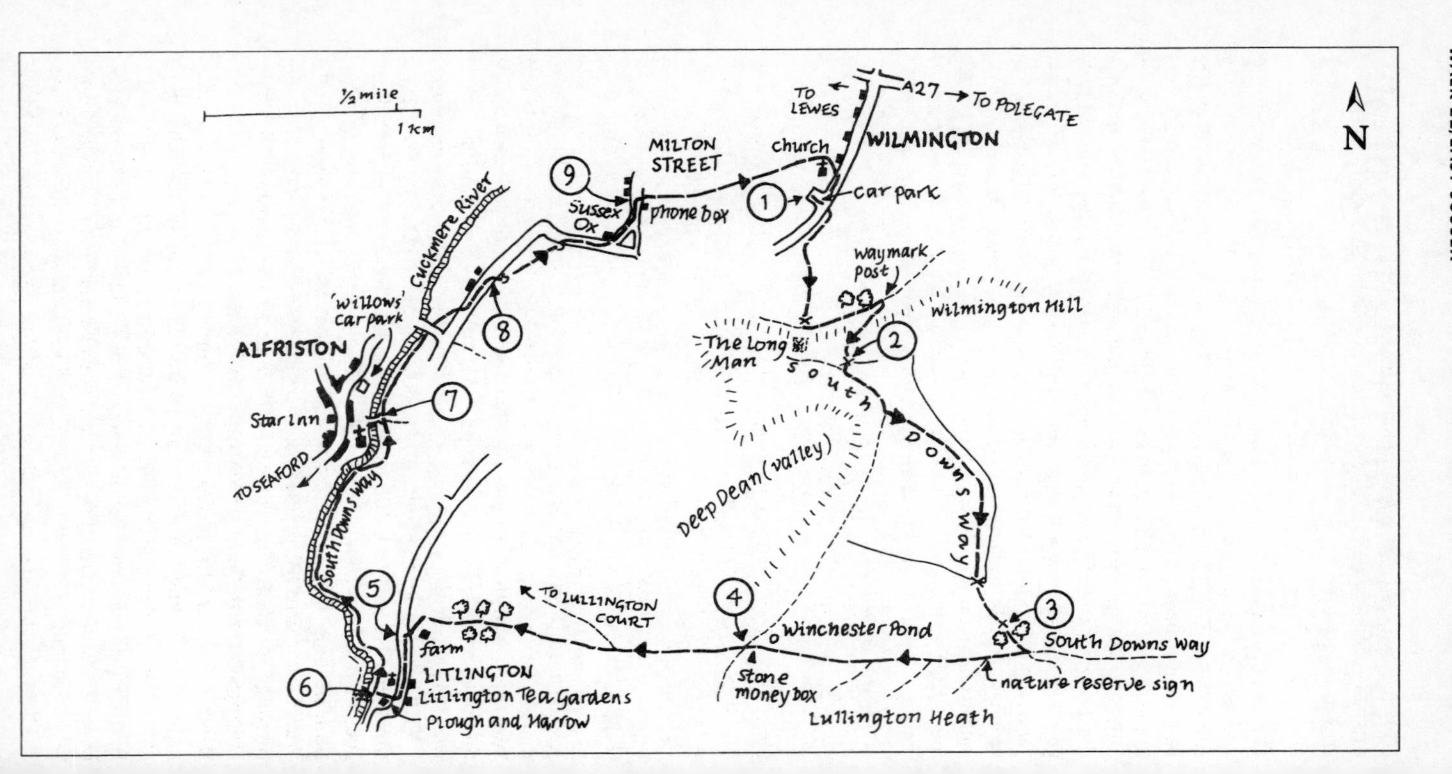

N
TO LEWES
A27 → TO POLEGATE
WILMINGTON
church
car park
MILTON STREET
phone box
Sussex Ox
Waymark post
Wilmington Hill
The Long Man
South Downs Way
Deep Dean (valley)
Cuckmere River
'willows' car park
ALFRISTON
Star Inn
TO SEAFORD
South Downs Way
TO LULLINGTON COURT
Winchester Pond
South Downs Way
farm
LITLINGTON
Litlington Tea Gardens
Plough and Harrow
Stone money box
Lullington Heath
nature reserve sign
½ mile
1 km
1
2
3
4
5
6
7
8
9

WC In Wilmington car park and Alfriston short stay car park.
PT Buses to Alfriston from Lewes, and to Alfriston, Litlington and Wilmington from Berwick railway station (hourly Sat and Sun, May to Sept).

❶ From the car park cross the road and take the signposted path opposite for the Long Man: the path runs beside the road then veers left to the foot of the great hill carving. Turn left beyond the gate beneath the Long Man. The path passes a group of trees on the left after 150 yards, then 200 yards later reaches a waymark post: turn sharp right on a path rising to the top of the escarpment ❷. The hummocky area on the top is the shafts and spoil heaps of a **Neolithic flint mine**; although flint nodules occur naturally on the chalk surface of the Downs, the best flint for tool-making, free from faults caused by frost damage, is found in seams underground.

Go through the gate and go forward to join a chalky track alongside a fence and at the top of a steep slope: turn left along it, past the head of a spectacular dry valley. Just beyond it fork left at a waymark post: this is the South Downs Way (marked with acorn motifs) – the route is marked with a series of wooden posts.

❸ After a mile, the route goes through a small wood. 100 yards later, turn right at a four-way junction (leaving the South Downs Way, which turns left here). Avoid turnings to the left as you skirt **Lullington Heath National Nature Reserve**, on your left. The reserve is unusual in having both acid and chalk-loving plants side by side. Beyond it lies Friston Forest and beyond that the chalk cliffs of the Seven Sisters.

The track dips and rises. ❹ Go forward (signposted Litlington) at a four-way junction by a stone money box in the shape of a pillar on the left (on your right just before this, not very apparent, is **Winchester Pond**, a haunt of dragonflies); this track now drops gradually. Keep left at the next fork, again signposted Litlington; the track drops steadily (in the distance, half left, you can see another chalk hill figure – of a white horse; this, however, is not of ancient origin), finally turning right at some farm buildings to reach the road ❺.

Turn left, passing the church and Litlington Tea Gardens, then 20 yards before the Plough and Harrow, take the signposted path on the right. ❻ Turn right on reaching the **Cuckmere River**, which has been canalised to prevent tidal flooding. Follow the river 1¼ miles to the long white bridge at Alfriston (cross it if you wish to see the village; see Walk 19 for further information about **Alfriston**); carry on, signposted Milton Street ❼. The river path leads to a road at another bridge. Here leave the river and take the path opposite and slightly right (signposted Milton Street), heading diagonally across two fields via kissing-gates.

Turn left on the next road, then after 200 yards ❽ take the signposted path on the right (or carry on along the road if you prefer; it makes a right bend) and go diagonally left to a stile and across a large field to rejoin the road. Turn right and left at the junction, signposted Wilmington; the Sussex Ox is placed on the corner here. Go through the little hamlet of Milton Street.

❾ 50 yards after the phone box take the field path on the right as signposted. There are more fine views of the Long Man away to the right. The path heads over to 12th-century **Wilmington church**, which is well worth a look. It has a carved Jacobean pulpit with a sounding board, and in the north chapel (behind the organ) a stained glass window depicting St Peter surrounded by 10 butterflies of different species (the window had been temporarily removed at the time of writing). In the churchyard a gigantic yew, held up by wooden props, measures 23 feet around its base and is believed to be 1,000 years old (so perhaps the oldest tree in Sussex).

Turn right on the road, past the entrance to **Wilmington Priory**. This house is made out of parts of a medieval Benedictine priory that belonged to Grestrain Abbey in Normandy and was seized by the Crown during war with France. It was later converted into a farmhouse and has been recently restored as holiday accommodation by the Landmark Trust. Just after the priory, also on the right, is the former **village pound**.

The Long Man of Wilmington

Formerly visible only in the early morning or evening light or after a snow shower, the Long Man of Wilmington is now marked out in concrete blocks. The first known drawing of the Long Man dates from 1710, but the origin of the figure is uncertain: he has been variously interpreted as a prehistoric boundary marker, a folly created by the monks of nearby Wilmington Priory or – despite his lack of male attributes – a fertility symbol. Couples hoping for a child are still rumoured to visit the site on summer nights. Just to the left of the Long Man is a long barrow, or Neolithic burial mound, dating from about 3500BC and known as **Hunter's Burgh**. Long barrows – nine are positioned conspicuously along the Downs between Eastbourne and Brighton – contain large quantities of human bones and were possibly associated with ancestor-worship. By contrast, the smaller oval or round barrows of the Bronze Age and Saxon periods, which are very common on the Downs, generally contain only a single burial.

Streat and Ditchling Beacon

EAST SUSSEX WALK 23

The route approaches the South Downs from the north, first gaining sight of them from a track along a slightly pronounced sandstone ridge, and skirting the edge of Plumpton race course (one of two visible en route). Once up on top of the Downs you have the option of diverting to Ditchling Beacon for one of the most majestic views in the county. Carline thistle, salad burnet, marjoram and common spotted orchid fleck the steep escarpment.

Jolly Sportsman, Chapel Lane, East Chiltington BN7 3BA. ☎ (01273) 890400. Open Tues to Sat (and bank hol Mon) 12 to 3, 6.30 to 11, Sun 12 to 4; closed 25 Dec; food Tues to Sun 12.30 to 3 (2.30 Fri), Tues to Sat 7 to 10. Rectory, 3 guest beers. The building is a rambling mixture of old and new, with a soft warm interior that is both modern and rustic. Food might be Dover sole with garlic and parsley butter or noisettes of pork. The bar menu includes items in smaller portions and at lower prices than the restaurant menu. Children welcome. Dogs welcome.

Half Moon Inn, Ditchling Road, Plumpton BN7 3AF. ☎ (01273) 890253. Open Mon to Sat 11 to 3, 6 to 11, Sun 12 to 10.30; food Mon to Sat 12 to 2.30, 7 to 9.30, Sun 12 to 2.30, 7 to 9.30. Badger beers. Large garden at the rear, children's play area with crooked house and five-a-side football; fine views of the Downs. Set menu, specials board and sandwiches. No children in bar. Dogs welcome.

Start: East Chiltington church (limited parking; during services on Sunday morning it may be easier to park by the phone box at the end of the lane unless you are a customer at the Jolly Sportsman and are using its car park. Turn off B2116 east of Ditchling into Novington Lane, signposted to East Chiltington, then after just over a mile take the first left to the church. Grid reference 370151.

Alternative start: Ditchling Beacon (large car park); start walk at ❼.

Length: Full walk 8 miles (13 kilometres), 4 hours; short walk omitting Ditchling Beacon 6 miles (10 kilometres), 3 hours.

Difficulty: Moderate to energetic. One steep climb on to the South Downs, but the rest is straightforward.

OS maps: 1:25,000 Explorer sheet 122; 1:50,000 Landranger sheet 198.

PT Buses to Plumpton and Streat (Mon to Sat) from Lewes and Haywards Heath; train to Plumpton (no Sun service). Go to the footbridge at the far end of the platform from the station building and follow the track around the right-hand side of Plumpton race course, keeping to the right of the grandstands, to emerge at a T-junction beyond the end of the race course. Turn right and join the walk at ❷ (to finish the walk retrace your steps from this point).

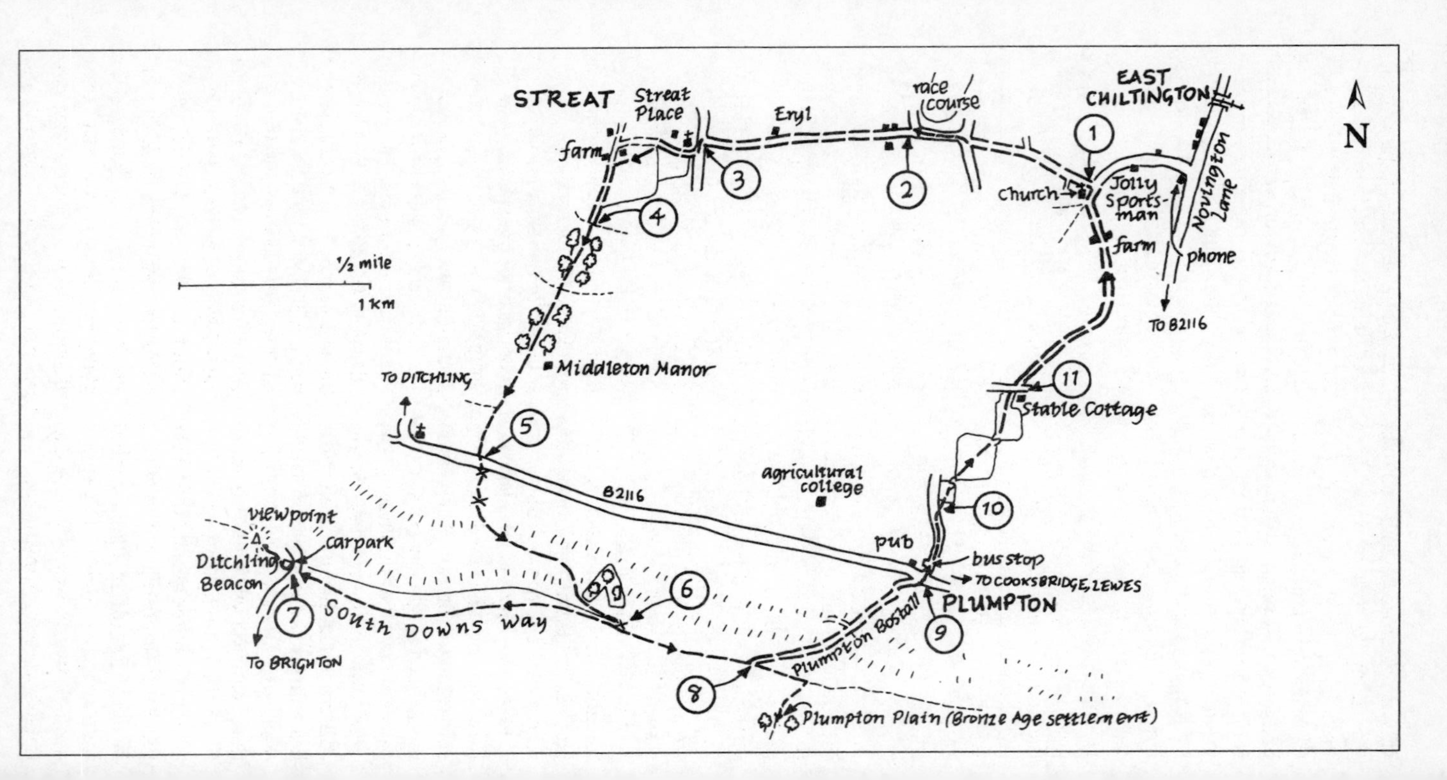
N
STREAT
Streat Place
farm
Eryl
race course
EAST CHILTINGTON
1
2
3
4
Church
Jolly Sports-man
farm
Novington Lane
phone
TO B2116
½ mile
1 km
Middleton Manor
TO DITCHLING
5
11
Stable Cottage
agricultural college
B2116
10
pub
bus stop
TO COOKSBRIDGE, LEWES
PLUMPTON
9
Viewpoint
Carpark
Ditchling Beacon
7
South Downs way
6
TO BRIGHTON
Plumpton Bostall
8
Plumpton Plain (Bronze Age settlement)

❶ With the road behind you, take the unmade track (signposted Bridleway) to the right of **East Chiltington church**, a simple building of Norman origins with a roof of four ancient beams. After the end of the churchyard, ignore a left turn but continue downhill, and ignore a right turn 300 yards later. You soon get fine views of the South Downs as the track follows a low greensand ridge, along the course of the **Roman Greensand Way,** which runs east–west from Barcombe to Hardham in West Sussex. It connects the iron production centres of the Weald with the Roman city of Noviomagus (Chichester), and goes through an ornate gateway. Cross the road and take the road ahead past the south end of Plumpton race course ❷. This becomes an unmade track and passes houses. On the Downs a pronounced V of woodland is visible; this was planted to commemorate Queen Victoria's Golden Jubilee in 1887. The intention was to plant the letters VR, but funds ran low and the scheme was left incomplete.

❸ At the tiny village of Streat turn left on the road past the entrance to Streat Place then immediately right on a track that passes to the left of the church.

Of Norman origins, **Streat church**, which has no dedication, has unusual cast iron memorials in the nave floor; one dated 1731 has the 3 cast the wrong way round. From the churchyard you can see the topiary in the grounds of **Streat Place**, an imposing house with a Jacobean façade of mullions and flint-knapped walls. The place name Streat derives from the Old English word for Roman road.

Beyond the end of the churchyard ignore a track to the right. After the end of the first field on the left, take a path half left* in the signposted direction across the field to a stile immediately to the left of barns, then turn left on the track towards the South Downs; keep forward at the junction just after the farm.

❹ At the end of the large field, go forward, now on a path between hedges. Continue in this direction for ¾ mile, avoiding all side turnings and glimpsing red-brick Middleton Manor (built about 1829) away to your left, to reach the B2116. ❺ Cross over and take the bridleway through the gate opposite. This climbs and beyond another gate reaches open downland, then continues above pronounced grassy banks, keeping slightly left, up through another gate and then up to the top (above a steep valley head down to your left, keep left at a fork, on the main path; you now pass above the V of woodland you saw earlier).

❻ At the top, go through a gate and reach a T-junction with the South Downs Way. Left is the continuation, but you can detour to the right along the South Downs Way to the prominent car park at **Ditchling Beacon** ❼, at 813 feet the highest point in East Sussex. The summit is beyond the road and car park and gives a superb 360-degree view. The rampart and ditch of an **early Iron Age hillfort** dating from about 600BC are visible in the scrub around the car park, but the site has been badly damaged by ploughing. Retrace your steps back along the South Downs Way, past the point where you joined it, and cross a small road. Brighton race course is in view to your right.

Half right you can see trees on the skyline of what is known as Plumpton Plain; these trees mark a celebrated early Bronze-Age settlement. ❽ The next track on the left, leading downhill, is the continuation; it is known as Plumpton Bostall, 'bostall' being a South Downs term for shepherds' roads or tracks that lead up to the top of the Downs like this one.

Before descending you can make an optional detour ahead and then to the right to get closer to the site of **Plumpton Plain settlement** (marked by trees on either side of the track), from where the view opens out to the coast at Newhaven and Seaford Head. Excavated in the 1930s, the settlement dates from 1,000BC to about 500BC and appears to have moved from one side of the track to the other over that time. It consisted of squarish banked enclosures, which surrounded huts. It is interesting that the place name of Plumpton appears from here all the way north to the race course near the start of the walk. Medieval administrative boundaries in Sussex (known as 'rapes') had the same long north–south shape and may have followed a more ancient pattern of land use, providing a good range of grazing, farming, forestry and hunting land for their inhabitants.

Now follow the route down Plumpton Bostall downhill, ignoring side turns; this becomes a concrete track. ❾ Cross the B2116 carefully, as this is a blind corner; the Half Moon is just to the left. Take the turning opposite signposted to Plumpton race course and walk on the left-hand then the right-hand verge (ignoring the first path on the right, which goes to Warningore Farm). After the road bends left you pass a tiny single-storey flint building, with a semi-legible plaque identifying it as the former **village school room**.

Just after this, turn right on a signposted path into a house garden, and keep half left to a stile, then through the garden of a shingle-hung house (keeping to the right of this house) and over a stile into a field ❿. Bear diagonally across this field and the next field to stiles in their far corners, and in the third field continue to a stile at the far fence between two houses.

⓫ Take the signposted stile beside a locked gate ahead (avoiding the driveway along the side of Stable Cottage) and follow this atmospheric pheasant-populated woodland track, with its ornate metal estate gates and glimpses of parkland, for nearly a mile to the end of a road at East Chiltington church, where the Jolly Sportsman is to the right along the road.

*It may be more tempting (and much easier underfoot) to keep forward along the track and turn left by houses to avoid this bit of field walking, but unfortunately there is no actual right of way along the track beyond the footpath signpost.

Friston and the Seven Sisters

EAST SUSSEX WALK 24

One of the most attractive stretches of coastal scenery in south-east England (illustrated on the front cover of this book), with sheltered mixed woodland in Friston Forest and two contrasting villages. Route-finding is easy, mostly on defined paths and tracks; keep well clear of the crumbly cliff edge.

For a much shorter walk (2½ miles/4 kilometres) start at Birling Gap and do the eastern loop of this walk to Belle Tout.

A recommended add-on is to drive past Beachy Head and down to Eastbourne, one of Britain's most endearing Victorian seaside resorts, with stucco-fronted hotels, bandstands and neat municipal gardens.

Tiger Inn, The Green, East Dean BN20 0DA. ☎ (01323) 423209. Open summer 11 to 11, winter Mon to Fri 11 to 3, 6 to 11, Sat 11 to 11, Sun 12 to 10.30; closed eves 25 and 26 Dec; food 12 to 2, 6.30 to 9 (9.30 Fri and Sat). Harveys Best, Adnams Best, Flowers Original, Morland Old Speckled Hen, Timothy Taylor Landlord. The bars are beamed with low ceilings and have traditional furniture and furnishings, with plenty of pewter, china and antique settles. Many of the meals incorporate local produce, and might include locally cured gravad lax with a mustard and dill sauce, smoked haddock, ginger and spring onion fish-cakes, sausage ploughman's, or a whole lobster. No children. Well-behaved dogs welcome on a lead.

Birling Gap Hotel, Eastbourne BN20 0AB. ☎ (01323) 423163. Open Mon to Sat 9.30 to 11, Sun 12 to 10.30; food Mon to Sat 12 to 3, 6 to 9.30, Sun 12 to 9.30. 2 real ales. Blackboard menu, sandwiches, Sunday carvery. Children welcome. Dogs welcome.

Start: Tiger Inn, East Dean village green. Free public car park on the edge of the village near the green; turn south from A259 (between Seaford and Eastbourne) by East Dean signpost (on the left if approaching from Eastbourne) at the bottom of a dip; the car park is signposted on the right. Turn right out of the car park to the village green by the Tiger Inn. Grid reference 557978.

Alternative start: Seven Sisters Country Park (pay and display car park) at Exceat on A259, 6 miles west of Eastbourne and 2 miles east of Seaford, at a bend near where the road crosses the Cuckmere River. Grid reference 518995. There are two car parks (if beginning from the one on the sea side of the A259, cross the A259 by the bus stop; if starting from the car park on the north side of the A259, leave by the car park ticket machine, go past the restaurant and visitor centre to a point close to the main road and turn left). Join the walk at ❼.

A free car park can also be found at Birling Gap (join the walk at ❹), and several along the road eastwards below Belle Tout.

Length: Full walk 10½ miles (17 kilometres), 5 hours; short walk omitting Birling Gap and Belle Tout 8 miles (13 kilometres), 4 hours.

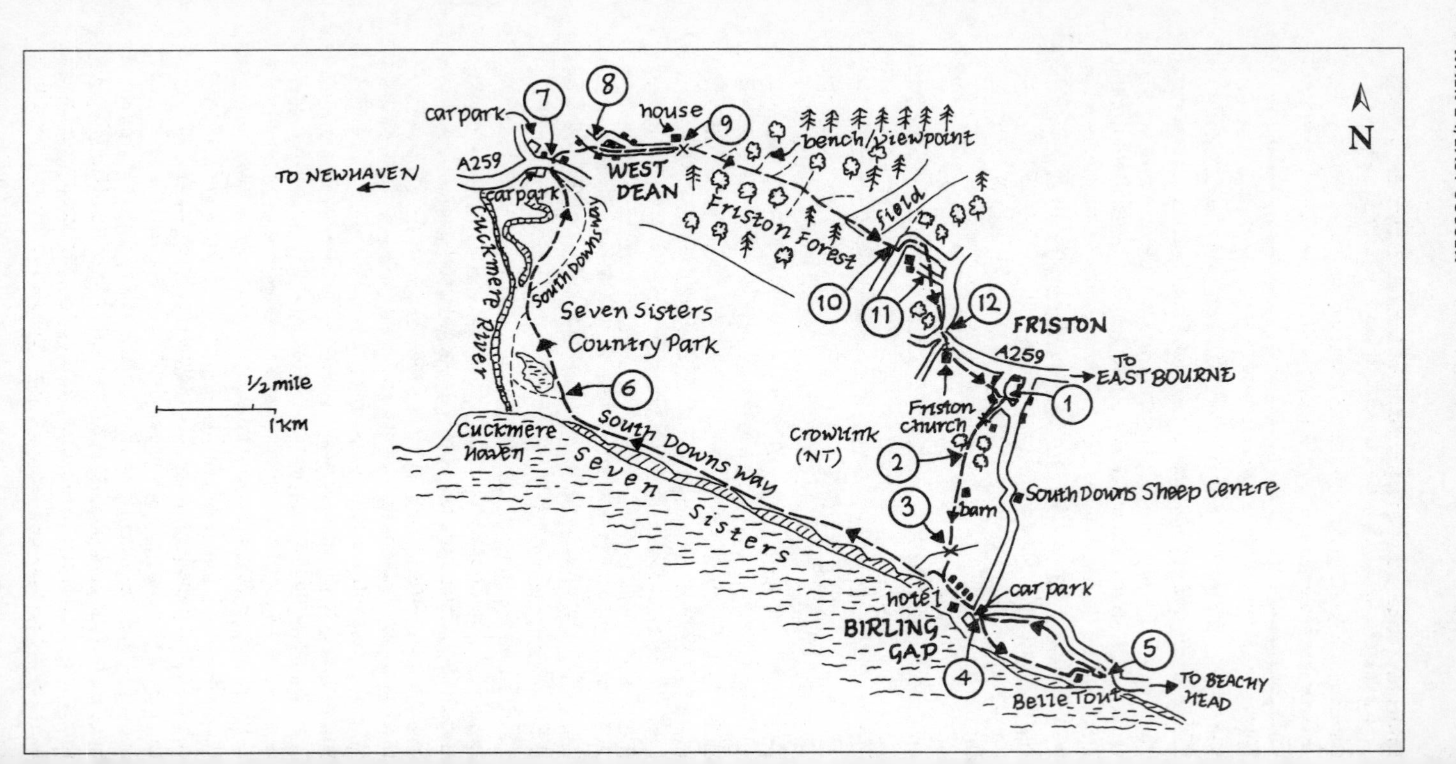
N
carpark
7
8
house
9
bench/viewpoint
A259
TO NEWHAVEN
WEST DEAN
carpark
Friston Forest
field
Cuckmere River
South Downs Way
Seven Sisters Country Park
10
11
12
FRISTON
A259
TO EASTBOURNE
½ mile
1km
6
1
Friston church
Cuckmere Haven
South Downs Way
Crowlink (NT)
Seven Sisters
2
South Downs Sheep Centre
3
barn
hotel
car park
BIRLING GAP
4
5
Belle Tout
TO BEACHY HEAD

Difficulty: Energetic. Usually tiring in the sea wind, and plenty of medium ascents and descents; firm underfoot.

OS maps: 1:25,000 Explorer sheet 123; 1:50,000 Landranger sheet 199.

Exceat Farmhouse Restaurant and Tea Rooms by A259 at Seven Sisters Country Park. Café at Birling Gap.

WC At Seven Sisters Country Park (by visitor centre) and Birling Gap.

PT Frequent daily buses to Exceat and East Dean from Eastbourne, Newhaven and Brighton.

---

❶ From the attractive green at East Dean, which is lined with flint-walled cottages near the simple Norman church with its Saxon tower, begin the walk with the Tiger Inn on your right. Go up the left side of the village green to the post office, pillar box and Grimaldi's Restaurant and turn left, immediately forking right into Went Way. At the end of the lane proceed straight on through a gate on to a path signposted Birling Gap. After 30 yards, where the wall on the left ends, go half left, up through a wood to emerge on to open downland (Went Hill) ❷. Head just to the right of a prominent small barn and pick up a slightly sunken track, which descends gradually towards the sea. ❸ After ¼ mile go through a gate, then take another gate near the top of the houses at Birling Gap. 30 yards later, just after Seven Sisters Cottage, you reach a gate on the right: this (the South Downs Way) is the continuation, unless you wish to detour to Belle Tout.

For the detour to Belle Tout go left down the track to Birling Gap ❹.

From Birling Gap car park (by the toilets and hotel) take the coastal path by the phone box (to the left of the cottages), up steps and over the steep banks of the huge **Belle Tout enclosure**. This is thought to have been used some 2,500 to 3,000 years ago for penning herds of cattle. Then it would have circled a hilltop about a mile inland: now the hill itself has been cut in half by erosion by the sea, which is nibbling away at the chalk cliffs to the extent of 20 inches a year. Continue on the coast path to pass to the left of **Belle Tout lighthouse**. Now a private house, it featured in the television series based on Fay Weldon's novel *The Life and Loves of a She-Devil* and hit the news in 1999, when it was moved back along special rails a short distance from the perilously close clifftop. Considering the rate of erosion, one wonders if the owner moved it far enough.

Descend from the lighthouse – the shore-level red and white striped tower of Beachy Head lighthouse is visible ahead. Between it and the cliffs lie the chalk boulders from a recent huge cliff fall. ❺ Just before the road turn left initially along the grass parallel to the road. Soon you pick up a well-defined level track that makes a much easier and swifter return to Birling Gap. Before leaving **Birling Gap** it is well worth descending the steps to the shore for a magnificent view of the cliffs from below.

Past Birling Gap car park return to the main route (if you have started from Birling Gap this point is found by beginning with the sea on your left, and taking the rising stony track from the corner of the main road, past some houses; this bends right, then just after take the South Downs Way via a gate on the left).

To continue the main walk beyond this gate the path soon turns right along the coastal cliff tops of the Seven Sisters for two miles.

❻ When descending from the last 'Sister' (above Cuckmere Haven) bear half right downhill (signposted Exceat), soon with a fence on the left. At the bottom, turn right on the prominent wide grassy track (signposted 'visitor centre'), which later becomes a concrete track (where you avoid the South Downs Way, which rises to the right).

Follow the track to a bus stop at **Exceat** by the A259. This was once a sizeable village, hit hard by the Black Death in the 14th century. Exceat now has a visitor centre for the Seven Sisters Country Park.

Cross the road and ❼ take the rising surfaced track (the South Downs Way), between buildings, cross a stile and ascend a steep grassy field straight ahead to a flint wall. Cross the wall and proceed into Friston Forest along a path. Descend the steps to **West Dean** village, ignoring a crossing-path at the bottom ❽. This secretive village in a wooded fold in the Downs all but closes out the rest of the world. King Alfred is thought to have had a manor house here, quite possibly at the ruined house by the dovecote in the village centre.

At the road junction turn right and follow the road past houses and then at the next road junction keep forward by the Friston Forest sign; to your left at this point, near the Norman church, the 13th-century rectory is visible. It is one of the oldest continuously inhabited houses in Britain.

❾ Bear right at a fork (signposted Friston), just after a barrier and 100 yards beyond an isolated white house. Continue straight along this broad stony track, ignoring side turnings. After ¾ mile, where the main track swings left, continue forward on a descending grassy track. Ignore side turns; later the track rises and enters a field, continuing along the right-hand side (signposted 'car park').

❿ Turn left at a T-junction (with a private drive opposite Friston Place, of which the mullioned 17th-century façade can be seen from a distance) and follow the road. This bends to the right; 250 yards later, by a signpost, take a gate in the right-hand wall and bear half left across the field and pass through a small gate in the wall on the far side ⓫. Cross the lane and take a stile into the next field, making for the top far left-hand corner. Cross a stile and go through a wood.

⓬ Emerge on to A259 at Friston. Cross the A259, go down the road opposite, signposted Crowlink. Follow the road for 40 yards, then enter the churchyard on the left by an unusual 'tapsel gate', pivoted in the centre to ease the passage of funeral processions. **Friston church** is worth a look, with its roof dating from 1450, and brasses and a fine alabaster memorial to the Selwyn family of Friston Place. The door is a memorial to the composer Frank Bridge (the teacher of Benjamin Britten), who died at Eastbourne in 1941. Look for the graffiti scratched by medieval pilgrims in the porch, and for a simple grave in the churchyard with the stark inscription 'washed ashore'.

Proceed through the churchyard and leave by the far right-hand corner. Walk downhill to East Dean through a grassy valley and through a gate at the village. At a T-junction turn right on the road and in a few yards reach the village green.

The Seven Sisters

This series of seven chalk spurs, with dry valleys between, abruptly ends at sheer 500-foot cliffs. Part of the area forms the Seven Sisters Country Park, while to the east is the National Trust's Crowlink estate, giving general public access to much of the area. On the way you pass memorials from those whose bequests have enabled the Trust to acquire the land and safeguard it for posterity.

From Birling Gap to Cuckmere Haven is good territory for bird-watching (especially for spring and autumn migrants), and the downland supports many butterflies, including the marbled white and five species of blue. Viper's bugloss, a tall blue and pink flower, is a common sight on the cliffs and is one of the most spectacular species of chalkland flora. At the western end, the land dips to **Cuckmere Haven**, the only estuary in Sussex to be undeveloped. During the Second World War, the beach was lit up at night as a dummy town to trick enemy bombers and confuse them into thinking they were flying over Seaford. Near the river mouth a Roman burial ground and mammoth's tusk have been found. The lagoon marshland, alluvial grassland and shingle bank are another rich habitat for wildlife and flora.

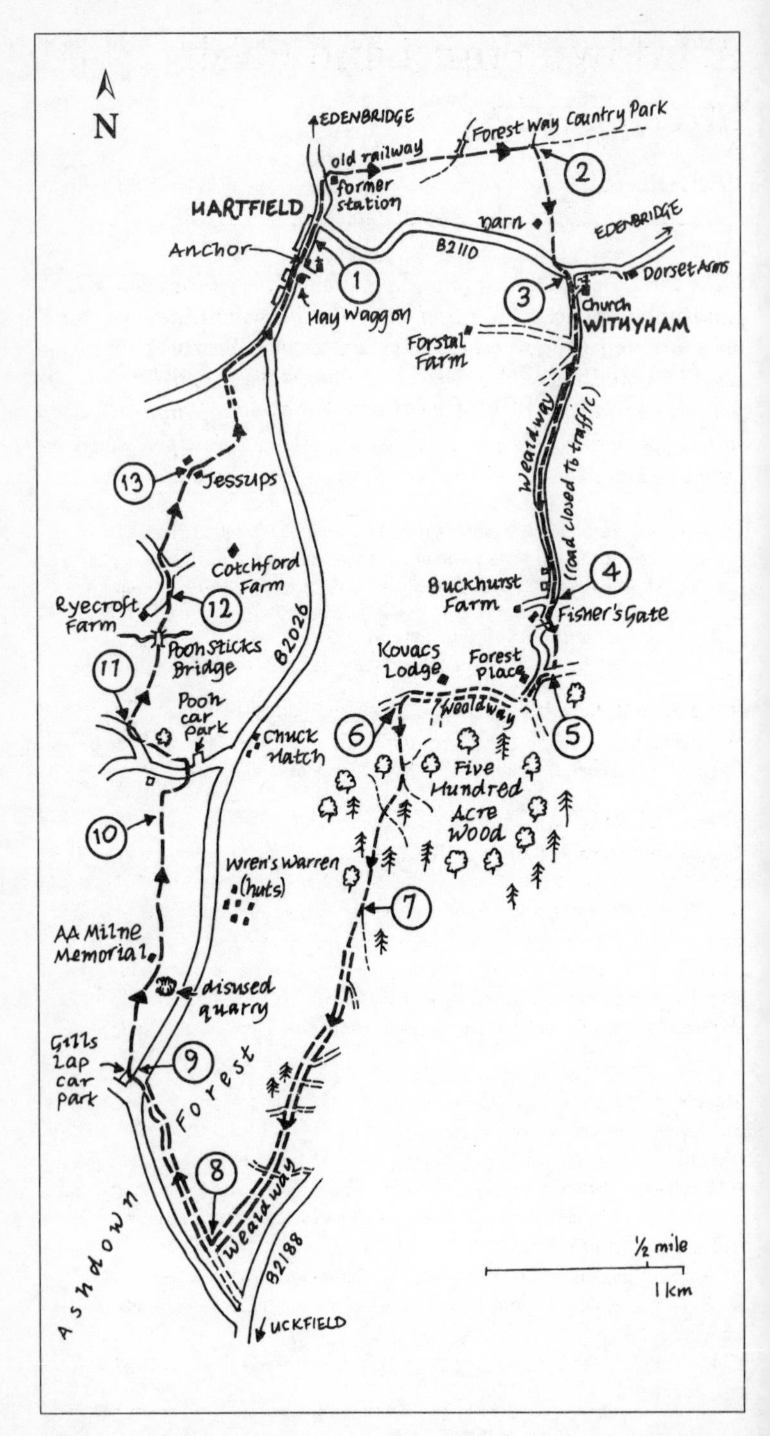
N
EDENBRIDGE
Forest Way Country Park
old railway
former station
HARTFIELD
barn
EDENBRIDGE
B2110
Anchor
Dorset Arms
Church
WITHYHAM
Hay Waggon
Forstal Farm
Wealdway
(road closed to traffic)
Jessups
Cotchford Farm
Buckhurst Farm
Fisher's Gate
Ryecroft Farm
Poohsticks Bridge
B2026
Kovacs Lodge
Forest Place
Wealdway
Pooh car park
Chuck Hatch
Five Hundred Acre Wood
Wren's Warren (huts)
AA Milne Memorial
disused quarry
Gills Lap car park
Forest
Ashdown
Wealdway
B2188
UCKFIELD
½ mile
1 km
1
2
3
4
5
6
7
8
9
10
11
12
13

Ashdown Forest and Pooh Sticks Bridge

EAST SUSSEX WALK 25

From the typical Wealden landscapes around the timber-framed and pantile-hung cottages of Hartfield, the route climbs on to Ashdown Forest, an area of unspoilt, elevated heathland unlike anywhere else in the south-east of England, and giving some of the finest walking in the region. The forest is instantly familiar to anyone who has read the Winnie-the-Pooh stories. For those who do not wish to tackle the full route, the path described from Gills Lap to the AA Milne Memorial is especially recommended.

Anchor Inn, Church Street, Hartfield TN7 4AG. ☎ (01892) 770424. Open Mon to Sat 11 to 11, Sun 12 to 10.30; food all week 12 to 2, 6 to 10. Harveys Best, Fuller's London Pride, Bass and Wadworth 6X. This mock Tudor pub serves bar food, including sandwiches, sausages, salads and ploughman's at lunch-time; an extended bar menu is available from 6pm; the restaurant menu with specials is available from 7pm. Children welcome. Dogs welcome in top bar.

Hay Waggon, The High Street, Hartfield TN7 4AB. ☎ (01892) 770252. Open Mon to Fri 11 to 3, 6 to 11, Sat 11 to 11, Sun 11 to 10.30; food Mon to Fri 12 to 2.30, 7 to 9.30 (10 Fri), Sat 12 to 3, 7 to 10, Sun 12 to 4, 7 to 9.30. Harveys beers. Blackboard specials, a la carte menu, steaks, traditional bar food, sandwiches (exc. Sat and Sun). No children in bar. No dogs in restaurant.

Dorset Arms, Withyham TN7 4BD. ☎ (01892) 770278. Open Sun to Fri 11.30 to 3, 5.30 to 11, Sat 11 to 3, 6 to 11, Sun 12 to 3, 7 to 10.30; food 12 to 2, Tues to Sat 7.30 to 9.30, light snacks Sun eves in summer. Harveys beers. This black and white tile-hung pub was originally an open hall farmhouse. Sandwiches and ploughman's are on the menu as well as soup, crispy mushrooms, and sausages, ham or fish served with chips. On the separate specials board might be ratatouille bake, mushroom Stroganov, toad-in-the-hole or fish pie. Children welcome in restaurant only. Dogs welcome in bar only.

Start: Hartfield, on B2026 and B2110 south of Edenbridge and east of Forest Row; park in the village centre near the Hay Waggon public house. Grid reference 478357.
Length: 8 miles (13 kilometres), 4 hours.
Difficulty: Moderate to energetic, with one long, gradual climb, but thereafter easy going along heathy tracks and pasture. Sandy soils underfoot; even in winter the terrain is well-drained.
OS maps: 1:25,000 Explorer sheet 135; 1:50,000 Landranger sheet 188.
Tea-room and shop in Hartfield; ice-cream van often in Gills Lap car park ❾ at weekends.
PT 2-hourly bus services from Tunbridge Wells to East Grinstead via Hartfield and Withyham.

❶ From Hartfield village centre, with the Hay Waggon pub and war memorial on your right, walk downhill along the B2026 in the Edenbridge direction, keeping left along the B2026 at the road junction. Just before the road rises and crosses a bridge, take a path (signposted 'pedestrian route') on the right into Forest Way Country Park (just left of the driveway to the former station). Avoid the path to the left going under the bridge but continue, 20 yards later taking the next path on the right, leading on to a dismantled railway by the platform of the former Hartfield station. The **Forest Way Country Park** occupies part of the former railway line from Three Bridges to Tunbridge Wells.

Follow the railway line for ¾ mile, ignoring a path crossing after ½ mile (where there is a stile and footbridge to the left) but ¼ mile after this, ❷ take the path over a stile on the right, waymarked with a WW sign denoting the **Wealdway** (an 80-mile long-distance walkers' route through a varied cross-section of the Weald, from Gravesend to Eastbourne), which you follow all the way to the top of Ashdown Forest.

The path crosses a field at 90 degrees in the direction of the railway track, to take a stile to the right of a gate at the far end of the field (and to the left of a brick barn); in the next field maintain the direction to reach a stile by a gate giving on to the road. Turn left along the road, then ❸ take the first turning on the right signposted to Withyham church.

After 100 yards ignore driveways to the left leading to the church and to houses (but for the detour to the Dorset Arms turn sharp left here, past Rectory Cottage to return to the road, follow the pavement to the pub and return the same way). **Withyham church**, rebuilt in 1663, is usually locked, but you may gain entry on a Sunday; it has a remarkable set of monuments to the Sackvilles, the earls of Dorset after whom Withyham's pub is named.

Keep along this quiet lane; later, ignore farm roads to the right but continue ahead ('private' notices refer to vehicles; there is no public vehicular access to this lane, but it is open to walkers).

❹ After 1 mile, at some houses at Fisher's Gate, keep forward at the fork (over a cattle-grid), then go past a partly weatherboarded house on the right. The path leaves the driveway to the left, as signposted, where the driveway ahead is gated and leads into a farm. The path is enclosed by fences and leads into woodland, reaching a junction with a track ❺; to the right is marked as private, while to the left the track forks into two. Turn left to take the right-hand of these forks, and keep right at the end of the triangle enclosed by the tracks. 50 yards later fork right just after a brick house (Forest Place) on the right, then 100 yards later keep on the surfaced track, taking the rightmost of three tracks; this bends right and descends. At the bottom, pass the hedged garden of Kovacs Lodge on your right, and keep right at a track junction, alongside a fence on your right.

❻ 30 yards after a field appears on the right, fork left on a path rising gently through **Five Hundred Acre Wood**. The wood was enclosed in 1693 and includes stands of oak and beech. This was the Forest (or Hundred Acre Wood) of the Winnie-the-Pooh stories. In the adjacent heathland, the sandy tracks leading to clumps of Scots pines are strongly reminiscent of the stories' illustrations by EH Shepard.

Keep to the main path, rising all the time (soon, ignore a minor descending sharp left-hand turn and keep right at a fork soon after). Go forward at a track crossing, taking the path through a break in a fence; the path continues to rise.

❼ Take special care to fork right as soon as open land momentarily appears on your right, into open heath. For the next 1½ miles follow Wealdway marker posts (notches cut into the top of posts indicate the direction), and ignore side paths (you are generally following the main track and maintaining the same direction). After ½ mile ignore a sharp left-hand turn and fork right soon after, on the main path. ½ mile on, at the next junction (by a group of trees down to the right; a road may be audible to the left), keep forward, joining a broad track coming from the left; fork right 80 yards later, and fork left 100 yards after that.

❽ ½ mile later reach a T-junction with a broad track (to the left this leads towards a road sign and mast) 50 yards before the road: turn right (the route now leaves the Wealdway) on this track, parallel to the road away to the left. As the track descends, Gills Lap car park is in view ahead, half left; the track bends left; keep right at the next fork (just below the road signpost) to cross the road and enter the car park ❾. Turn immediately right on a path, passing to the right of a stone plinth/information board, and then passing benches and following the top of the ridge with the road parallel to right (but not visible). The path drops gently (ignore any side turns) and later passes a small abandoned quarry with a pool on your right and (just off to the left – not immediately visible) a **memorial to A.A. Milne**, the author of the Pooh stories and father of Christopher Robin, on the left just after. This grand viewpoint is the 'enchanted place', or Galleon's Lap of the stories (Gills Lap in real life).

❿ ½ mile later, fork left in front of a wooden barrier, and keep right on the main path just after. Cross a small road, take the path opposite, forking right after 30 yards, then left 20 yards later at a marker post for Pooh Bridge. Keep to the main path, which drops; later a field appears on the right, and ⓫ the path reaches a road by Andbell House on the right. Turn right on the road, then after 50 yards take a bridleway on the right which drops through woodland to **Pooh Sticks Bridge**. In *The House at Pooh Corner*, Pooh, Piglet and Christopher Robin played Pooh Sticks by dropping twigs into the brook and seeing which came out first on the other side of the bridge. The Milnes lived nearby at Cotchford Farm (not open).

Beyond the bridge, the path rises to reach the end of a small road (coming from Ryecroft Farm, to the left) ⓬: keep right along it, ignoring the first turning on the right; 100 yards later, take a path over a stile by the gate on the right.

Head across the field to a stile (turn round for a fine view, with the Milnes' Cotchford Farm visible in the middle distance half left); cross the next field keeping to the left of a prominent house, to find a stile in the top right-hand corner ⓭.

Keep right, to take a path between driveways to Jessups and South Cottage. Enter a field, follow its left edge (past Landhurst, a white house); as soon as you enter the next field, turn left to cross a stile and walk down a narrow field to a stile in the middle at the bottom, leading on to a track down to the bottom of the next field. Turn right on the road, and keep left by a huge oak tree at the next junction, into Hartfield. You may like to finish by browsing the memorabilia on every conceivable Pooh theme (including the rulebook for players of poohsticks) at the shop known as **Pooh Corner.**

Ashdown Forest

Nearly half of the Ashdown Forest's 6,420 acres is heathland – the largest heath in south-east England. The forest was created as a Royal Hunting Ground and formally disafforested in 1662; parts were subsequently enclosed and re-forested. The forest is part woodland and part heath, with a substantial covering of heather. No buildings or pylons detract from the views; the land is maintained by the Conservators of Ashdown Forest.

Ling heather predominates in the open areas, and gorse presents a bright blaze of yellow through much of the year. Adders and silver-studded blue butterflies are found on the heath, while dragonflies and damselfies frequent the bog pools and valley floors. Profusions of fungi – including the unmistakable red and white fly agaric toadstool – appear in autumn in the woodlands, which shelter many fallow and roe deer as well as a herd of sika deer.

Arundel Park and the Arun Valley

WEST SUSSEX WALK 26

The hilly parkland of Arundel Castle's estate spreads right up to the edge of Arundel, and this route steps out of the bustle of the attractive old town into the 1,000 acres of former deer park. The reedy, canalised Arun provides the theme for the opening and closing sections of the walk (including a fine stretch between the idyllically peaceful villages of South Stoke and Burpham), and there are spectacular views across to the castle itself.

Within close reach is the Wildfowl and Wetlands Trust reserve, in Mill Road, just outside Arundel. Founded by the great naturalist Sir Peter Scott on the banks of the Arun, the path-laced reserve features ponds and other wildfowl habitats, with a worldwide collection of ducks, geese and swans.

George and Dragon, Burpham BN18 9RR. ☎ (01903) 883131. Open Mon to Sat 11 to 2.30, 6 to 11, Sun 12 to 3, Easter to Sept Sun 7 to 10.30; bar food Mon to Sat 12 to 2, 7 to 9, Sun 12 to 2, restaurant all week 7.15 to 9.30. 3 real ales. A la carte menu including, for example, panache of sea scallops or terrine of wood pigeon to start and breast of pheasant or roast rump of lamb as main courses. Daily specials and set Sunday lunch are also available. Children welcome if eating. No dogs.

Red Lion, 45 High Street, Arundel BN18 9AG. ☎ (01903) 882597. Open Mon to Sat 10.30am to 11pm, Sun 12 to 10.30; food Mon to Fri 12 to 2.15, 6 to 9, Sat 12 to 2.15, Sun 12 to 2. Fuller's London Pride, Young's Special. Salads, sandwiches, traditional pub food with chips; specials board including soup, fried liver, cold beef with garnish and mash potato. Children welcome in dining area. Dogs welcome on a lead.

Start: Burpham, signposted off A27 just west of Arundel. Free public car park next to the George and Dragon.

Alternative start: Arundel town centre; car park (expensive for a full day) in Mill Road (turn right after crossing the bridge); begin at river bridge and join walk at ❻.

Length: 8 miles (13 kilometres), 4 hours.

Difficulty: Energetic.

OS maps: 1:25,000 Explorer sheet 121; 1:50,000 Landranger sheet 197.

Shops and tea rooms in Arundel.

WC Arundel.

PT Train to Arundel. Leave the station, go left along the main road, then fork right at the roundabout; just after a modern brick guesthouse called Port Reeves and just before the first house on the left, turn right on a signposted footpath, then left along the river to cross the bridge into the town centre; join walk at ❻.

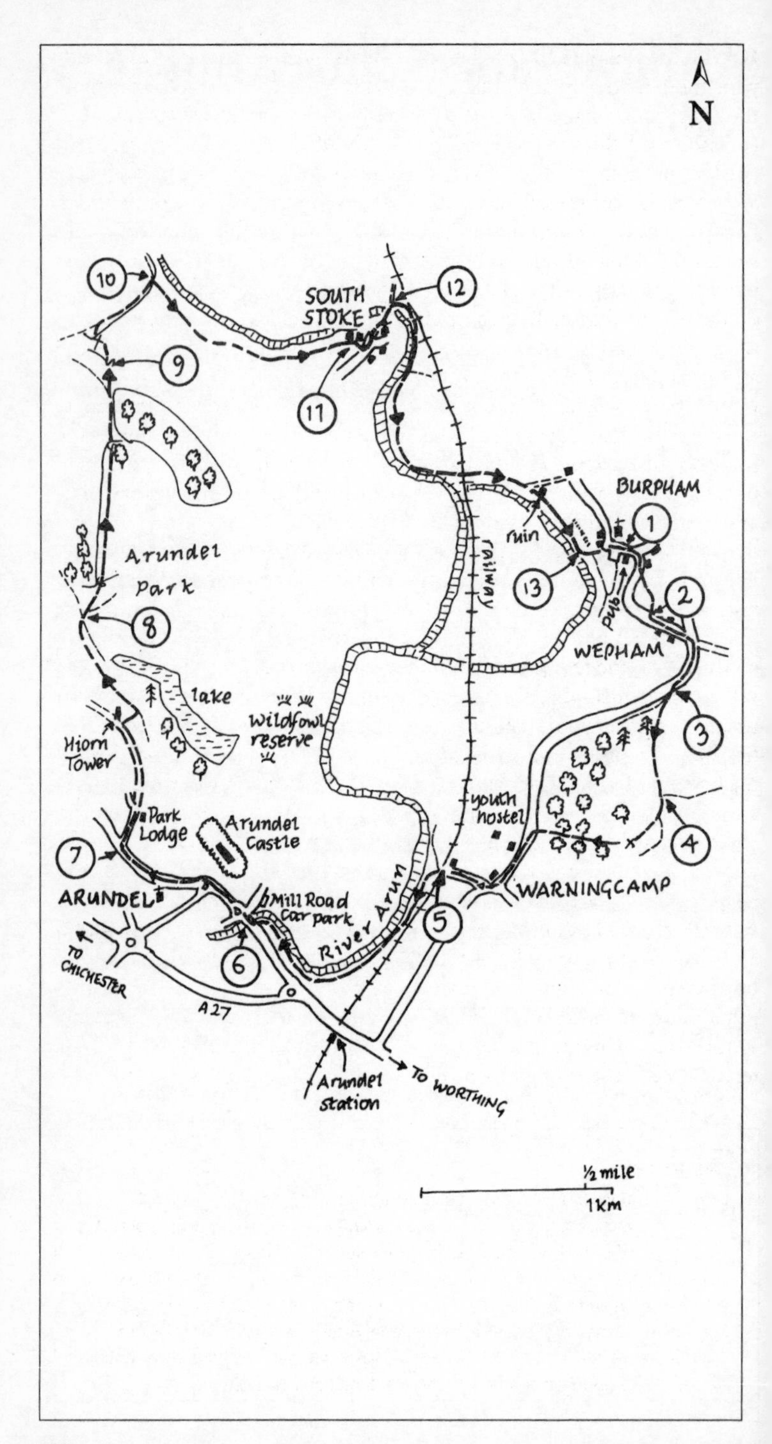
N
SOUTH STOKE
BURPHAM
ruin
railway
pub
WEPHAM
Arundel Park
lake
Wildfowl reserve
Hiorn Tower
Park Lodge
Arundel Castle
youth hostel
WARNINGCAMP
ARUNDEL
Mill Road Car park
River Arun
TO CHICHESTER
A27
Arundel station
TO WORTHING
½ mile
1Km

❶ With the George and Dragon on your right, follow the road through the flint-built village of Burpham (pronounced Burfam); turn right (just after houses called Rycroft and Pensway on the right) at the first junction on an unmarked small road. After 50 yards, where it bends right, take a signposted stile on the left. Go diagonally right over a marshy meadow, over a bridge and up a flight of steps; turn right in the next two fields along the right edges, then down steps to a road ❷. Turn left, then right at a T-junction. Pass a thatched cottage and thatched barn on your right, then ❸ 50 yards after the Wepham village sign (facing the other way) take a bridleway on the left way-marked with a blue arrow (do not confuse with the footpath with the yellow arrow just after). This goes up through the woods, across the field, and beyond a gate to drop to the bottom of a grassy dry valley by a signpost ❹.

Go forward slightly uphill for 30 yards to the next signpost then fork right along a path just above the valley floor, later leading into a wood and then reaching a road. Turn left on the road, and right at the next junction, signposted Youth Hostel. Ignore side turnings, pass a shuttered white house, and go over railway with care. **Arundel Castle** suddenly appears in the most dramatic fashion beyond the reed beds.

❺ After the railway fork left, soon joining the river bank, which you follow all the way to Arundel, with boat jetties providing the theme for the last few yards. Just past an open-air swimming pool, the path finally leaves the river and goes through a yard to reach the street.

❻ Turn right over the bridge. Just on the right are remains of the south range of **Blackfriars**, a 13th-century Dominican priory dissolved in 1538.

Go straight up Arundel's fine, and distinctly steep, High Street. Ignore turns to the left, and pass the massive castle wall on the right, then the French Gothic-style Roman Catholic cathedral (1873) on the left. ❼ Where the stone wall on the right reaches a corner turn right on a road into Arundel Park, past a castellated estate building with Gothic windows on the right and past Park Lodge and a gate, where you keep forward on a metalled drive. **Arundel Park** includes one of the most delightful cricket grounds (not visible from this route) used in the first-class game; it traditionally hosts the first match of the touring team, who

Arundel

From a distance this hilltop town has something of the appearance of a fortified French settlement with its spikily ornate Gothic Catholic cathedral and massive castle. The Normans established the stronghold here, but the castle is predominantly a Victorian country house, and is the residence of the Duke of Norfolk's son and his wife, the Earl and Countess of Arundel. It is open to the public and hosts many events in the Arundel Festival in August. A small local museum is beside the tourist office in the High Street; also explore the historic buildings around Tarrant Street, Maltravers Street and Arun Street.

play against the Duchess of Norfolk's XI (a side made up of first-class players).

A swathe of green parkland appears on the left. Just before a prominent folly known as Hiorn's Tower, turn right at a marker post with a yellow arrow, and cross the grass and woodchip track used for training horses to another marker post, then go down to a track where you turn left over a stile, and go down again to a track junction at the bottom of the valley ❽.

Go ahead 20 yards then fork left on a small path rising steeply to a woodland fence, which you follow up (above the track you have just left) to the next stile. From here the path is not visible, but the route is easy to find if you head along the middle of the ridge towards the left end of a distant woodland belt on the horizon. Cross a stile in a clump of trees and turn left at a signpost at the edge of the woodland belt. Where the woodland reaches a corner by a cattle trough and signpost, go forward (leaving the track which swings slightly left) roughly towards a distant chalk pit to find a stile ❾, beyond which you follow a track downhill into a wood.

Go right (signposted) at a triangular junction in the wood, still downhill, and just after emerging into the open, turn left as signposted, down alongside a fence on your right (which is later replaced by a wall).

❿ Turn right through a kissing-gate in the wall then right slightly uphill. This goes through delightful mixed woodland, with yews and plenty of woodland birds, then along the bottom edges of fields to reach buildings at the sleepy, back-of-beyond hamlet of South Stoke ⓫.

Turn right past a church-like red brick building, then turn left along the road and left again at a road fork. Where the road metalling ends you can detour right to **St Leonard's Church**. This simple building, with its ancient timber roof and slender 13th-century lancet windows, dates from the 11th century; it has no electricity.

Carry straight on along the track, over the river bridge then ⓬ go right over a stile to follow the riverside path. After crossing the railway you pass a brick and stone ruin on the left; after this there is a flat meadow and high bank away to the left. ⓭ Just after the high bank ends, the path leaves the river and rises up through trees and bushes. Turn left at the next junction to reach the end of the road by a farrier's in Burpham. The George and Dragon is a short distance ahead.

St Mary's Church, Burpham dates from Norman times, and has Roman tiles in its flint fabric; a Roman pavement was found near the north transept, and the 13th-century chancel has a vaulted stone roof. The flat field behind the pub is fringed by the steep banks of a Saxon promontory fort built to guard the Adur.

Kingley Vale and the Devil's Humps

WEST SUSSEX

WALK 27

This is a magnificent, slightly arduous walk: if you start from Stoughton (as we recommend you do), the initial climb is rewarded with a surprise as you come across a row of large bell barrows with superb views over the ancient yews of Kingley Vale below. This forest is another, very special, highlight but you must make a second climb out of it before the final, easy descent.

Hare and Hounds, Stoughton PO18 9JQ. ☎ (01705) 631433. Open Mon to Fri 11 to 3, 6 to 11, Sat 11 to 11, Sun 12 to 3, 6 to 10.30; food Mon to Sat 11 to 2, 6 to 10, Sun 12 to 2. Regularly changing guest beers. This brick and flint pub has a garden with views of the South Downs; the interior is compact, comfortable and well-cared for, with beams and brick walls. On the menu might be venison sausages or pheasant casserole, smoked mackerel paté, or grilled Mediterranean prawns with salad. Shepherd's pie and half a roast chicken are also on offer. Children welcome. Dogs welcome.

Start: Hare and Hounds, Stoughton, on minor road off B2146 north-west of Chichester. Roadside parking in village. Grid reference 813115.
Alternative start: (If you prefer to visit the pub halfway round the walk; note the finest parts of the walk are in the early stages – we much prefer to start at Stoughton). West Stoke car park (turn off B2178 at East Ashling, north-west of Chichester, signposted West Stoke). Take the first turning (Downs Road) left at a signpost and grassy triangle; the car park is almost immediately on the right. Grid reference 825088. To start the walk, turn right out of the car park, then go straight on where the road bends left, following a path signposted to Kingley Vale. Fork right where this enters woodland and keep forward over the stile beside the gate and by the bridleway signpost (pointing left and right) and past a wood sculpture and museum on the right; join the directions at ❺.
Length: Full walk 6 miles (9.5 kilometres), 3½ hours; short walk omitting nature trail 4 miles (6.5 kilometres), 2 hours.
Difficulty: Moderate.
OS maps: 1:25,000 Explorer sheet 120; 1:50,000 Landranger sheet 197.

❶ With the Hare and Hounds on your right, follow the road, avoiding a right fork to the church – although the church is worth a detour. It was built in the 11th century, some time before the Norman conquest, and has survived as an almost purely Saxon church, distinguished by its remarkably tall, thin walls, its small, high windows and its large corner stones. The graveyard has many fine and varied

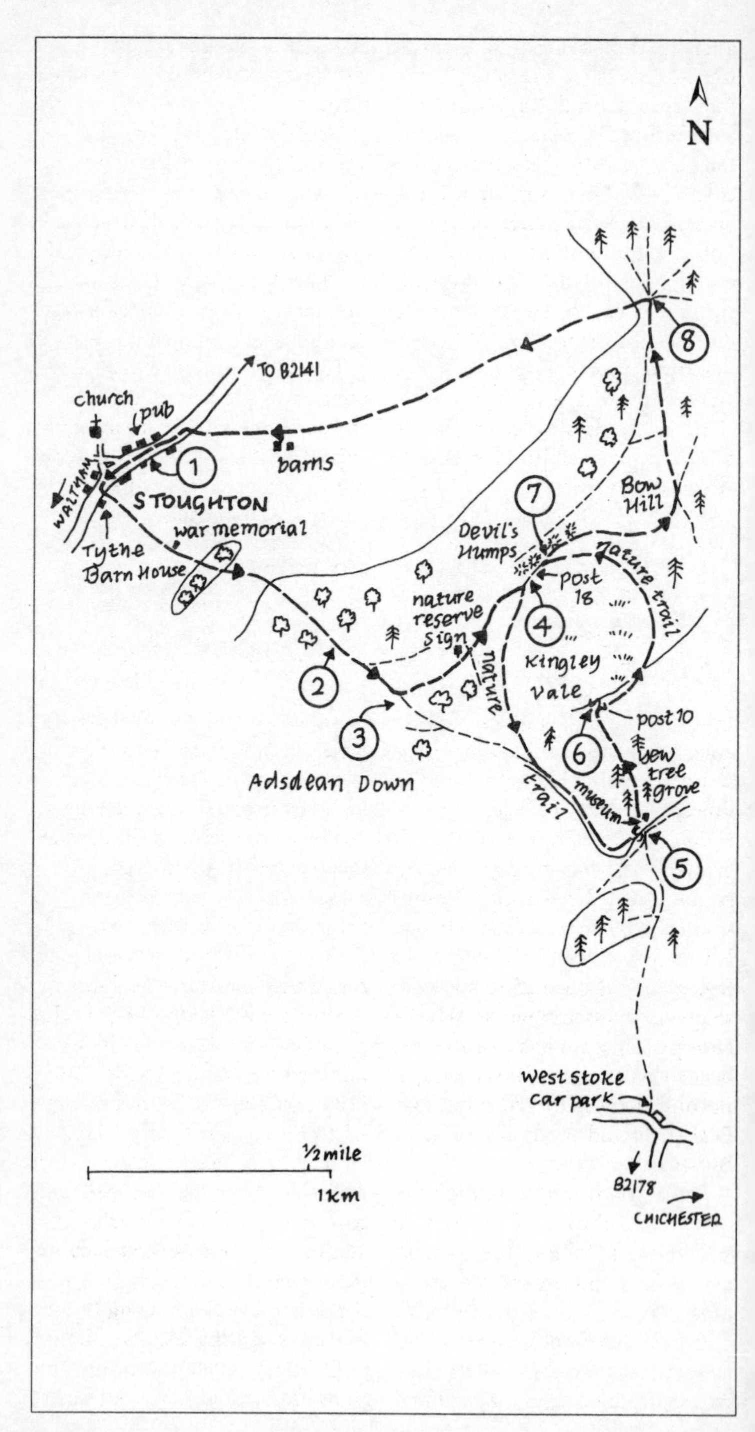
N
TO B2141
church
pub
barns
1
WALTHAM
STOUGHTON
Tythe
Barn House
war memorial
8
7
Bow
Hill
Devil's
Humps
nature trail
post
18
4
nature
reserve
sign
Kingley
Vale
2
nature
post 10
3
6
yew
tree
grove
Adsdean Down
trail
museum
5
West Stoke
car park
½ mile
1km
B2178
CHICHESTER

ancient tombstones. 100 yards later, turn left on a concrete track (signposted bridleway) immediately before Tythe Barn House (on the right is a driveway flanked by chains). This becomes a stony track and rises, passing a **memorial** to a Polish pilot shot down in aerial combat in 1940. After passing through a belt of trees, the track enters beech woods. ❷ Where a field appears on the right, keep forward, now with a fence on your right. 100 yards later keep right at a fork of signposted bridleways, still alongside the fence.

❸ Just as the track begins to drop very slightly, turn left at the next fork of bridleways (a distant view of Chichester Harbour appears ahead), later passing a Kingley Vale nature reserve sign at a junction (where you keep forward). ❹ Eventually, and suddenly, you emerge from the trees to a stunning sight ahead. In front of you is an open downland plateau. To the right, over the tops of the yews growing in the forested valley below, are far-reaching views towards Chichester Cathedral and Harbour, and the Isle of Wight. To the left are two huge, distinctly bell-shaped tumuli, known as **Devil's Humps**. They are believed to have been burial mounds for early kings. Beyond them is the view towards Petersfield and the radio masts of Butser Hill.

For the short walk (omitting the nature trail through Kingley Vale yew forest) go forward on the main grassy track and resume directions at ❼.

For the full walk turn immediately very sharp right as soon as you emerge from the woods by the first bell barrow. Follow the numbered nature trail marker posts down through the yew forest to the bottom, where you ignore a stile and locked gate to the right by a signpost (unless you started from West Stoke car park, in which case cross it and retrace your steps to the car park) but turn left past the wooden sculpture and past a small 'field museum' on the right ❺.

The field museum has a few information boards on the reserve, and a sandpit where you can stamp animal 'footprints'. Now follow the numbered marker posts of the nature trail through the most magical part of Kingley Vale (after post 4).The trail loops in and out of woodland, passing some spectacularly shaped trunks of immense antiquity. ❻ At a stile by marker post 10 at the foot of the large grassy downland follow the trail to the right (it is possible to cross the stile, but it is a steep and not particularly rewarding slog up the downland and through woodland, where you turn left at the top; a not very recommendable short cut). The trail passes around the edge of a field, with the woods on your right, then turns left, starts to climb and crosses a stile. Follow the marker posts in and out of woodland. At marker post 16, the **Tansley Stone** is up to the right. This is a memorial to Sir Arthur George Tansley, who set up Kingley Vale as a nature reserve. Reach the two bell barrows, and just before marker post 18 (before the first bell barrow) turn sharp right on the most defined grassy track along the top of the down (very slightly rising).

❼ You pass a less prominent third bell barrow on the left, then a modern stone pillar just behind it, then a fourth bell barrow (less prominent still) – also on the left. ¼ mile later turn left at a cross-junction of bridleways, and ignore a bridleway to the left 300 yards later. Keep right on joining a track where the view opens ahead. ❽ At a six-way junction, take the left-most track, proceeding with a fence on the left and woodland on the right. Where the woods end, you will find a strategically sited bench with a fine view northwards. The track drops gradually for an easy final mile to Stoughton. Turn left on the road to the village centre.

Kingley Vale Nature Reserve

Yews usually grow singly or in mixed woodland, so Kingley Vale, with its groves made up purely of yew trees, is unique in Europe. Some of the trees – great gnarled giants with shallow, twisting roots – may be the oldest living things in Britain. Some are thought to have been planted to celebrate a victorious battle against the Vikings. The canopy is dense, with little light penetrating it, so not much grows on the floor of the yew groves, but you may see grey squirrels and you should listen for nuthatches, goldcrests and, in autumn, thrushes that feed on the berries (yew bark, berries and foliage are poisonous to many mammals, but not to birds).

Kingley Vale is on chalk, so in the more open areas of the nature reserve, expect flora and fauna associated with chalk downland. Plants include round-headed rampion, milkwort and several orchids, notably frog, fly and bee. Among the 33 species of butterflies that thrive here are chalkhill blue, Adonis blue, various skippers, silver-washed fritillary and purple emperor.

Devil's Dyke

WEST SUSSEX WALK 28

Easy field walking connects two characterful old small villages – Poynings and Fulking, ensconced at the foot of the South Downs and each with a good pub. The second part of the walk is completely different, with a steep haul up on to the Downs, followed by an exploration of an imposing prehistoric earthwork and one of the most tucked away and beautiful of all the area's numerous dry valleys.

For even more of a contrast, it is only a short drive into central Brighton, where you can take in a stroll along one of England's best Regency seafronts and visit the Royal Pavilion or the excellent (and free) Brighton Museum, with its art deco and art nouveau furniture, costumes and displays about Brighton in the past.

Royal Oak, The Street, Poynings BN45 7AQ. ☎ (01273) 857389. Open Mon to Sat 11 to 11, Sun 12 to 10.30; food Mon to Fri 12 to 2.30, 6 to 9.30, Sat and Sun 12 to 10 (9.30 Sun). Harveys, Morland Old Speckled Hen, Courage Directors, Bass beers. Bar menu and specials board, steaks, sandwiches, bar snacks. Children welcome in restaurant. Dogs welcome in bar area.

Devil's Dyke, Devil's Dyke Road, Poynings BN1 8JJ. ☎ (01273) 857256. Open Mon to Sat 11 to 11, Sun 12 to 10.30; food Mon to Sat 11.30 to 10, Sun 12 to 10. Flowers beers. Traditional pub menu, including potato skins or soup to start with, and steak, lasagne, scampi or chicken Tikka Masala as a main course. Roasts on Sundays, and sandwiches and salads are also available. Full restaurant menu. Children welcome in play area and if eating. Guide dogs only.

Shepherd and Dog, The Street, Fulking BN5 9LU. ☎ (01273) 857382. Open Mon to Sat 11 to 11, Sun 12 to 10.30; food 12 to 9. Badger beers. The pub has a garden right beneath the escarpment of the South Downs. Traditional pub food, pies, ploughman's and sandwiches. Also specials board. No children in the bar. No dogs in eating area.

Start: Poynings (roadside parking near the Royal Oak), south of A281, and between Brighton and Henfield. Grid reference 263120.
Alternative start: Car park on Devil's Dyke; join the route at ❼. Grid reference 259111.
Length: 5 miles (8 kilometres), 2½ hours.
Difficulty: Moderate, with one long climb up on to the Downs.
OS maps: 1:25,000 Explorer sheet 17; 1:50,000 Landranger sheet 198.
WC Devil's Dyke (next to pub).

❶ With the Royal Oak on your right, follow the main street, past a phone box, then just after the entrance to Dyke Farm and just before a driveway to Green Acres (both on the right), turn right

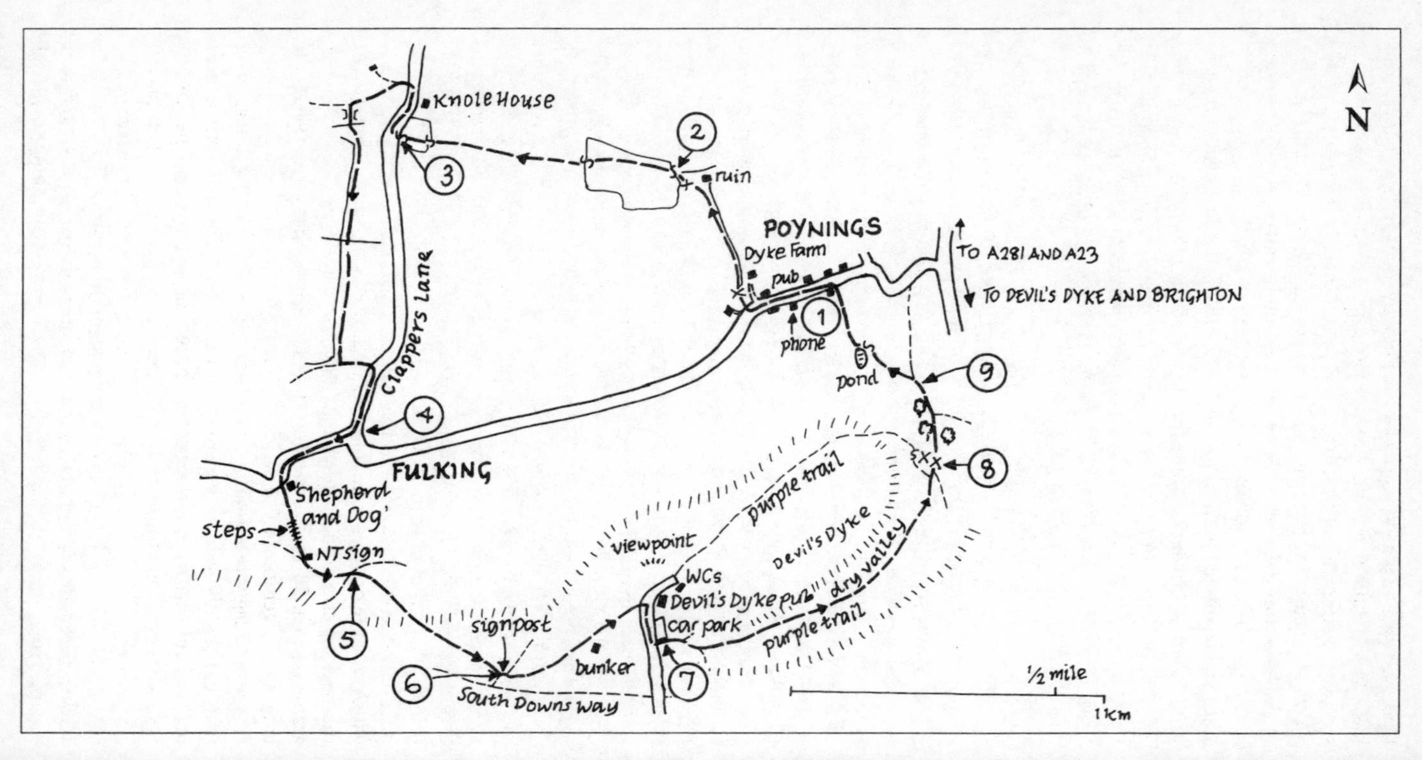
N
Knole House
2
ruin
3
POYNINGS
Dyke Farm
pub
TO A281 AND A23
TO DEVIL'S DYKE AND BRIGHTON
1
phone
pond
9
Clappers Lane
4
FULKING
8
'Shepherd and Dog'
steps
NT sign
purple trail
Devil's Dyke
viewpoint
WCs
Devil's Dyke pub
dry valley
car park
purple trail
5
signpost
bunker
6
South Downs Way
7
1/2 mile
1 km

through a gate on a cobbled track – it is not particularly obvious, but is signposted from the other side of the road. Keep going past the yard of the house until you enter a field by a gate, where the cobbling ends. The grassy track leads downhill (there is a pleasant view of the Weald immediately, with the South Downs to your left). Ignore the track to the left at the bottom, and carry on past a white gabled house (a short distance away to the right) and a ruined brick and flint building and go through a gate and over a ditch. Just after, ❷ turn left over a waymarked stile and follow the yellow arrows along a grassy track. Beyond a redundant footbridge it narrows to a path as you are directed half left across a rising field to a stile, then over a large field (two fields now one), then forward to a stile on to a lane (Clappers Lane) ❸.

To reach Fulking by quiet road-walking you can turn left along this quiet lane for ½ mile to Fulking to avoid any seasonal mud.

To reach Fulking by field paths turn right along the lane, then just after the lane bends left (opposite Knole House) and crosses a small bridge, turn left at a footpath signpost. Take the stile to the left of the gated concrete driveway and follow the path, over a small footbridge across a ditch. 30 yards later, turn left over a larger footbridge across a stream at a signposted path junction. Go slightly left as signposted to the hedge corner, and in the next field carry on along the right-hand hedgerow.

To the left in the distance **Wolstonbury Hill** is slightly separate from the rest of the downland ridge, topped by the grassy ramparts of a 3,000-year-old Bronze Age hill fort. One of the earliest Sussex hill forts, Wolstonbury is unlikely to have been a defended settlement as its ditch, unlike the more common Iron Age hill forts, is on the inside of its bank. It may have been used for keeping cattle in times of danger, or for carrying out ritual ceremonies. To the right you can see the broken woodland crown of **Chanctonbury Ring**. The famous trees were planted by the landowner in the 18th century and badly damaged in the Great Storm of 1987. A Romano-British temple, apparently dedicated to the wild boar, stood on top of the hill 2,000 years ago: small bronze boar figures and a pit full of pig and boar teeth have been found there.

Cross a farm track and take the stile opposite, follow the right edge of the next field and turn left at a path T-junction after the end of the field. Go through a gate, and turn right on the lane into Fulking.

Both routes ❹ Turn right along Fulking village street. It has a most appealing combination of thatched roofs – ancient and modern – and building materials that include timber, large pebbles and tiles. You pass a Gothic Victorian roadside well, then the road drops to the **Shepherd and Dog**. This pub name dates from the days when the stream here was dammed each year for the washing of the flocks prior to shearing. The adjacent Gothic pump house, with its psalm lettered in Victorian tiles, was part of a scheme to pump the water supply around the village.

Just after the Shepherd and Dog turn left through the pub car park and take the signposted path just to the left of the pub garden. This leads up to a flight of steps; follow steeply up the Fulking Escarpment, ❺ keeping forward halfway up at a junction of deeply sunken tracks – the slope gets less steep now, and the views are glorious. ❻ At the top go forward at a signpost and go past the wartime bunker on your right to the **viewpoint** by the Devil's Dyke pub. Popular with kite-fliers and hang-gliders, this is one of the best-known viewpoints on the South Downs (so it is not exactly off the beaten track). The panorama, described fully on the information board, includes Selborne Hanger in Hampshire (see Walk 40), Butser Hill, Black Down, Ashdown Forest (see Walk 25), Leith Hill (in Surrey, and the highest point in the south-east of England at 965 feet), and Toys Hill (in Kent). Slightly down from the viewpoint, and all round the hill, run the banks of the late Iron-Age hill fort which occupied the entire ridge.

❼ Follow the road, past the Devil's Dyke pub on your left, then just after the pub car park on your left turn left on a path with green, orange and purple waymarks. At the next T-junction turn right, following the purple marker (through a gate), to reach the head of a superb dry valley. This is the **Devil's Dyke** itself, reputedly rent apart by the Devil in his foiled attempt to drown the churches in the Weald by cutting a gap in the Downs. Before turning left downhill along the floor of the valley, pause to enjoy one of the best views (for character rather than scope) in the South Downs. This was where the first cable car in Britain crossed over in the early 1900s – one of three attractions built hereabouts by the owner of the Devil's Dyke Hotel to lure day trippers about a hundred years ago: Devil's Dyke also had a funicular railway (closed 1897) and a railway line from Hove, which functioned from 1887 until the 1920s. Now the valley is completely unspoiled and is a classic example of what the Downs once looked like.

❽ At a fence at the bottom, take the right of two gates (leaving the purple trail which goes left over a stile) and follow the bridleway, soon ignoring a climbing path to the right (which has a yellow waymark; keep to the blue waymark).

❾ Fork left at the next signpost, taking a path round field edges and then left over a stile and past the end of a pond. In the next field turn right into Poynings, and left to return to the Royal Oak.

Poynings itself takes its name from the medieval family that held the manor for three centuries. Michael of Poynings (d.1369) left money for the building of the imposing Perpendicular church.

The Chidham Peninsula

WEST SUSSEX WALK 29

This is a superb coastal walk around one of the peninsulas in Chichester Harbour, a designated Area of Outstanding Natural Beauty. The inter-tidal mudflats are an extremely important wintering ground for birds, and in summer there is plenty of boating bustle to watch. Note that a small section of the walk is normally cut off for an hour or so either side of high tide.

The Old House at Home, Cot Lane, Chidham PO18 8SU. ☎ (01243) 572477. Open Mon to Fri 11.30 to 3, 6 to 11, Sat 12 to 3, 6 to 11, Sun 12 to 4.30, 7 to 10.30; food Mon to Sat 12 to 2, 6 to 9.30, Sun 12 to 3.30, 7 to 9.30. 5 real ales. At lunch-time traditional pub fare and daily specials, for example, venison casserole in red wine and apple mash. A la carte menu in evenings. Starters might be fresh Selsey crab or parfait of pork liver and brandy served with an apple and celery salad, while main course could include Cajun spiced swordfish steak with fried potato wedges and mixed leaves dressed with sour cream or half a duckling, roasted and served with a Dubonnet and orange sauce, roasted potatoes and seasonal vegetables. Children welcome in designated area. Dogs welcome.

Start: Public car park on the right-angled bend at the southern end of Chidham Lane, which runs south from the A259 between Nutbourne and Bosham. Grid reference 793035.
Length: 5 miles (8 kilometres), 2½ hours.
Difficulty: Easy/moderate. Level walking throughout. Easy, except for the 2-mile stretch down the western side of the peninsula, where you either take a narrow (sometimes slippery) path on top of the sea wall or, if the tide permits, walk on the shingle. **For about an hour either side of most high tides, the south-west tip of the peninsula is impassable**. Check tides before setting out (Chichester Tourist Information, ☎ (01243) 775888, has tide timetables). The approach to the sea wall across fields from Cot Lane can be very muddy.
OS maps 1:25,000 Explorer sheet 120; 1:50,000 Landranger sheet 197.
Shops in Nutbourne.
PT Train to Nutbourne. Turn right out of the station approach to reach the A259. Cross the road and continue for ⅗ mile (1 kilometre) down Cot Lane, to start the walk at ❷.

❶ Turn left out of the car park and follow the road round a corner, past Chidmere Pond and round a left-hand bend into Cot Lane. Follow Cot Lane as it winds through Chidham past the church and the Old House at Home, a pub surrounded by farm buildings.

❷ ¼ mile north of the pub, turn off the lane (due west), at a wooden signpost, on to a shingle footpath alongside a line of poplars. This

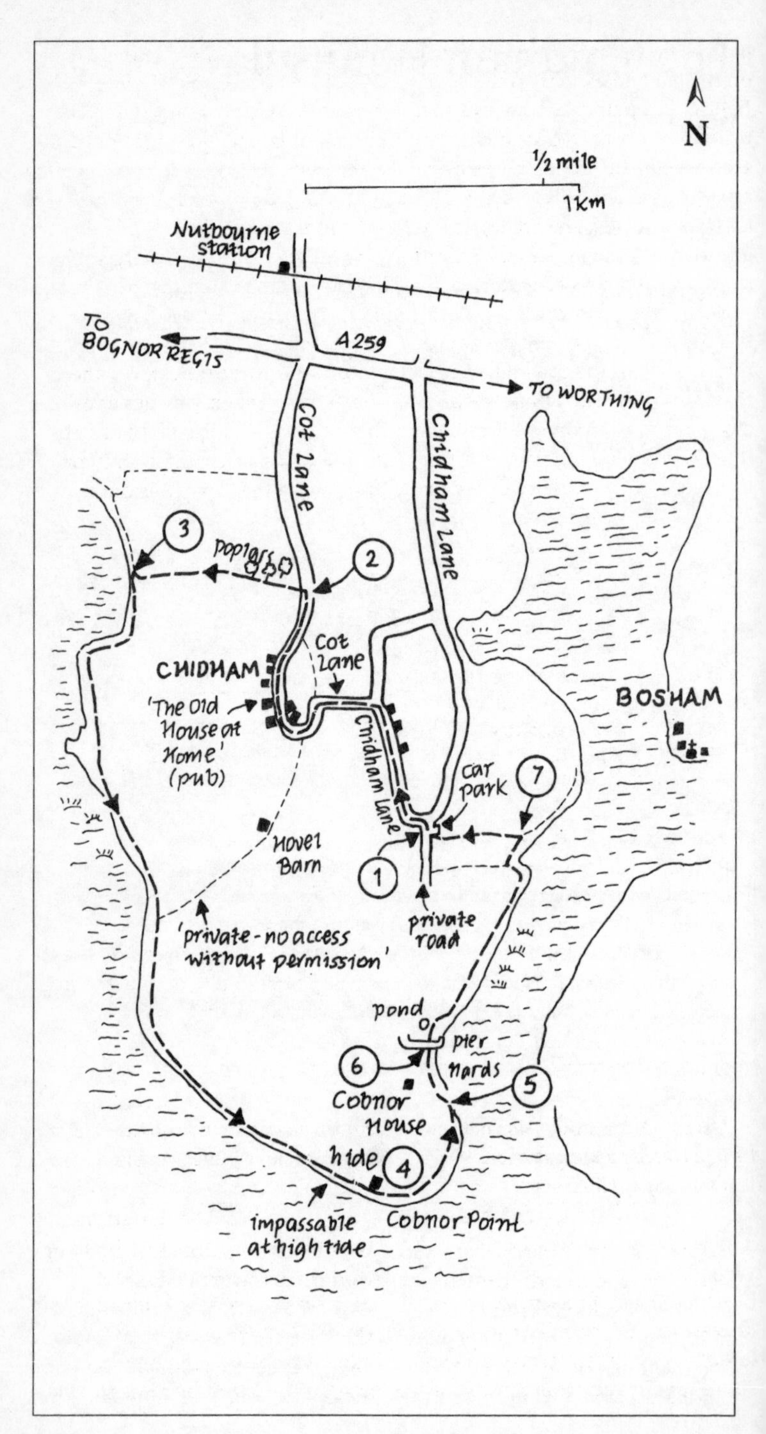
N
½ mile
1km
Nutbourne station
TO BOGNOR REGIS
A259
TO WORTHING
Cot Lane
Chidham Lane
3
2
poplars
Cot Lane
CHIDHAM
'The Old House at Home' (pub)
Chidham Lane
Car park
7
BOSHAM
1
Hovel Barn
private road
'private - no access without permission'
pond
pier
hards
6
5
Cobnor House
hide
4
impassable at high tide
Cobnor Point

narrows to a grass path with a fence on the left and a ditch on the right. Follow the path across a wooden bridge over a drainage ditch (this section can be extremely muddy after prolonged rain) and round the edge of the field to cross another drainage ditch. Climb steps to join the shore path ❸.

Turn sharp left and walk along the narrow grassy path on top of the sea wall or on the shingle beach to Cobnor Point, about 2 miles away. For most of the way drainage ditches run alongside the sea wall to its left, while to the right are the mudflats. It is dangerous to walk on the inter-tidal mudland. If you leave the sea wall, keep to the shingle near the foot of it. The mudflats are rich in bird life.

After about a mile, pass the end of a private track on the left which leads back to Chidham. There are views across the marshes to Thorney Island, with plenty of yachts moored. Nearing the bottom of the peninsula, as you draw level with some barns on the left, the path drops down on to the shore to cross an inlet before continuing on the bank the other side. As you reach a patch of trees, you have to drop down on to the shingle (this is normally covered at high tide) past or under some wonderfully gnarled oak trees growing on the shoreline.

❹ Reach Cobnor Point, at the bottom of the peninsula, where there is a notice board, beside a hide, with information about Nutbourne Nature Reserve, and a bench from which you can admire the sea views. Climb a flight of steps up the bank. Turn right and continue along the top of the sea wall. This becomes a tarmac path, created for wheelchair users. There are good yacht scenes across the water in West Itchenor and Bosham Hoe.

❺ Just before Cobnor House, the path turns inland, then bends right to go through a boat club park. The tarmac path comes to an end at the trolley park. Here keep straight ahead, following a footpath sign, across the grass, keeping close to a hedge on the right. Go through a gap in the hedge over a plank bridge. Turn right on to the tarmac road ❻ and almost immediately

Chichester Harbour

This vast natural harbour, used commercially as far back as Roman times, is now almost exclusively the preserve of recreational sailing boats. For wildlife, its significance lies in the huge areas of mud that are exposed at low tide, with the numerous plants and invertebrates providing rich pickings for birds, who commute with the tides between the muflats and the inland fields. The thousands of overwintering birds include waders such as curlew, redshank and dunlin, ducks such as shelduck, teal and red-breasted merganser, and brent geese. In summer look out for breeding black-headed gulls and terns, as well as oystercatchers, redshanks, curlews and plovers. As for plant life, in summer, sea lavender, yellow horned poppy, golden samphire and sea holly provide a colourful display.

take the footpath signed to the left, a narrow path between hedges, with a sailing school over the hedge. At the end, turn right along the edge of the field. Climb some steps and turn left on to the sea wall again. The views across to the pretty village of Bosham are good.

❼ Just under a mile north, at a signposted junction of paths at the head of a small inlet, keep right. Take the next footpath left (not signed), to reach the car park. To return to the station, continue from ❶ and retrace your steps up Cot Lane.

Hooksway and Harting Downs

WEST SUSSEX WALK 30

The Royal Oak, tucked away all by itself in a grassy valley at the bottom of a narrow, dead-end lane, is an auspicious starting point for this superb South Downs walk. A long but gradual climb out of the valley brings you on to wide, open, chalk downland, where you join the South Downs Way as it makes its way along the top of a steep escarpment. The views here are a dramatic prelude to those rewarding you after the short, sharp ascent first of Pen Hill, then of Beacon Hill. After this excitement, it is a relaxed return to base.

Royal Oak, Hooksway, Chilgrove PO18 9JZ. ☎ (01243) 535257. Open Mon to Sat 11.30 to 2.30, 6 to 11, Sun 12 to 3; food Mon to Sat 12 to 2, 7 to 10, Sun 12 to 2. Badger Tanglefoot, Gale's HSB, Hookways. The Royal Oak sits in the valley bottom in a delightful, very remote setting. It is popular with walkers and has tables outside. Steak, mixed grill, fish, pies and ploughman's. Children welcome. Dogs welcome.

Start: The Royal Oak, Hooksway, at the end of a minor, dead-end road signed off the B2141 Petersfield–Chichester road, approx 3½ miles south-east of South Harting and ¼ mile east of North Marden. Parking: immediately beyond the pub. Grid reference 816163.
Length: 4 miles (6.5 kilometres), 2 hours.
Difficulty: Moderate. Gentle climb with a couple of short, steep stretches.
OS maps: 1:25,000 Explorer sheet 120; 1:50,000 Landranger sheet 197.

❶ With the road behind you and the pub on your left, take the track through a gate in the far right-hand corner of the parking area. A short way along the valley bottom, meet a track that has been running parallel on the left. Continue ahead with the steep, wooded valley side on the left. At the end of the track, go through a gate and continue up the foot of the valley on open grassland. Keep ahead as another track joins from the left, and shortly, when the track divides, take the right fork. With views to the right of Buriton Hanger, the path passes between the flint buildings of Buriton Farm, where it may well be muddy underfoot.

Continue between fields and approximately 150 yards beyond the farm, turn left over a stile on the bridleway signed South Downs Way ❷. The 101-mile national trail makes its way across the Downs from Eastbourne to Winchester. The grassy path runs between wire fences. At the end of the fence, ignore a path down into the trees to the right and keep ahead on the South Downs Way, veering slightly left. Continue round the edge of woodland and look right for excellent views over Treyford Manor Farm to the folds of distant hills. Thickly wooded Elsted Hanger drops away steeply beside the path.

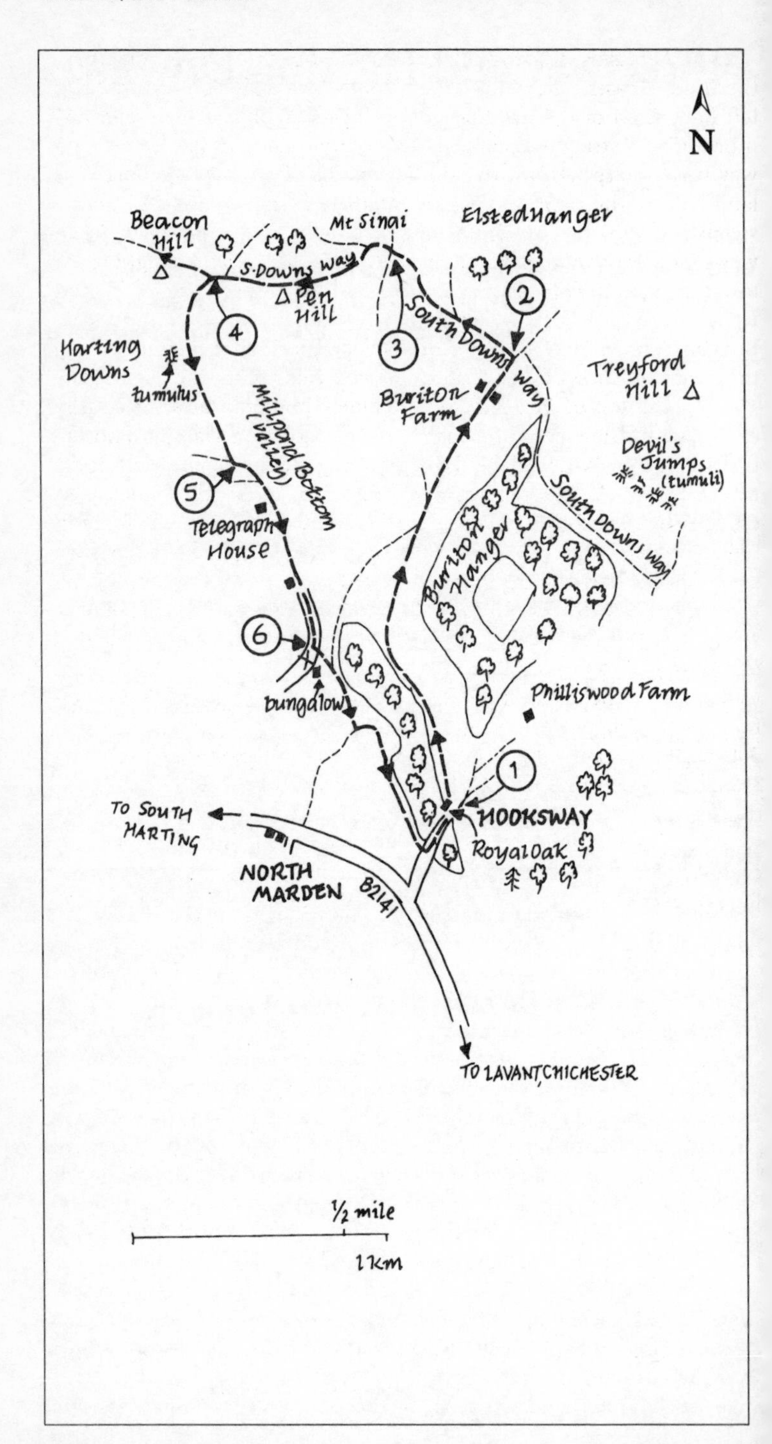
N
Beacon Hill
Mt Sinai
Elsted Hanger
S.Downs Way
Pen Hill
South Downs Way
Harting Downs
tumulus
Mill-pond Bottom (Valley)
Buriton Farm
Treyford Hill
Devil's Jumps (tumuli)
South Downs Way
Telegraph House
Buriton Hanger
Bungalow
Philliswood Farm
TO SOUTH HARTING
HOOKSWAY
Royal Oak
NORTH MARDEN
B2141
TO LAVANT, CHICHESTER
½ mile
1 Km
1
2
3
4
5
6

❸ At a crossing of paths, follow the South Downs Way, which is the left-hand path of the two that go more or less straight ahead. The way turns sharp left, with woodland still on the right, to begin a steepish climb up Pen Hill. The views back over your left shoulder towards the scarp slope are magnificent: Treyford Hill, behind Buriton Farm, is at 775 feet one of the great eminences of West Sussex.

From the top of Pen Hill, the chalky path drops down through the summer chalk-downland flora to a National Trust **Harting Downs Nature Reserve** noticeboard, where the broad track swings left ❹. It is well worth leaving this briefly, to take the path straight ahead for a short, steep climb to the top of Beacon Hill (800 feet). At the top, take the left fork for the trig point and superb 360-degree, distant views. **Uppark House**, now fully restored after the disastrous fire of 1989, is 2 miles west; Petworth House is 10 miles east; Chichester Harbour south. Return to ❹.

The South Downs Way turns south, gradually climbing the side of Beacon Hill and then following the contours as its passes the scant remains of an **Iron Age fort**. The path goes into woodland before coming to a junction ❺. The South Downs Way is signed right, back round the western side of Beacon Hill, but go left and soon pass Telegraph House behind a tall beech hedge on the right. The name commemorates the nearby site of part of a naval semaphoring system used during the Napoleonic Wars to link the docks in Portsmouth with the Admiralty in London. Continue down the drive with trees on either side. Immediately before a white bungalow to the left of a pair of wooden gates, turn left off the tarmac drive on to a narrow grassy path between fences ❻.

Continue ahead as the path joins a track from the left. Ignore a path to the right as the track bends left and narrows into a tunnel of trees. Meet the road and turn left, downhill, to return to the Royal Oak.

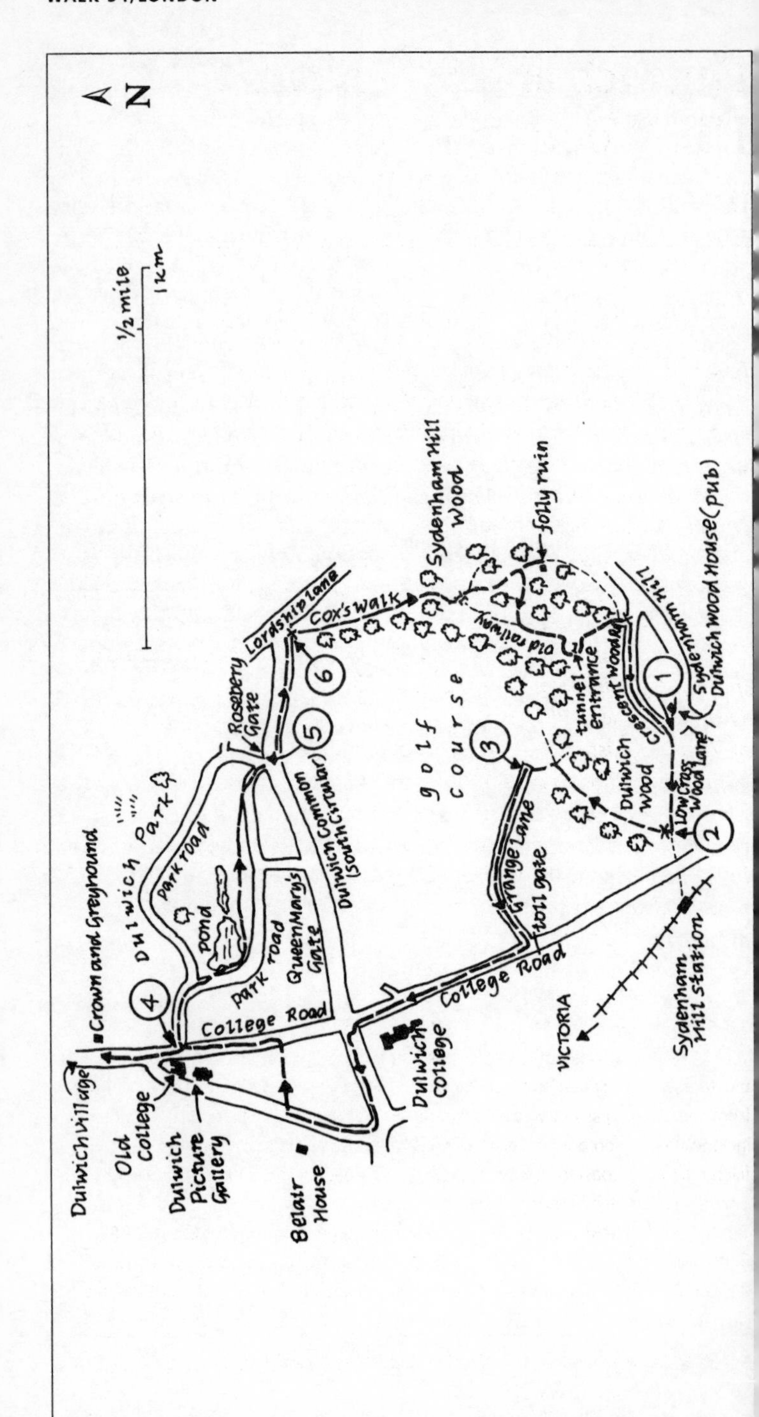
N
1/2 mile
1 km
Dulwich Village
Crown and Greyhound
Old College
Dulwich Picture Gallery
Belair House
4
College Road
Dulwich Park
Park Road
Pond
park road
Queen Mary's Gate
Dulwich Common (South Circular)
Rosebery Gate
5
Lordship Lane
6
Cox's Walk
Sydenham Hill Wood
folly ruin
old railway
tunnel entrance
Crescent Wood Rd
Sydenham Hill
1
Dulwich Wood House (pub)
golf course
3
Grange Lane
toll gate
Dulwich Wood
Low Cross Wood Lane
2
College Road
Dulwich College
VICTORIA
Sydenham Hill station

Dulwich and Sydenham Hill Wood

LONDON — WALK 31

A real surprise in the heart of the inner suburbs: leafy, patrician Dulwich Village and an unexpected survival of rural woodland side-by-side. Dulwich Wood together with neighbouring Sydenham Hill Wood form the largest remaining fragment of the great North Wood which once covered what is now South London. The nearby suburb of Norwood takes its name from this. Seemingly against the odds the developers have been kept at bay in Sydenham Hill Wood, and the long-term future for a priceless London asset at last looks safe.

Short stretches of the walk involve walking along the pavement by the South Circular; do persevere with the traffic noise, as there are much better things to come later on. Note that Dulwich Park closes at dusk.

The walk can be tacked on to a visit to Crystal Palace Park, the site of the Great Exhibition after it was moved there in 1854; apart from the terraces where the Crystal Palace stood, the most striking survival is the set of Victorian cast-iron dinosaurs, life-size and prowling the undergrowth of the park. Or you can head to nearby Forest Hill, where the Horniman Museum is another hit with children (in fact a firm favourite of the author since his own childhood), with an entertaining miscellany including musical instruments from round the world, an aquarium and a famous ethnographic collection – much of it most imaginatively displayed.

Crown and Greyhound, 73 Dulwich Village, London SE21 7BJ. ☎ 020-8693 2466. Open Mon to Sat 11 to 11, Sun 12 to 10.30; food 11 to 2, 6 to 10. Bass, Young's beers. Lunch menu may include leek and potato soup to start, with chicken in mustard sauce or spinach and potato pie to follow. In the evening you could choose from starters such as prawn cocktail or farmhouse paté and main courses, which might include steak, Dijon pork or vegetarian lasagne. Also available during the evening are filled croissants, toasted sandwiches, jacket potatoes, salads, curry or fish and chips. Children welcome in family area. No dogs.

Dulwich Wood House, 39 Sydenham Hill, London SE26 6RS. ☎ 020-8693 5766. Open Mon to Fri 11 to 11, Sat and Sun 12 to 10.30; food Mon to Sat 12 to 2.30, Sun 12 to 3. Young's beers. Baguettes, blackboard specials, roasts, set menu. No children. No dogs.

Start: Dulwich Wood House (pub), Crescent Wood Road, SE26 (at corner with Sydenham Hill).

Length: 3½ miles (5.5 kilometres), 2 hours.

Difficulty: Easy.
Map: Any London street atlas.
Shops in Dulwich; café in Dulwich Park.
WC In Dulwich Park.
PT By train to Sydenham Hill. Leave the station on the 'Down side' (Orpington-bound trains), follow the walkway to reach College Road. Cross the road and take the woodland track opposite, beyond the barrier. Turn left after 100 yards through a gate and start walk directions at ❷. Bus 63 passes the starting point.

---

❶ Take the broad path known as Low Cross Wood Lane opposite Dulwich Wood House (Crescent Wood Road side), behind a picket fence and descending between woods. ❷ 100 yards before reaching the road at the bottom, take the gate on your right into Dulwich Wood and follow the broad path ahead.

After 300 yards turn half left at a big junction of paths (by a seat and bin) and follow this path, eventually going through a gate at the end of **Grange Lane** ❸. This lane retains the appearance of a rural lane, fringed with hedgerows and with allotments and golf course on either side. There is a big view ahead of central London, with the Palace of Westminster and the British Telecom tower among the landmarks; the Dulwich College campanile is in the foreground. The huge Crystal Palace TV transmitter aerial is to your left.

Go down the lane to reach College Road by the **toll-gate**, which dates from 1789 and is the only one in use left in London; it still displays its old charges board.

Turn right along College Road. On the left of College Road, **Dulwich College**, a leading public school, is a richly ornamented complex in North Italian Renaissance style. Its design by the younger Charles Barry in 1870 made one of the earliest uses of terracotta on such a large scale. Opposite, the 18th-century Pond Cottages and old mill-pond make an attractive scene. French impressionist Camille Pissarro painted the pond and college while staying in the area in 1871.

Turn left at the crossroads (cross over by means of the traffic lights to the left) into busy **Dulwich Common**. You pass several fine houses on your right: Northcroft (early 1800s); then Old Blew House (rendered Georgian three-storey); then Elm Lawn (18th-century).

Past the junction with Alleyn Park, turn right into Gallery Road. Pass on your left **Belair House**, a small Adam-style mansion built in 1785 and now a restaurant; the park is now municipally owned.

100 yards later turn right through a kissing-gate and follow an enclosed path to College Road, where you turn left. **Pickwick Cottage**, opposite where you emerge into College Road, is a Regency house renamed after Charles Dickens made it the fictitious retirement home for Mr Pickwick in *Pickwick Papers*. Along **College Road** on the right are Bell House (No. 27, with belfry), dating from 1767 – and a boarding house for the college – and Bell Cottage, weatherboarded, built in the early 1700s with Doric door-case; Nos. 13 and 15 are ivy-clad Georgian, with fine porches.

❹ You will soon reach Dulwich Picture Gallery and the almshouse-like Old College (see box). Here the continuation of the route is to your right into Dulwich Park (through Old College Gate), but first detour ahead past the roundabout along Dulwich Village; the Crown and Greyhound is ahead on the right. At the roundabout, the old **Grammar School** (designed by Charles Barry in 1842) is on your left. This functioned until 1858 as a charitable free school for local boys after the college became fee-paying. In **Dulwich Village**, the right side is grander (Nos 97–105 are particularly fine, with 103 and 105 dating from about 1700) and the left more rustic and cottagey with some 18th-century shop-fronts.

Return to Old College Gate and cross **Dulwich Park**, making your own way to Rosebery Gate: the easiest route to find is to fork right where to the left is sealed off to traffic by bollards; keep left where the right turn goes to Queen Mary's Gate and immediately take the path on the left, past the pond on your left and a sculpture *Two Forms (Divided Circle)* by **Barbara Hepworth** on your right. At the end of the pond fork right (or in late May to early June detour ahead to see the famous display of **rhododendrons**) and go left on the road, which leads to the Rosebery Gate ❺.

Cross the main road (Dulwich Common) and turn left along it. ❻ Just before the traffic lights, take Cox's Walk on the right (through a gate) and follow the broad, rising woodland path; as soon as you cross a footbridge over the dismantled railway, fork right

Dulwich Picture Gallery and the Old College

Dulwich Picture Gallery (Open from 25 May 2000 Tuesday to Friday 10 to 5, Saturday and Sunday, and bank holidays 11 to 5, closed Monday) is England's oldest art gallery (opened in 1814), with a noted collection including works by Rembrandt, Murillo, Gainsborough and Reynolds. In 1790 King Stanislaus of Poland commissioned art dealer Noel Desenfans to build a collection for a projected Polish National Gallery. Pictures were acquired but the plan was aborted when the king was deposed five years later. After the death of Desenfans the collection was left to his wife under the care of a fellow collector, Francis Bourgeois.

The paintings were added to a collection left by actor-manager Edward Alleyn, and after Bourgeois' death Margaret Desenfans had the gallery built to the design of John Soane, complete with a mausoleum to Bourgeois and the Desenfans. Later extensions were added in 1910 in Soane pastiche; heavy bombing destroyed most of Soane's original building but the gallery and mausoleum has been rebuilt as it was.

Adjacent, the **Old College** is the original site of Dulwich College of God's Gift, set up by Edward Alleyn in 1619 as a charitable foundation of almshouses for 12 poor men and a school for 12 poor scholars. Entry was gained by drawing lots; successful boys drew a slip of paper inscribed 'God's Gift'. The tower and cloister date from 1870, and the almshouses have mostly been renewed, although part of the west wing is original. The chapel is still used by the college.

through a gate on to a path up some steps.

This **footbridge** crosses an old railway track which operated 1865–1954 from Nunhead to the terminus at Crystal Palace. From the bridge, Pissarro painted Lordship Lane Station, erroneously titled 'Penge Station, Upper Norwood' until 1972; it depicts a view to your left, of a train approaching, with trailing steam drifting to the left and houses in the middle distance, but the site is now overgrown and very different.

Follow this path through Sydenham Hill Wood. You are now on a nature trail, which is marked with white and green topped posts; always keep to the best-defined path. After 200 yards, reach a fork. Detour on the left fork for 60 yards to see the ruined 'chapel' – in fact a romantic garden feature built to look like a ruin, but which has decayed further. Return to the other fork, go past a small railed-off wetland site and turn left on a straight path; this is the old railway track, which runs along a marked ridge.

Just before the tunnel, turn right and take the path over the tunnel mouth and up to the gate on to Crescent Wood Road, along which you turn right. Just before the Dulwich Wood House, on your left, is **Six Pillars**, built by Harding and Tecton in 1935 in International style: a rendered concrete block with a partly revealed brick drum of the staircase. Opposite, set back, is a large house with a plaque to **John Logie Baird**, pioneer of television broadcasting.

Sydenham Hill Wood

This is the largest area of ancient woodland left in inner London. Its oaks and hornbeams are direct descendants of a 10,000 year old post-Ice Age tree cover. Fifty three species of bird have been recorded (including all three varieties of British woodpecker) as well as 52 species of tree and 40 of butterfly and moth. Towards the top of the wood the trees are more mixed and contain some trees that have survived from the gardens of large 19th-century houses once on the site; prominent are a large cedar of Lebanon and a monkey-puzzle tree.

Richmond and Ham

LONDON WALK 32

The route explores Richmond's wealth of Georgian (and earlier) streets and follows the edge of Richmond Park where it slopes abruptly towards the Thames, whose towpath provides the return route. You look over Petersham Meadows, which are still used for grazing farm animals.

Victoria Inn, 78 Hill Rise, Richmond TW10 6UB. ☎ 020-8940 2531. Open Mon to Sat 11.30 to 11, Sun 12 to 10; food 12 to 3. 3 real ales. Sandwiches, bar snacks, blackboard specials. No children. No dogs.

Roebuck, 130 Richmond Hill, Richmond TW10 6RE. ☎ 020-8948 2329. Open Mon to Sat 11 to 11, Sun 12 to 10.30; food 12 to 3, 6 to 10. Courage, Theakston. Sandwiches, bar snacks, pies, scampi, steak and chips, blackboard specials, traditional Sunday lunch. Children welcome if eating. Dogs welcome.

New Inn, 345 Petersham Road, Richmond TW10 7DB. ☎ 020-8940 9444. Open Mon to Sat 11 to 11, Sun 12 to 10.30; food 12 to 2.30 hot and cold buffet, 3 to 10 cooked set menu. 3 real ales. Pies, stews, chicken, salads and quiche can be ordered at the lunch-time counter. Sausage and mash, pasta, nachos, sandwiches and specials are also available. Children welcome if eating. Dogs welcome.

White Cross, Water Lane, Riverside, Richmond TW9 1TH. ☎ 020-8940 6844. Open Mon to Sat 11 to 11, Sun 12 to 10.30; food 12 to 4. Young's beers. Salads, sandwiches, blackboard specials. Children welcome in upstairs room. Dogs welcome.

White Swan, Old Palace Lane TW9 1PG. ☎ 020-8940 0959. Open Mon to Fri 11 to 3.30, 5.30 to 11, Sat and Sun 12 to 10.30; food 12 to 3 (4 Sun). 3 real ales. Blackboard menu, Sunday carvery, sandwiches, snacks available all day. Children welcome in conservatory. Dogs welcome.

Start: Richmond station (mainline and Underground District line); car parks in town centre.

Alternative start: Car park at Pembroke Lodge in Richmond Park (start with Pembroke Lodge Gardens to your left, follow the path parallel to the road until the next junction and join the walk at ❸); there is also roadside parking around Ham Common.

Note: Richmond Park closes to vehicles at dusk. High tides can partly submerge cars parked close to the river at Ham and elsewhere.

Length: Full walk 6½ miles (10 kilometres), 3½ hours; short walk omitting Isabella Plantation and Pen Ponds 5 miles (8 kilometres), 2½ hours.

Difficulty: Easy.

Maps: Any London street atlas.

Full range in Richmond. Café in Pembroke Lodge. Drinking fountain at Ham Gate. Several riverside cafés in Richmond.

WC Signposted near the start of the walk in Richmond town centre; in Richmond Park, where the walk enters the park, and by Ham Gate. By the river near the Terrace Gardens, shortly before Richmond Bridge.

PT Trains and District Line Underground to Richmond.

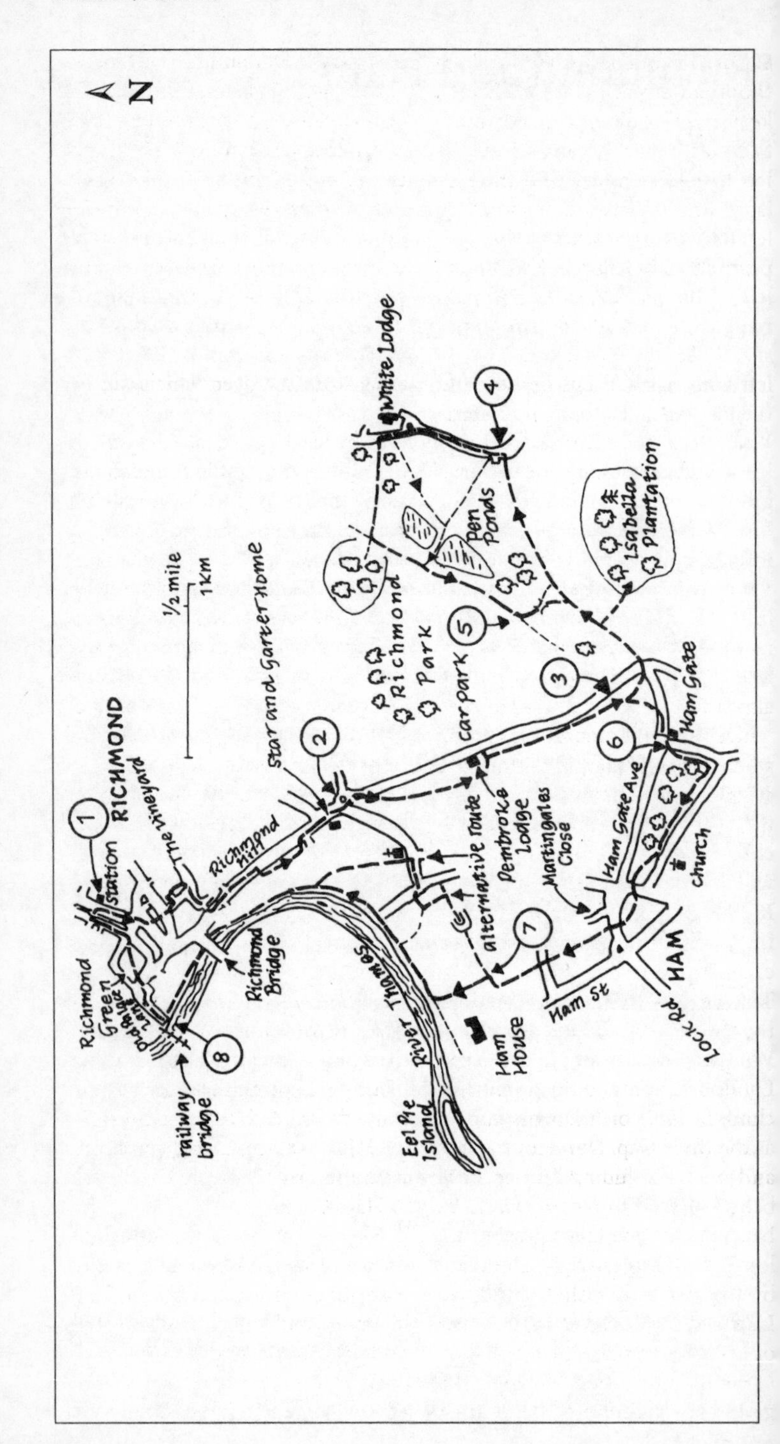
N
RICHMOND
1
station
The Vineyard
Richmond Green
Old Palace Lane
Richmond Hill
Richmond Bridge
railway bridge
8
River Thames
Eel Pie Island
Ham House
7
alternative route
Pembroke Lodge
Martingales Close
Ham St
Lock Rd
HAM
Ham Gate Ave
church
6
Ham Gate
3
car park
5
Richmond Park
2
Star and Garter Home
1/2 mile
1KM
Pen Ponds
Isabella Plantation
4
White Lodge

❶ Turn left out of the station, along the main street (The Quadrant); keep right at the next major junction (with The Square, where the left fork is signposted to the registry office/toilets), then soon turn left into Church Court by the signpost to Parish Church. Keep to the left of the church, cross the main road and take Halford Road opposite. Where the road bends left, fork left into a small cul-de-sac, and turn right at the end along Vineyard Passage, a path with railings that runs alongside a burial ground behind the houses. At the top turn right by a phone box, immediately keeping left into **The Vineyard** avoiding the right fork into Halford Road. The Vineyard's name is probably historically accurate. The street has two groups of almshouses.

Keep straight on past the church where the road markings indicate a compulsory left turn for traffic, then turn left at a pocket handkerchief of a green into Hill Rise, which immediately becomes **Richmond Hill**. Soon a walkway to the right of the pavement gives excellent views. The Queen's Terrace is a 17th-century feature; there is a grand prospect of Windsor, the Thames, the park, London airport and the prominent chink in the North Downs known as the Mole Gap. Numerous artists and poets, including Turner, have been attracted to record this view. No. 116 (Downe House) was once leased to the playwright Sheridan; by the junction with Nightingale Lane is Wick House, once the home of Joshua Reynolds.

Follow up to pass through the gates of **Richmond Park**, just beyond the Star and Garter Home. Covering 2,358 acres, this magnificent expanse was enclosed in 1635 by Charles I as a hunting park, and encompassed by a 10-mile wall. Public access was gained in the 18th century after a vigorous campaign by brewer John Lewis. It remains one of London's largest semi-untamed areas, with rough pasture, woodlands and ponds. Keep well away from the deer, which can be aggressive.

❷ Inside the park, take the path to the right of the traffic roundabout, along the top of the slope, walking parallel to the road; drop down just after the toilets and follow the path that runs along the foot of the steep slope. You later pass a fenced brick building, and soon after can go through a gate into **Pembroke Lodge Gardens**. Pembroke Lodge, the 18th-century former home of Bertrand Russell, is now a café.

If you prefer to skip the gardens, carry on along the foot of the slope, turning left uphill at the end of the fence around the gardens, then right along the path that runs along the top of the slope. Either way, beyond the gardens, follow the path closely parallel to the road (if you are heading for Ham Gate, there are alternative paths leading half right beneath the slope but the route described is easier to find).

❸ Just before a road junction, where the right turn is signposted to Ham Gate:

For the short walk bear downhill on a gravel path just before the road junction to reach Ham Gate by a pond and toilet block, and pick up walk directions at ❻.

For the long walk further into Richmond Park proceed to the road junction, and take the track opposite, signposted Isabella Plantation. Ignore side-turns; however, the detour right after 200 yards to the **Isabella Plantation** is recommended for a superlative show of azaleas (best in May to June) and heathers in a plantation crossed by an attractive stream.

Continuing along the main track for ¾ mile, you reach a road by a car park ❹. Turn left, up to porticoed **White Lodge**, a splendid villa of 1729 built as a rural retreat and with a specially created vista down a broad ride. The birthplace of Edward VIII in 1894, it now houses the Royal Ballet School.

At White Lodge turn left on a grassy track to Pen Ponds.Take the causeway between the two ponds. After you cross the causeway between **Pen Ponds** a surprise view of the British Telecom Tower appears. Turn left on the far side. Ignore side-turns, and 600 yards later ❺ join a broad horse track, which crosses a tiny brick bridge over a channel; immediately after, bear right and soon join the track you were on earlier. Follow this back to the road junction, and take the path to the right of the road opposite Ham Gate.

❻ Just after Ham Gate, turn left into Church Road, on a path alongside the right side of the road. Opposite pillars for a driveway to Wilmer House, and just before Church Road bends right at a junction with Latchmere Lane, turn right, inside woods and parallel with the road. Later, some houses are visible through the trees away to the left, and the path almost joins the road. When you are level with the church, either follow the road or take any of several paths leading half right through woods; both routes soon lead to the main road and a large green flanked by mainly 18th- and 19th-century houses (**Ham village**), still rural in feel, with a pond at its far end.

Follow the right edge of the green; 100 yards after Martingales Close (on your right), and where the right-hand wall ends, take the broad path on your right marked by a wide white fence leading towards Ham House; the path (known as Melancholy Walk) crosses a road halfway along. In front of Ham House gates, turn right, then ❼ left at the corner of the wall towards the river. Where the track bends left in front of the house carry on forward across the grass and turn right along the towpath.

Ham House (NT, open daily except Thursdays, April to end October. Garden open daily 10.30 to 6) is Jacobean, dating from 1610 and remodelled some 60 years later. The interiors are celebrated for their showy woodwork, intricate plaster ceilings and furnishings; the Great Staircase displays carved bowls of fruit. The gardens have been restored to their original formal elegance. The archives of the Lauderdale family, who owned the house at the time of these alterations, assisted the building's renovation by the National Trust and the Victoria and Albert Museum.

At high tide the towpath may be flooded, in which case see directions at the end of the walk. Follow the towpath. Seen first is **Eel Pie Island**, so called because a now demolished hotel on it used to sell eel pies to visitors. Later, **Marble**

Hill, a stucco Palladian mansion of 1729, is seen on the other side of the river. Near a toilet block you pass a grotto-like entrance to **Terrace Gardens**, which has a café and a restored statue of a 'River God'. You pass under **Richmond Bridge**, built in 1777 of Portland stone and now London's oldest bridge; you can hire a boat here. **Heron Square** (1986), immediately after Richmond Bridge, is Quinlan Terry's controversial neo-classical creation.

Just before the next bridge ❽ turn right on a road by a sign for the White Swan pub. Just after the pub turn right into **Old Palace Yard**. The gate-house and various brickwork now incorporated into adjacent houses are remains of Richmond Palace built by Henry VII, former Duke of Richmond (the Yorkshire town giving its name to this one), on the site of the priory of Shene, first occupied by Henry I in 1125. Edward III, Henry VII and Elizabeth I all died here. Much of the palace's destruction was wrought by Cromwell's men.

Leave Old Palace Yard by an archway, then cross **Richmond Green**, aiming for the Richmond Theatre (with prominent green copper domes). The Green is a former knights' jousting ground belonging to the palace. It is worth taking in each side for the exceptional quality of its predominantly 17th- and 18th-century houses. The theatre (built in 1899) is an exuberant piece of late Victoriana, with two mock burning torches at the entrance.

Continue past the theatre, over the railway, then opposite Park Lane take the path (signposted Toilets) on the right into Richmond town centre, emerging opposite the station.

If the Thames towpath is flooded return to the corner of the wall at ❼, turn left on a long straight path towards a gatehouse (1898 mock-Jacobean), 50 yards before which you cross the school driveway on the left and take the track opposite. 200 yards later, turn right on a path between fences, to reach River Lane, where you turn right to join the main road. Turn left along the main road for 200 yards through the village of **Petersham**, which has some outstanding houses, including 16th-century Montrose House with superb wrought-iron gates.

Turn left on a path signposted to St Peter's church, a Saxon foundation, rebuilt in 1266 and altered every century since the 16th. Internally it is very much early 19th-century in appearance, with late 18th-century box-pews. Beyond the church continue forward by the remains of an old lamp-post, on a path. After crossing a field, the path reaches the river, where you turn right and resume the walk directions at ❽.

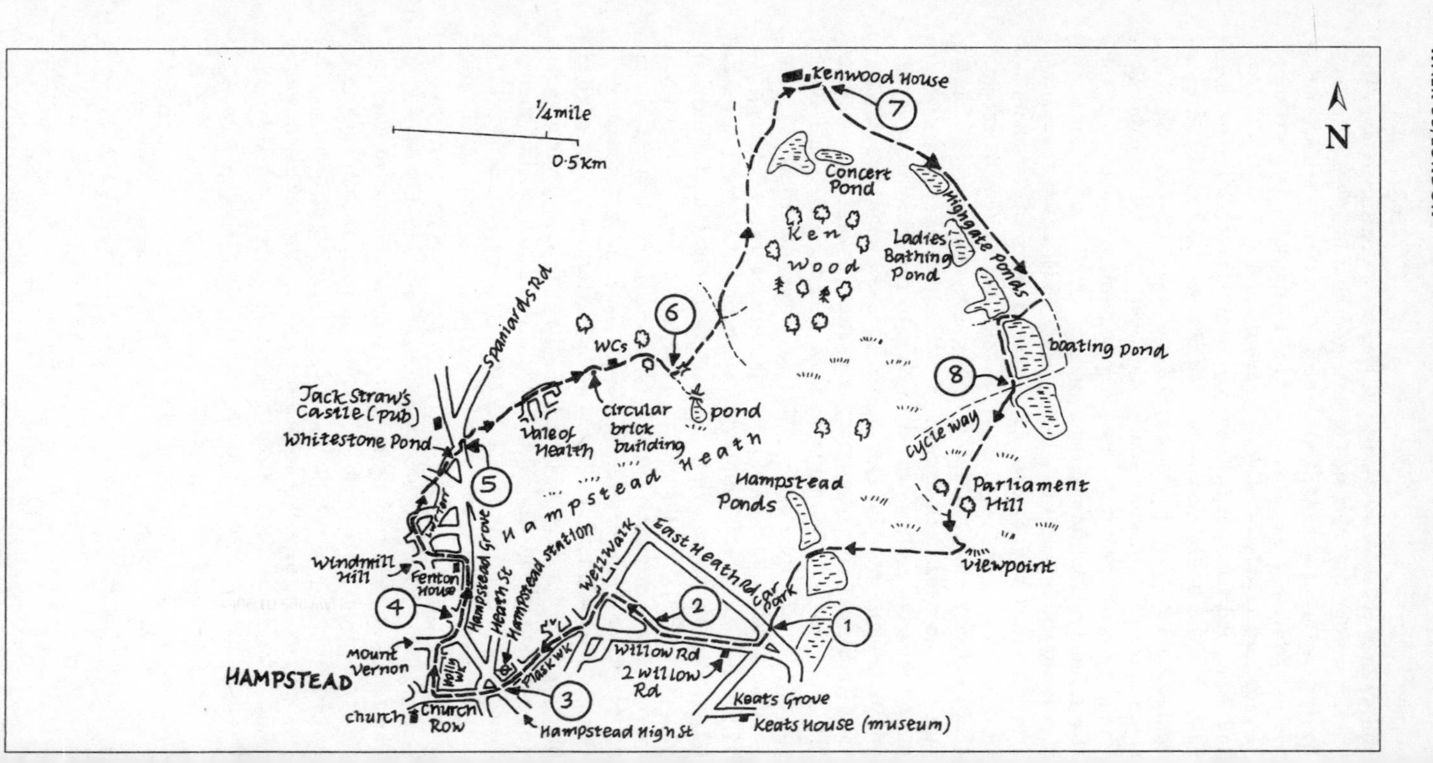
N
1/4 mile
0·5 Km
Kenwood House
Concert Pond
Ken Wood
Ladies Bathing Pond
Highgate Ponds
boating pond
cycle way
Parliament Hill
Viewpoint
Hampstead Ponds
Hampstead Heath
Spaniards Rd
WCs
pond
Jack Straw's Castle (pub)
Whitestone Pond
Vale of Health
circular brick building
Windmill Hill
Fenton House
Hampstead Grove
Heath St
Hampstead station
Well Walk
East Heath Rd
car park
Mount Vernon
Holly Wk
HAMPSTEAD
Flask Wk
Willow Rd
2 Willow Rd
Keats Grove
church
Church Row
Hampstead High St
Keats House (museum)
1
2
3
4
5
6
7
8

Hampstead and Kenwood House

LONDON WALK 33

Endowed with a blend of intricate townscape and semi-rural heathland, historic Hampstead lies on a hillside, laced with a maze of 18th-century and early 19th-century streets, stepped alleys, small greens and sloping lanes. The grand town mansions, luxuriant suburban villas and intimate terraces are and have been homes to many famous people.

Route-finding across the Heath is rather involved as there are a great number of paths, so we have tried to take a route that is reasonably easy to find, passing Highgate Ponds and the viewpoint at Parliament Hill Fields.

Open houses in Hampstead include Fenton House, and the former houses of the psychologist Sigmund Freud (not on this route), the poet John Keats and the architect Arno Goldfinger.

The grounds of Kenwood House are open daily 8 to 8 in summer and 8 to 4 in winter. This walk passes through them; if they are closed it is possible to skirt the grounds by keeping to the left as you near the house.

Freemasons Arms, Downshire Hill, Hampstead NW1 1NT. ☎ 020-7433 6811. Open all week 12 to 10; food Mon to Sat 12 to 10, Sun 12 to 9.30. Greene King Abbot Ale, Greenalls beers. Large garden. Pies, steaks, bar snacks, sandwiches, Sunday roasts. No sandwiches on Sunday. Children welcome in family area. No dogs.

Wells Tavern, Well Walk, Hampstead NW3 1BX. ☎ 020-7794 2806. Open Mon to Sat 11 to 11, Sun 12 to 10.30; food 11 (12 Sun) to 7. 2 real ales. Set menu including fish/sausage/scampi and chips, Sunday roasts, sandwiches. Children welcome. Dogs welcome in bar area.

Flask, 4 Flask Walk, Hampstead NW1 1HS. ☎ 020-7435 4580. Open Mon to Sat 11 to 11, Sun 12 to 10.30; food Mon to Sat 12 to 3 (4 Fri and Sat), 6 to 9, Sun 12 to 4. Young's beers. Traditional pub food, blackboard specials, fresh fish and chips, sandwiches. Sunday roast. Children welcome in dining area. Dogs welcome.

Three Horseshoes, 28 Heath Street, Hampstead NW3 6TE. ☎ 020-7431 7206. Open Mon to Sat 11 to 11, Sun 12 to 10.30; food 11 to 10, Sun 12 to 9.30. 5 real ales. Traditional pub food, jacket potatoes, specials board, Sunday roast. No children. No dogs.

Holly Bush, 22 Holly Mount, Hampstead NW3 6SG. ☎ 020-7435 2892. Open Mon to Sat 11 to 11, Sun 12 to 10.30; food Mon to Fri 12 to 3.30, 5.30 to 10.30, Sat and Sun 12 to 10. 5 real ales. Food might be soup of the day, sausage sandwich, pheasant and rabbit casserole or grilled squid. Sunday roasts are also on offer. Children welcome in eating area. Dogs welcome.

Start: Car park opposite the junction of East Heath Road and Downshire Hill, on the south-west edge of Hampstead Heath.

Length: 3 miles (5 kilometres), 2 hours, but with much to see on the way.
Difficulty: Easy.
Map: Any London street atlas.
Full range in Hampstead. Restaurant/café with outdoor sitting area at Kenwood House.
WC On Hampstead Heath and at Kenwood House.
PT Hampstead Underground station (Northern Line). Turn left out of the station, along Hampstead High Street, then right into Oriel Place and join the walk at ❸.

❶ Cross the road from the car park, into Downshire Hill (some houses, particularly Nos 16, 26 and 27, have good examples of **fire-marks** denoting the insurance company the owner had used to insure against fire), then go first right into Willow Road (near the Freemasons Arms).

(You can detour to **Keats House** by continuing along Downshire Hill and taking the next left, by the church, into Keats Grove; the house is on the right. Here Keats fell in love with his neighbour's daughter, Fanny Brawne, composed love letters to her and wrote 'Ode to a Nightingale'; he learned here that he was dying of consumption. Ring 020-7435 2062 opening times).

You pass **No. 2 Willow Road**, a Modernist terrace house designed by the architect Erno Goldfinger for his own use in 1939, now owned by the National Trust and open to the public (end March to end October, Thursday to Saturday 12 to 5; November to mid-December and March Saturday only). Goldfinger, after whom the James Bond character was named, designed the once notorious 31-storey Trellick Tower (1972) in west London, now only posthumously being recognised as a masterpiece.

❷ Fork right into Christchurch Hill, marked by a horse trough and no-entry traffic signs, continuing with the edge of the heath on your right. Turn left by the Wells Tavern into **Well Walk.** A short distance to the right a plaque on the right side of the road records the site of the wells that turned Hampstead into a health spa in the 18th century, soon bringing an often raucous clientele; gambling-parlours and beer-houses sprang up to satisfy a new demand. By the early 1800s Hampstead's spa days had declined. Numerous plaques record celebrated residents: historian Henry Hyndman (No. 13), birth-control pioneer Marie Stopes (14), J. B. Priestley (27), D.H. Lawrence (32) and John Constable (40).

The road forks right at a junction near the red-brick Wells and Campden Baths of 1888 and continues as Flask Walk. Carry on up past a small green, with **New End Square** on the right. Here Flask Cottages have a curious external bird-cage, hanging from the upper storey, and sport comically shaped chimney-stacks. Burgh House, a little further up, is a fine three-storey house of 1703 and hosts changing art exhibitions. **Flask Walk** itself is so named because this was where spa water from Well Walk was put into flasks for sale at the Eagle and Child in Fleet Street. Bottling was carried out in the Thatch'd House Inn on the site of the present-day Flask Tavern.

Cross High Street and take Oriel

Place opposite and slightly to the left ❸. Pass the Three Horseshoes, cross Heath Street and take **Church Row**, again opposite and slightly to the left. This is one of Hampstead's finest streets – a row of tall houses built of a handsome brown brick with plum-coloured dressings in the 1720s during Hampstead's emergence as a health resort. The railings are original and some front entrances have torch stands. It leads to St John's Church, dating from 1745 with a gilt, barrel-vaulted interior, unusual pew-ends and Ionic columns; unusually the tower is at the east end. The gates came from the Duke of Chandos' demolished mansion at Stanmore in Middlesex. The artist John Constable and his family are buried here: the tomb is in the bottom corner of the churchyard, surrounded by iron railings.

Just by the church, turn right up **Holly Walk**, where escapees from the French Revolution settled – hence St Mary's Catholic Church of 1816, looking surprisingly foreign. In the 1830s Holly Berry Lane (leading off to the right from Holly Walk) had a watch-house for the recently formed Hampstead police force; down the lane is a plaque to the composer William Walton.

At the top of Holly Walk, turn right at the T-junction into Mount Vernon, where Abernethy House has a plaque to R.L. Stevenson. You soon bend round to the left, along railings above Holly Hill, coming down to road level at the road fork in front of the wrought-iron gates of Fenton House ❹. Off Holly Hill, itself one of Hampstead's steepest streets, is **Holly Mount**, a charming little alley where stands the Holly Bush pub, originally a stable block for Romney's House next door. It was here that James Fenton of Fenton House organised local residents to fight the long-running but ultimately successful battle to preserve Hampstead Heath.

At the above-mentioned fork by Fenton House, fork right into **Hampstead Grove**. On the right Romney's House (1797) was built for the portrait artist George Romney. Further on, New Grove House has a plaque to George du Maurier, 19th-century novelist and cartoonist for *Punch*: he originated the celebrated 'curate's egg' cartoon of 1895 (on being presented with a bad egg at breakfast the curate insists 'parts of it are excellent'). Opposite is **Fenton House**, (1693–5), Hampstead's oldest house and is now owned by the National Trust and open to the public (3 March to 2 April weekends only, 9 April to 29 October Wednesday to Sunday); an outstanding example of William and Mary period architecture, it contains a collection of early keyboard instruments, as well as paintings, porcelain and furniture.

Take the next left, into **Admiral Walk**. Here Admiral's House, a rambling five-storey Georgian building, has a plaque to George Gilbert Scott, the 19th-century architect who designed the Albert Memorial and St Pancras Station. The street was named after Admiral Matthew Benson, who reputedly fired a cannon from the roof on appropriate occasions. John Galsworthy wrote much of *The Forsyte Saga* (1922) while living at adjacent Grove Lodge, 1918–35.

Turn right into Windmill Hill,

following it past the junctions with Lower Terrace (plaque to Constable on No. 2) and Upper Terrace (keeping just to the right of No. 4, Fountain House). Cross over Judges Walk – allegedly named because in the 1660s High Court judges fled here to escape the plague and held court – and cross through a line of trees to reach the edge of Hampstead Heath. Constable painted the view from here.

Immediately turn right by a bench, with the wooded hollow on your left, and soon walk beside a fence on your right. Reach the road at Whitestone Pond and fork left, along Whitestone Walk. Cross the main road by the zebra crossing (Jack Straw's Castle, a pub, is just to the left here), and turn left for 40 yards.

❺ Turn right by the sign for Spaniard's Road, just before the road fork by the obelisk (at 442 feet, this is the highest point in London), and go right down some steps. Fork right after 50 yards and follow the path with gorse bushes on your left for 100 yards and then branch off right to a residential road. Turn left along it. This cluster of streets is the **Vale of Health**, originally an area of malarial swamp known as Hatches Bottom, drained in the 18th century and given a more wholesome-sounding name. Its development hints at what might have been had not the rest of the Heath been saved. As it is, the area has become a desirable enclave; celebrated residents have included James Leigh Hunt (with whom Byron, Coleridge, Lamb and Shelley stayed), D.H. Lawrence, Compton Mackenzie and Edgar Wallace.

Where the road bends right, carry forward on a paved path along the edge of the Heath. Where the fence on the right ends, go forward at a path junction (avoiding a path to the right), passing a small circular brick building. This path soon joins a broader track coming in from the left; ignore any side turns.

❻ 150 yards after you pass a toilet block on the left, turn left over a bridge (if you reach a large bridge over the end of a lake, you have overshot by 50 yards), and carry on up to a large junction of paths with railings and an Iveagh Bequest Kenwood sign ahead. Turn half left (this path ascends for the first two or three yards, then levels), soon being joined by the railings on your right. 100 yards later go through a gate by another Iveagh Bequest sign. This path emerges into the open and becomes a broad stony path.

Fork right on another stony path shortly before the path ahead enters woodland and passes a white house. You reach a gateway near a Henry Moore sculpture (*Two piece reclining figure No. 5*, 1964), where you turn left to reach **Kenwood House** (open daily 10 to 6; November to March 10 to 4). The seat of the Earl of Mansfield in the reign of George III, it was rebuilt in 1767 by Robert Adam and given to the nation in 1927. It is now owned by English Heritage and, wonderfully for such a nationally important collection of paintings and furniture, is open free of charge; among the most familiar are Rembrandt's *Self Portrait* and Vermeer's *Guitar Player*. In summer the lakes in front of the house make a spectacular setting for open-air concerts with fireworks.

Carry on along the gravel track past the front of the house, with the lakes down to your right, and past the toilets and Brewhouse restaurant entrance on your left. Just after these, fork left through a gateway in the railings and ❼ immediately turn right, alongside the railings on your right, on a descending path. This later becomes a tarmacked track; avoid any side turns. The track (now unsurfaced) passes close by a pond and then the entrance to the Kenwood Ladies' Bathing Pond (the pond itself is hidden among the trees). Opposite a house and shortly before the track reaches a road, turn right, passing the right side of the boating-pond, and turn left around its second side.

❽ At the end of the pond cross a cycleway and 30 yards later take the surfaced path half right that heads up to a clump of trees, where you branch off left across the grass to the summit of **Parliament Hill Fields**. From here Guy Fawkes' fellow conspirators supposedly met on the evening of 5 November 1605 to watch the blowing-up of Parliament. It gives one of the best free views in London, with Highgate to the north-east, the City and the West End (the NatWest and Telecom towers prominent) and the distant Crystal Palace ridge beyond with its two TV transmitter masts.

From the summit turn right on the tarmacked path (towards a distant church spire). Go forward at two path crossings (at the second you have back gardens close by on your left), and carry on the main tarmacked path which goes between two lakes, then fork right to join the road on the left side of the car park.

Saving Hampstead Heath

The 800-acre Heath is a much-revered expanse of woods and parkland within metropolitan north London, joined on to Parliament Hill Fields, the Kenwood estate and Golders Hill Park. The nearest countrified area to central London, it owes its survival to a fierce campaign by local residents from 1830 to 1890. They formed the Heath Protection Committee when Thomas Marlon-Wilson, Lord of the Manor, wanted to develop the Heath. His private Parliamentary bills were constantly frustrated by the committee, whose members' influence in Parliament was considerable. He managed to fell many trees and ran sand-extraction operations. But after his death, tracts of the Heath were sold to public ownership and the former sand-pits now appear as attractive hollows.

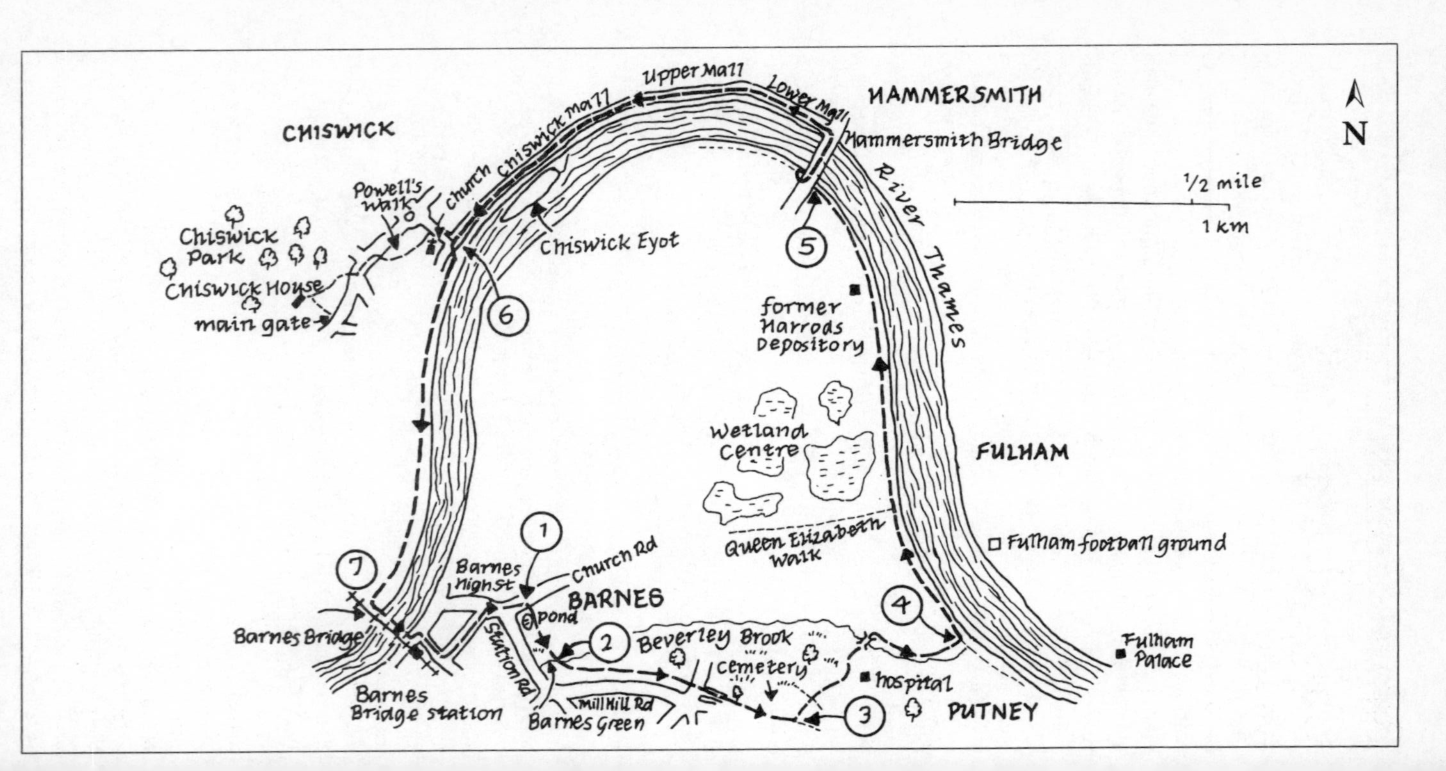
N
HAMMERSMITH
Upper Mall
Lower Mall
Hammersmith Bridge
CHISWICK
Chiswick Mall
Church
Powell's Walk
Chiswick Park
Chiswick House
main gate
Chiswick Eyot
River Thames
1/2 mile
1 km
5
6
former Harrods Depository
Wetland Centre
FULHAM
Queen Elizabeth Walk
Fulham football ground
7
1
Barnes High St
Church Rd
BARNES
pond
Barnes Bridge
Station Rd
2
Beverley Brook
cemetery
4
Fulham Palace
hospital
3
PUTNEY
Barnes Bridge station
Mill Hill Rd
Barnes Green

Barnes Common and Chiswick Mall

LONDON WALK 34

The village pond at Barnes and the woods of Barnes Common introduce the mostly rural theme of this walk in the south-west suburbs. It explores a great loop of the Thames, including some of the old riverside houses at Chiswick's Lower and Upper Mall. Optional diversions take in the recently created Wetland Centre and the grounds of Chiswick House, one of England's finest Palladian villas.

Sun Inn, 7 Church Road, Barnes SW13 9HE. ☎ 020-8876 5256. Open Mon to Sat 11 to 11, Sun 12 to 10.30; food Mon to Sat 12 to 2.45, 6 to 10, Sun 12 to 3.45. Bass. Salads, ploughman's, specials board, Thai food, Sunday roast. Sandwiches Mon to Sat. Children welcome in eating area but not bar. Dogs welcome.

Blue Anchor, 13 Lower Mall, Hammersmith W6 9DJ. ☎ 020-8748 5774. Open Mon to Sat 11 to 11, Sun 12 to 10.30; food Mon to Sat 12 to 3, 6 to 9, Sun 12 to 3.30. 4 real ales. Cold food counter, including mackerel, pâté, beef, ham, egg mayonnaise, prawn and chicken platters and turkey and ham pie. Jumbo wholemeal baps and salad with ham, beef, tuna, pâté, Stilton or Brie, ploughman's, sausage rolls or pasties are also on offer. Other dishes might be steak and kidney pie or chilli chicken with rice. Roasts on Sundays, sandwiches. Children welcome. Dogs welcome.

Dove, 19 Upper Mall, Hammersmith W6 9TA. ☎ 020-8748 5405. Open Mon to Sat 11 to 11, Sun 12 to 10.30; food Mon to Fri 12 to 2, 6.30 to 9, Sat 12 to 3, 6.30 to 9, Sun 12 to 4, 6.30 to 9. Fuller's beers. Traditional pub food, blackboard specials; jacket potatoes, baguettes, ploughman's at lunch-time, Sunday roasts. No children. Dogs welcome.

Old Ship, 25 Upper Mall, Hammersmith W6 9TD. ☎ 020-8748 2593. Open Mon to Fri 10am to 11pm, Sat 9 to 11, Sun 9 to 10.30; food Mon to Fri 10am to 10.30pm, Sat 9 to 10.30, Sun 9 to 10. Fuller's beers. Set menu, bar snacks, Sunday roasts, sandwiches and salads. Children welcome. Dogs welcome.

Black Lion, 2 South Black Lion Lane, Hammersmith W6 9TJ. ☎ 020-8748 2639. Open Mon to Sat 11 to 11, Sun 12 to 10.30; food Mon to Sat 11 to 11, Sun 12 to 10.30. Courage Best, Theakston, Greene King IPA. The 200-year-old building is reputedly a former piggery. It has a garden and bar billiards. The menu might include chicken wings, scampi and chips, beef and ale pie, coq au vin, burger and chips, cheese and pasta bake, Sunday roast or soup. Sandwiches and bar snacks are also on offer. Children welcome. Dogs welcome.

Bull's Head, Lonsdale Road, Barnes SW13 9PY. ☎ 020-8876 5241. Open Mon to Sat 11 to 11, Sun 12 to 10.30; food 12 to 2.30, 7 to 9, bistro Thur to Sat 7 to 11, Sun 1 to 5, sandwiches served all afternoon. Young's beers. The Bull's Head has live jazz every evening at 8.30 and at lunch-time on Sunday. On the pub menu you might find devilled chicken, Scotch pies and stew. These are served with fresh vegetables and potatoes. On the bistro menu might be Arbroath smokies, chicken and duck liver pâté, cheese fondue, escalope of pork or fillet of beef en croûte. Well-behaved children welcome. Well-behaved dogs welcome.

Start: Pond at Barnes Green (junction of Barnes High Street, Church Road and Station Road SW13).

Length: 4 miles (6.5 kilometres), 3 hours. Detour to Chiswick Park adds about a mile.

Difficulty: Easy, all on the level.

Map: Any London street atlas.

Café just to the right at ❹. Full range in Barnes.

WC At ❹, just to the right where you join the Thames path.

PT Barnes Bridge station (mainline): Turn right out of the station, right into Cleveland Gardens, and second left into Cleveland Road to reach the pond at ❶.

Barnes station (mainline): Turn left out of the station, signposted Barnes Village; turn right at signpost to Ranelagh Path/bottle and can banks/Rocks Lane Tennis Centre; join the walk at ❸.

---

❶ Begin at the **original village centre of Barnes**, with the pond immediately on your right and with the 17th-century Sun Inn on your left (across the road). The stocks stood here until 1835; overlooking the Green are timber-framed Essex Lodge and early-18th-century Nos 66 and 68 Station Road.

Walk round the pond, turning right on the tarmacked path by a fanciful gabled Gothic cottage, then past the end of the pond go forward along the left edge of Barnes Green, with a residential road on your left.

❷ Cross a footbridge and turn left on the other side, on a tarmacked path with lamp-posts. After 200 yards fork left (by a lamp-post on the left side of the path) on to another tarmacked path (where the right fork goes towards a main road), also with lamp-posts. Ignore a left fork after 60 yards and soon cross the main road (Rocks Lane). Take the small road opposite, signposted to Ranelagh Path/bottle and can banks. Where the road ends by the recycling banks, go forward on a path along an avenue of trees; on the right is Barnes Common, a local nature reserve. After 100 yards, and 30 yards after the avenue ends, turn left opposite a bench on a woodland path ❸. This immediately joins a path coming in from the left; 100 yards later keep forward at a crossing of paths in a semi-open area. Go forward, making towards the left end of a hedge in front of hospital buildings (with a large chimney), along the left side of a flat grassy area. 100 yards before this hedge, bear left to find a metal footbridge over the Beverley Brook (with the floodlights of Fulham football ground beyond). Turn right on the other side, on an enclosed path leading to the River Thames.

❹ Turn left on the path beside the river. Putney Bridge, to the right, is the start of the University Boat Race; opposite and to the right are the grounds of 16th-century Fulham Palace (now municipally owned), residence for 1,000 years of the Bishops of London. Proceeding towards Chiswick, exactly one mile from Putney Bridge, the towpath passes a memorial to Steve Fairbairn, founder of the Head of the River Race. The former Harrods Furniture Depository, a Boat Race landmark, has been converted into flats.

You can detour into Queen Elizabeth Walk on the left for the **Wetland Centre** (ring 020-8876 8895 for opening times) where the former Barn Elms Water Works have been converted into the biggest bird table in London, as the largest wetland habitat creation project in Europe. The old concrete-edged reservoirs have been broken up into a wetland area of 30 re-formed lakes, ponds and marshlands, with special bridges, boardwalks, a visitor centre with a viewing tower and birdwatchers' hides constructed for the purpose. Thousands of trees have been planted and some 200,000 aquatic plants have been introduced. This centre breaks new ground in London in maximising feeding, roosting and breeding opportunities for a range of water birds, including endangered species such as the Hawaiian goose or Nene, which was rescued from the brink of extinction by a captive breeding programme.

❺ Go under Hammersmith Bridge, then up the path the other side and cross the bridge itself to the north bank. Turn left along the river; this is Lower Mall (see box for **Lower Mall and Upper Mall**). You pass the Blue Anchor, then after a small park briefly lose sight of the river as you pass The Dove. You then walk along Upper Mall, one of the most desirable riverside stretches in London. After Upper Mall Open Space you again lose sight of the river for a short distance as you enter Hammersmith Terrace.

❻ Reach **Chiswick Parish Church**. This is heavily restored, but the churchyard is famous for the grave of satirical artist William Hogarth, with epitaph by David Garrick, which was much criticised by Dr Johnson; the tomb, surrounded by railings, is easily located.

For detour to Chiswick House and Park (see box) turn right into

Chiswick House and Chiswick Park

(English Heritage, open April to September 10 to 6 daily; October to end March 10 to 4, Wednesday to Sunday; Chiswick Park free, fee for house). The house is approached through the lovely grounds of **Chiswick Park**, landscaped by Richard Boyle (the third Earl of Burlington) and William Kent in the naturalistic style that was to become the essence of English landscape gardening. The **Park** includes an Inigo Jones arch, a camellia house, an ornamental 'Cascade', a temple and an obelisk. Burlington had Chiswick House built more as an architectural essay and object of admiration than a residence, using it mainly for parties and as a library; it became a leading social venue. This immaculately proportioned design of 1727–9 by Burlington was partly modelled on Palladio's Villa Capra near Vicenza, but also draws from elsewhere – the portico columns, for example, are copied from Palladio's drawing of the Roman Temple of Castor and Pollux in Naples. The interiors by Kent incorporate some designs of Inigo Jones.

Church Street, then just after the church left into Powell's Walk; keep to the left side of the churchyard, and then follow the path between walls to the main road. Turn left and almost immediately cross the road by a pelican crossing, then go left and right into **Chiswick Park**. Return via the pelican crossing and then along Corney Road to a roundabout; turn left on Corney Reach Way, go past an octagonal pavilion-like building and then turn right on the riverside path.

To continue take the riverside path just to the left of Chiswick Wharf (a modern housing estate); this is a private path, but is open to the general public in daylight hours.

Carry on along the river and ❼ cross by Barnes Bridge. Turn right

Lower Mall and Upper Mall, Chiswick

Lower Mall Forms part of a charming riverside promenade. This group of Georgian houses is part rendered, part 'London Stock' brick, with much variation in detail (fanlights, balconies and so on). Nos 11 and 12, built in the 17th century as fishermen's cottages, are the oldest. After passing Furnival Gardens is **The Dove** tavern, once a coffee house. It claims numerous historical connections. James Thompson supposedly wrote the words for *Rule Britannia* upstairs, Ernest Hemingway and Graham Greene were customers, and A.P. Herbert used the pub as the model for 'The Pigeons' in *The Water Gypsies*. Prince Augustus Frederick, son of George III, was so fond of the view that he bought part of the building as a smoking-box for planning his anti-slave trade campaign. The bar on the right as you enter is reputedly London's smallest.

Into **Upper Mall**, No. 26 has a plaque to poet and novelist George MacDonald and was also the home of **William Morris**, designer and champion of the Arts and Crafts movement. Engraving for Morris and his Kelmscott Press was carried out by Emery Walker in Sussex House, opposite The Dove. Above the coach-house door, a plaque commemorates the first electric cable (laid in 1816). By the Black Lion, you enter **Hammersmith Terrace**, losing sight of the river temporarily. You pass the house of **Edward Johnston** (No. 3), the calligrapher who designed the pioneering sanserif lettering used by London Transport from the 1930s. Another blue plaque identifies the former home of **A.P. Herbert**, lawyer and author of *Misleading Cases*, who ran a passionate (but unsuccessful) campaign for the commercial use of the Thames. You may get a wholesome whiff from the nearby **Fuller's Brewery** near Chiswick Lane South. Continue along **Chiswick Mall**, where riverside gardens belonging to the houses form a strip on the left-hand side, looking on to the island **Chiswick Eyot** with its population of ducks and swans. Notice, particularly, Regency Cedar House, Strawberry House (1700) and 17th-century **Walpole House** (once the residence of Barbara Villiers, one of Charles II's mistresses, shunned by all by the time of her death here in 1708). Eynham House, with its almost comically narrow windows, was formerly part of Bedford House. At **Greenash** lived the parents of John Thorneycroft, who used the river to carry out underwater weaponry experiments that resulted in his invention of the torpedo.

on emerging on the road, along The Terrace, with the river on your left. Just before house No. 12, with a plaque to **Gustav Holst**, turn right into Cleveland Gardens (this cuts out a noisy stretch along the main road), then second left (Cleveland Road) to reach the pond at Barnes.

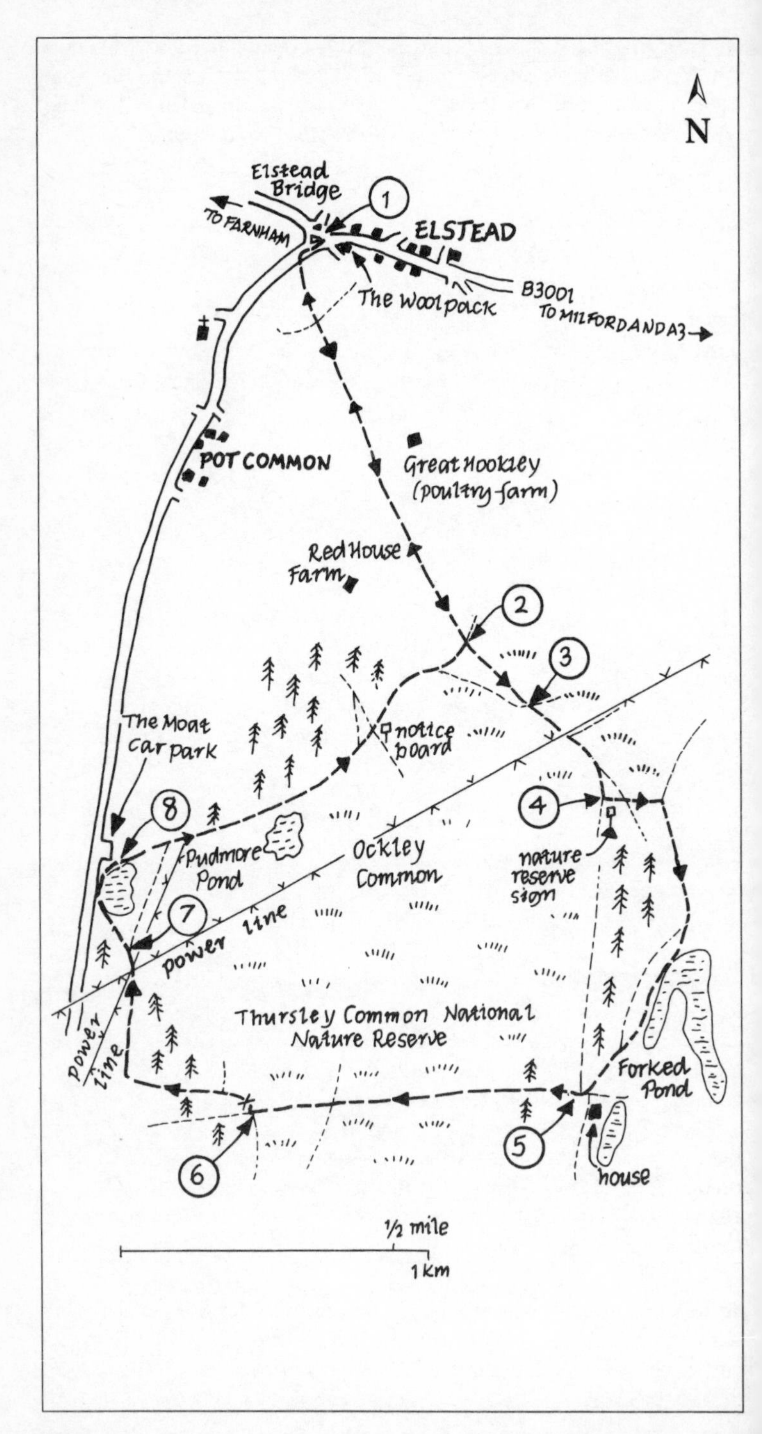
N
Elstead Bridge
1
TO FARNHAM
ELSTEAD
The Woolpack
B3001
TO MILFORD AND A3
POT COMMON
Great Hookley (poultry farm)
Red House Farm
2
3
The Moat Car park
notice board
8
4
Pudmore Pond
Ockley Common
nature reserve sign
7
power line
Thursley Common National Nature Reserve
power line
Forked Pond
5
6
house
½ mile
1 km

Elstead, Ockley Common and Thursley Nature Reserve

SURREY WALK 35

Deep in suburbia between Elstead and the A3 lies, amazingly, a barren expanse of heathland hidden by the surrounding woodland. This is an easy, level walk on white sandy paths, past bogs and ponds, through patches of woodland and dry expanses of heather and gorse, all rich in wildlife. There is a picnic site by a large pond known as The Moat, the alternative starting point.

The Woolpack, The Green, Elstead GU8 6HD. ☎ (01252) 703106. Open Mon to Sat 11 to 2.30, 6 to 11, Sun 12 to 3, 7 to 10.30; food Mon to Sat 12 to 2, 7 to 9.45, Sun 12 to 2, 7.15 to 9; closed 25, 26 Dec. Greene King Abbot Ale and Fuller's London Pride. Both bars in this much-modernised pub have log-burning fires. One has low ceilings and beams, while the other, more modern bar has high ceilings and a lighter, brighter feel to it. Wool trade memorabilia are dotted around the walls along with Victorian black and white engravings and country prints. Deep-fried Camembert in port and cranberry sauce or an avocado and seafood salad could be among the starters, while a main course might be pork steak in apricot, schnapps and thyme sauce or a casserole. Ploughman's, sandwiches and light snacks are available in the bar. Children welcome in children's room and dining-room. No dogs in dining-room.

Start: Elstead village green, in front of The Woolpack pub. Roadside parking. Grid reference 907437.
Alternative start: (for those who do not want to do the stretch ❶ between Elstead and the common at the start of the walk). The Moat car park, on a minor road south of Elstead (turn off B3001 at Elstead village green, in front of The Woolpack pub). With the road behind you, take the path from the right-hand side of the car park on to a walkway to the pond known as The Moat. Start the walk at ❽, ignore ❶ and continue from ❷ to the end of ❼. Grid reference 899417.
Length: Full walk 6 miles (9.5 kilometres), 3 hours. Shorter walk, starting at The Moat and omitting the leg to and from the pub at Elstead, 4 miles (6.4 kilometres), 2 hours.
Difficulty: Easy, though sometimes boggy on Ockley Common.
OS maps: 1:25,000 Explorer sheet 145; 1:50,000 Landranger sheet 186.
PT Hourly buses (not Sun) to Elstead from Guildford, Godalming, Farnham, and Aldershot.

❶ To start the walk from Elstead, with the Woolpack pub behind you, walk along the left-hand side of the triangular village green. Opposite a letterbox on the other side of the road, turn left into Staceys Farm Lane. Immediately, look out for a signposted, narrow footpath on the left, up some steps and between wooden fences. At the top, cross a stile and, keeping close to the hedge on your left, walk straight ahead over a rounded, grassy field to a stile. Turn left over the stile, immediately meet a track at a corner, cross it diagonally right and continue on a narrow footpath with a fence on the left and a hedge on the right. Continue over several fields of peaceful pasture, keeping the hedge on the right and passing a poultry farm over to the left. As you approach woodland and reach the gate into the private drive to Red House Farm, the footpath heads diagonally left across the field to a gate/stile halfway along the far side of the field (ignore the gate in the right-hand corner of the field). Cross the stile and continue with a hedge on the right to a stile that leads into the wood. Keep straight ahead between trees to a crossing of ways.

❷ *If you started from Elstead*, keep ahead at the crossing. *If you started from The Moat*, turn right.

Emerge from the woods into open heathland, with strikingly white-stemmed birches over to the left, to join a broad vehicle track at ❸. Pass under power lines and immediately afterwards keep straight ahead, leaving the vehicle track, which swings left. Ignore side tracks until you reach a sign for Thursley National Nature Reserve ❹; here turn left. Ignoring a small path to the right, reach a T-junction and turn right. As a green barn comes into sight on your left, the path divides. Take the left fork to follow the path round the edge of the **Forked Pond**, a secretive expanse of water surrounded by trees and reeds and dotted with kingcups. The other route goes to the right of the pond. The paths merge just before the start of some fencing on the left. Keep ahead where a path forks right, and pass under some telegraph wires. About 10 yards after, when a house comes into view on the left, take the right-hand fork, past a nature reserve board, and continue straight over a crossing of ways by a bridleway waymark post ❺.

Continue ahead up the broad sandy track, with telegraph wires alongside you on the left. The heath here is rather hillier than the section already crossed, and as the track rises you gain fine views of the Weald and North Downs. At the third crossing of ways turn right through a barrier preventing access to cyclists ❻.

Follow the main (narrow) path, which immediately bends left through gorse and heather, and then reaches more open heath, planted out with young Christmas trees. Soon the power lines seen at the start of the walk are visible to the right. The path later bends right as it joins a wider track.

❼ About 100 yards past a point where two sets of power lines cross, fork left on a narrow path leading into the trees. Go through a barrier and immediately turn right to reach the edge of the pond, known as **The Moat**. The Moat is named after the Anglo Saxon 'moot' or meeting place. Mallards, little grebes and moorhens inhabit the pond, but it is the dragonflies, including the rare white-faced dragonfly, as well as water beetles and spiders on or around the ponds that Thursley is noted for.

Take the path along the left-hand edge of the pond. This brings you to a picnic area and a walkway. To return to the Moat car park, turn left on the walkway.

❽ From the end of the walkway, with the car park behind you and the pond in front, turn left through trees for 20 yards. Where the path opens out keep straight ahead (ignoring a path to the right) and emerge from the trees on to a sandy/grassy vehicle track. Pass under small power lines (in the far distance on the right are some larger power lines). About 100 yards later a path joins from the right. There are nature reserve signs on the right, and to your left is a military training area. Follow the track across the heathery expanse of Ockley Common for ¾ mile: this can be boggy in places, but generally the sandy track is easy to walk on. The nearby ponds are a legacy of the medieval iron-smelting industry that made the Weald the industrial belt of England (see Walk 36).

(If, as you draw near the woodland ahead, the track is impassably wet and boggy, you can briefly detour left through the heather, on a narrow path that starts just before a dead tree stump, skirting left of a grassy, boggy area and heading for 11 o'clock. When you meet a broad, sandy track, turn right to get back to your original track.)

Enter the woodland and keep ahead over a crossing of paths with a warning sign about wet conditions on Thursley Bog. This is a soft, broad path through open woodland, mainly coniferous. Meet a broad vehicle track, with a smaller path straight ahead, at a waymark post, and turn right. After 100 yards or so, the main track swings right, and a lesser track

Thursley Common National Nature Reserve

This is one of the finest lowland heaths in Britain. The common was once woodland, cleared during Neolithic times, and later became grazing land. In the 1920s it began to be used for military training. The Whitbreads, the famous brewing family to whom it reverted after the Second World War, loved its open character, and the heath escaped afforestation. In the 1970s the Whitbreads sold it to the Nature Conservancy Council (now English Nature), who designated it a National Nature Reserve. It is a famous site for dragonflies, with 26 recorded species, as well as grayling and silver-studded blue butterflies (both of which are heathland species). Summer migrant birds include woodlarks, nightjars and hobbies, while Dartford warblers are present all year round. On the wet heath in early summer, marsh orchids burst into pale pink flowering spikes, while from July onwards there are yellow carpets of bog asphodel. Sundews make an appearance throughout the summer. These plants resemble miniature red frying pans and have sticky hairs to trap insects that provide nitrogen. The dry areas of heath are dominated by bell heather (in flower from June to September) and by common heather (June to October).

forks left. Take the left fork and, after 100 yards, reach a crossing of tracks ❷.

To return to Elstead, turn left and retrace your steps over the stile by the 'Out of Bounds to Military' sign, out of the woods and across the fields back to Elstead.

If you have started from The Moat, continue from ❷.

Abinger Roughs and Friday Street

SURREY WALK 36

This is a well cared-for and cherished landscape between the North Downs and the heights of the greensand, a swathe of woodland speckled with ponds and dotted with old farmhouses and peaceful hamlets. The contrast is striking between the secretive, folded country around Friday Street and the more open views of the chalk escarpment of the Downs after Abinger Hammer.

Wotton Hatch Hotel, Guildford Road, Wotton RH5 6QQ. ☎ (01306) 732931. Open Mon to Sat 11 to 11, Sun 12 to 10.30; food Mon to Wed 12 to 3, 6 to 10, Thur to Sat 12 to 10, Sun 12 to 10.30. Bass, Fuller's London Pride, Hancock's beers. Set menu and blackboard specials, sandwiches, small dishes, summer ploughman's. Children welcome but not in bar area. No dogs.

Stephan Langton, Friday Street, Abinger Common RH5 6JR (just off the route near the lake at Friday Street). ☎ (01306) 730775. Open Mon to Sat 11 to 3, 6 to 11, Sun 12 to 6, 7 to 10.30; food all week 12 to 3.30 (2 Mon), Mon to Sat 6 to 9.30. Harveys, Fuller's London Pride, Bass. Mock Tudor pub with patios at front and rear. A la carte menu and blackboard specials, ploughman's, bar snacks and sandwiches. Children welcome in restaurant. Dogs welcome in bar area.

Abinger Hatch, Abinger Common RH5 6HZ. ☎ (01306) 730737. Open Mon to Fri 11.30 to 3, 5 to 11, Sat 11 to 11, Sun 12 to 10.30; food all week 12 to 2.30, Tues to Sat 6 to 9.30. 6 real ales. A la carte and blackboard menus, filled rolls, ploughman's and bar snacks. No children after 8pm. Dogs welcome.

Start: Abinger Roughs National Trust car park (turn north off A25 between Abinger Hammer and Westcott, on a road signposted to Effingham and Surrey Cycleway Link; if approaching from Westcott, pass the Wotton Hatch pub on your left and turn right at a crossroads a mile later). The car park is on the left opposite a more prominent sign saying 'Wotton Estate Private Track, Access to 5–8 The Deerleap only'. Honesty box for contributions. Grid reference 111480.

Alternative start: Friday Street free car park, just west of the hamlet of Friday Street, south of Westcott. Grid reference 125458. Follow the road downhill towards the pond at Friday Street, using the path on the right side of the road; after 100 yards from the car park, as the road is about to bend left (just before Copse Cottage on the left) take a deeply sunken path on the right and join the walk at ❻.

Length: 8 miles (13 kilometres), 4 hours.

Difficulty: Moderate, with gradual ascents. All on well-drained sandy soil, so quite feasible after prolonged rain.

OS maps: 1:25,000 Explorer sheet 146; 1:50,000 Landranger sheet 187.

PT Daily buses from Dorking, Guildford and Redhill; alight at the Wotton Hatch pub, and join the walk at ❹.

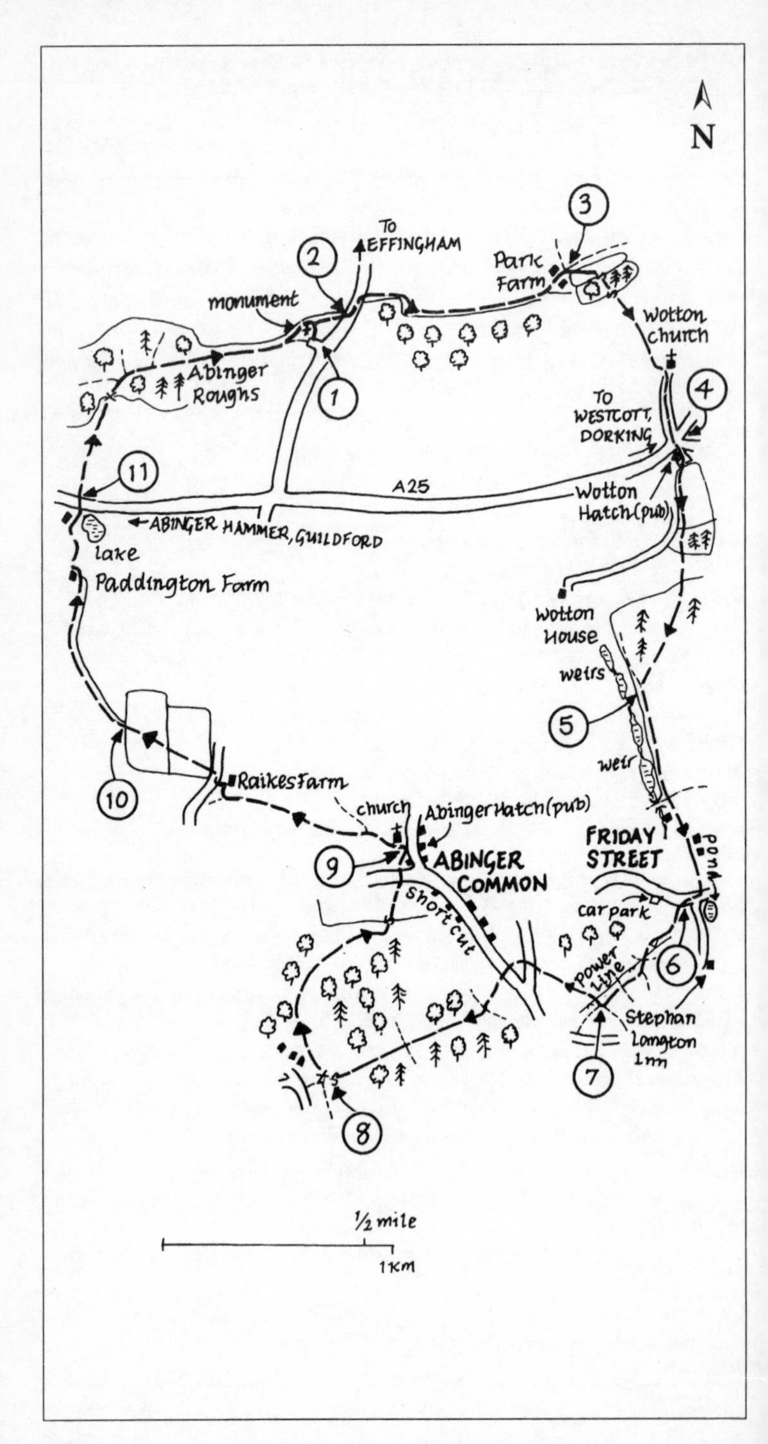
N
To EFFINGHAM
Park Farm
monument
Wotton Church
Abinger Roughs
To WESTCOTT, DORKING
A25
Wotton Hatch (pub)
ABINGER HAMMER, GUILDFORD
lake
Paddington Farm
Wotton House
weirs
weir
Raikes Farm
church
Abinger Hatch (pub)
FRIDAY STREET
pond
ABINGER COMMON
car park
short cut
power line
Stephan Langton Inn
½ mile
1 km
1
2
3
4
5
6
7
8
9
10
11

❶ From Abinger Roughs car park, with your back to the road, walk past the roofed information board and take the path on the right (avoid the track ahead through the broad barrier). This leads down to the granite **monument to Samuel Wilberforce**, an erstwhile bishop of Winchester who had a fatal fall from his horse at this spot in 1873. He campaigned for Anglican orthodoxy against the Oxford Movement, which aimed to revive English Roman Catholicism. His father was William Wilberforce, the MP who famously promoted the bill that abolished slavery in the British empire.

Turn right along the level sandy track by the monument. ❷ Turn left on the road. Ignore a signposted woodland footpath on the right, but just after turn right on a signposted bridleway. This leads into a field and skirts the edge of it, between the field fence on the left and the woodland on the right. The escarpment of the North Downs is seen to the left and ahead, with the spire of **Ranmore Common church** just peeping above the trees on top. Known as the 'Church of the North Downs', it was built in 1859 by Giles Gilbert Scott, architect of the Albert Memorial and St Pancras Station.

❸ After ½ mile pass between weatherboarded barns at Park Farm (just before them, ignore a right fork), with the old farmhouse seen to the left. Just after these barns, keep forward at a crossing of tracks then immediately take a path half right (waymarked with a yellow arrow) into a field, heading up into a wood of predominantly Scots pines, then on through a field to **Wotton Church**. Here is buried (with many others of his family) John Evelyn (1620–1706), whose famous diary covers the last 66 years of his life. He was a founder member of the Royal Society and a friend of that other great diarist Samuel Pepys. Many of the woodlands from here to Leith Hill are descended from his plantings.

Turn right at the churchyard (either walk through the churchyard or along the field edge), then go along the road and cross the A25 ❹. Take the small road to the left of the Wotton Hatch pub, immediately forking right through the pub car park and leave by a stile at the far end. Cross the field diagonally right, and take the stile in the very far right-hand corner of the field (avoid another stile in the right-hand fence on to a driveway just before this). This leads through woods, down into a small, open valley with **Wotton House** just glimpsed to the right. Now a training college, the house was home to John Evelyn, who died there. He recorded that it was 'sweetly environed with delicious streams and venerable woods . . . It has rising grounds, meadows, woods, water in abundance.'

The path goes up into more woodland, then drops to a T-junction of tracks just inside the woods ❺. Turn left. Through the trees on your right you have views of a chain of small lakes linked by weirs that supply water for the hammer pond at Friday Street. ¼ mile later, keep forward, avoiding a track to the right over a bridge and a stile to the left. Your track soon passes a brick cottage on the right; avoid left turns as you pass further houses and eventually reach the road at **Friday Street**. The tranquil tree-shaded hammer pond, made for the former iron industry, is just opposite, and you can detour along the road on its right-hand side for 200 yards to the Stephan Langton Inn.

To continue the walk, turn right on the road uphill, then after 50 yards, just after Copse Cottage on the right, where the road bends right take a deeply sunken path on the left ❻. Follow this path up through the woods. 70 yards after you cross an open strip beneath power lines, turn half right at a five-way path junction, continuing between slightly raised banks. 80 yards later, keep forward at the point you are rejoined by the power lines on your right.

❼ A further 150 yards after the power lines have rejoined the path, turn right at a crossing of paths and carry on in this direction until you emerge on a road (with a bus shelter away to the right on the opposite side). Cross over and take the path opposite along the right edge of a triangular green (to the left you can see **St James's Well**, dated 1893, with its quaintly decorative cover). At the next road cross to the signposted path opposite (or you can make a short cut by turning right along the road to the church and pub at Abinger Common; this saves about ¾ mile but the section is uninteresting; resume directions at ❾). This enters woodland: keep forward and ignore all side turns. Eventually the path narrows and drops steeply to a junction beyond a stile ❽.

Turn right to take the stile beside the gate (with a 'Private Property – Public Footpath Only' sign erected by Wotton Estate). The track soon bends right and heads along a quiet woodland valley, crossing beneath power lines after ½ mile (where ignore a path forking right along the power lines), then soon rising to a stile into a field. Carry on to the stile in the opposite hedgerow, cross the road and take the path opposite along the edge of **Abinger Common** village green to the pub and church ❾. Stocks still stand on the green of this unspoilt village, which can trace its history back some 10,000 years: Mesolithic remains of a human amputation have been unearthed locally. In recent years the church has had its share of misfortune and had to be substantially rebuilt twice: a flying bomb exploded nearby in 1944, and just twenty years later a bolt of lightning caused further damage.

Take the path through the churchyard, passing to the left of the church, then continue through an ornate gate on an enclosed path. This soon enters a field and continues beyond a cattle-grid as an enclosed track (ignore another path half right). Just before Raikes Farm ignore a path ahead and continue to the right into the farm. Just after the cottage and first barn on the left (just before a brick and timber cottage and where road surfacing begins), turn left on a short (easily missed) path to the road.

Turn right (avoid the track opposite) and then after 20 yards left on a signposted field path, heading diagonally across two fields and through a hedgerow ❿. In the third field immediately turn right and right again on an enclosed path between field boundaries (if stinging nettles are a problem, continue along the field edge and join this path at the next power post). This broadens and drops. At Paddington Farm it bends left and immediately right (by the farmhouse), then right past a pond and Paddington Mill of 1867 to the A25 ⓫. Cross over to the rising woodland path opposite. This soon crosses a field and enters the woods of **Abinger Roughs**, home to many woodland birds including great and lesser spotted woodpeckers, wood warbler, tree-creeper and nuthatch.

50 yards later turn right at a track junction and follow the main, sandy track past a glade (where you avoid a lesser track immediately to the right and another waymarked path just after to the left). This track soon drops gently; later fields appear a few yards to the left: carry on just inside the woods to reach the monument to Samuel Wilberforce. Here either turn right to the car park, or if you started from Friday Street car park continue ahead and pick up the directions at ❷.

The Wealden iron industry

For more than 2,000 years, from the late Iron Age to the early 19th century, the clay and sandstone area of the Weald between the North and South Downs was the major industrial area of Britain, the Black Country of its day.

From Tudor times, chains of ponds such as those near Friday Street were used to store water to power furnace bellows or for hammering the iron – hence the term 'hammer ponds'. They were also stocked with carp to provide for the compulsory 'fish days' ordained by Henry VIII in his bid to boost the fishing industry.

The ironstone was burnt with charcoal, then melted in the furnace; lumps of iron called 'pigs' could then be drawn off and hammered into marketable lengths. The scene must have been one of heat, noise and smoke, day and night – except when summer drought cut off the power supply.

The Wealden industry peaked in the early 1600s. It was gradually eclipsed by competition from cheaper imported Swedish iron and the new coke-fuelled processes developed in the Sheffield-Derby area and the West Midlands. But the Weald remained the specialist supplier of ships' guns for the Royal Navy throughout the 18th century.

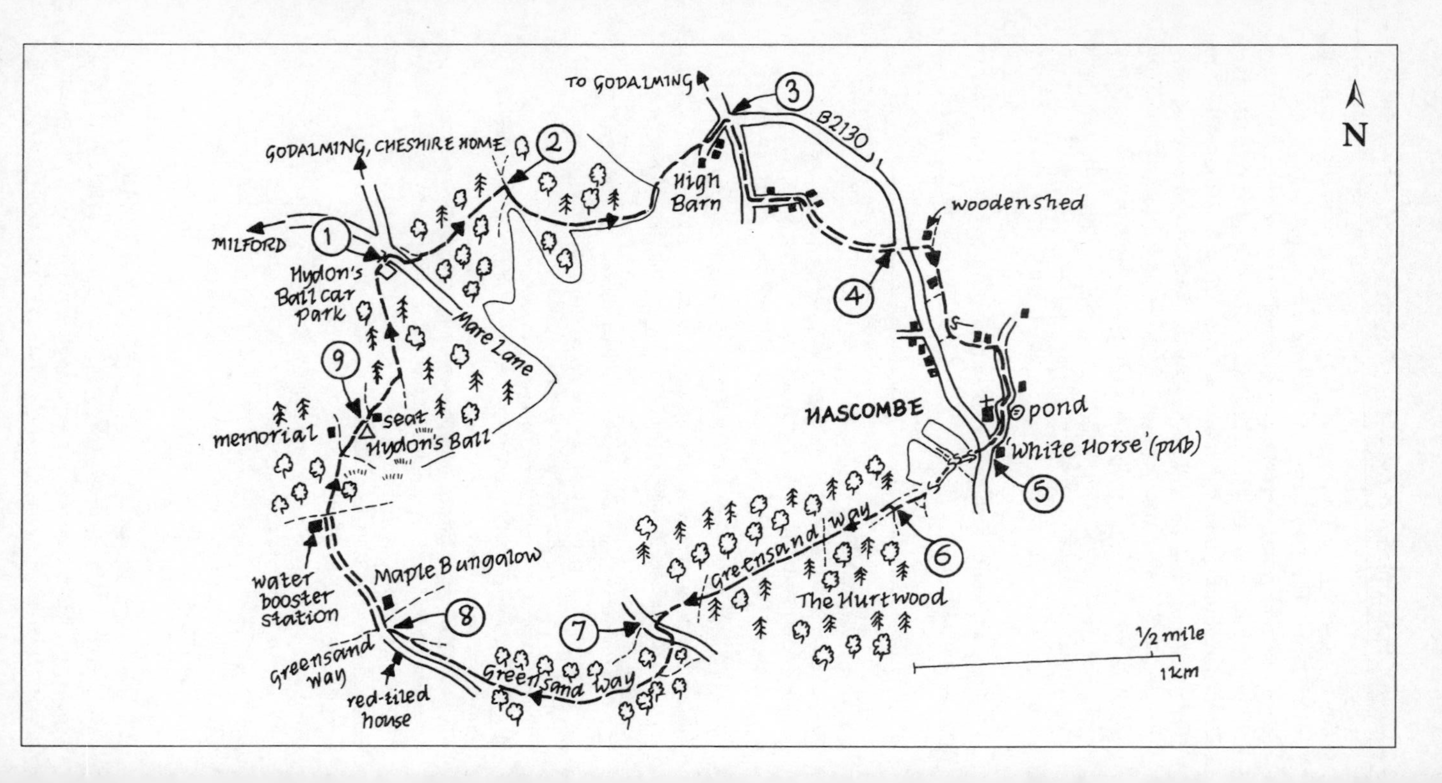
N
TO GODALMING
B2130
GODALMING, CHESHIRE HOME
High Barn
woodenshed
MILFORD
Hydon's Ball car park
Mare Lane
HASCOMBE
pond
'White Horse' (pub)
seat
memorial
Hydon's Ball
Greensand Way
The Hurtwood
water booster station
Maple Bungalow
Greensand Way
red-tiled house
Greensand Way
1/2 mile
1km
1
2
3
4
5
6
7
8
9

Hascombe and Hydon's Ball

SURREY WALK 37

This walk is half under the cover of trees, through the forest of The Hurtwood and Hydon's Ball, but opens out around the conspicuously attractive village of Hascombe, with its sumptuous Victorian church and pretty pond. The best of the views are reserved for later, from the Greensand Way and the bilberry- and bracken-clad summit of Hydon's Ball. One of the finest tree collections in the UK is just a mile north from Hascombe, at Winkworth Arboretum (National Trust; open daily during daylight hours), famed for its autumnal tints, shows of azaleas and carpets of bluebells.

White Horse, Hascombe GU8 4JA. ☎ (01483) 208252. Open Mon to Fri 11 to 3, 5.30 to 11, Sat 11 to 11, Sun 12 to 10.30; food 12 to 2.30, 7 to 10 (9.30 Sun). Castle Eden, Flowers IPA. This pub is well known for its attractive setting, child-friendly atmosphere and riverbank moorings. It is thoroughly traditional, with a virtually unaltered old bar room, and a larger dining area round the back. A la carte menu in restaurant, bar menu including traditional pub food, steaks, sandwiches, ploughman's, soup and bar snacks. Children welcome in eating area at back of pub. Dogs welcome.

Start: Hydon's Ball car park (inconspicuously marked by a small National Trust sign beside an approach track in the woods), off Salt Lane and 2½ miles south of Godalming. From Milford, take the turning for Milford Station; past the station, carry on at the crossroads at Hydestile (left is Godalming and a Cheshire Home) and continue along Salt Lane towards Hascombe and Dunsfold, into woodlands. Immediately after another left turn to Godalming and Cheshire Home turn right into Hydon's Ball car park.

From the B2130 from the east, take Markwick Lane, just south of Hascombe (signposted Hydestile and Milford), and follow it until you turn left at the National Trust sign for Hydon's Ball, just before a turn on the right to Godalming and Cheshire Home. Grid reference 979402.

Length: 6 miles (9.5 kilometres), 3 hours.

Difficulty: Moderate, with some steep sections; can be muddy or waterlogged.

OS maps: 1:25,000 Explorer sheets 133, 134 and 145; 1:50,000 Landranger sheet 186.

PT Buses (hourly, not Sun) from Guildford and Godalming pass the White Horse, Hascombe at ❺.

❶ Follow the track out of the car park and back to the road, along which turn right. After 50 yards, turn left on a signposted path, over a stile, then after only 10 yards turn right on a broad track. This gently drops for about 500 yards (about 5 minutes' walk). ❷ Turn right at the next junction, by a waymark post, and fork left uphill 30 yards later. This mostly fenced path takes a course through woodlands and more open areas, rising and dropping over more than ½ mile, finally joining a surfaced driveway coming from the Old Dairy and other houses. ❸ Just as you are about to reach the main road, turn right on a small road signposted 'Bridleway' (soon ignore driveways to High Leybourne and Garden Cottage).

At the next junction (after ¼ mile), by a power post on the right, turn left (signed with a number of house names, including Whinfold and High Hascombe). This road soon bends right in front of High Hascombe and continues as an unmade track, dropping and becoming increasingly uneven.

❹ Cross the main road and take the rising bridleway opposite. After 150 yards, by a wooden shed on the left, turn right at a T-junction of paths, and follow this for 500 yards (past two pet graves on the left), avoiding a right turn and then a stile on the left. By a second right turn (which you also avoid), the main path bends slightly left, and eventually reaches the end of a small road by cottages on the left (unusually pointed with nodules of ironstone). Turn right along the road, into Hascombe. You pass the **pond** – one of the best picnic spots on the walk (benches provided) – and **St Peter's Church**. This is a striking Victorian building of 1864 by Henry Woodyer, a pupil of the famous architect Butterfield; the push-button light switch is high up to the left as you enter (not obvious). The walls of the nave are painted with 153 fishes being caught in a net held by the six disciples, and the 500-year-old oak screen has been lavishly and quite spectacularly repainted (giving a good idea of how brightly such features would originally have appeared). The chancel is even more ornate, with a reredos depicting the Adoration of the Lamb, and its ribbed and gilded ceiling topped by a golden dove. Carry on past the church to the White Horse, on the main road.

❺ With your back to the White Horse, cross the road and take the signposted path slightly to the left. Cross a stile and walk along the left edges of two fields. Over the next 1¼ miles you are following the mostly waymarked **Greensand Way**. On entering woodland carry on up for 15 yards, then fork right on a narrow, very steeply rising path to reach a waymark post, where you turn right (it may be easier to keep left 15 yards after entering the woodland, on the main path, then turning right at the first junction, and keeping straight on at the waymark post).

❻ 200 yards later turn sharp right on a path marked with a blue arrow, and 15 yards further on turn left at a marker post (again with blue arrow/Greensand Way). This broad path leads straight through the forest (known as **The Hurtwood** – 'hurts' are a Surrey term for bilberries); ignore any side turns (mostly marked 'Walkers Welcome'). The path eventually drops.

❼ Turn left at the road and follow it downhill for 120 yards, then turn right on a signposted bridleway (still on the Greensand Way; this section can be muddy). This leads through rhododendron bushes (soon ignore a footpath signposted sharp left), and later emerges into the open, with **views** spreading southwards, encompassing the prominent escarpment of Black Down, the highest point in Sussex at 918 feet. Eventually the path re-enters woodland; where a lane appears on the left near a red-tiled house, avoid joining it but follow the path uphill. Ignore the next path waymarked to the right, and 20 yards later at the top turn left inside a field. The path skirts the field and drops to a lane ❽.

Turn right on the lane (at the point at which it becomes an unmade track), immediately avoiding a path crossing it (the route leaves the Greensand Way, which goes off to the left here), and follow the track, which passes to the left of Maple Bungalow. This section may be flooded after prolonged rain. At the edge of a wood by a brick Thames Water booster station on the left, carry on forward at a four-way junction, on a sunken path uphill. 300 yards later keep forward uphill at another four-way path crossing (the left branch passes a **stone memorial**, recording the donation of part of the Hydon's Ball estate to the National Trust in memory of soldiers killed at Hanover and in the Somme during the First World War). Turn right at a prominent manhole cover (marking part of an underground reservoir) to the stone bench at the summit of **Hydon's Ball** ❾. You gain another exceptionally attractive view of the Surrey and Sussex Weald from here, with the South Downs in the far distance. The woodland and scrub support nightingale, sparrowhawk and three varieties of woodpecker, and redpoll, brambling and siskin winter on the common. Take the path to the left of the stone bench; immediately behind the bench fork right, and descend to a T-junction with a broader path, along which you turn left and follow it down to the car park.

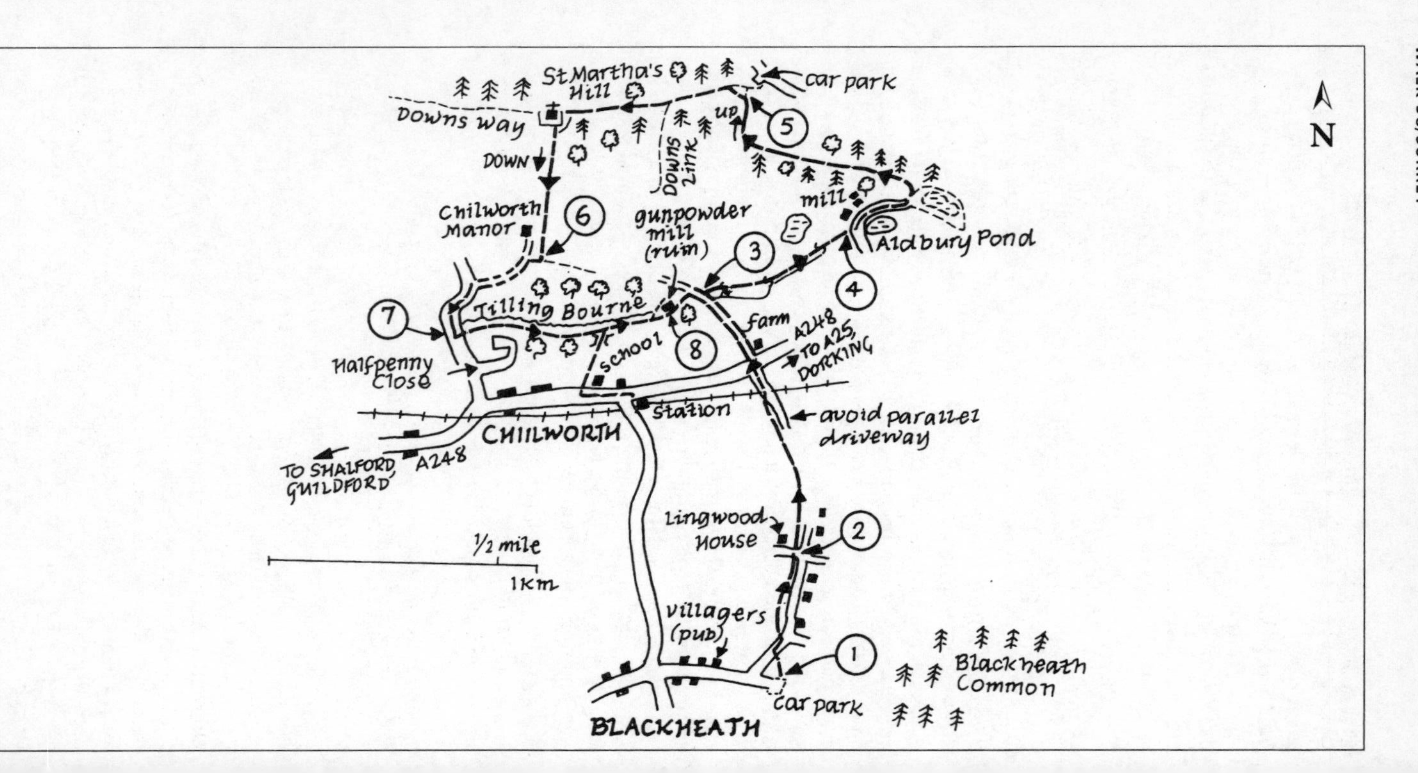
N
St Martha's Hill
car park
Downs Way
DOWN
up
5
Downs Link
mill
Chilworth Manor
6
gunpowder mill (ruin)
3
Aldbury Pond
4
7
Tilling Bourne
farm
A248
TO A25, DORKING
8
school
Halfpenny Close
station
avoid parallel driveway
CHILWORTH
TO SHALFORD, GUILDFORD
A248
Lingwood House
2
1/2 mile
1Km
Villagers (pub)
1
Blackheath Common
car park
BLACKHEATH

St Martha's Hill and the Gunpowder Mills

SURREY WALK 38

This short walk is packed with interest. It begins mildly enough, through attractive forest and then with more open views of a sandstone ridge. Past some former mill ponds, the route climbs on to St Martha's Hill, with its lone church perched on the summit. A very steep descent precedes the remarkable finale beside the Tilling Bourne, where eerie ruins of long defunct gunpowder mills stand in the woods. To keep route-finding as easy as possible (other paths through the woods around Blackheath can be confusing) and to avoid the main road, we have steered the walk to return the same way from the A248 to the car park at Blackheath. The walk also passes Chilworth Manor, where the gardens are occasionally open.

Villagers, Blackheath Lane, Blackheath Village, Surrey GU4 8RB. ☎ (01483) 893152. Open Mon to Sat 11 to 3, 6 to 11, Sun 12 to 4; food Mon to Sat 12 to 2.30, 7 to 9.30 (exc. Mon), Sun 12 to 2.30. Fuller's London's Pride, Courage Best, local Hogs Back beers. This is a low-ceilinged old pub in a peaceful location by the edge of the forest. Starters might include crispy whitebait or deep fried Camembert, while examples of main courses are fillet of lamb casserole or vegetarian pesto lasagne. Fresh fish is a speciality, and steaks and home-made steak and kidney pie are also on offer. Children welcome in dining area. Dogs welcome in village bar.

Red Lion, Shamley Green GU5 0UB (off the route on B2128, 4 miles south-east of Guildford). ☎ (01483) 892202. Mon to Sat 11 to 11, Sun 12 to 10.30; food Mon to Sat 12 to 3, 6.30 to 10, Sun 12 to 3, 7 to 9.30. Neat, white-painted pub opposite village green. Young's Bitter, Flowers Original and Greene King Abbot Ale. A la carte menu in restaurant, daily specials, toasties, sandwiches, jacket potatoes, ploughman's and salads. Restaurant menu has traditional food. Children welcome if eating. No dogs.

Start: Free car park at Blackheath Common, south-east of Guildford. Turn south from the A248 at Chilworth railway station (signposted Blackheath and Shamley Green), and after ¾ mile turn left along Sample Oak Lane at the crossroads (signposted Farley Heath). The car park is at the end of the road and is marked by a Waverley Countryside sign for Blackheath Common. Grid reference 036463.

Alternative start: Chilworth (limited roadside parking in village; start either by the station (see public transport details for directions) or turn off the A248 at the level crossing into Blacksmith Lane and then park along Halfpenny Close on the right (begin the walk by turning right out of Halfpenny Close, along Blacksmith Lane, then just before the road crosses a stream turn right through a gate into the woods at ❼. Grid references 031473 and 025474.

Length: Full walk 5 miles (8 kilometres), 2½ hours; short walk from Chilworth omitting sections ❶ and ❷ 3 miles (5 kilometres), 1½ hours.

Difficulty: Moderate, on clearly marked paths and all on sandy terrain. The steady climb up St Martha's Hill is followed by a very steep descent, but the soil is virtually pure sand and grips very well even after rain.
OS maps: 1:25,000 Explorer sheet 145; 1:50,000 Landranger sheet 186.
Shops in Chilworth.
PT Train to Chilworth. Go to the main road in front of the station, and turn left along it. After 100 yards, just past a primary school, turn right on an enclosed path (signposted Vera's Path), which you follow into the woods. Just after the footbridge, turn right at the path T-junction and join the walk directions at ❸.

❶ With the road behind you, find a path on the left (marked by a blue-topped post), midway along the car park (avoid the more obvious broad track beyond the barrier at the far end of the car park by the notice board), leading through woodland. Reach a small road and turn right along it. 75 yards later (just before the road divides) turn left on a woodland path to the right of the bridleway signpost and to the left of the 'private road' sign.
❷ Cross an unmade road and take the enclosed path opposite (to the right of Lingwood House). Keep left on a yellow-arrowed footpath (avoiding the potentially muddy blue-arrowed bridleway parallel on the right; the two routes later merge). This emerges into the open. You join a driveway coming in from the right, and cross a bridge over the railway. Cross the A248, where there are views of St Martha's Hill (with its hilltop church), which you will later reach. Take the track opposite, signposted Downs Link.

Just before the track is about to cross a stream (the Tilling Bourne) turn sharp right over a stile and ❸ follow the signposted direction across the field to the next stile, and maintain the same direction in the second field to a stile near a power post. The path then proceeds close to a fence on the right.

❹ Emerge on a road by Postford Pond and turn left along it, past the former mill. At the beginning of the next pond (Waterloo Pond) keep left, and fork left 40 yards later on a woodland path just after a bridge and at the end of the pond. The path eventually bends right and rises steeply. ❺ Bear left at a fork, and soon after turn left at a T-junction on the ridge (where the view opens out ahead) and follow the sandy track that rises to the church on the summit of **St Martha's Hill**. There is a lovely southerly outlook over the Weald and towards the South Downs from here. The church, largely rebuilt in carrstone (coarse ironstone and sandstone) in 1848 after its predecessor had collapsed, can be reached only by footpath. Its dedication may be to the St Martha who is said to have come here with Joseph of Arimathea; or the name may be a corruption of St Martyr's – a legend tells of a massacre of Christians hereabouts. The summit marks the northern end of the long-distance **Downs Way**, which links the North Downs Way and the South Downs Way, and ends at Shoreham-by-Sea.

Go into the churchyard of St Martha's, and turn left once you are level with the benches beneath the tower. Leave the churchyard between the pair of yews at the bottom and continue steeply down, by a fence corner on your right. Ignore a crossing-path and continue down to the bottom. ❻ Just after passing Chilworth Manor, seen away to the right, turn right at a path T-junction, and soon after turn left at a T-junction with the drive coming from the manor. Alternatively, you can detour to the right to visit the walled garden of **Chilworth Manor**, with its lavender walk, wisteria and herbaceous border; there is also a woodland area with azaleas and rhododendrons (open occasionally from April to July, phone for times, tel (01483) 561414).

Turn left on joining the public road (known as Halfpenny Lane). You pass a fishing pond away to the left. Just after passing over the brick road bridge over the Tilling Bourne, turn left through a gate ❼. Follow this path through the woods. A panel by the entrance has a map showing the location of the former **gunpowder mill**, as well as remains of its wharf. You later pass a line of eight millstones on the left. Just before two picnic benches on the left, the swing bridge and path to the right mark the line of a former tramway of 1888 that served the gunpowder works (if you have started from Chilworth station, return along this path back to the start). Gunpowder was made here for three centuries up to 1920; the valley must have been a noisy place, with frequent explosions, the biggest killing half a dozen people in 1901.

❽ Keep to the right of the large derelict mill of 1885 and reach an unmade track.

For the short walk omitting Blackheath turn right over the bridge and immediately left over the stile and resume the walk at ❸.

For the full walk turn right over the bridge and retrace your steps to the start (go over the A248, then just after the railway keep right on a sandy track, avoiding the private driveway parallel to the left. Later, where you enter the woods, keep right along the footpath, avoiding the potentially muddy bridleway parallel to the left. After the fence on the right ends, cross over an unmade road and take the bridleway ahead – avoiding another bridleway half right, and walking parallel to a driveway on the left. At the next road, opposite an electrical substation, it is simplest now to turn right along it to reach a T-junction at Blackheath Common – the Villagers pub is to the right, and the car park is to the left.

Blackheath Common has plenty of scope for strolling after you have finished the main walk, with a maze of broad, sandy tracks through the forest. Nightjars and woodlarks are summer residents, and the heathland supports populations of adders and sand lizards.

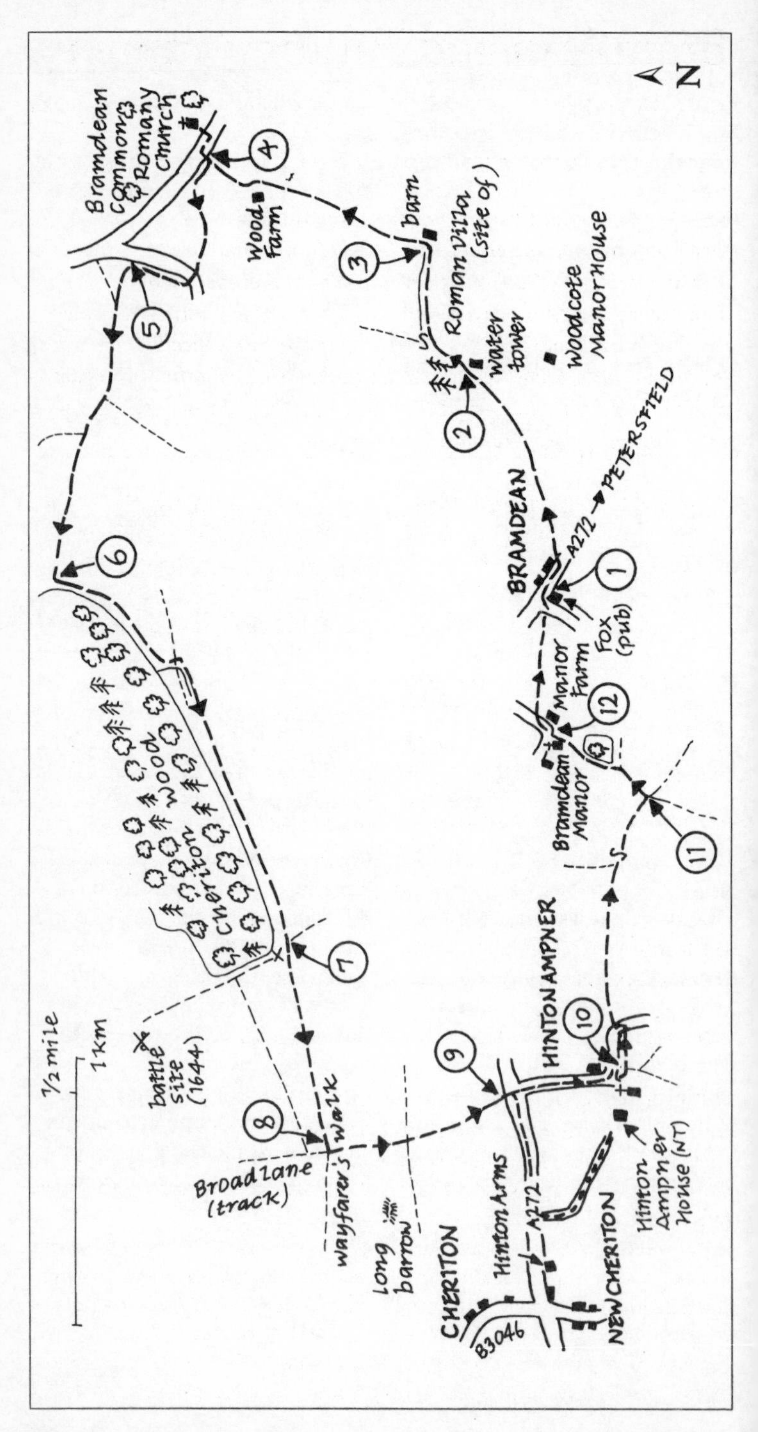
N
Bramdean Common
Romany Church
4
Wood Farm
barn
3
Roman Villa (site of)
water tower
2
Woodcote Manor House
PETERSFIELD
BRAMDEAN
A272
1
Fox (pub)
Manor Farm
12
Bramdean Manor
11
5
6
Cheriton Wood
7
½ mile
1 km
battle site (1644)
8
Wayfarer's Walk
Broad Lane (track)
Long barrow
9
HINTON AMPNER
10
Hinton Ampner House (NT)
Hinton Arms
A272
CHERITON
B3046
NEW CHERITON

Bramdean and Hinton Ampner

HAMPSHIRE WALK 39

This gently undulating and fairly undemanding walk, mainly across farmland, links a variety of highlights. Bramdean Common has long been popular with the Romany people, and in the woodland here is their own tiny gem of church. Next you pass the site of the particularly bloody Civil War battle of Cheriton, where fields are now peacefully grazed by sheep and cattle. Finally, a short detour takes in a delightful shrub garden at Hinton Ampner (closed in the winter), a 20th-century creation with superb views of the surrounding countryside.

Fox Inn, Bramdean SO24 0LP. ☎ (01962) 771363. Open Mon to Sat 11 to 3, 6.30 (6 summer) to 11, Sun 12 to 3, 7 to 10.30; food 12 to 2, 7 to 9 (no food Sun D Jan and Feb). Greene King Abbot Ale. The pub is neatly kept and comfortable with cushioned benches, warm-coloured brick walls, a roaring log fire, low ceilings and a large three-sided bar. Fish is the speciality here, with perhaps avocado and prawns, red snapper or locally smoked trout on offer. Non-fish options might be mushroom soup, braised beef in red wine or roast rack of lamb. It is advisable to book for meals, especially at Sunday lunch-time. No children. Small dogs welcome.

Hinton Arms, Petersfield Road, Hinton Ampner SO24 0NH. ☎ (01962) 771252. Open Mon to Sat 11 to 3, 6 to 11, Sun 12 to 3, 7 to 10.30, closed Mon Jan to Easter; food Mon to Sat 11.30 to 2.30, 6.30 to 9.30, Sun 12 to 2.30, 7 to 9. Beers from 8 local breweries. Bar food, daily specials, restaurant, seasonal food, Sunday roast. No children under 14 in bar. No dogs in restaurant.

Start: The Fox Inn, Bramdean, on the A 272. Grid reference 616278.
Length: 6 miles (9.5 kilometres); 3 hours.
Difficulty: Easy to moderate.
OS maps: 1:25,000 Explorer sheet 132; 1:50,000 Landranger sheet 185.
Hinton Ampner House.
PT Irregular bus service to Bramdean from Winchester and Petersfield (not Sun).

❶ Turn right out of the Fox Inn on to the A272, walking on the pavement, as far as the speed derestriction signs. Cross the road to turn left up a track. As the main track swings left behind houses, keep ahead, up the right-hand edge of the field and to the right of a clump of trees, with views over the hedge on your right of 17th-century Woodcote Manor House. As you draw parallel with a water tower on the right, the path may be a bit overgrown, but keep heading for the right-hand end of the trees ahead ❷.

Go into the trees and at the first yellow waymark keep straight ahead. At the next waymark post, at the end of the trees, turn left over the stile and then keep right, to follow the edge of the field with a hedge on your left. Ignore the stile on the left after 50 yards, continuing round the field. Over to the right of the barn ahead of you is the site of a Roman villa. Early 19th-century excavations revealed two good mosaic floors, but it has all been reburied.

❸ At the barn turn left on to a track to Wood Farm, noting the elegant green-copper cupola on a building to the left, and an old horse-drawn caravan overrun with brambles on the right. At the junction with the drive to the house, keep right. At the end of the drive ❹, turn right on to the road for a few yards to a sign, on the other side of the road, indicating a path through the trees to the **Church in the Woods**, a Romany church founded in about 1900, when Bramdean Common was home to numerous gipsy families. The area is still popular with the Romany people, and services are held in the corrugated tin church. Its tiny graveyard is carefully kept.

Retrace your steps to the end of Wood Farm drive and turn right on to Bramdean Common. Bear left and take the left-hand path where the way divides, to pass in front of several houses. Meet an unsurfaced track and keep ahead to the road. Cross the road, turn right, walking on the wide grass verge as far as a broad track leading off to the left ❺.

Follow this across the common and then along the edge of woodland beneath beech, hazel, oak and holly trees. A short patch may be muddy after rain. Views through breaks in the hedge are over the downland to the south.

Reach a T-junction at the edge of Cheriton Wood ❻ and turn left on to a path running along the edge of the trees. Keep straight on through a gate, reach an open field and turn left with the path as it narrows round the corner. In 50 yards keep ahead at a crossing of paths and follow the path as, almost immediately, it turns right, edging the long, narrow field on your right. On the left are superb views over a comfortable landscape of arable fields and hedges to the rooftops of Bramdean village and, further right, the bell-tower of Hinton Ampner House.

❼ At the end of the long field, keep ahead to emerge on a track. Turn right and after 25 paces reach a waymarked gate on the left.

To continue the walk, turn left through the gate.

For a short detour, keep ahead on the track to the brow of the next hill. The fields of pasture all around you make a peaceful scene now, but in 1644 they were the site of a gory Civil War encounter, the **Battle of Cheriton**. The battle (won by the Roundheads) was a violent one, with some 2,500 men killed. The lanes are said to have run with blood, and farmers occasionally plough up relics even today. Retrace your steps to the gate and go through it.

Walk along the left-hand edge of the field, with clear views right towards the battle site.

❽ Turn left on to Broad Lane and join the **Wayfarer's Walk** on its way from Inkpen Beacon in Berkshire to Emsworth on the south coast. At the next crossing of paths, stand on the stile on the right to get a view of a Neolithic long barrow. Keep ahead to the A272 ❾.

*To visit **Hinton Ampner House and Garden*** (National Trust; garden open April to September, Tuesday,

Wednesday, Saturday, Sunday, bank holiday Monday 1.30 to 5.30; house open April to September, Tuesday, Wednesday, and August Saturday and Sunday, 1.30 to 5.30), cross the road and walk along the grass verge for ¼ mile to the bottom of the ¼-mile drive (about 100 yards beyond the drive is the Hinton Arms, a comfortable pub with a large garden). Leave the grounds by taking the path to the right of the church (entrance to the gardens is not permitted here) and turn right on to a footpath opposite the gate at the east end of the church. Continue from ⑩.

If you are not visiting Hinton Ampner, cross the A272 and walk up the lane opposite. Where the lane swings left, keep ahead to the ancient Church of All Saints, Hinton Ampner. The door to the vestry is Saxon, as is the long-and-short stonework in the north-east corner of the nave. (There is no access to Hinton Ampner House or Garden from here.) Opposite the church gate, turn left on a footpath.

⑩ Go through a kissing-gate and walk straight ahead across the field. At the road, turn left and immediately right on a footpath. Keep ahead through a five-bar gate, with a hedge on the left. After crossing a stile and as you draw up with a line of trees on your right, turn left on to a waymarked bridleway across the middle of a field ⑪.

Where a path joins from the right, keep ahead downhill, with a hedge on your right. In the bottom corner go right, through trees and a kissing-gate. Keep to the right-hand edge of the field. Go through a waymarked kissing-gate, turn left and go through another kissing-gate into the churchyard of **St Simon and St Jude**, Bramdean, originally Norman, with a lot of 19th-century work.

⑫ Leave the churchyard by the lych-gate. Just past Manor Farm, turn right on a footpath that takes you straight across fields to meet a track. Cross this and follow the path over one more field to the Fox Inn car park.

Hinton Ampner Garden

The garden at Hinton Ampner is testimony to the claim of its creator that what he wanted above all else from a garden was tranquillity. It also belies his description of himself as 'not a very knowledgeable plantsman'. When Ralph Dutton, eighth and last Lord Sherborne, inherited the estate in 1936 and embarked on remodelling both house and garden, he laid out the garden to take full advantage of the views over the surrounding countryside, siting trees and statues to give unexpected vistas from the terraced walks. The design is formal, but the planting, mainly shrubs, is informal, with colours kept subtle and muted. The house was ravaged by fire in 1960 but has been restored, and displays Ralph Dutton's collection of Italian paintings.

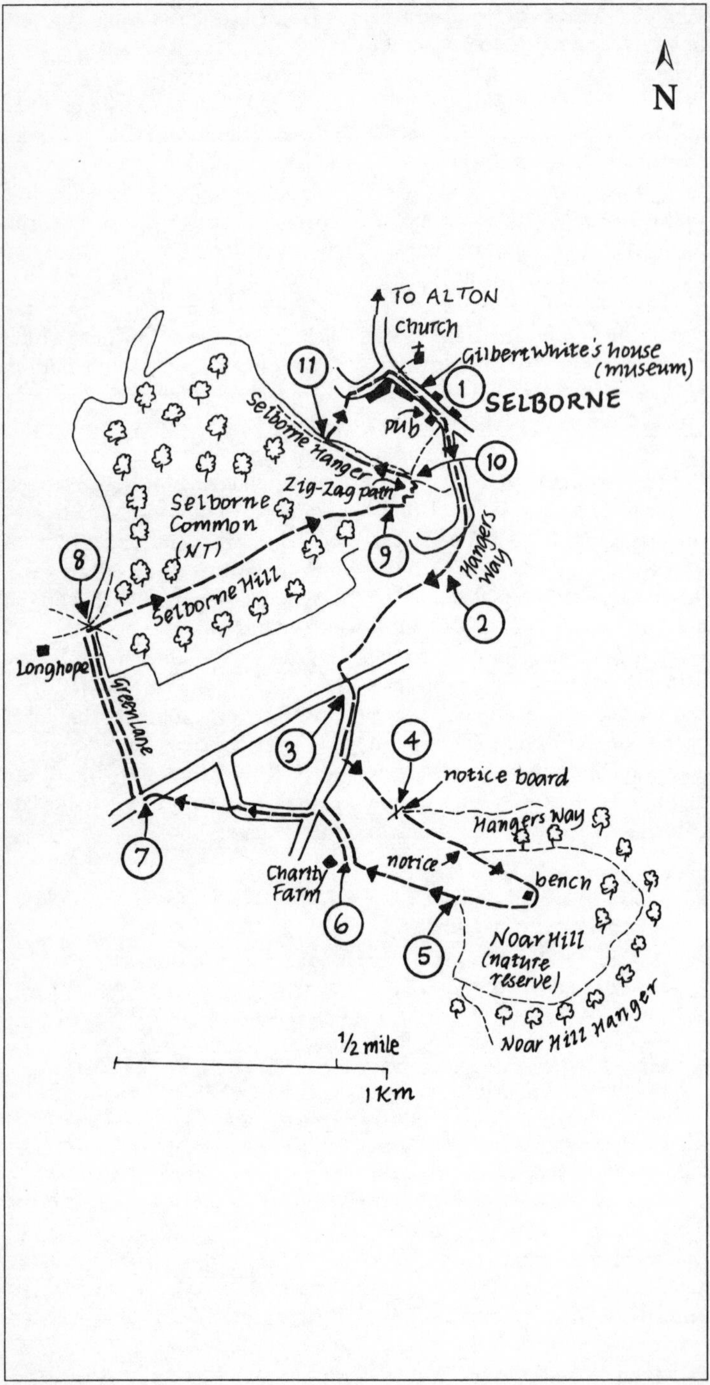
N
TO ALTON
church
Gilbert White's house
(museum)
SELBORNE
pub
Selborne Hanger
Zig-Zag path
Selborne Common
(NT)
Selborne Hill
Hangers Way
Longhope
Green Lane
notice board
Hangers Way
notice
bench
Charity Farm
Noar Hill
(nature reserve)
Noar Hill Hanger
1/2 mile
1Km
1
2
3
4
5
6
7
8
9
10
11

Selborne and Noar Hill

HAMPSHIRE WALK 40

The countryside in and around Selborne was a constant source of inspiration to its most famous resident, the 18th-century naturalist Reverend Gilbert White. This walk begins by heading out of the village to Noar Hill. Preserved as a nature reserve, it is as delightful a habitat for chalk grassland fauna and flora now as it must have been in White's day. The walk then makes its way through the beech woods of Selborne Hill to descend back into the village via the Zig-Zag, a flight of steps cut into the side of Selborne Hanger by Gilbert White and his brother.

Selborne Arms, High Street, Selborne GU34 3JR. ☎ (01420) 511247. Open Mon to Thur 11 to 3, 5.30 to 11, Fri to Sun all day; food 12 to 2/2.15, 7 to 9.30 (10 Fri to Sun). Fuller's London Pride, Courage Best, Gilbert White, Leywood. Steak, game, venison, pasta, curry, chicken, soup. Children welcome. Guide dogs only.

Queen's Hotel, High Street, Selborne GU34 3JJ. ☎ (01420) 511454. Open Mon to Sat 10am to 11pm, Sun 10 (for coffee) to 10.30; food 12 to 9.20. Ushers beers. Set, specials, à la carte and round-the-world menus, sandwiches. Children welcome. Dogs welcome.

Start: Village car park behind the Selborne Arms; grid reference 742335.
Length: 4 miles (6.5 kilometres); 2 hours.
Difficulty: Moderate.
OS maps: 1:25,000 Explorer sheet 133; 1:50,000 Landranger sheet 186.
Cafés in the village, including Gilbert White's House Tea Parlour (Open 11 to 5 daily).
WC In car park.
PT Train: Alton station is 4 miles away. Limited bus service to Selborne from Alton (Mon to Sat).

❶ At the car park entrance, with the village high street on your left, take the tarmac lane signed 'Unsuitable for motors' and 'Hangers Way'. Fork left off the tarmac road on to a gravelly track, following the Hangers Way sign. At a bungalow called Lavenham take the waymarked path immediately to the left of a five-bar gate. This narrow path skirts the fields beneath the trees on Selborne Hill.

❷ Continue straight on through a stile and a gate over fields of grazing land. As the Way climbs slightly, catch views over the hedge on your left of wooded Noar Hill and the countryside beyond. Crossing more stiles, the route runs between a house and its paddocks and then follows the right-hand edge of a paddock to reach a stile with the Hangers Way signed left. Do not cross the stile, but turn left along the edge of the field to the road ❸.

Cross the road and walk down the lane opposite, signed Noar Hill. Past Lower Noar Hill Farm, take a track, signed 'Bridleway', on the left that leads up towards the trees on the top of Noar Hill.

❹ At the notice board, keep straight on up the broad chalky track. Reach a pair of gates by another notice board and go through the small gate. Follow the broad grassy track gently uphill and round to the left across scrub and grassland. When the way divides into four paths, take the second one from the right, more or less straight ahead, with a grassy mound and then an overgrown pit on your left. This is one of several **medieval chalk quarries** on the hill. Come to a clearing at a T-junction, with a bench conveniently placed to pause and admire the distant views beyond the hangers at the far side of the field in front of you. Turn right along the path, back into trees.

❺ High Common is to the right and it is well worth leaving the path now and then to explore a little. **Noar Hill** is one of Hampshire's best examples of chalk grassland, notable for its numerous species of orchid – notably musk orchids – and its variety of butterflies, including Duke of Burgundy. Numerous humps and bumps around the old chalk pits are home to scores of rabbits, who skitter away into the bushes at your intrusion. There's a wonderful feeling that nature has the upper hand here, with birds singing lustily, and butterflies relishing the multi-coloured carpet of wild flowers. Find a spot to sit and drink it all in for a few restorative moments.

The path continues westwards broad and clear. Charity Farm comes into view at the foot of the hill; ahead is Selborne Hill and to the left of it a big house called Longhope. The path drops down to a gate near another disused chalk pit. Leave the nature reserve through the gate ❻, with farm buildings to the left. Meet the unmade road that leads to the farm and turn right. Turn left on to the road at the end, then almost immediately right, for a short stretch of road walking. There is no pavement, but it is a quiet road. Just after the road takes a right-angled bend, go left at a footpath sign through a gap in the hedge and walk diagonally across the field to a gap in the hedge opposite ❼.

Cross the road carefully and enter the seductive Green Lane

Gilbert White

The Revd Gilbert White was born in the vicarage in Selborne in 1720 but spent most of his life in the Wakes, dying there in 1793. After completing his education, he become curate at nearby Farringdon, and then Selborne. A man of charm, with a wide circle of friends, he loved his garden and his frequent rides on horseback around the neighbourhood, observing and recording with freshness and humour every minute detail of natural life. His notebooks and letters are immortalised in *The Natural History and Antiquities of Selborne*, published first in 1788 and in numerous later editions, and are a delightful read.

opposite. This is an ancient track, with beech, ash and sycamore on either side arching over to form a tunnel. It starts to climb more steeply as it reaches the edge of the trees on Selborne Hill, with Longhope House on the left.

❽ At a clearing and a meeting of ways, take the second path on the right, signposted as a footpath. Follow the wide grassy path through the trees, mainly beech and oak, ignoring paths to the left or right. Eventually reach a point where there is a view over the valley ahead, as you draw parallel with a house behind a hedge on the right. Take the left-hand fork here. This brings you to a short flight of wooden steps, at the top of the **Zig-Zag**, a path cut by Gilbert White and his brother in 1753. Sit on the seat and enjoy the view over the village, as Gilbert White did so often ❾.

Walk left from the seat a couple of paces, then turn right to take the steps behind the large boulder and follow the Zig-Zag path down to the foot of the hanger. As you descend you get a clear view of White's 18th-century house, **The Wakes**, with its polygonal gable and half-timbering.

❿ At the bottom of the Zig-Zag, with a notice board and map on the left, go straight ahead on to Love Lane, immediately to the left of a concrete National Trust collection box.

To return directly to the car park take the path on the right, through the gate.

To continue With a wooden fence on your right and the beech hanger on your left, Love Lane is a pretty path along the edge of the parkland, grazed by sheep, at the back of The Wakes. Here, on a barrel set on a little mound, is White's revolving '**Wine Pipe**', through which he surveyed the park and the hanger. Between the park and the house, the garden has been restored to its 18th-century form.

⓫ At the hedge, turn right over a stile and follow the right-hand edge of the field. Turn right on to the quiet lane at the end. At the main road through the village, turn right. Cross over to The Plestor (the word means Play Place) to visit the pottery and the **Norman church**. Gilbert White is buried in the churchyard. The famous Selborne yew fell down in the storm of 1990. It was replanted but failed to survive. A cutting taken from the original tree has been planted opposite the church door. Across the street is Gilbert White's house and garden, **The Wakes**, housing the **Gilbert White's House Museum**, the **Oates Museum** and a tea parlour (you do not have to pay admission to the museum to take tea here. The museum is open all week 11 to 5; closed 25 December to 1 January). The Oates Museum commemorates Captain Lawrence Oates, who accompanied Scott to the South Pole, and his uncle Frank, a Victorian explorer. Continue along the street to the Selborne Arms and the car park.

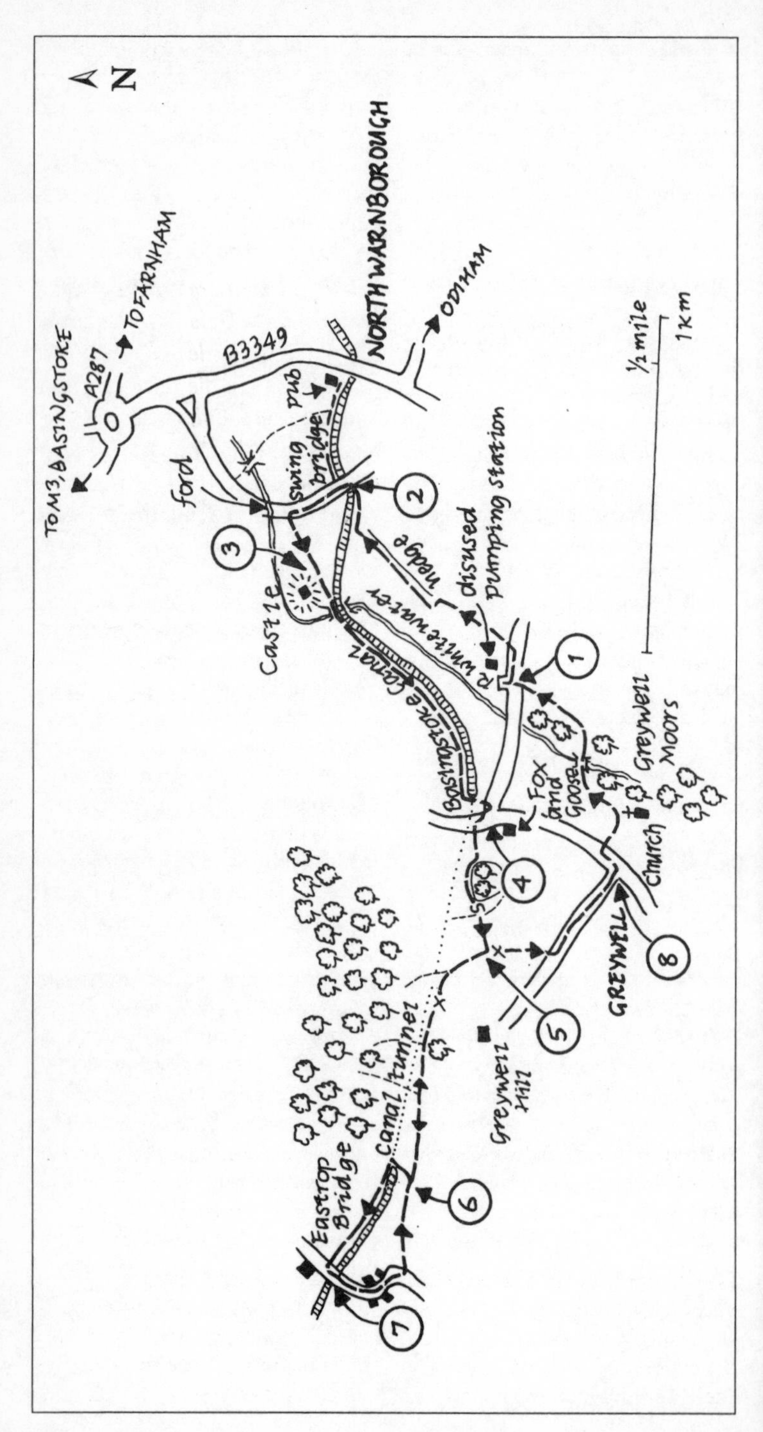
N
TO M3, BASINGSTOKE
A287
TO FARNHAM
B3349
NORTH WARNBOROUGH
ODIHAM
ford
swing bridge
pub
Castle
hedge
disused pumping station
R Whitewater
Basingstoke Canal
Fox and Goose
Greywell Moors
Church
GREYWELL
Greywell Hill
canal tunnel
Eastrop Bridge
1
2
3
4
5
6
7
8
½ mile
1 km

Greywell and the Basingstoke Canal

HAMPSHIRE — WALK 41

Two very different stretches of the Basingstoke Canal are explored in this walk. The first stage, popular with local walkers, follows the towpath alongside a navigable stretch of water by St John's Castle and ends at the eastern portal of the Greywell Tunnel, famous for the bats that have colonised it since its collapse. After crossing Greywell Hill, the second stage of the walk picks up the canal again at the tunnel's western portal, deep in woodland, silent and all but secret. It is an area rich in wildlife, and the walk will be of particular interest to nature-lovers. Walking is mainly level apart from the gradual climb up Greywell Hill.

The Swan, Hook Road, North Warnborough RG29 1EX. ☎ (01256) 702727. Open Mon to Wed 11.30 to 3, Thur 11.30 to 3, 5.30 to 11, Fri and Sat 11.30 to 11, Sun 12 to 10.30; food Mon to Sat 12.30 to 2.30, Mon to Thurs 7 to 9, Fri and Sat 7 to 9.30, Sun 12 to 2.30. Courage Best and 3 guest ales. Bar snacks, à la carte menu plus specials, ploughman's and sandwiches. Children welcome. Dogs welcome.

Anchor, The Street, North Warnborough RG29 1BE. ☎ (01256) 702740. Open Tues to Sat 11 to 3, Mon to Sat 5.30 to 11, Sun 12 to 4, 7 to 10.30; food Tues to Sat 12 to 2, 5.30 to 8, Sun 12 to 2. Courage Best. Set menu and blackboard specials, sandwiches. Children welcome. Dogs welcome.

Fox & Goose Inn, The Street, Greywell, RG29 1BY. ☎ (01256) 702062. Open Mon to Sat 11 to 11, Sun 12 to 10.30; food 12 to 10. Beers change regularly. Home-cooked food, game, fish, daily specials, cream teas and ice-cream. Children welcome if eating. Dogs welcome on a lead.

Start: Entrance to Greywell Pumping Station (disused), on the minor road leading from Greywell to North Warnborough and Odiham. Grid reference 723514.
Length: 4¼ miles (7 kilometres) with an additional ¼ mile each way on towpath to The Swan, North Warnborough; 2½ hours (additional 15 minutes if including The Swan).
Difficulty: Easy (except for a short scramble down to the west portal of the canal).
OS maps: 1:25,000 Explorer sheet 144; 1: 50,000 Landranger sheet 186.
PT Irregular bus service to Greywell from Basingstoke and Alton (not Sun).

❶ With the Pumping Station behind you, turn left on to the road and take the first footpath on the left, immediately beyond the first house after the pumping station. Follow this round to its end, cross the stile and turn right along the right-hand edge of the field. Over to the left the ruins of **King John's Castle** rise above the trees. At the end of the field, cross the stile and turn right on to the canal towpath to the swing bridge ❷. If you are lucky you may see this being raised to allow a narrowboat through. Cross the bridge.

For a short detour (¼ mile each way) to The Swan in North Warnborough, cross the bridge and turn right down to the towpath. Immediately after passing under a road bridge, leave the towpath, taking the steps on the left up to the road. The Swan is opposite. Retrace your steps from the pub and continue the walk.

To continue go along the lane to a ford, where the River Whitewater flows across the lane. Just before the ford, take the signed footpath to the left, over a stile and across the field to the canal towpath. Turn right on to the towpath. Shortly, leave the towpath to walk round the ruins of the **castle** keep ❸ built in 1207 by King John as a hunting lodge and stopover point en route between Windsor and Winchester. the castle's moat and outer baileys.

Return to the towpath and continue right, soon crossing over the River Whitewater, which here flows underneath the canal bed, at right angles to it. Shortly after this, reach what is now the end of the navigable stretch of the canal, a turning area for narrowboats. Beyond this point, the canal gets increasingly overgrown, with ducks, dabchicks, coots and moorhen, as well as watervoles, stickleback and perch quietly busying themselves in the weed. Over the decades the canal has become a nature reserve in its own right, supporting some 26 types of dragonfly and a profuse and fascinating variety of water plants.

The bridge ahead marks the point where the canal goes into the famous bat tunnel under Greywell Hill. Steps lead down to the tunnel entrance, but take care as they are slippery. Follow the towpath up to the right, cross the bridge and follow the path to the road ❹.

The Greywell Tunnel

The Basingstoke Canal, completed in 1792 and 37 miles long, linked Basingstoke with the Wey Navigation at West Byfleet. A 1,230-yard tunnel was constructed to take the canal through, rather than around, Greywell Hill. In 1932 the roof of this tunnel collapsed and, although for some years after that canoes could get through, the tunnel is now thought to be totally blocked for about a quarter of its length. Chalk springs, which feed the canal, keep the temperature in the tunnel constant, and the blockage ensures it is both draught-free and undisturbed. The unique micro-climate that has developed is ideal for hibernating bats and, as home to an estimated 12,500 bats, the tunnel is now the largest bat roost in Britain, supporting the second-largest colony of Natterer's bats in the world. The tunnel has been declared a Site of Special Scientific Interest.

A notice board gives a full history. The route of the Basingstoke Canal, constructed in 1792, went through

To return directly to your car turn left along the road.

To continue the walk, turn right

on the road and reach a T-junction. The Fox & Goose Inn is diagonally left.

To continue the walk, turn right at the T-junction and after a few yards turn left at a footpath sign. Trees give way to the open parkland of Greywell Hill, the large house visible ahead. Cross a stile and keep straight on, along the left-hand edge of the field to a small gate on the left at the edge of the woodland ❺. Here, turn right across the park in front of the house, following a handpainted sign 'Tunnel' and heading for a large oak tree. At the second large tree, go left, as signed, to reach a gate at the edge of woodland. Through the gate, follow the path ahead downhill, into the trees.

You are now walking almost on top of the tunnel, which lies to the right, parallel to your path. Keep ahead across two tracks, following the bridleway and tunnel signs. Pass a pond in the trees on your left, and then another small pond on the right. Continue ahead on the bridleway, now a narrow path, with fields on your left and deep, silent woodland on the right. Think of those boatmen 'legging' it for six hours to get their boat through the tunnel beneath these trees. Look out for a tree with a 'Tunnel' notice (at the time of writing, this was broken) pinned to it and, immediately before it, on the right, a notice board saying 'Permissive footpath. Walkers only' ❻.

Take the steep path downhill into the trees (it may be slippery), with a wooden fence on the right, and suddenly, in the depths of the woods, there on the left is the canal again, a flat ribbon of bright green duckweed running between tall trees. Over the portal of the canal is a notice board about the canal. Walk over the bridge on top of the portal and take the path down on to the towpath, to the left of a retaining wall (again, this may be slippery). Look back, carefully, at the tunnel entrance – it is very overgrown, and gridded and fenced off for safety.

Continue ahead along the towpath, with trees high on either side. The canal is restored but is not navigable; the silence, deep in the woods, is slightly spooky, and this is a very different canal scene from that at North Warnborough.

❼ At the first bridge, Eastrop Bridge, leave the towpath on the path up to the right and walk left over the bridge. Follow the lane past some attractive old houses, and on the corner where the lane bends to the right keep straight ahead on the signed bridleway, back into the woodland, passing point ❻, where you went down into the trees to the canal's west portal. Retrace your steps to the gate at the edge of the woods, up to the large tree, and across the parkland to the small metal gate to the left of trees at ❺.

Keep ahead through this gate, following the right-hand side of the field, with views of Greywell village to the left, and soon drawing parallel with the private road to Greywell Hill. Go through the right-hand of the two gates at the end of the field and continue down to the road ❽.

Turn left, walking on the right-hand side of the road (no pavement) to the church lych-gate. For the Fox and Goose Inn, keep ahead.

To return to your car directly from the pub, turn left out of the pub, and then right down the road.

To continue the walk, turn right through the lych-gate to the pretty little church, **St Mary the Virgin**, Greywell, of 12th-century origin. Go through the lych-gate opposite the west door and keep ahead across the field overlooked by the attractive row of brick, tile-hung and half-timbered houses along **The Street**. Turn right just beyond a lone tree and cross the River Whitewater on a footbridge to **Greywell Moors**, where rare plants, including the marsh helleborine orchid, flourish in the alkaline fen habitat. As you emerge from the trees, turn left to walk between the hedge on the right and a line of telegraph wires on the left. Return to the pumping station.

East Meon and the Downs

HAMPSHIRE WALK 42

A gentle climb out of the valley of the River Meon leads to a bracing walk along a chalk downland ridge that overlooks the ancient village of East Meon. The Norman parish church is one of the best in England, with a precious and vividly carved Tournai font.

The Olde George Inn, Church Street, East Meon GU32 1NH. ☎ (01730) 823759. Open Mon to Sat 11 to 3, 6 to 11, Sun 12 to 3, 7 to 10.30; food 12 to 2.30, 7 to 9.30. 4 real ales. Ploughman's, sandwiches, pies, chilli, curries, gammon, scampi, pasta. Children welcome. Dogs welcome.

Izaak Walton, High Street, East Meon GU32 1QA. ☎ (01730) 823252. Open Mon to Sat 10 to 2.30, 6 to 11, Sun all day; food Mon to Sat 12 to 2, 7 to 9 (8.30 Wed), Sun 12 to 2, 6 to 8. Ringwood, Webster's, John Smith's beers. Pies, lasagne, steak and fish. Children welcome. Dogs welcome.

Start: Signposted village car park, Workhouse Lane. Grid reference 677223.
Length: 5½ miles (9 kilometres); 3 hours.
Difficulty: Moderate.
OS maps: 1:25,000 Explorer sheet 132; 1:50,000 Landranger sheet 185.
Shop in the centre of the village.
WC At the Izaak Walton pub.
PT Petersfield station 5 miles. Buses to East Meon (not Sun) from Petersfield and Southampton (2-hourly) and Winchester (irregular).

❶ Leave the car park, walking straight ahead through the entrance on to the road, towards the village centre. At the T-junction, turn left and pass the shop. At the next junction either turn left, past the Olde George Inn and make for the church ahead, or, to see more of the village before continuing on the walk, take the road straight ahead, walking to the left of the infant River Meon, which flows down the side of the street. The Izaak Walton pub is named after the famous 17th-century angler who sang the praises of this trout stream in *The Compleat Angler*. Retrace your steps to the memorial cross and turn right, with the church straight ahead. The village is an attractive mix of thatched, flint, tile-hung, brick and colour-washed houses.

❷ At the end of the road, in front of the church, turn right for a few yards (no pavement) to get a view of the steeply roofed **Court House**, built as a hunting lodge for the Norman lords of the manor. Return to the church and go through the lych-gate. **All Saints' Church** was built during the 100 years or so after the Norman conquest and is a treasure for anyone who appreciates the Romanesque style. Follow the tarmac path past

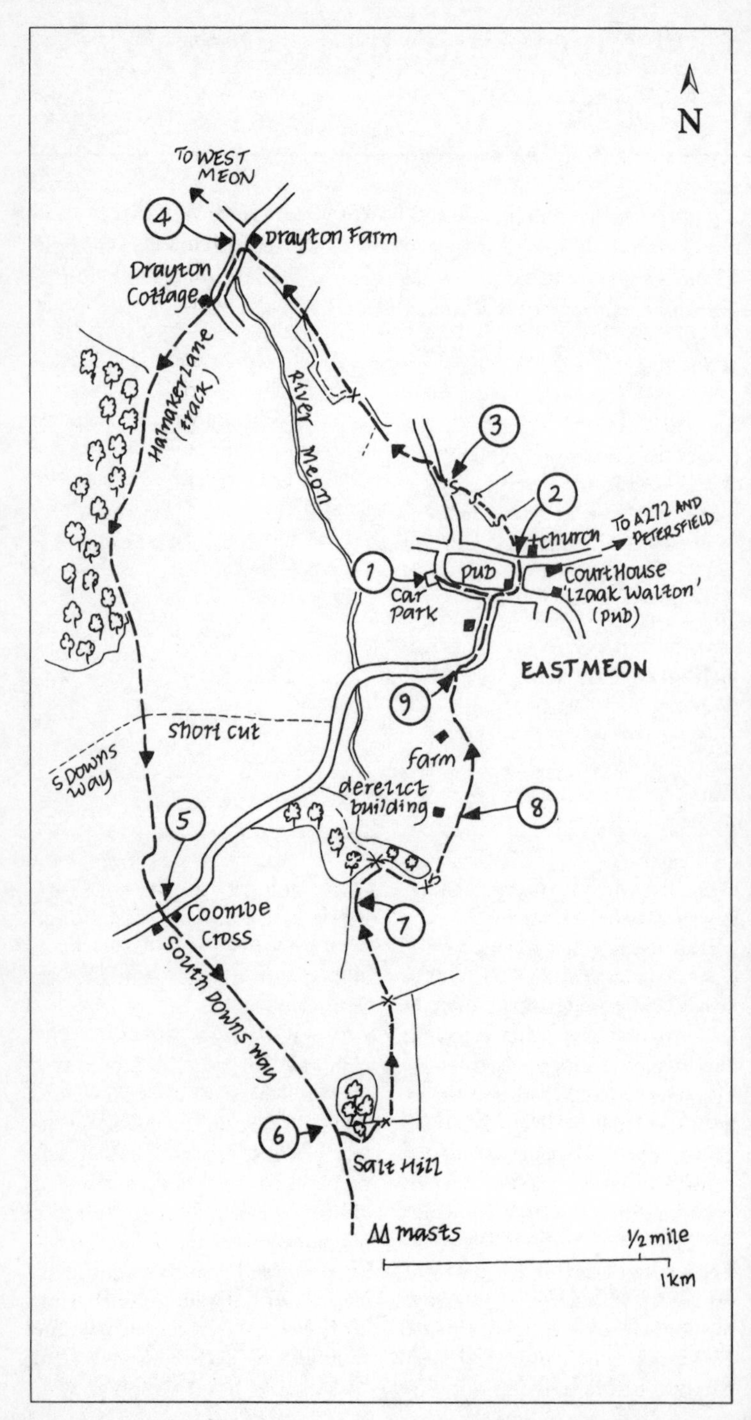
N
TO WEST MEON
4
Drayton Farm
Drayton Cottage
Halnaker Lane (track)
River Meon
3
2
church
TO A272 AND PETERSFIELD
1
pub
Court House
Car Park
'Izaak Walton' (pub)
EASTMEON
9
Short cut
S Downs Way
farm
derelict building
8
5
Coombe Cross
7
South Downs Way
6
Salt Hill
masts
1/2 mile
1km

the early Norman west door and follow the footpath sign to the left, edging the graveyard and then going between a fence on the left and a high bank on the right. Ignore steps on the right and continue over a stile, with the fence still on your left. Cross a stile and walk straight ahead up and over the middle of a field of pasture to another stile. Cross this and skirt left of a gravel drive to meet a lane ❸.

Turn right up the lane and almost immediately turn left over a stile to follow the right-hand edge of two fields. Cross the stile beside a metal gate and, if crops allow, follow the right of way across the middle of the next field to a stile in the hedge opposite (alternatively go round the edge of the field, to the left, to the same stile). Cross the stile and keep ahead with a hedge on your left. This is typical 'rolling' downland, with grazing sheep and calling pheasants for company, and good autumn colour in the woods to the left. At Drayton Farm follow the narrow path, with barns on your right, to the road ❹.

Turn left on to the road (quiet, but no pavement) for a short stretch. A bridge takes you over the River Meon, winding its way along the valley. Immediately after Drayton Cottage (bed and breakfast) turn right up Halnaker Lane. Ignore the private drives to the right and keep forward on the broad stony/grassy path, which soon goes into trees. Go left of the five-bar gate straight ahead of you, on a path that takes you through the edge of some delightful mixed deciduous woodland. The path narrows before opening out with sight of some derelict barns across the field to the left. At a crossing of paths, with the masts of the radio station on Butser Hill at 10 o'clock, keep ahead. This is the **South Downs Way**, the 101-mile national trail between Winchester and Eastbourne, which joins from Old Winchester Hill, the wooded escarpment of which is soon visible to the right.

To return to the start, at the crossing turn left, skirt right of the barns and keep ahead to a lane. Turn left and follow the lane back to the centre of the village, rejoining the walk at ❾.

❺*To continue*, at Coombe Cross, cross the road and follow the South Downs Way sign straight ahead, with chalk downland views to right and left. The path now climbs gently between trees until suddenly, at the top, two more masts pop up ahead of you, this time belonging to the **HMS *Mercury*** naval base at the far end of Salt Hill. At this point, leave the South Downs Way, turning left over a stile with a dog-gate at a footpath sign. Perch on the stile and imbibe the distant **views** north and east, towards Alton, Petersfield and the South Downs ❻.

Having crossed the stile, skirt right of the trees in the combe below, then continue with a fence on your left as far as a metal gate on the brow of the hill. Turn left through the gate and walk ahead along the brow of a grassy spur. Keep ahead through a gate, ignoring a footpath signed to the right. This is an exhilarating stretch, with birds, butterflies and quite possibly sightings of deer. The views are wide, with East Meon's silvery broach spire and the steep, red-tiled roof of the Court House standing out from the village below. From this viewpoint, it is easy to visualise the scene as it was at the time of Domesday, with thatched huts in place of the houses we see today.

❼ As you begin to drop downhill, a fence joins from the left. Keep close to the fence, go through a gate, and follow the left-hand edge of the field of pasture to the trees. Continue round the bottom of the field, with the trees on your left, ignoring a gate in the corner. At the next gate, turn left down a track. Cross the stile on the left and keep to the right-hand edge of the field with a tall hedge on your right and a small derelict flint building at 11 o'clock.

❽ As you draw parallel with this building, in the bottom right-hand corner of the field, follow a footpath sign straight up and over the field ahead. At a hedge, keep left, following the footpath sign, with the hedge on your right. Continue straight ahead across the middle of the next field to a row of red-roofed houses. Cross a stile and meet the road ❾. Turn right and follow the road past the school and thatched, flint, brick, and colour-washed houses.

East Meon – Domesday village

Visitors to Bayeux in northern France may be surprised to find among the exhibits accompanying the Bayeux Tapestry a model of East Meon as it must have looked in the days of the Normans. Made at the time of the 900th anniversary of the Domesday book for an exhibition held in Winchester – where the Domesday Book was actually written – the model was subsequently presented to the Bayeux Tapestry museum.

East Meon's church was mainly the work of Bishop Walkelin, who also rebuilt Winchester Cathedral, and has a splendid Romanesque tower. The black Tournai marble font, brought over from Belgium in 1150 and one of four in Hampshire, is delightfully carved with the story of Adam and Eve. Across the road from the church is the Court House. Built in about 1400, this belonged to the Lords of the Manor, the Bishops of Winchester.

Dorchester-on-Thames and Wittenham Clumps

OXFORDSHIRE WALK 43

This figure-of-eight route explores a fine Thames valley village and takes in the unspoilt woodlands and impressive hillfort and viewpoints on Wittenham Clumps. The walk concludes with a delightful amble along the Thames towpath. Other classic Thames scenery nearby can be seen on an idyllic two-mile walk from Streatley to Moulsford.

George Hotel, Dorchester-on-Thames OX10 7HH. ☎ (01865) 340404. Open Mon to Sat 11 to 11, Sun 11 to 10.30; food all week 12 to 2.15, 7 to 9. Brakspear beers. The George Hotel is a late 15th-century coaching inn with a timber-framed black and white structure, oak antiques, polished brass and interesting old prints and photos. Bar food, including soup, baguettes, steak, pan-fried calves' livers, smoked salmon, duck. On the à la carte menu could be halibut, guinea fowl or roast lamb. Children welcome in restaurant. No dogs.

Fleur de Lys Inn, The High Street, Dorchester-on-Thames OX10 7HH. ☎ (01865) 340502. Open Mon to Sat 11 to 3, 6.30 to 11, Sun 12 to 3, 7 to 10.30; food 12 to 2, 7 to 9.30, (Sun in winter 12 to 3 only). 4 real ales. Set menu and blackboard specials, bar snacks, ploughman's. Children welcome in restaurant. Dogs welcome in bar.

Start: Dorchester-on-Thames, just off the A4074 (north-west of Wallingford and south-east of Oxford). Free car park by public toilets signposted from main street, near the abbey, in a side turning called Bridge End. Grid reference 579941.
Length: 5 miles (8 kilometres), 2½ hours (or two separate walks of 2½ miles each).
Difficulty: Easy, with two very short ascents. Waymarking is thorough, and all of the walk is on well-tramped and visible paths.
OS maps: 1:25,000 Explorer sheet 170; 1:50,000 Landranger sheet 164 or 174.
Full range in Dorchester-on-Thames.
WC In the car park in Dorchester-on-Thames.
PT Daily buses from Abingdon and Wallingford via Culham rail station (operated by Thames Travel Mon to Sat ☎ (01491) 874216, Chiltern Buses on Sun, ☎ (01491) 680354).

❶ Turn left out of the car park and walk along the main street in Dorchester, passing the Fleur de Lys Inn and the George Hotel, both on your left. ❷ Turn left opposite the White Hart Hotel into Malthouse Lane; ignore a right turn into a garage, but turn right in front of a row of black-and-white thatched cottages; the lane here narrows to path width.

Emerge on to a small road, turn left along it for 250 yards, then ❸ fork right on to a signposted path

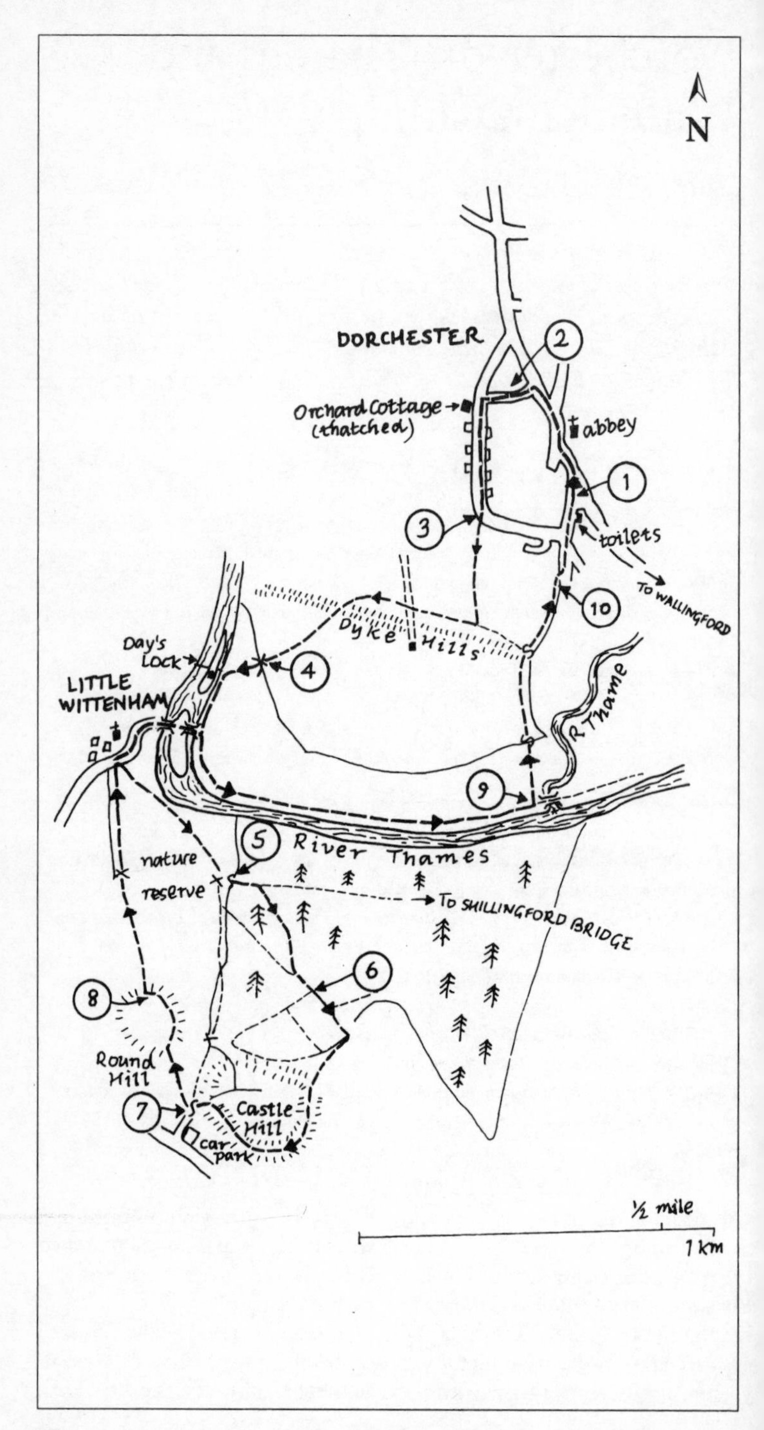
N
DORCHESTER
Orchard Cottage (thatched)
abbey
toilets
TO WALLINGFORD
Dyke Hills
Day's Lock
LITTLE WITTENHAM
R Thame
River Thames
nature reserve
TO SHILLINGFORD BRIDGE
Round Hill
Castle Hill
car park
½ mile
1 km
1
2
3
4
5
6
7
8
9
10

(for Day's Lock), which passes just to the left of house no. 50 (Sinodun), and between garden fences, then crosses a field. Turn right at a T-junction with a path in front of a fence and **Dyke Hills** (a prominent grass bank). These substantial grassy ramparts are the remains of an Iron Age town, sited on a strategic bend in the river. They consist of a double line of banks, with a ditch in between. Originally, wooden palisades would have been built around them, protecting the community and its livestock. After 150 yards cross over a track and continue forward, now on a path between fences.

❹ At the end of the fenced section, go through a gate and cross a field, heading to Day's Lock on the River Thames. Turn left along the river, soon crossing it by bridges, then proceed on the far bank on a lane. You go through the tiny hamlet of **Little Wittenham**. The church in this tiny hamlet is largely Victorianised, but its tower is 14th- and 15th-century. Within the tower are memorials to the Dunch family. A brass plate of 1597 commemorates the older William Dunch, sheriff of the county, auditor to the mint and MP for Wallingford. His grandson (also William Dunch, and an MP) died in 1611 or 1612 and is represented by an alabaster carving, together with that of his wife, who was related to Oliver Cromwell, and their children.

As soon as you pass the church, take the gate on the left into **Little Wittenham Nature Reserve**, immediately forking left on a grassy path (marked by blue and yellow waymarks) across a large field known as Church Meadow (the right-hand path leads towards Round Hill, the prominent hill ahead; you will later return this way).

The nature reserve includes Castle Hill and Round Hill (together forming Wittenham Clumps, each being capped by trees), over which there is open access. It is an area of grassland and woodland, crisscrossed by public rights of way and permissive paths. 30 species of butterflies and 120 species of bird have been seen here, and the flora includes orchids; there is a bird-watchers' hide. Parts of the woodland are coppiced.

❺ At the end of the field, take the left-hand of two gates to enter Little Wittenham Wood. After 60 yards fork right through a wooden barrier; ignore the left turn after 150 yards, but 100 yards later turn left at the T-junction with a hard track, downhill along it.

❻ Just after the track begins to rise, and as it is about to veer left, fork right on to a path rising to a stile leading into a field. Turn right on the path along the field edge, uphill. The path crosses a stile; turn right and immediately left on to a grassy bank. This is the outer rampart of **Castle Hill fort**, which like Dyke Hills was an important Iron Age site. The two sites are very likely linked. In the middle of Castle Hill, a plaque identifies the Poem Tree, carved with a poem written by Joseph Tubb, 1844–5. The original inscription has, sadly, deteriorated.

Follow the path along the top of this rampart until ❼, taking a stile on the left; do not proceed on the track that heads down to the car park, but bear right up **Round Hill** to join the fence that surrounds the woodland crowning its summit. The hill rises to only 393 feet but gives a fine view over the Thames Valley, and across to Coombe Hill, the highest point in the Chilterns. The British Leyland Works at Cowley and Culham Laboratory are also prominent.

Turn right ❽, alongside the fence, until you reach a bench and view indicator. From the view indicator, take the path down towards Little Wittenham church, through a gate at the bottom, then along the left edge of Church Meadow, to reach the gate you passed through earlier. Turn right on the lane, to re-cross the bridges over the Thames. On the other bank, turn right along the river (you have to pass under the bridge to do this), in the other direction from Day's Lock.

❾ After ¾ mile, just before the river path crosses a footbridge over a tributary river (confusingly called the Thame), turn left, initially along the Thame, then forward as the Thame bends to the right, to take a stile. Proceed forward through a long strip-shaped field, passing a brick pill-box on the right (Dyke Hills are again seen to the left) and crossing another stile. Proceed forward, along the right edge of a field.

❿ At the unmade lane at the edge of Dorchester, go forward (ignoring minor side turns) for 30 yards, then take the path between hedges on the right opposite a thatched cottage. Turn left at the end, passing a triangular green on your right, then go forward, to pass between the Chequers Inn and the Roman Catholic church, and reach the car park.

Dorchester-on-Thames

This handsome village retains many thatched, tiled, half-timbered buildings. Now bypassed, this was formerly a busy staging-post on the London to Oxford road; the George Hotel and the White Hart are two imposing coaching inns from this period. The 18th-century yellow coach standing outside the George is a reminder of the village's former importance as a stopping point; the interior of the pub is comfortably unpretentious in tone.

Dorchester Abbey is an Augustinian foundation dating from the 12th century but greatly extended in the two centuries following. It has a lofty interior, with some magnificent arcades. Above all it is noted for its Norman lead front, its Jesse window with its stained glass and remarkable tracery embellished with stone figures, and the 14th-century sedilia beneath the south window. Adjacent to the abbey, the former abbey guest house and grammar school, dating from about 1400, house a small museum (open in summer, except Mondays and Sunday mornings). A Roman settlement was sited between modern-day Dorchester and the Thames, on a road linking Silchester and Alcester; nothing remains of it, but an altar to Jupiter and Augustus has been discovered, along with pavements and Roman coins.

Henley, Hambledon Lock and the Regatta Course

BERKSHIRE/OXFORDSHIRE WALK 44

We begin with a brief, bustling river scene, but a much longer, very beautiful stretch of Thames towpath is reserved for the second half of this walk. After climbing gently through woodland and unspoilt farmland, with quite easy route-finding, the walk drops to the riverbank, passing Hambledon Lock, Temple Island and the famous regatta course.

The new, award-winning River and Rowing Museum in Meadow Road (near the car park) is worth a visit. It covers every aspect of the Thames throughout history, from source to sea; there is also a gallery devoted to rowing.

Angel on the Bridge, Thameside, Henley-on-Thames RG9 1BN. ☎ (01491) 410678. Open Mon to Sat 11 to 11, Sun 11 to 10.30; food Mon to Fri 12 to 2.30; 6 to 10, Sat 12 to 3.30, 6 to 10, Sun 12 to 3.30. Brakspear beers. A la carte menu, with perhaps cream of tomato and basil soup or a plate of smoked salmon with lemon and brown bread to start, and lamb curry with basmati rice, asparagus and Stilton quiche with salad and sauté potatoes, or salmon en croûte with vegetables and new potatoes as a main course. Children welcome. Dogs welcome on terrace only.

Little Angel, Remenham Lane, Henley-on-Thames RG9 2LS. ☎ (01491) 574165. Open Mon to Sat 11 to 3, 6 to 11, Sun 12 to 3 (summer 7 to 10.30); food Mon to Sat 12 to 2.30, 7 to 10.30, Sun 11 to 3, 7 to 10.30. Brakspear beers. Modern English and Continental food. Starters might be Brie parcels on a cranberry and orange compote, calamari salad or dim sum. Main courses – moules marinière, tuna with roasted vegetables or escalope of veal. Brasserie menu includes garlic bread or soup of the day to start, nachos, steak sandwich with chips or penne with tuna. Main meals might be farmers' steak pie, stir-fried chicken with noodles or sausages and mash. Well-behaved children welcome. Guide dogs only welcome.

Flower Pot Hotel, Aston RG9 3DJ. ☎ (01491) 574721. Open Mon to Sat 10.30 to 3, 6 to 11, Sun 12 to 3, 7 to 10.30; food Mon to Sat 12 to 2, 6.30 to 9, Sun 12 to 2, bar snacks 7 to 9. Brakspear beers. A pleasant pub with a good garden in a peaceful location. Bar snacks such as pies, burgers, lasagne and steak. Well-behaved children welcome. Dogs welcome in public bar only.

Start: Mill Meadows long-stay car park, in Meadow Road. In the centre of Henley, at the traffic lights on the western end of the river bridge, turn off the A4130 down the side of the Angel on the Bridge pub (Thameside); turn left at the T-junction and follow signs to car park and museum. Grid reference 766822.

Length: 7 miles (11 kilometres), 3½ hours.

Difficulty: Easy/moderate.

OS maps: 1:25,000 Explorer sheet 171; 1: 50,000 Landranger sheet 175.

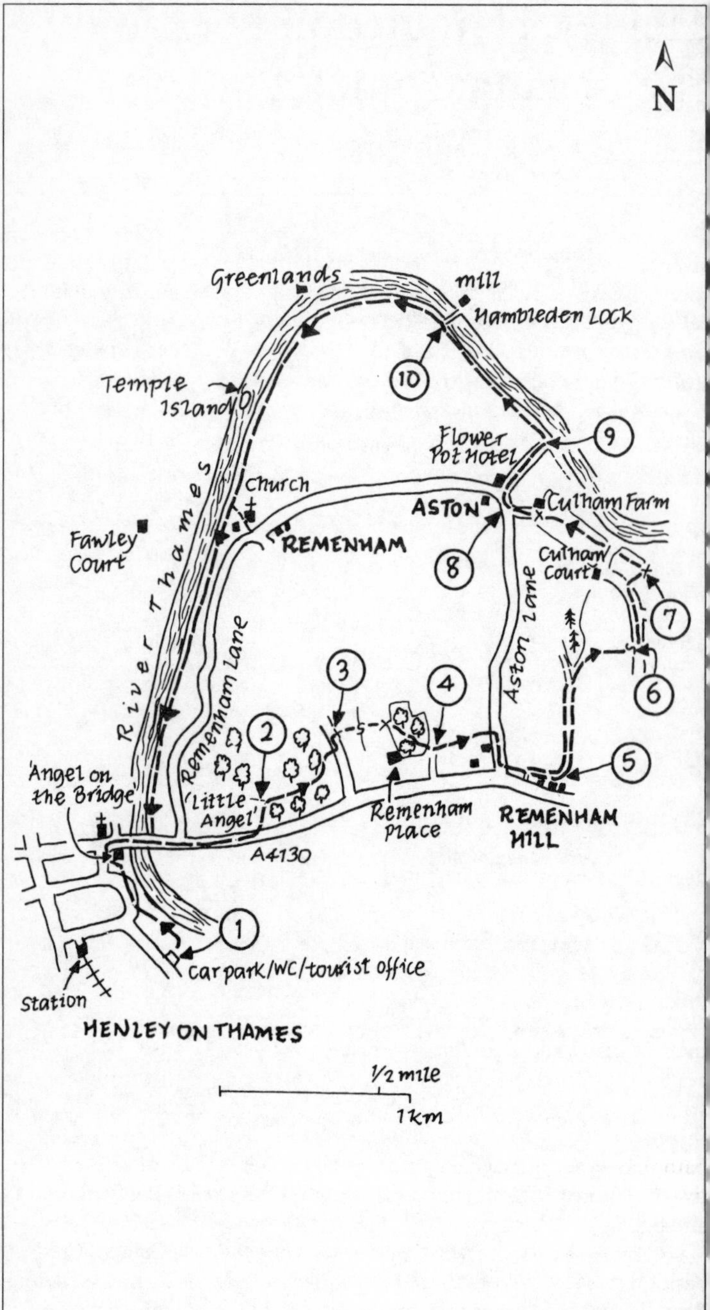

N
Greenlands
mill
Hambleden Lock
10
Temple Island
Flower Pot Hotel
9
Church
ASTON
Culham Farm
Fawley Court
REMENHAM
8
River Thames
Culham Court
Remenham Lane
Aston Lane
7
6
3
4
2
5
'Angel on the Bridge'
'Little Angel'
Remenham Place
REMENHAM HILL
A4130
1
Car park/WC/tourist office
Station
HENLEY ON THAMES
1/2 mile
1km

Full range in Henley.

WC Mill Meadows car park.

PT Trains to Henley Station (adjacent to the start of the walk). Turn right out of the station building, and right on to the road to a boat hire centre by the riverbank. Turn left on the towpath and continue round the Angel on the Bridge pub and over the bridge, as in ❶.

---

❶ Standing in the car park, face the river and walk across the meadows to the riverbank. Turn left on to the towpath and follow it to the Angel on the Bridge pub. Skirt the pub using the pavement and cross the river bridge (walking away from Henley). Cross the road with care, pass the Little Angel Inn and continue, with allotments below on your left, to the end of the footway; here turn left up a flight of steps into woodland.

Emerge at a meeting of private drives ❷. Ignoring two drives on your left, take the footpath almost directly opposite you, to the right of a tree with an arrow painted on it. Follow this past a tennis court to a T-junction. Turn right and after 25 yards, keep straight ahead over a crossing of paths. The beautiful beech woodland is particularly rewarding in spring, when it is full of bluebells. The well-defined path continues beside a fence past a house to reach a stile. Turn left along the road for about 20 yards, then ❸ turn right through a gate across the middle of a field to a stile, across a second field and through a gate on to a well-defined path that winds through an attractive area of mixed beech, holly, oak and birch.

❹ Emerge from the woodland beside a gate and drive to Common Barn. Turn left, following the footpath sign, along a track and then a path between a fence and a hedge, with views of fine rolling parkland to the left. Arrive at Aston Lane and turn right to the junction with the main road (A4130); immediately before the road, turn left over a stile into a field and follow the edge of the field with conifers and houses and gardens on the right.

❺ At the end of the houses, turn left at a signpost along the right-hand edge of a field with trees and a hedge on your right. Just before the copse ahead, turn right through a gap in the hedge at a waymark post and continue left along the edge of the next field with the hedge and copse of trees on your left. As Culham Court comes into view ahead, and the edge of the field curves left, turn right, downhill, with a line of oak trees, to reach a tarmac farm road ❻.

Turn left along the road and fork left at a small clump of trees; at the bottom of the dip in the drive up to Culham Court turn sharp right at a footpath sign with a wire fence on the left and fields either side. As you approach a house, follow the Thames Path sign through a gate on the left, across a field. The Thames Path runs for 180 miles from the source of the river in Gloucestershire to London.

Go through a second gate and continue towards Culham Court, a fine neo-classical house dating from 1770. With the river close by on the right, and the formal clipped yew hedges of the gardens on the left, reach a gate just to the right of iron railings. Following a Thames Path sign and with the iron railings on your left, pass through two iron gates. The Thames passes wide and slow to the right. Leaving the house behind, keep ahead across the middle of a long, narrow field to a gate just to the left of distant red-roofed buildings. In spring this path is lined with daffodils. Follow a tarmac track ahead down to a road ❽.

Turn right at the T-junction. Just ahead, where the road bends left, is the Flower Pot Hotel, Aston, a pleasant pub with a good garden, in a peaceful location. Fork right here on a minor cul-de-sac down to the river ❾. Turn left along the river-bank, a tranquil scene with coots and moorhens, and trees on either bank. At the end of a field go through a gate and join a track to reach **Hambleden Lock** ❿. Take a short detour here, turning right on a footbridge, across the lock and then on a long footbridge, with a weir thundering and swirling beneath you, to an attractive weather-boarded watermill and mill house on the opposite bank. Return to the lock and continue along the signposted Thames Path.

On the opposite bank, as the river bends south, is the **Greenlands** estate, bounded by some fine topiary hedging. The house, a Victorian mansion built in the Italian style by the newsagent WH Smith, was formerly the home of Viscount Hambleden. Soon the path draws level with **Temple Island**. The delightful folly and old fishing lodge was designed by James Wyatt to improve the view from Fawley Court, which he classicised in 1771. **The Court** itself, seen on the opposite bank a little further on, has gardens created by Capability Brown. Temple Island is the start of the **Henley Royal Regatta**. The regatta was established in 1839 as 'a source of amusement and gratification to the neighbourhood and the public in general'. It acquired the 'Royal' from the Prince Consort's patronage in 1851. The first Oxford and Cambridge Boat Race was rowed here in 1829, when Oxford won. There is normally plenty of rowing activity on the river between here and Henley.

Remenham is a pretty hamlet just off the path to the left. From here the towpath is tarmac. A few houses and a couple of boat clubs are on the left bank, but the opposite bank remains undeveloped right into Henley. At the end of the towpath, follow the path back to the main road. Turn right to cross the bridge and return to the car park.

Cookham, Winter Hill and the Thames

BERKSHIRE WALK 45

Literary and artistic associations add to the interest of this Thames Valley walk. Its varied route begins over fields, continues through the beech woods that inspired the Wild Wood of The Wind in the Willows *to the dramatic viewpoint of Winter Hill, then descends to join the Thames towpath into Cookham, home of the artist Stanley Spencer. Route-finding is intricate in parts, but paths are well signposted.*

Uncle Tom's Cabin, Hills Lane, Cookham Dean SL6 9NT. ☎ (01628) 483339. Open Mon to Sat 11 to 3, 5.30 to 11, Sun 12 to 3, 7 to 10.30; food Mon to Fri 12 to 2, 7.30 to 10, Sat and Sun 12.30 to 2.30, 7.30 to 10. 3 real ales. Full restaurant menu, bar snacks and sandwiches. Children welcome in restaurant. Dogs welcome in bar area.

Inn on the Green, The Old Cricket Common, Cookham Dean SL6 9NZ. ☎ (01628) 482638. Open Mon to Sat 12 to 3, 5.30 to 11, Sun 7 to 10.30; bar food Mon to Sat 12 to 2.30; restaurant 12 to 2.30, 7.30 to 10, closed 25 Dec and 1 Jan. Brakspear, Fuller's London Pride. This characterful mock-Tudor pub is set back from the large village green. Starters might be potato and goat's cheese gratin, Thai crab parcels or terrine of wild boar, while main courses include dishes such as steamed lobster, pot-roast quail or Roquefort and apple strudel. Starters can be served as light meals in the bar in the evenings, in addition to dishes such as club sandwiches, goat's cheese gratin or venison sausages and mash. Children welcome in restaurant and bar eating area. Dogs welcome in bar only.

Bel and the Dragon, High Street, Cookham SL6 9SQ. ☎ (01628) 521263. Open Mon to Sat 11 to 11, Sun 11 to 10.30; food 12 to 2.30 (3 Sun), 7 to 10. Brakspear beers. This is a 15th-century inn with wattle-and-daub walls. Modern bistro-style menu with chargrilled daily specials. Children welcome. Dogs welcome in bar area.

Start: Cookham Moor car park, off the B4447 at the western end of the village. Grid reference 893854.
Length: 6½ miles (10.5 kilometres), 3½ hours.
Difficulty: Moderate.
OS maps: 1:25,000 Explorer sheet 172; 1:50,000 Landranger sheet 175.
Full range in Cookham.
WC Cookham village (on the A 4094 just south of junction with the B4447).
PT Train (limited Sunday service in summer) to Cookham. Leave the station on the side by some shops, follow the road ahead, then go left just before The Gate pub into Poundcroft Lane; proceed ahead along a gravel track to reach the road. Turn left then immediately right on to a gravel track for 50 yards to a gap in a fence at a footpath sign. Go through on to the golf course at ❷.

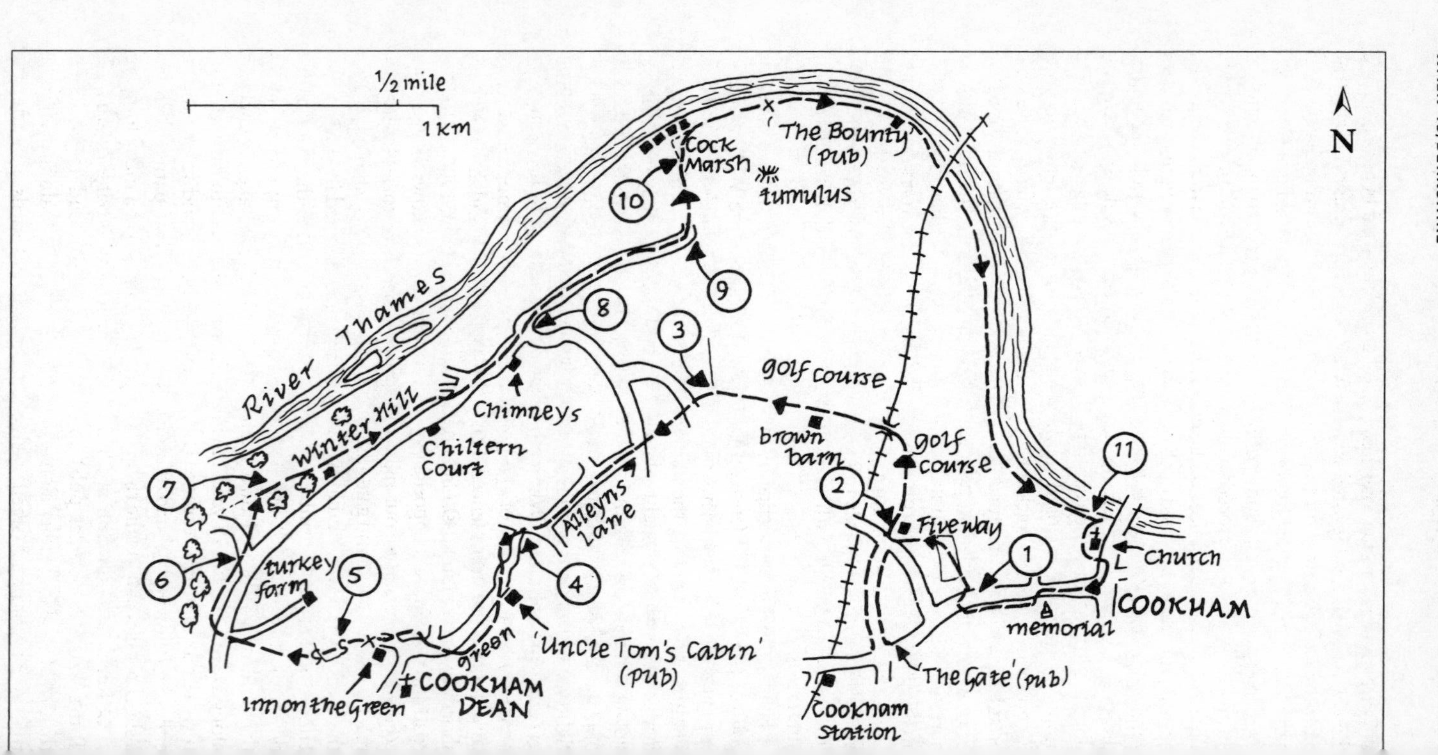
N
1/2 mile
1km
River Thames
Winter Hill
Chiltern Court
Chimneys
turkey farm
Inn on the Green
COOKHAM DEAN
green
'Uncle Tom's Cabin' (pub)
Alleyns Lane
golf course
brown barn
golf course
Cock Marsh
tumulus
'The Bounty' (pub)
Fiveway
Cookham Station
'The Gate' (pub)
memorial
COOKHAM
Church
1
2
3
4
5
6
7
8
9
10
11

❶ With your back to the road, leave the car park on a signposted footpath through the trees on the left-hand side, crossing a low footbridge over stagnant water, and going through a stile/gate to proceed along a narrow path with a fence and field on your left and a tree-lined ditch on your right. When the field ends and the path divides, turn left up the slope to a kissing-gate, then continue along a narrow enclosed path. Emerge where a gravel track meets a broader gravel track and road.

To return to the station, turn left here on to the road, then immediately right along Poundcroft Lane.

To continue the walk, turn right on the gravel for 50 yards to a gap in a fence at a footpath sign, to enter the golf course ❷.

Follow the left-hand edge of the golf course. Where the fence on the left ends, look right for views of the Thames before crossing the railway bridge. Continue straight ahead, slowly climbing through the middle of the golf course, passing just to the right of a brown barn and then with a hedge on your left. Where the hedge ends at the end of the golf course, turn left on to a fenced path, shortly to reach the road ❸. Cross the road and take the path opposite: proceed with the fence on your right, to reach a road by a stile and gate, just to the right of the white buildings of Hillgrove Farm. Continue ahead down Alleyns Lane to a T-junction at the bottom, where you turn right along Dean Lane for 70 yards, then turn left steeply up Warners Hill, either by following the road or using a short parallel path on the right.

❹ Reach a T-junction at Uncle Tom's Cabin (a popular pub) and turn right (walking either along the road or on Hardings Green). After the green, the road bends right; at a junction just after this bend, keep left on the road, then immediately turn right across the middle of Cookham Dean village green in the direction of the sign for The Inn on the Green. The pub is 50 yards to the left of the sign. Take a narrow signposted path to the right of the pub, through a copse, to reach a stile ❺, where you walk down the edge of the field ahead, with a wire fence on your right, past a turkey farm, to reach a track at the valley bottom. Continue straight ahead up the other side of the valley to a double power-post.

Emerge on the road and go into the woods on a narrow path directly opposite. Turn right after 25 yards on a path that runs closely parallel to the road ❻. **Quarry Wood** is believed to have been the inspiration for the Wild Wood in Kenneth Grahame's *The Wind in the Willows*. As a child, Kenneth Grahame used to stay in Cookham Dean with his grandmother. His uncle used to take him on the river, where he discovered the attractions of messing about in boats. In later life, when he became Secretary of the Bank of England, he came back to live at Mayfield, 1906–1910. *The Wind in the Willows* began as a series of bedtime stories for his son, Alastair, and was shaped into a book and published in 1908.

At the far end of the wood, come to a road junction; cross Quarry Wood Road and take an enclosed path opposite, just to the right of a thatched house, and follow this to the T-junction of paths. Turn left for 15 yards and at a metal footpath sign turn right (NB if the path from Quarry Bank Road is too overgrown, turn left along the road, then after 100 yards, just after the last house, turn right on a narrow path, and 70 yards later, turn left at a metal footpath sign.)

Follow the path through the woods (white arrow-markers on the trees) to reach the top of the escarpment, where the path bends to the right and narrows ❼. A fence begins on your right as a path joins from the left by a waymark post. Join a gravel drive for 20 yards, then, just before the road, turn left along a narrow path to emerge at the top of **Winter Hill**, with excellent views across the valley to Marlow and the Chilterns. Continue on the grass along the top of the hill, joining the road near a house called Chiltern Court; ignore the left road turn (Stonehouse Lane and Gibraltar Lane) and opposite a house called Chimneys, fork left down a broad gravel track ❽.

Soon after passing a gate beside a stile, ignore a minor left fork (which descends) and keep along the level; 100 yards later ignore the minor right fork (which ascends). Soon the main track drops gently with views of the peaceful river scene ahead.

❾ At the bottom of the slope bear left to a gate by a signpost and continue ahead across a field towards some houses (may be muddy). Reach the corner of a concrete farm road ❿, where you turn right on a footpath across the grass to join the River Thames towpath at the last bungalow (Ferry Cottage).

Keep beside the water's edge (this stretch is particularly reminiscent of *The Wind in the Willows*), with views to the right of the steep escarpment beyond Cockmarsh. **Cockmarsh**, 130 acres of flat, marshy meadows and steep chalk slopes, has been common land since at least 1272. It is now preserved by the National Trust and is designated as a Site of Special Scientific Interest. It had five ancient burial mounds, only one of which is visible now. An excavation in the 19th century revealed two cremated bodies. Continue along the well-defined towpath close to the river, with houses on your right. Pass The Bounty pub, go under a railway bridge, and continue on the towpath for 1 mile.

⓫ 100 yards before the next bridge, turn right at a high redbrick wall signed to **Cookham churchyard**. Walk straight ahead through the churchyard and you should pass Stanley Spencer's tombstone. Leave from the far left corner. Turn left and continue ahead to reach the road; turn right, then right again along the length of Cookham High Street, passing the **Stanley Spencer Gallery** (see box). After the war memorial, walk along the surfaced path (a raised causeway). Just before the causeway crosses a brick bridge, turn right down steps and cross the road to return to the car park. *To return to the station, see* ❶.

Stanley Spencer

The artist Stanley Spencer was born in Cookham in 1891; the village was an essential source of inspiration throughout his life. Such paintings as his *Resurrection,* set in Cookham churchyard, and *Swan-Upping* (see Walk 49) are firmly rooted in the village scene (both are in the Tate Gallery in London). The Stanley Spencer Gallery, housed in a disused chapel, displays many of his drawings and paintings, and memorabilia (open Easter to October daily 10.30 to 5.30; November to Easter, Saturday, Sunday, bank holidays 11–5). He died in 1959.

Windsor Great Park

BERKSHIRE/SURREY WALK 46

Some good walking is to be found in this vast wooded park. A nature reserve in itself, Windsor Great Park also has some magnificent gardens. This is a figure-of-eight walk, so you can do either one or both of the loops, starting at the Savill Gardens. The southern loop takes in a Totem Pole, the banks of Virginia Water and the Valley Gardens, where camellias, azaleas and rhododendrons are spectacular in spring, and the Pinetum Valley and Heather Gardens are a delight in winter. The northern part takes in the tranquil Cow Pond, which is covered in waterlilies in summer, the famous Copper Horse statue, glimpses of royal residences, and an avenue of liquidambar trees that are stunning in autumn.

Fox and Hounds, Bishopsgate Road, Bishopsgate, Englefield Green TW20 0XU. ☎ (01784) 433098. Open Mon to Sat 11 to 11, Sun 12 to 10.30; food Mon to Sat 12 to 3, 6.30 to 9.30, Sun 12 to 3, 7 to 9.30, bar meals Mon to Fri 12 to 2.30. Courage, Brakspear beers. Restaurant with à la carte menu served in the evenings only, bar meals and specials at lunch-times from Mon to Fri, sandwiches on Saturdays, and Sunday roasts. Children welcome. Dogs welcome.

Sun, Wick Lane, Englefield Green TW20 0UF (just off route, 500 yards north of Savill Gardens entrance). ☎ (01784) 432515. Open Mon to Sat 11 to 11, Sun 12 to 10.30; food 12 to 3, 6 to 9.30, Sun 12 to 3. Courage Best. Pies, ploughman's, bar snacks, specials, Sunday roasts. Children welcome in family room. Dogs welcome.

Start: Car park (fee payable) at Savill Gardens, Wick Lane, signposted off the A30 at Englefield Green, just north of Virginia Water. Free roadside parking from November to February near the entrance to Savill Gardens. Grid reference 976705.
Length: Southern loop 4 miles (6.5 kilometres), 2 hours. Northern loop 4½ miles (7 kilometres), 2 hours.
Difficulty: Easy, mostly level walking, partly on tarmac paths; one or two potentially muddy patches (avoidable).
OS maps: 1:25,000 Explorer sheet 160; 1:50,000 Landranger sheet 175.
Savill Gardens restaurant.
WC Savill Gardens, Valley Gardens.
PT Nearest railway station Virginia Water – 1½ miles from Virginia Water entrance to park.

Southern loop, for the Totem Pole, Virginia Water and Valley Gardens

❶ Facing the entrance to Savill Gardens, with the car park behind you, turn left along the broad tarmac track to the **obelisk**, erected by George II to commemorate his son William, Duke of Cumberland. Here fork right off the tarmac track ❷ and take the path that swings

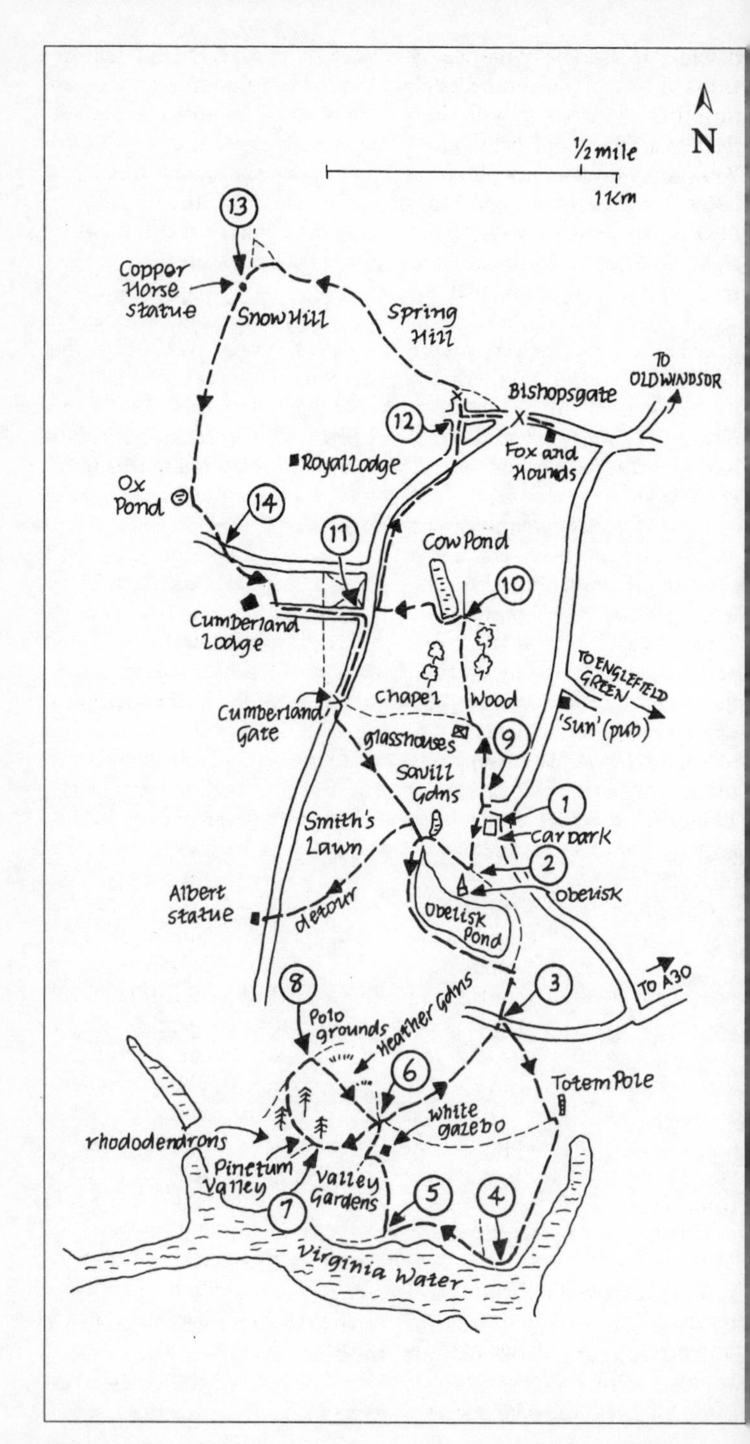
N
½ mile
1 Km
13
Copper Horse statue
Snow Hill
Spring Hill
TO OLD WINDSOR
Bishopsgate
12
Fox and Hounds
Royal Lodge
Ox Pond
14
11
Cow Pond
10
Cumberland Lodge
Chapel Wood
TO ENGLEFIELD GREEN
Cumberland Gate
'Sun' (pub)
glasshouses
9
Savill Gdns
1
Smith's Lawn
car park
2
Albert statue
detour
Obelisk
Obelisk Pond
8
3
TO A30
Polo grounds
Heather Gdns
6
Totem Pole
white gazebo
rhododendrons
Pinetum Valley
Valley Gardens
7
5
4
Virginia Water

downhill to the right of the obelisk. Cross a bridge and immediately turn back sharp left, to walk along the western bank of Obelisk Pond. You gain glimpses, through breaks in trees and across the pond, of the obelisk. Ignoring a path to the right, follow the bank round to meet the tarmac track that has come from the obelisk. (After heavy rain it may be very muddy beside the bridge; an alternative route avoiding this would be to return to the obelisk and continue on the tarmac track round the eastern side of the pond to ❸).

Turn right and reach a five-way junction ❸. Cross the vehicle road and take the second path on the left, a tarmac path signposted to the Totem Pole. Stick with the tarmac path as it winds its way downhill through rhododendron bushes, ignoring paths to the right and left, to arrive at the brightly painted **totem pole**. This was erected in 1958 to commemorate the centenary of British Columbia becoming a British colony.

Continue straight ahead, following the sign for Virginia Water North Ride, through woodland to Botany Bay Point. Here the path reaches a clearing on the banks of the lake, **Virginia Water**. The 150-acre lake was created in the 18th century by the Duke of Cumberland. On the opposite bank you can see some Roman ruins from Leptis Magna, in Tripoli, donated by the Prince Regent in 1816.

❹ With the lake behind you, return to the path and turn left. Immediately fork left again, to the left of a sign for Valley Gardens, following the path along the northern bank of the lake. On the right, at a break in the trees, a grassy bank leads up to an area planted with camellias, at their peak in late spring/early summer.

Continue on the broad path along the edge of the lake, passing fine specimens of ancient trees, some dating from the 18th century. In a dip ❺, turn right off the path, up a wide grassy avenue to a white **gazebo** with a seat offering uninterrupted views back down to the lake. Facing the seat, turn left and at a junction turn right. This brings you to a signposted meeting of six paths ❻.

Turn left down the path signed for **Azalea Valley**, an area at its best in spring. Continue past a path to the right to the Heather Gardens. Where the gravelly path ends in grass ❼, the **Rhododendron Species Collection** is ahead. Turn right along **Pinetum Valley**, which is particularly attractive in winter, with its collection of pines, spruces and other coniferous trees of varied shape and habit. At the top of the rise, turn right on to a tarmac road, with the polo grounds to the left. Take the first right, through a gate into the **Heather Gardens** ❽. Bear left through the gardens, planted with ericas, cedars and junipers under conifers and birch, to return to a gate by the six-way signpost.

Take the Savill Gardens and car park path (passing WCs), an undulating path through open woodland, back to the meeting of five ways at ❸. Continue across the vehicle road back to the Obelisk Pond and **Savill Gardens**, a 35-acre woodland garden, at its peak in spring but with interest year-round.

Northern loop, for Cow Pond, Copper Horse, Cumberland Lodge and Smith's Lawn

❾ Facing Savill Gardens entrance, with the car park behind you, turn right along a broad vehicle track, lined with rhododendrons. Where the track swings left at glasshouses, continue ahead on a narrower path through Chapel Wood. Where a minor path crosses ❿, turn left to **Cow Pond**. In summer this is a beautiful sight, its surface covered with pink, white and cream water lilies. At all seasons this is a peaceful spot, surrounded by trees and popular with waterbirds. Follow the path round the edge of the pond, taking the path off to the left halfway up the left-hand side. Follow this up an avenue of trees, with Cumberland Lodge ahead. Turn right at a road crossing ⓫, to walk alongside the road, which swings right to the crossroads ⓬. *For the Fox and Hounds pub*, turn right and go through Bishopsgate. The pub is 100 yards along on the road.

To continue the walk from the crossroads at ⓬, with gates to Royal Lodge on your left, take the road to the large metal gates at the entrance to the Deer Park. Go through the kissing-gate and continue on the broad tarmac track, with views right over Old Windsor and soon skirting right of Spring Hill to gain views of Windsor Castle. At times this lies under a Heathrow flight path.

After crossing a stone bridge, leave the track and walk left up Snow Hill to the large **Copper Horse statue** ⓭, a bronze George III put up in 1831 by George IV and sitting side-on to the 3-mile, oak-lined Long Walk leading to the castle.

With the statue and the castle directly behind you, walk straight ahead downhill, between two clumps of trees, through a gate and along a drive between hedges. To the left is Royal Lodge. At Ox Pond the path narrows. Meet a tarmac road, turn left to a signpost ⓮ (Cumberland Lodge), where you turn right. At the entrance to Cumberland Lodge, skirt left of its grounds and meet a drive to the Lodge. Turn left on to this (this is the western end of the avenue to Cow Pond), and keep ahead to meet the tarmac road at ⓫. Turn right and go through Cumberland Gate.

Ahead is Smith's Lawn. Take the broad grass avenue that runs between a tarmac road to the left (to Savill Gardens) and the road that runs straight ahead down the length of **Smith's Lawn**. This grassy avenue is lined on the right-hand side with liquidambar trees, a truly glorious sight in autumn, with leaves of every colour from yellow through orange and red to deep purple. At the far end, the obelisk (see ❷) is visible. (From the avenue, you could detour right, to see a fine **equestrian statue of Prince Albert** on the other side of Smith's Lawn, modelled by Demund Boehm, in commemoration of Queen Victoria's jubilee in 1887.) Keep ahead over a bridge and up to the obelisk. Turn left on the path back to Savill Gardens and the car park.

The Chess Valley

BUCKINGHAMSHIRE WALK 47

The walk takes in three attractive villages and two imposing houses as well as varied and unspoilt country in and around the Chess Valley. Paths are well walked but because of the intricate nature of the terrain the directions should be followed carefully.

Cricketers, The Green, Sarratt WD3 6AS. ☎ (01923) 263729. Open Mon to Sat 11 to 11, Sun 12 to 10.30; food Mon to Sat 12 to 2.30, 6 to 9, Sun 12 to 4. 5 real ales. Bar menu, jacket potatoes, ploughman's, home-made specials, no sandwiches. Children welcome in separate area. Dogs welcome in bar.

Boot, The Green, Sarratt WD3 6BL. ☎ (01923) 262247. Open Mon to Sat 11 to 3, 5.30 to 11, Sat 11 to 11, Sun 12 to 10.30; food Tues to Sat 12 to 2, 6 to 9, Sun and Mon 12 to 2. 4 real ales. Full bar menu, specials, baguettes and jacket potatoes at lunch-time, à la carte menu in evenings. Children welcome at lunch-time. No dogs during food times.

Plough, Belsize, Sarratt WD3 4NP. ☎ (01923) 262800. Open Mon to Sat 11 to 3, 6 to 11, Sun 12 to 3, 7 to 10.30; food Mon to Sat 11 to 3, 6 to 11, Sun 12 to 3. Pubmaster pub, 2 real ales. Traditional pub food, blackboard specials, sandwiches, baguettes, ploughman's, bar snacks. Children welcome in dining area. No dogs in dining area.

Cock Inn, Church Lane, Church End, Sarratt WD3 6HH. ☎ (01923) 282908. Open Mon to Fri 11 to 3, 5.30 to 11, Sat 11 to 11, Sun 12 to 10.30; food Mon to Sat 12 to 2.30, 6 to 9, Sun 12 to 2.30, 7.30 to 9.30. Badger beers. Set bar menu and specials board, sandwiches, à la carte menu in restaurant. No children in bar area. Dogs welcome in bar area.

Red Lion, Chenies WD3 6ED. ☎ (01923) 282722. Open Mon to Sat 11 to 3, 5.30 to 11, Sun 12 to 3, 6.30 to 10.30; closed 25 Dec; food 12 to 2, 7 to 10 (9.30 Sun). Vale Notley Ale, Wadworth 6X, Benskins beers. In the L-shaped bar are old advertising signs, prints of traction engines, interesting old photos, and a brass model of Stephenson's Rocket. Food offerings are filled baguettes and baps, jacket potatoes, soup and salads. For a more substantial meal, you might choose turkey escalopes or grilled Mediterranean tomatoes with mozzarella, olives and basil and ciabatta bread. No children. No dogs in dining-room.

Start: Car park, ¼ mile north of A404, 2½ miles north-west of Chorleywood; turn off the A404 at the east end of Little Chalfont into Stony Lane (signposted Latimer and Flaunden); the car park is on the left just where the woods begin. Grid reference 005982.

Length: Full walk 6½ miles (10.5 kilometres), 3 hours. Short walk omitting Sarratt 3 miles (5km), 1½ hours.

Difficulty: Moderate, over rolling terrain but with no steep slopes.

OS maps: 1:25,000 Explorer sheet 172; 1:50,000 Landranger sheet 176, or 165 and 166.

Shop at Sarratt.

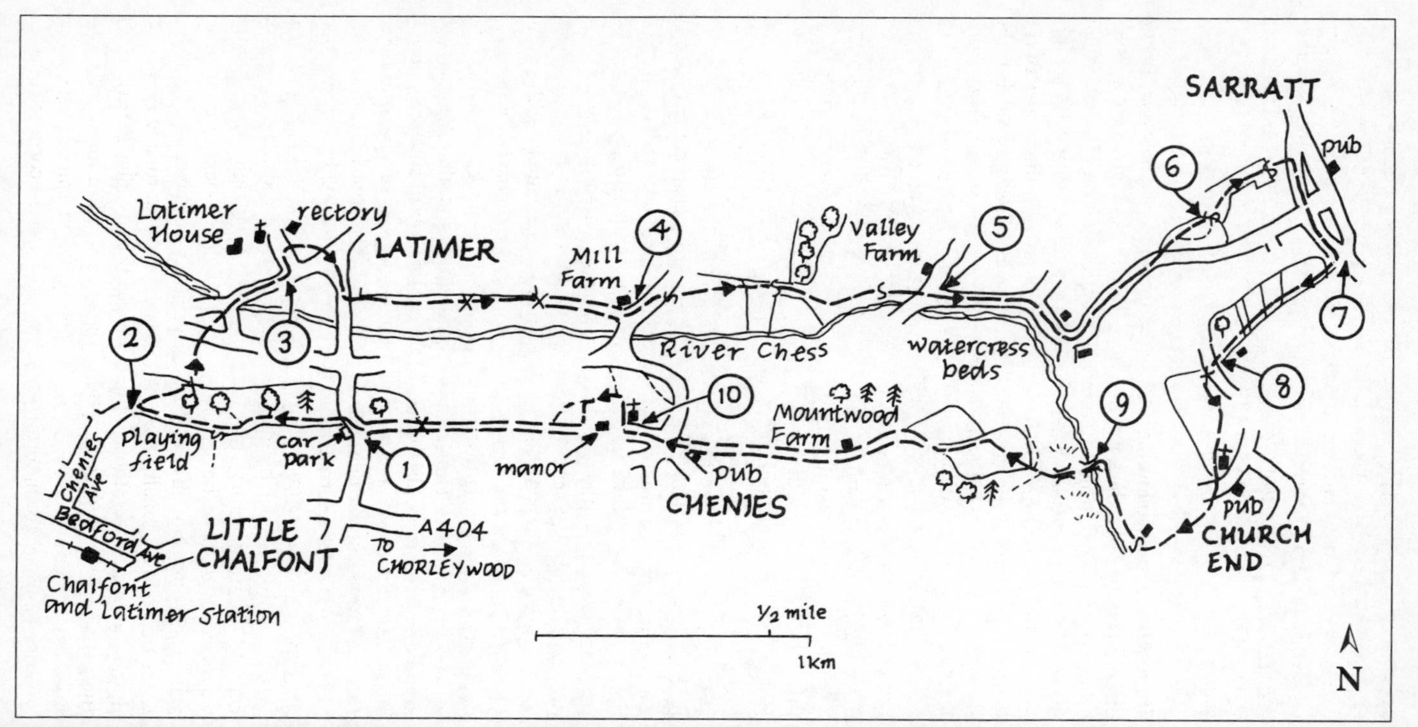
SARRATT
pub
Latimer House
rectory
LATIMER
Mill Farm
Valley Farm
River Chess
watercress beds
Mountwood Farm
manor
pub
CHENIES
pub
CHURCH END
Playing field
car park
Chenies Ave
Bedford Ave
LITTLE CHALFONT
A404
TO CHORLEYWOOD
Chalfont and Latimer Station
½ mile
1km
N
1
2
3
4
5
6
7
8
9
10

PT Chalfont and Latimer station. Leave by the exit on the London-bound platform, turn right outside the station, left into Bedford Avenue, then right into Chenies Avenue, which you follow to its end, ignoring side turns. Where it becomes unsurfaced continue into the woods, where you pass to the far side of a fence 20 yards away and take the right-hand of two paths which descend through the woods; join the walk at ❷. To return to the station, follow the directions at ❶, turning left through the barrier into Chenies Avenue 100 yards after a modern house.

---

❶ From the car park follow the road downhill for 50 yards, then take the bridleway on the left, which follows the top edge of the woods. After ¼ mile, ignore a stile into a playing field on your left, but continue inside the edge of woods. After ¼ mile pass close to a modern house, then 100 yards later turn sharp right to the other side of a fence on a descending woodland path ❷.

At the bottom of the woods, go through a barrier (with Latimer House visible on the hill ahead), follow the right edge of a field, then cross the road and take the signposted gate opposite, along the left edge of the small field to a road junction, where you continue forward, over the bridge, along the road. You now gain the first of a series of fine views over the **Chess Valley**; the Chess in this section has been dammed to create a landscaping effect for Latimer House, the grandiose 19th-century, Elizabethan-style mansion (now a National Defence College) on the hillside.

❸ At a T-junction, turn left, then opposite a path to Latimer church (which stands near a handsome early 18th-century rectory), take the waymarked path (Chess Valley walk) on your right into a field. Cross this field diagonally, heading down to some houses, then follow the path between hedges into the main part of Latimer.

Cross its village green, turn right on a road, then left 80 yards later by a signpost, and go into a field. Follow the fence on your left until it reaches a corner, then carry on forward 80 yards to the corner of the next fence, walking parallel to the River Chess away to your right; proceed alongside this fence. After the next field, continue on a farm track, through a farm, to reach the road ❹.

For the short walk turn right and follow the road over the river, then bear right where the road divides, to reach a T-junction, where you take the path opposite into woodland. Immediately fork left and follow the path up the left edge of woods, then proceed on a path between hedges to reach Chenies church and manor house; this is point ❿ (resume the walk directions with the church on the right; you will now return to the woods).

For the full walk turn left on the road, then right after 100 yards to take a signposted stile: the route is along the top of a pronounced grassy bank (marking a former field boundary). Follow the left edge of the second field, then go through the woods, on the far side of which keep right, soon joining the river; in the next field continue alongside the river to reach the corner of a farm road ❺ (to the left this leads past Valley Farm), where you keep forward for ¼ mile – on the right you can see watercress beds – to join the corner of another road. Turn right along this, then left at the next junction (ahead is a no through road), 50 yards after the woods begin, take a signposted footpath on the left; keep left at a fork, close to the edge of the woods.

❻ Ignore a gate beside a stile on the left leading out of the woods but continue forward to a stile into a field: follow the right edge of the field, then at the end take the path into **Sarratt**. Turn right along the ½-mile-long village green, which is flanked by mostly 18th- and 19th-century cottages.

❼ Just after a pillar-box and the post office, take a lane on your right, signposted Church End; after Forge Cottage cross a stile and follow the left edges of four fields, enter the woods and fork left 20 yards later. The path runs along a fence then in the same direction behind back gardens, before reaching a road ❽.

Take the kissing-gate opposite, turn left in the field alongside woods, then go forward to the church. Emerge by the church gate on to a road. The Norman church, early 19th-century almshouses and pub at **Church End** make an appealing group. The next section is one of the walk's visual highlights, with views over the Chess Valley, and a descent to the river, which is marshy and remote-feeling.

Cross this road and bear half right (over a stile) towards a signpost (for Chorleywood) 30 yards away, where you cross the driveway and take the stile into a field. Turn right in the field, along its edge, to the bottom corner, then go forward on a track; turn right a few yards later to pass below a cottage and over a stile. Walk close to the river.

❾ At the end of the field, turn left, over a footbridge. The path then crosses another footbridge (over a channel); immediately after this avoid a right fork. On entering the woods, fork right, enter the bottom of a field and cross it diagonally, uphill (waymarked). On reaching the opposite hedgerow, follow it uphill, and in the next field proceed along its left edge to pick up a farm track leading past the left-hand side of a farm, then on ⅓ mile to Chenies.

Take the gravel driveway on the opposite side of the village green to the church ❿, just after which turn right on a path between walls. Descend into the woods, where you turn left, along the top edge. 120 yards later, fork left to continue along the top edge. Emerge from the woods just beyond a house on your left and continue straight ahead until the path joins the road at the car park.

Chenies

Chenies has a triangular village green flanked by estate cottages built in the 1850s by the Earl of Bedford. The church is heavily restored, but worth a look for the spectacular array of 16th-century and 17th-century monuments in the Bedford Chapel. Adjacent is the step-gabled and brick-turreted Elizabethan manor house, with a shell of one wing at the rear open to the elements. The main part of the manor is still a residence (open April to October, bank holidays, Wednesday and Thursday; afternoons only). It contains tapestries, a doll collection and a priest's hole, while in the grounds are a physic garden and a maze.

Turville and Stonor Park

BUCKINGHAMSHIRE/OXFORDSHIRE WALK 48

This quiet corner of the Chilterns offers an enjoyable blend of mixed woods and open farmland; the route passes through the deer park of Stonor House. The rolling nature of the terrain gives changes of altitude, and the walk begins from Turville, a small village with a number of attractive half-timbered houses and a flint church of Norman origin with a 16th-century tower.

Bull and Butcher, Turville RG9 6QU. ☎ (01491) 638283. Open Mon to Sat 11 to 3, 6 (6.30 Sat) to 11, Sun 12 to 4, 7 to 9.30; food Tues to Sun 12 to 2 (2.30 Sat and Sun), Tues to Sat 7 to 9.45. Brakspear beers. This small 17th-century black-and-white timbered pub featured in *The Vicar of Dibley* and *Chitty Chitty Bang Bang*. Barbecues are occasionally held on the front lawn on summer weekends. Inside, beams from captured Spanish Armada ships provide extra counter space for drinking. Food, which is cooked to order, is an eclectic mix: perhaps tapas or stir-fried calamares to start, and scallops with lemon grass and garlic or steak Wellington for a main course. Starters are available as bar snacks. No children. Dogs welcome.

Crown Inn, Pishill RG9 6HH. ☎ (01491) 638364. Open Mon to Sat 11.30 to 2.30, 6 to 11, Sun 12 to 3, 7 to 10.30; food all week 12 to 2, 7 to 10. Brakspear, Fuller's London Pride. Bar snacks, including ploughman's, soup and sandwiches, à la carte menu including fillet steaks, pigeon, chicken and fish. No sandwiches in evenings. Children welcome in dining-room by prior appointment. No dogs.

Stonor Arms, Stonor RG9 6HE. ☎ (01491) 638345. Open Mon to Sat 11 to 11, Sun 12 to 10.30; bar food all week 11 to 9, restaurant all week 12 to 2, 7 to 9.30. Bass, Brakspear beers. On the bar snacks menu are sandwiches, soup, ploughman's, steaks. The restaurant menu might include warm goat's cheese and green tomato chutney or country-style pork and pistachio terrine to start, and lobster fish cake with roast cod and shellfish sauce or pan-fried calves' liver with parsley mash as a main course. Children welcome. Dogs welcome.

Start: Turville, west of High Wycombe and south of M40 (junction 5). Grid reference 767912.

Length: 8½ miles (13.5 kilometres), 4 hours.

Difficulty: Moderate, over rolling farmland and through woods, all on good paths and tracks. Can get muddy.

OS maps: 1:25,000 Explorer sheet 171; 1:50,000 Landranger sheet 175.

❶ Start on the village green in Turville, between the church and the Bull and Butcher pub. Walk down the village street to the left of the church; at the end of the village, by Turville village sign, turn left down a track marked by a public bridleway sign. Follow this track through a belt of trees and for 300 yards along the left-hand edge of a

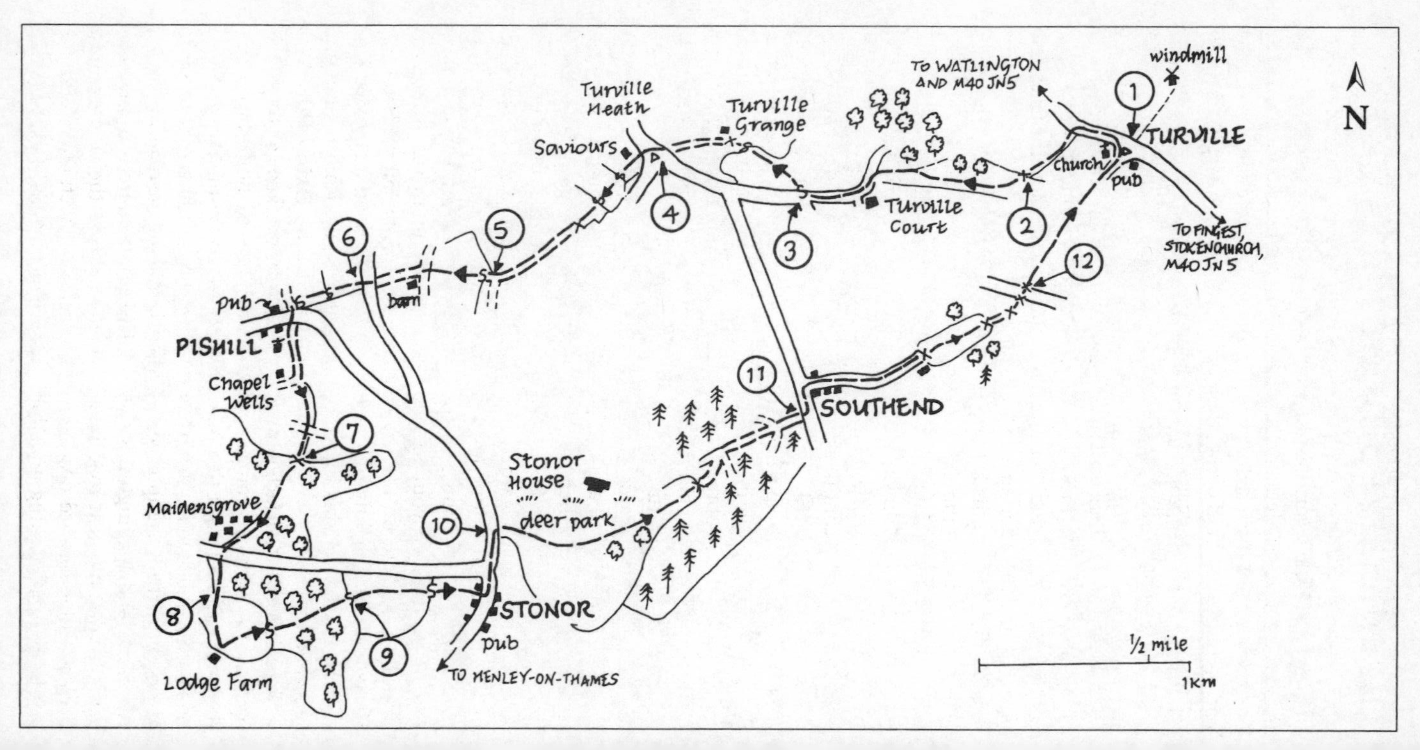
N
windmill
TURVILLE
1
TO WATLINGTON AND M40 JN5
TO FINGEST, STOKENCHURCH, M40 JN 5
Church
pub
2
12
Turville Court
Turville Grange
3
Turville Heath
Saviours
4
5
6
barn
pub
PISHILL
Chapel Wells
7
Maidensgrove
8
Lodge Farm
9
10
STONOR
pub
TO HENLEY-ON-THAMES
Stonor House
deer park
11
SOUTHEND
1/2 mile
1km

field, ignoring a turn to the left half the way along.

❷ At the field corner (which is not very clear-cut), turn left into the wood on a well-defined path, but after 10 yards turn sharp right and slightly uphill. Follow this narrow path, as indicated by an arrow on a tree, and go diagonally uphill.

At the top of the slope turn right along a woodland track, which continues to ascend and then runs along just inside the top edge of the wood, with a field on the left. After 500 yards, just before the end of the wood, turn left at a T-junction of tracks towards buildings, where you turn right on a surfaced farm road by a house and continue down this to a road junction ❸.

At the junction, go up a bank to the right and over a stile into a field, following a public footpath sign. Cross the field to the closest point in the far hedge, then turn left following the hedge towards Turville Grange. Shortly before a house, go right over a stile and then turn left towards another house. Soon cross another stile into a garden and maintain this direction down a track to the left of a house. At the end of the wall on your left, go through a gate out on to Turville Heath then bear slightly right and emerge in front of this fine 18th-century house.

Turn left on a surfaced track, opposite the wrought-iron gates to the house, and follow it to a junction with a public road. Turn right along the road signposted to Northend and Watlington. ❹ 70 yards later, at the next road junction, continue forward on a signposted footpath, taking direction from signs to Saviours. The path goes to the left of the gate to Saviours and immediately enters the first field by a gate. Stay to the left of the house, keeping level and making for a stile into the second field. Continue forward to a stile into the third field, then maintain direction (diagonally) to reach a kissing-gate and turn right on to a fenced track. The track soon enters a field (but continues with a fence on the right). Follow the track into the next field.

❺ After 100 yards, the track divides (with the left fork leading towards Stonor village, visible in its valley); take the right-hand fork, marked by white arrows. Soon, cross a stile and descend to the bottom of valley on a well-defined field path to an open-sided barn. Keep right of this barn and then ascend to the ridge, ignoring a cross-path. Your path broadens to become a track.

❻ At the top of the rise, cross the surfaced lane. Continue downhill alongside a hedge on the left to cross a stile at the corner of a field and continue on a broad path (past a house and garden on your left) to a further stile. Turn left on a track, soon reaching a road, where you turn right. After 50 yards on this road, turn left on a surfaced lane signposted to Pishill church and marked as the **Oxfordshire Way** (sometimes marked as OW), a 65-mile path, from Bourton-on-the-Water to Henley-on-Thames. (The Crown Inn is 100 yards' detour to the right along the road.)

Pass Pishill church on your right then, at end of the lane, take the footpath to the left of the entrance to Chapel Wells (still on the

Oxfordshire Way). After 75 yards, take the left-hand fork (OW), then go down the left-hand edge of a field. At the bottom, ignore a cross-track and continue up the edge of the field to enter a wood ❼.

Continue forward into the woods on a footpath going uphill, and at the top of the rise maintain direction, keeping the field visible on your right. ¼ mile into the woods, fork left (the right fork goes towards a nearby house), now descending gently. Cross a road and take the right-hand path opposite (the narrower of two paths); this ascends through the woods, with the edge of the woods close on your right.

After 200 yards, and shortly before the end of the woods, ignore a stile to the right. Continue another 20 yards to emerge into a field ❽. Continue straight ahead across the field towards farm buildings, but at the end of the field do not leave it; instead turn sharp left on to a path running diagonally across the field, keeping just to the left of a pylon, to a stile.

Cross this stile into the woods and continue forward downhill on a woodland path marked by white arrows. ❾ To enter the field by the stile, continue forward and make for the village of Stonor, clearly visible at the bottom of the slope (crossing this and the next field, then following an enclosed path into the village). Turn left on the road (or detour 100 yards to the right for the Stonor Arms pub).

❿ After 300 yards, iron railings around Stonor Park start on the right: here enter the parkland through a gate by a 'Private Deer Park' sign and take the grassy path heading uphill and away from the fence towards a line of trees. Follow the line of trees as this path becomes better defined and is marked by white arrows.

From here you get a good view of **Stonor House**, its walled garden and private chapel. Home of the Stonor family for 600 years, the original Tudor manor was extended in Tudor times, and a new roof and windows were added in 1760. During the Elizabethan religious troubles, the Jesuit Edmund Campion had a secret printing-press here.

After ½ mile, leave the deer park by a gate into the wood. Ignore side turns (keep forward at the first junction; ¼ mile later, near the edge of the woods, avoid left and right turns) and proceed up to a road. ⓫ Turn left along the road for 100 yards to a minor junction at the hamlet of Southend, where you turn right on a surfaced track marked as public footpath, keeping a small common on your right. At the end of the common, keep to the left of a pair of brick houses and take the farm road signposted to Southend Farm.

Follow this concrete track to the end of the farm buildings, and when the track swings right around the buildings continue forward over a stile beside a gate (marked by white arrows). Cross a field, keeping just to the right of the pylons to a gate beside a stile in the middle of the far edge, then go steeply down a fenced track through a wood. At the end of this wood, take a gate beside a stile directly ahead (ignore a gate to the left), then descend the left-hand edge of the field to a gate beside a stile on to a road ⓬.

Cross this road and enter a field by a gate beside a stile, then head forward across a field; when inspected, this path was very well defined but if it is unclear take the direction from **Cobston Windmill** on the hill ahead. This smock mill was constructed in the 18th century; its top part was designed to rotate separately.

At the end of the field, an enclosed path continues ahead, emerging after 200 yards on the road by some bungalows. Follow this down to the main village street in Turville.

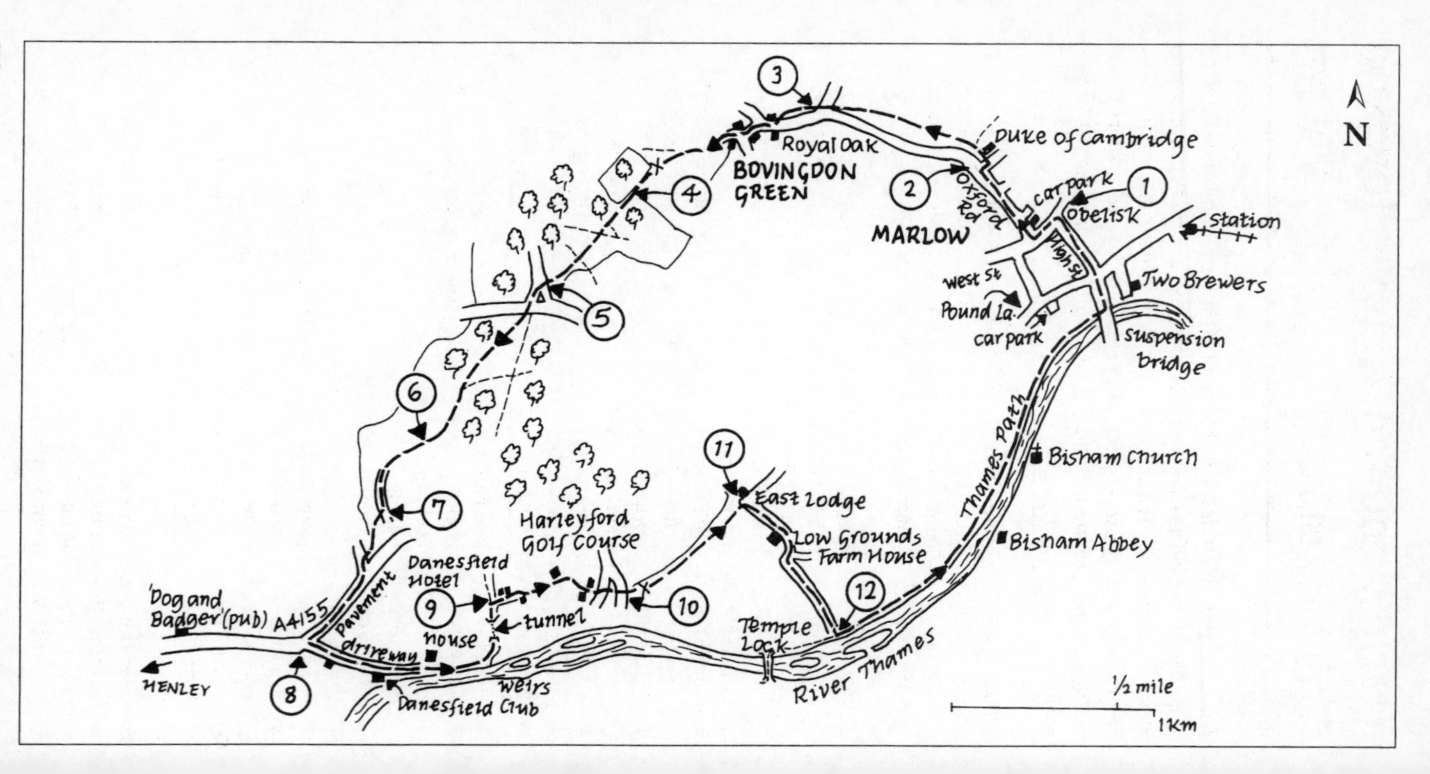
N
Duke of Cambridge
1
car park
Obelisk
Station
MARLOW
Oxford Rd
2
High St
Two Brewers
West St
Pound La.
car park
Suspension bridge
3
Royal Oak
BOVINGDON GREEN
4
5
6
7
Thames Path
Bisham Church
Bisham Abbey
11
East Lodge
Low Grounds Farm House
12
Harleyford Golf Course
Danesfield Hotel
9
tunnel
10
house
Temple Lock
River Thames
'Dog and Badger' (pub)
A4155
Pavement
driveway
HENLEY
8
Weirs
Danesfield Club
1/2 mile
1 Km

Marlow and the Thames Towpath

BUCKINGHAMSHIRE WALK 49

The handsome riverside town of Marlow is the base for a varied walk that heads out through fine Chilterns beech woods, particularly attractive in spring and autumn. White arrows on trees make route-finding easy. Then comes a surprise – some sheer chalk cliffs (and a short tunnel through them) – before the finale, a beautiful stretch along the Thames towpath.

Hogshead, 82 High Street, Marlow SL7 1AZ. ☎ (01628) 478737. Open Mon to Sat 11 to 11, Sun 12 to 10.30; food Mon to Thurs 11 to 9, Fri and Sat 11 to 8, Sun 12 to 9. 12 real ales including Whitbread, Theakston, Hogshead beers. Traditional pub food, set menu, à la carte menu, specials board and sandwiches. No children. Guide dogs only.

Royal Oak, Frieth Road, Bovingdon Green SL7 2JF. ☎ (01628) 488611. Open Mon to Fri 11.30 to 3.30, 5.30 to 11, Sat 11 to 11, Sun 12 to 10.30; food Mon to Fri 12 to 2.30, Sat 11 to 11, Sun 12 to 4. Brakspear, Wadworth 6X and 1 guest beer. A la carte menu, blackboard specials, bar meals, sandwiches, baguettes, Sunday roast. Children welcome. No dogs in restaurant.

Two Brewers, St Peter's Street, Marlow SL7 1NQ (first right turning off Station Road from High Street, or follow Thames Footpath signs east of suspension bridge). ☎ (01628) 484140. Open Mon to Sat 11.30 to 3, 5 to 11, Sun 12 to 10.30; food Mon to Sat 12 to 2.30, Sun 12 to 1.45. 4 real ales. A la carte menu, which might include moules marinière, crispy duck leg confit or ginger-crusted red bream fillets. Daily specials, bar snacks, baguettes and Sunday roasts are also served. Children welcome. Dogs welcome in bar area.

Start: Marlow town centre, by the obelisk and Crown Hotel in the High Street. Grid reference 866848. Car park in Pound Lane, adjoining the Leisure Complex, is convenient: turn right out of the car park entrance/exit into Pound Lane and left into the High Street to the obelisk ❶.
Length: 7½ miles (12 kilometres); 4 hours.
Difficulty: Moderate.
OS maps: 1:25,000 Explorer sheet 172; 1:50,000 Landranger sheet 175.
Full range in Marlow; kiosk at Temple Lock.
WC Pound Lane, Marlow; Oxford Road, Marlow; Temple Lock.
PT Train to Marlow. At the end of Station Approach, turn right into Lock Road, left into Station Road, right into the High Street to the obelisk ❶.

❶ From the obelisk (which commemorates the opening of the Hatfield-to-Bath road) in the High Street, with the Crown Hotel on your right, turn left into West Street. At No. 47 West Street is the house where the poet **Percy Shelley** lived from 1817 to 1818; Mary Shelley wrote *Frankenstein* here. Turn right into Oxford Road (signposted Bovingdon Green). Turn right into Queen's Road, then ❷ take a path on the left up the side of the Duke of Cambridge pub (the path runs to the right of a concrete track); carry on uphill, with allotments on the right, then levelling off between fences between fields.

❸ At a surfaced lane, with private drives to the right and a house on the left, turn left and immediately fork right on a footpath that reaches a road opposite the Royal Oak, a pub with a good garden adjoining the village pond. Bear right along the road and take the next left turn after the pub into the pretty hamlet of **Bovingdon Green**. Take the signposted stony track that leaves from the far right-hand corner of the green, with a hedge on the left and a barn behind a wall on the right. Keep ahead on the track, which swings right and becomes a path between fences through fields of pasture with beech woods all around. Keep ahead through a kissing-gate.

❹ The path enters woods through a gate marked with a white arrow: keep forward, initially with a fence on your right. At the end of the fence, keep ahead, following the white arrow, and drop downhill. At the first path crossing, in the dip, go forward, up a rise, and 20 paces later bear left, following white arrows on trees. The path narrows but is reasonably clear through beautiful beech woodland full of birdsong. Soon a broad path crosses at right angles in front of a tree marked with white arrows. Keep straight ahead following a succession of white arrows. The path stays fairly close to the left edge of the woods. Keep forward with more arrows.

❺ Emerge at a road, turn left and at a fork take the right-hand road to a T-junction. Cross the road on to a broad path ahead, but immediately leave this path and bear diagonally right on to another signed footpath that initially goes downhill then rises through Hollow Hill Wood, with plenty of white arrows on trees to indicate the way ahead.

❻ After ½ mile this path bends right to skirt houses. Pass a large white house on the left, then join a track, which is initially gravel and soon tarmac. Proceed past glasshouses on the left until you reach a large multi-gabled white house on the right, just before which ❼ you take a narrow, paved path on the right, down to the edge of the woods. Here turn left on a path to reach a driveway. Keep left and meet a main road. Turn right on to this (cross the road and use the pavement on the other side).

❽ Immediately before (not after) the Medmenham village sign, turn back sharp left up a driveway to the right of West Lodge, with a Danesfield (Thames) Club sign. At the end of the driveway, find an enclosed path to the right of the red-brick house facing you, close by the river, and soon pass beneath tall, sheer, white chalky cliffs on the left. As you reach some weirs in the river, a popular spot for canoeists to practise their rolls, the path climbs steeply away from the river, with superb views down over the river, and goes through a short, brick-lined tunnel.

❾ Where a wall on your right ends at a wooden gate with a white arrow, turn right, with a fence on your right, through a patch of woodland. Go through a gate at the end, right, following the edge of Harleyford Golf Course close to a tall evergreen hedge and passing a redbrick house to enter the Harleyford leisure complex. Follow the footpath round the clubhouse, straight over the tarmac drive, and down a footpath that leads through a workshop yard to a road ⑩.

Cross the road and take the signposted path opposite (look back for a view of Harleyford Manor). This runs along beneath woodland on the left, with views right over grazing land to the Thames, and cruisers moored along the bank.

⑪ Go through the stile/gate by East Lodge, turn right on to the signposted public footpath, to pass Low Grounds Farm House on your right. Just after it, fork right on a broad vehicle track.

⑫ At the river, the walk turns left along the riverbank, but a short detour to the right brings you to **Temple Lock.** Here you can sit on benches and watch the comings and goings in the lock (there is a refreshment kiosk and a toilet). Continue the walk eastwards along the towpath. This is part of the Thames Path, which runs for 180 miles from source to sea.

The views across the river to **Bisham Abbey** (now a sports centre) are excellent. Its pretty church is said to be haunted by the ghost of Lady Elizabeth Hoby, who is buried here. As you near the suspension bridge, designed by William Tierney Clark in 1832, you can fork left through public gardens to return to the Pound Lane car park or the High Street. Alternatively, continue to the bridge and follow Thames Path signs across the causeway and through to the Two Brewers pub in St Peter's Street, where Jerome K. Jerome sketched out ideas for *Three Men in a Boat*, his comic story of three men and a dog making a trip along the Thames.

Swan Upping

Every year since the days of Elizabeth I a voyage has taken place on the Thames to mark the beaks of cygnets on the river. All swans are royal property apart from some on the Thames, which belong to the Vintners and the Dyers, two ancient London livery companies. In the third week of July, the Royal Keeper of Swans and the Swan Markers of the Vintners and Dyers row from Sunbury to Pangbourne, with the oarsmen colourfully attired in traditional livery and the boats festooned with flags. Roast swan forms the focus of an ensuing banquet.

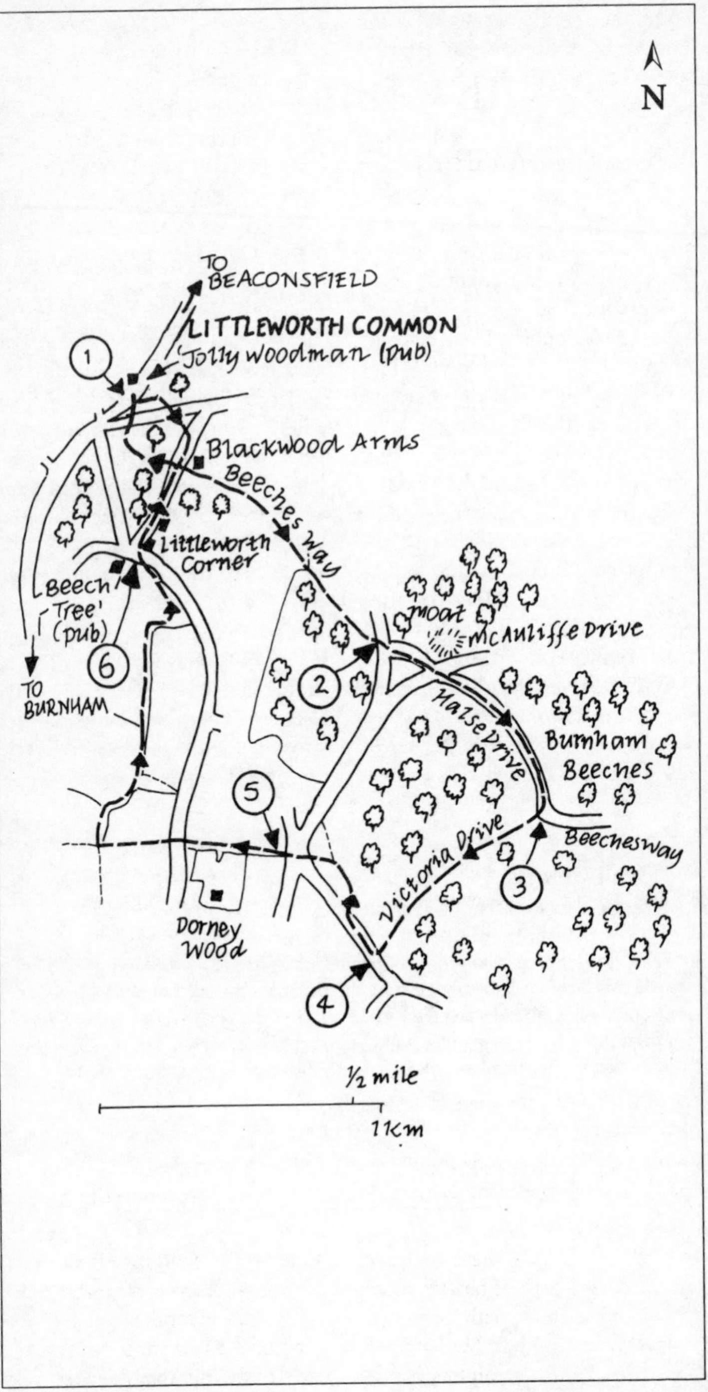

N
TO BEACONSFIELD
LITTLEWORTH COMMON
Jolly Woodman (pub)
1
Blackwood Arms
Beeches Way
Littleworth Corner
'Beech Tree' (pub)
6
TO BURNHAM
moat
McAuliffe Drive
2
Halse Drive
Burnham Beeches
5
Beechesway
Victoria Drive
3
Dorney Wood
4
½ mile
1Km

Burnham Beeches and Littleworth Common

BUCKINGHAMSHIRE WALK 50

There can be few patches of woodland that rival Burnham Beeches for beauty. In spring it is beautiful, in autumn spectacular. This walk picks out some of many paths that wind through the ancient, semi-natural woodland with its huge pollarded beech trees and open grassy glades. This is an undemanding walk, beginning and ending through fields of pasture.

Jolly Woodman, Littleworth Road, Littleworth Common, Burnham SL1 8PF. ☎ (01753) 644350. Open Mon to Sat 11 to 11, Sun 12 to 10.30; food Mon to Sat 12 to 2.30, 6.30 to 9.30, Sun 12 to 4. Whitbread, Flowers, Brakspear beers. Traditional pub food with daily specials, baguettes. Children welcome if eating. No dogs during meal times.

Blackwood Arms, Common Lane, Littleworth Common, Burnham SL1 8PP. ☎ (01753) 642169. Open Mon to Fri 11 to 3, 5.30 to 11, Sat 11 to 11, Sun 12 to 10.30; food all week 12 to 2, 6 to 9. 6 guest beers. A small pub deep in the woods serving platters and sandwiches at lunch-time, and a set menu, blackboard specials and steaks in the evenings. Children welcome. Dogs welcome.

Beech Tree, Dorneywood Road, Littleworth Common SL1 9PX. ☎ (01628) 661328. Open Mon to Sat 11 to 11, Sun 12 to 10.30. Greenalls beers. Traditional pub food, sandwiches, blackboard specials, including casseroles and pasta. Children welcome. Dogs welcome.

Start: Car park beside the Jolly Woodman, Littleworth Common. Grid reference 935865. The pub is on the minor road that runs south-west off the A355 immediately south of M40 Junction 2 (Beaconsfield). Follow signs to Littleworth Common and Burnham. The pub is 2 miles south of the A355 junction, on the left (east) side of the road. Alternatively, from the centre of Burnham (3 miles west of Slough), follow signs for Beaconsfield (Dropmore Road) for 2½ miles due north. The Jolly Woodman is on the right-hand side of the road, almost opposite Dropmore Parish Hall, Littleworth Road.

Length: 4½ miles (7 kilometres), 2½ hours.

Difficulty: Easy.

OS maps: 1:25,000 Explorer sheet 172; 1:50,000 Landranger sheet 175.

PT Nearest railway stations: Beaconsfield or Burnham (both approximately 3 miles).

❶ With your back to the road, leave the car park from the far left-hand corner, on a narrow path, passing a bungalow on the left. Swing right (ignoring a path straight ahead) and cross the road into the woods. Meet a road, turn right on to it and pass the Blackwood Arms. Turn left over a stile a few yards beyond the pub, following the Beeches Way over stiles and across fields to enter Dorney Wood. Keep ahead on the clear, waymarked path to emerge at a road ❷.

Cross straight over the road and continue into **Burnham Beeches National Nature Reserve**. A notice board gives information on the practice of pollarding (see box). The danger is that if left uncut too long (and many trees in Burnham Beeches have not been cut for 150 years), pollarded trees grow top-heavy and fall. At the time of writing a pollarded tree has collapsed some 300 yards along the path on the right-hand side. Meet a tarmac 'drive' and turn left, then left again at a large notice board into McAuliffe Drive. About 50 yards on, turn left into the trees to a metal plaque marking Hartley Court or Hardicanute's Moat, a moated homestead dating from the 12th to 14th century. Cross over the moat and stand in the central, square homestead. Retrace your steps to the large notice board at the end of McAuliffe Drive and turn left onto Halse Drive.

Follow Halse Drive through rhododendrons and beech trees. At the bottom of a dip ❸, leave the tarmac road, turning right on to Victoria Drive, a broad woodland path. In autumn you kick your way through a carpet of leaves while the beech trees on all sides are aflame with every shade of red, orange and yellow. You may well see evidence of woodland management, both in the form of pollarding and by allowing dead trees to lie where they fall, thus providing sanctuary for insects and birds such as the green woodpecker, which nests in decaying tree trunks.

Visible to the left of the path are the ramparts of an ancient settlement; trees now grow up its banks. Reach a road, Pumpkin Hill ❹, by a large Corporation of London notice board, and turn right. After 150 yards pass a drive to a private house on the left and 50 yards beyond this leave the road by taking a path on the right at a metal gate, back into the woodland. At a clearing with a junction of paths, keep ahead, parallel to the road. Emerge by a big black notice board at a crossroads ❺.

Cross Park Lane and then Curriers Lane, and take a signed footpath over a stile to the left of an electricity substation and down the left-hand side of a field (this may be muddy). On the left is **Dorney Wood**, a property donated to the National Trust as a residence for a Secretary of State or Minister of the Crown, currently used by the Chancellor of the Exchequer. The 1930s-style gardens are open to the public on a handful of days each summer, by written appointment. Cross straight over a road and continue ahead across the middle of another field. Meet the corner of a hedge, go through the gap and turn right along the edge of the field, keeping the hedge on your right. Follow the path along the right-hand edge of a succession of crop fields, going through more gaps in the hedges. The path eventually curves right, round a field of pasture with woodland on the right. A stile in the hedge brings you on to the road ❻.

Turn left and in 50 yards is the Beech Tree pub. Turn right into Common Lane, with some pretty houses and a tiny bungalow on the right and then with the beech and birch trees of Littleworth Common on either side. Just before the Blackwood Arms, turn left through the car-parking area and take the path beside a notice board into the woods. As you draw level with the church, turn right, cross the road and take the path to the right of the churchyard back to the start point.

Pollarding

Pollarding and coppicing are woodland management practices dating from medieval times. Through these techniques a continuous supply of wood was produced for firewood and craft purposes. Every few years the trees were felled, and the new shoots put out by the stumps would provide the next crop of wood. Coppiced trees, cut just above ground level, were grown in areas protected from grazing animals, who would eat the new young shoots. Pollards, cut about 8 feet (2.5 metres) above the ground so the new shoots were safe from browsing animals, are an indicator of ancient pasture-woodland, in which trees were grown and cattle grazed in the same place. Many of the splendidly gnarled specimens in Burnham Beeches have not been cut since the mid-19th century and have become dangerously top heavy. The trees are now being cut again to prolong their lives.

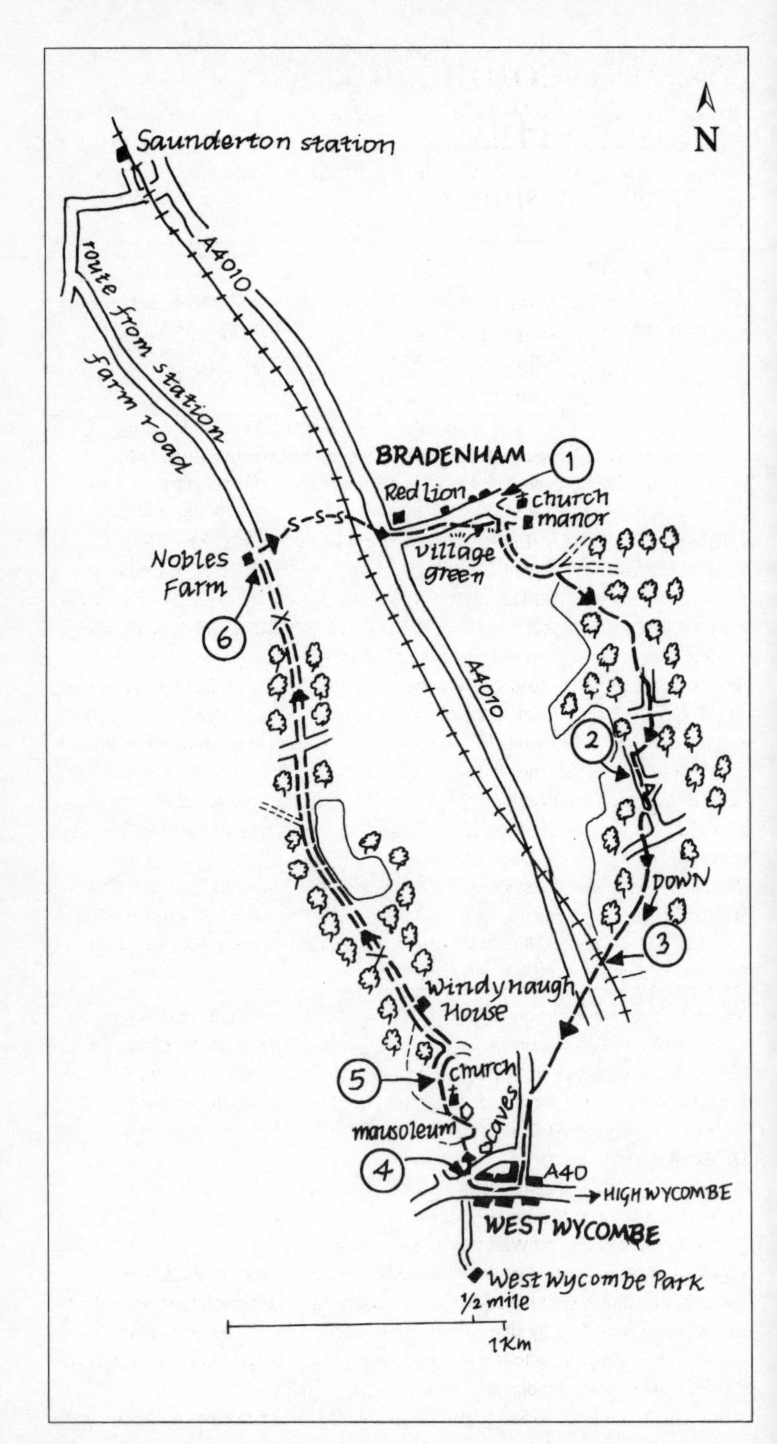
N
Saunderton station
A4010
route from station
farm road
BRADENHAM
1
Red Lion
church
manor
village green
s-s-s
Nobles Farm
6
A4010
2
DOWN
3
Windynaugh House
5
church
caves
mausoleum
4
A40
HIGH WYCOMBE
WEST WYCOMBE
West Wycombe Park
1/2 mile
1Km

West Wycombe and the Chiltern Hills

BUCKINGHAMSHIRE WALK 51

Waymarked tracks through Chiltern beechwoods link the small, peaceful village of Bradenham and the larger, attractive, National Trust village of West Wycombe, notable for various colourful legacies of Sir Francis Dashwood, an 18th-century eccentric.

George and Dragon Hotel, High Street, West Wycombe HP14 3AB. ☎ (01494) 464414. Open Mon to Sat 11 to 2.30, 5.30 to 11, Sun 12 to 3, 7 to 10.30; food Mon to Sat 12 to 2, 6 to 9.30, Sun 12 to 2.15, 7 to 9. Courage Directors, Charles Wells Bombardier, Fuller's London Pride. The George and Dragon is a grade II listed Tudor coaching inn, with blackened beams, Windsor chairs and window seats. On the printed menu might be soup, chicken goujons or potted Stilton to start, while main courses could be beef Wellington, steak or specials such as grilled goats' cheese salad or pancakes. Children welcome in family room. Dogs welcome.

Red Lion, Wickham Road, Bradenham HP14 4HF. ☎ (01494) 562212. Open Mon to Fri 12 to 3, 4.30 to 11, Sat 12 to 11, Sun 12 to 10.30; food 12 to 2. 2 real ales. The Red Lion is an old whitewashed flint building with a pleasant dining room extension and serves bar snacks, sandwiches and Sunday roasts. No children in bar. Dogs welcome.

Old Plough, West Wycombe HP14 3AG. ☎ (01494) 446648. Open Mon to Sat 11 to 11, Sun 12 to 10.30; food 12 to 10. 3 or 4 real ales. Sandwiches, basket meals, roasts. Children welcome. Dogs welcome.

Swan, High Street, West Wycombe HP14 3AE. ☎ (01494) 527031. Open Mon to Fri 11 to 2, 5.30 to 11, Sat 11.30 to 2.30, 5.30 to 11, Sun 12 to 2.30, 7 to 10.30; food 12.15 to 1.30. 3 real ales. Roasts Mon to Fri, sandwiches only at weekends. Children welcome in dining room. Dogs welcome in bar.

Start: Bradenham village green, just off the A 4010, 1½ miles north of the junction with the A40 at West Wycombe, and 3½ miles north-west of High Wycombe. Park on the north side of the green, opposite the path to the church. Grid reference 827972.

Length: 4½ miles (7 kilometres), 2½ hours. Start/finish at Saunderton station: 6½ miles (10 kilometres), 3½ hours.

Difficulty: Moderate.

OS maps: 1:25,000 Explorer sheet 172; 1: 50,000 Landranger sheets 165 and 175.

West Wycombe village stores makes up sandwiches.

WC In West Wycombe, off West Wycombe Hill Road.

PT Trains to Saunderton Station (1¾ miles from start of walk). Grid reference 812982. Turn right out of the station approach and walk up Slough Lane (away from the railway bridge). Shortly after a right-angled bend to the left leave the road, following the tarmac drive to Nobles Farm. At the farm, continue from point ❻ to the start point ❶ opposite Bradenham church.

Frequent buses (Mon to Sat) to West Wycombe from High Wycombe, Oxford and

Uxbridge. 2-hourly service on Sun to West Wycombe from Oxford, High Wycombe, Amersham, Stansted Airport and Cambridge.

❶ Standing with the Norman Church of St Botolph to your left and the village green in front of you, walk across the green (owned by the National Trust) to a pavilion, where you turn left on a gravel track that runs alongside the boundary wall of 17th-century **Bradenham Manor**, childhood home of Victorian statesman Benjamin Disraeli (open March, Saturday and Sunday, April to October, Wednesday to Sunday). After 200 yards, at a corner of the wall on the left and immediately before a footpath/bridleway sign, turn right uphill on a narrow woodland path just inside the edge of the woods (avoid the wider track half-right actually next to the signpost). The path through the woods is waymarked – look for white arrows painted on trees. After 100 yards, where a broader track comes in from the left, bear right, following the white arrow on a tree. Keep following the white arrows on the trees and join a broader track. Ignore a path to the left immediately before a tree with a white arrow at a point where the path drops downhill. Keep forward at the crossing of tracks in the dip, going uphill on a narrow, winding path. Meet a wide track and turn left, still following white arrows. Shortly the track divides, forming a triangle of grass, with a pylon to the left ❷.

Take the right fork, a wide grassy track on the edge of the woodland, with views to the right across the valley. About 300 yards from the triangle, pass an ash tree with a white arrow opposite a 'Private Please Keep Out' sign. Continue for another 20 paces, then, just before a second 'Private Please Keep Out' sign, turn right off the track on to a narrow path between trees, soon starting to drop downhill slightly. Join a wider track on a corner. About 50 yards on, as the track bends away to the right, take the footpath off to the left (the white arrow on the beech tree here may be obscured when the tree is in full leaf). The path goes downhill, through a dense clump of yews, down an avenue of beech trees and then between fencing. Leave the wood through a gate ❸.

Cross the railway line with great care, go down half left across the field to cross the road and continue (still half left) up a large field on the other side. The golden orb in the church tower, in which the notorious Hell-Fire Club (see box) used to meet, is visible above the trees to the right. In the far left-hand corner of the field, emerge by a gate on a tarmac road. Turn left on to the road down Church Lane into **West Wycombe village.** At the end of Church Lane note Church Loft House, a medieval hospice whose upper storey projects over the pavement. The large yellow mansion ahead is **West Wycombe Park**, the Palladian mansion built for Sir Francis Dashwood in 1750 (see box). Turn right along the main street, an attractive mix of 15th- to 18th-century buildings, including the George and Dragon, a village shop and a chair restoration works, a reminder of the long-established Chilterns chair-making industry. The whole village is owned by the National Trust.

❹ At the western end of the main street and opposite the entrance to

West Wycombe Park, turn sharp right into West Wycombe Hill Road. Follow it up as far as the school (passing toilets on the right), where the road bends right to the resplendent entrance to West **Wycombe Caves** (see box).

To continue the walk, go straight up the hill from the corner, on a steep path across grassland. Turn right on to a chalky cross-track by trees. After climbing a little further, you will see **West Wycombe Church and Mausoleum** on the left. Turn left uphill to pass around the left side of Dashwood's octagonal, flint-built mausoleum, then up to the church. Leave by a gate at the far side of the churchyard ❺.

Outside the gate, continue forward on a wide track (ignoring the path to the right), which soon becomes surfaced. Just after it bends right, take the first of the two tracks on the left, signposted to Saunderton. After ½ mile, when the broad track swings to the left just past a tree with a white arrow on it, continue ahead (slightly right) on a narrower path through glorious beechwoods. Keep straight on at a crossing of tracks, with another white arrow. The views to the right are over to the village of Bradenham. The track goes through a gate, then between woods on the right and a field hedge on the left to reach the restored flint buildings of Nobles Farm ❻.

At the farm, turn right, beside an electricity pylon, as indicated by a white arrow.

To return to the station, keep straight on to the end of the farm drive and turn right on to the lane.

To continue, follow the narrow footpath as it goes steeply downhill into woods, initially with a fence on the right. Fork left just after an old telegraph pole with a white arrow, and leave the woods by a stile. Descend close to the right-hand edge of a field and across a second field to a stile. Cross the railway with care, then proceed across the next field to the main road. Again cross with care, diagonally right, and turn left at The Red Lion, Bradenham, to return to the start point.

Sir Francis Dashwood

Perhaps our most colourful Chancellor of the Exchequer ever (1762), Sir Francis Dashwood was the creator of West Wycombe Park. Both the Italianate mansion and the rococo landscaped gardens reflect his theatrical leanings. (House and grounds open June to August, Sunday to Thursday; grounds only also open April and May, Wednesday and bank holidays.)

He was the founder of the Society of Dilettanti and, more notoriously, the Hell-Fire Club, a fraternity of knights who are said to have held secret revelries and black magic meetings in various local venues. One of these was West Wycombe church tower, on top of which Dashwood had a large golden orb built. Another was the caves (open March to October, daily, November to February Saturday, Sunday and bank holidays), dug on Dashwood's orders and extending one-third of a mile under the hill beneath the church. A brick tunnel leads from the flint-lined forecourt to various chambers, in which tableaux and a variety of curiosities are now displayed. Also on top of the hill, near the church, is the huge Dashwood family mausoleum.

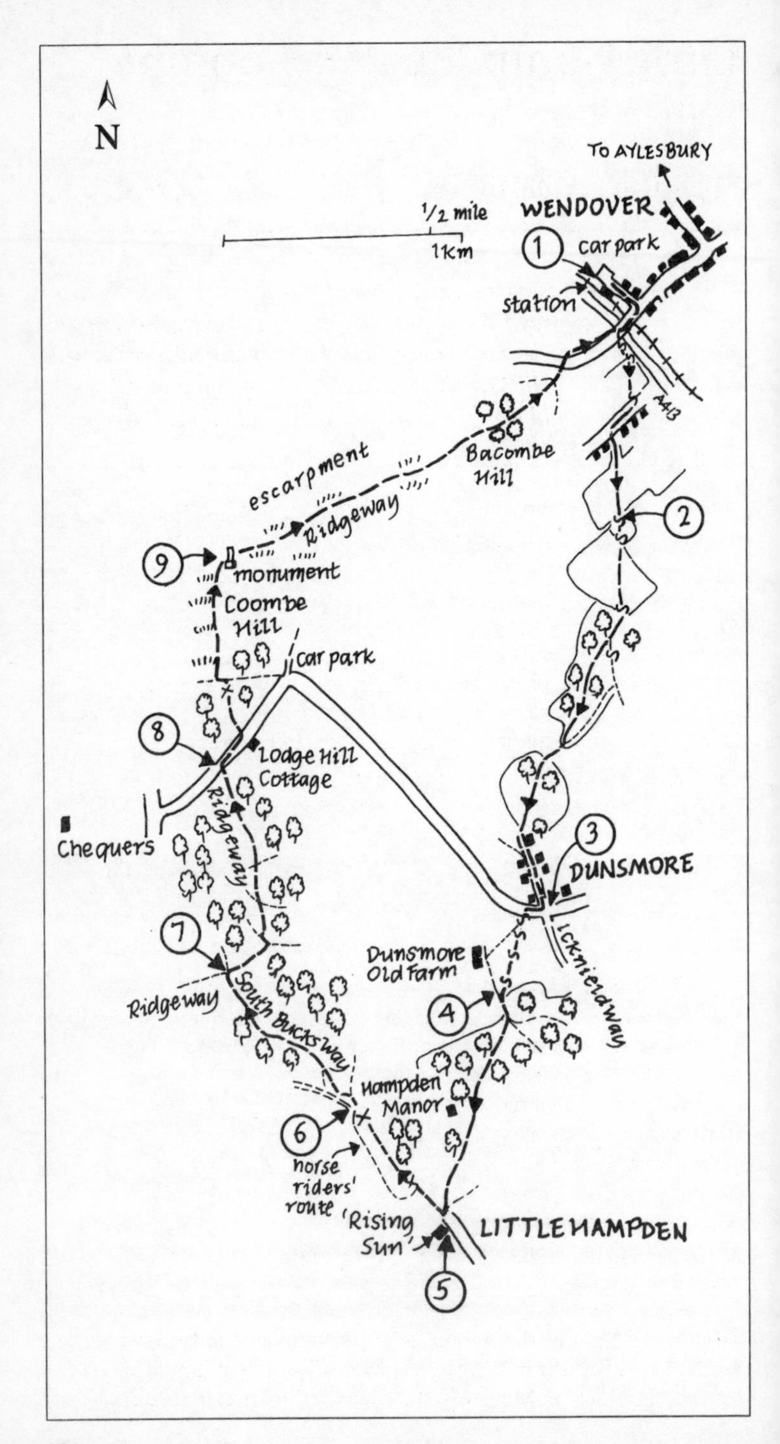
N
TO AYLESBURY
WENDOVER
1/2 mile
1km
1
car park
station
A413
Bacombe Hill
escarpment
Ridgeway
2
9
monument
Coombe Hill
Car park
8
Lodge Hill Cottage
Chequers
Ridgeway
3
DUNSMORE
Icknield Way
7
Dunsmore Old Farm
Ridgeway
South Bucks Way
4
Hampden Manor
6
horse riders' route
'Rising Sun'
LITTLE HAMPDEN
5

Little Hampden and Coombe Hill

BUCKINGHAMSHIRE WALK 52

Most of the route is along well-marked paths through majestic beech woods, with good waymarking and signposting to guide you. You gain glimpses of the outside world though, and the final section opens out gloriously at Coombe Hill. The route from the Rising Sun pub follows the South Bucks Way and joins the Ridgeway, which is thoroughly signposted all the way back to Wendover.

Shoulder of Mutton, 20 Pound Street, Wendover HP22 6EJ. ☎ (01296) 623223. Open Mon to Sat 11 to 11, Sun 12 to 10.30; food Mon to Sat 12 to 2.30, 5.30 to 9.30, Sun 12 to 9. 4 real ales. Bar menu including sandwiches and lasagne, à la carte menu, Sunday roasts. Children welcome if eating. No dogs.

Red Lion Hotel, 9 High Street, Wendover HP22 6DU. ☎ (01296) 622266. Open Mon to Sat 11 to 11, Sun 11 to 10.30; food Mon to Sat 12 to 2, 6 to 10, Sun 12 to 2.30, 7 to 9.30. Brakspear, Courage Directors, Young's beers. Bar food includes scampi, burgers and pasta, while restaurant menu might offer shank of lamb, chicken, fish or steak. No children in bar in evenings. No dogs in eating areas.

Rising Sun, Little Hampden HP16 9PS. ☎ (01494) 488393. Open Tues to Sat 11.30 to 3, 6.30 to 11, Sun 12 to 3; food Tues to Sun 12 to 2, Tues to Sat 7 to 9. Adnams, Brakspear, Marston's beers. Starters might include pan-fried curried prawns with mango and orange salad or baked avocado filled with crab meat with parmesan cream sauce. Main courses might be breast of chicken filled with blue cheese and prawns with lemon and tarragon sauce or roast shoulder of lamb served with rosemary and honey sauce. Blackboard specials are also available during the day. Children welcome. No dogs.

Start: Wendover railway station, on the edge of Wendover (south-east of Aylesbury). Station car park (fee); roadside parking in the village can be very limited, but is much easier on Sundays. Grid reference 865077.
Length: 6 miles (10 kilometres), 3 hours.
Difficulty: Moderate, with some short climbs and along some potentially muddy woodland paths.
OS maps: 1:25,000 Explorer sheet 181; 1:50,000 Landranger sheet 165.
Shops and restaurants in Wendover.
WC Wendover (in the short-term car park by the library).
PT Train to Wendover.

❶ Turn right out of the station to reach the main street in Wendover, by the Shoulder of Mutton pub. Turn right, crossing the bridge over the railway, then immediately after take the signposted stile on the left, beneath power lines. This leads along a short track and into a field, where you go diagonally right as signposted to a stile. Turn right on the residential road, then after 120 yards, just after a house called St Benedict's, turn left on a signposted bridleway. After a section between back gardens this leads between field fences.

❷ At the end of the fenced section, take the stile ahead (avoiding the bridleway between fences to the right), and go diagonally right in the waymarked direction to the next stile in the far corner of the field. Maintain the same direction across the next field to enter the woodland. The path is well marked by yellow arrows painted on trees. After 100 yards fork right (where the left fork goes to a stile and into a field), and carry on up; the path dips, then rises; soon after keep right (uphill) at an oblique junction with a broader path. This soon passes between fields.

After the woodland resumes on the right, keep left past a house on the left, ignoring a path joining from the right, and go past more houses at Dunsmore. ❸ Turn right at the crossroads in Dunsmore, signposted Kimble. After 75 yards take a signposted stile on the left: ignore the path signposted half right, downhill, but go roughly along the level to the stile visible in the left-hand fence. Carry on in the same direction down through three more small fields, through a belt of woodland and then ❹ turn left at a T-junction of paths at the bottom of the valley. On entering the woodland, take the right-hand of three tracks ahead. This rises (ignore any minor side turns), swinging left at the end of the main ascent, and after ½ mile reaches the Rising Sun pub at Little Hampden ❺.

Turn right (if you are starting from here you begin with the Rising Sun on your left) along the lane, and after 50 yards fork left on the South Bucks Way (the right fork is a private driveway to Hampden Manor). 200 yards later go past a barrier (where a sign indicates that horse riders are diverted to the left) and follow the South Bucks Way across the woodland of Little Hampden Common.

❻ Past the next barrier, where a field appears on the left, go forward and slightly right at a junction of paths and tracks, taking the South Bucks Way (clearly waymarked to the right of the main track ahead). This soon joins a broader track and turns right along it. The track later bends right and descends, with views over the valley to the left.

❼ Turn right, uphill, at a signpost for the Ridgeway, which you follow all the way to Wendover and is very clearly marked through a maze of woodland paths by signposts and waymarks with acorn symbols. It turns left, and then turns right 50 yards later and proceeds through the woods past further junctions to a road ❽. Turn right along the road, then left opposite a house (Lodge Hill Cottage).

Beyond a kissing-gate, the Ridgeway goes left downhill for 20 yards, then turns right into the open. Behind you to the left, above the far side of the valley is **Chequers**, the 16th-century country home of British prime ministers since 1921, when Lord Lee of Farham made it over as a gift to the nation.

Reach the Boer War Memorial at the summit of **Coombe Hill ➒**, at 852 feet the highest point in the Chilterns. You have an extensive view over the Oxfordshire plain, the Berkshire Downs, and the eastern Cotswolds. The hilltop is a Site of Special Scientific Interest, and its chalkland flora – such as dropwort, bird's foot trefoil and harebell – supports a range of butterflies. This point is the start of the 23-mile South Bucks Way, which leads via Amersham to Denham, finishing on the towpath of the Grand Union Canal.

The path bends right and gradually descends (avoid all side turns), passing through **Bacombe Hill Local Nature Reserve** (where you fork left on entering woodland). At a sign for the reserve, carry on forward to the road, where you cross over and turn right along the pavement alongside the road to Wendover.

Wendover itself is lined with brick and timber houses, some thatched and others with Georgian façades concealing older structures. The broad High Street drops to the Clock Tower of 1842, now home to the tourist information office.